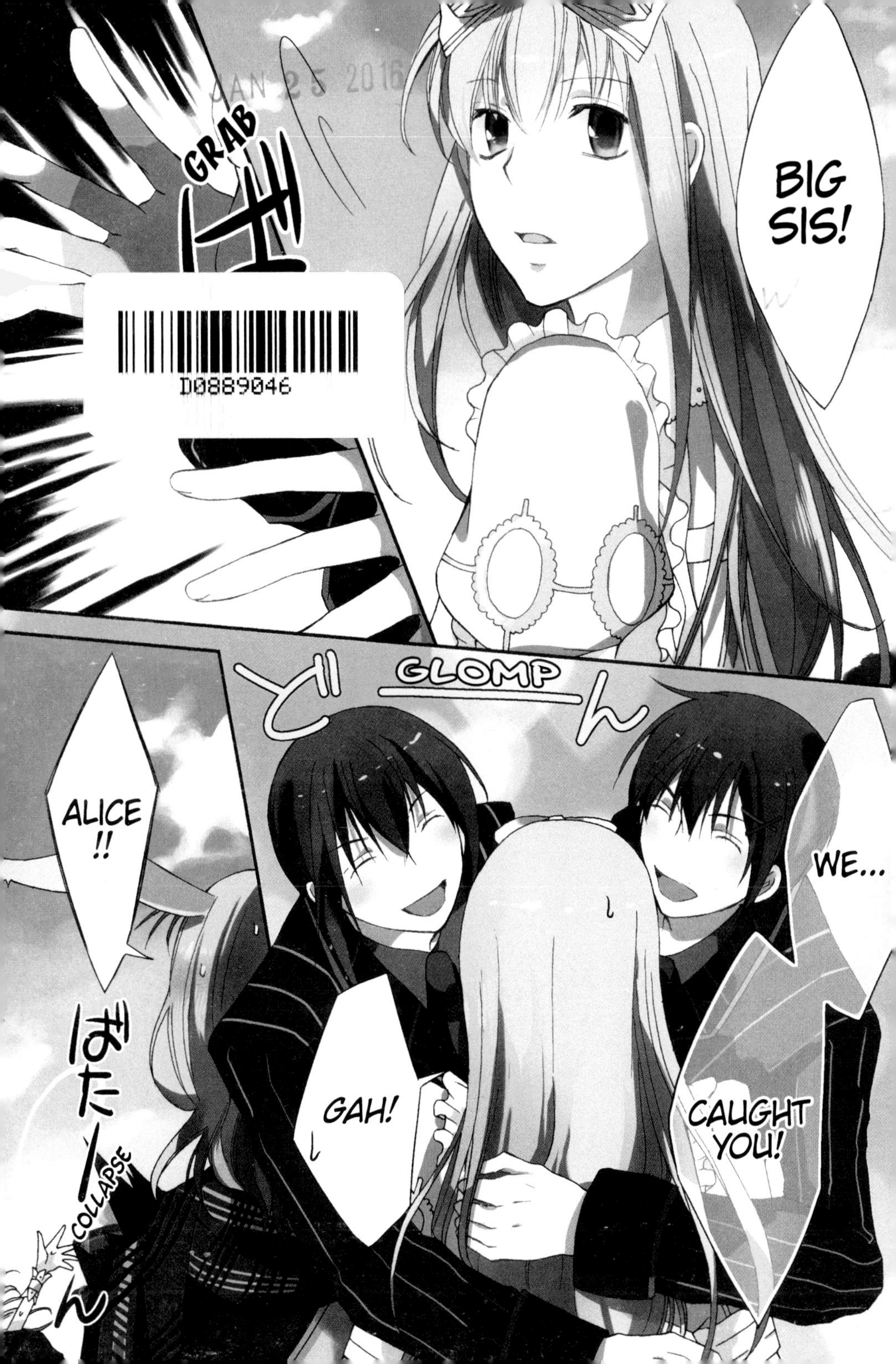
BIG SIS!
GRAB
どーん
GLOMP
WE...
CAUGHT YOU!
ALICE!!
GAH!
ぱたーん
COLLAPSE

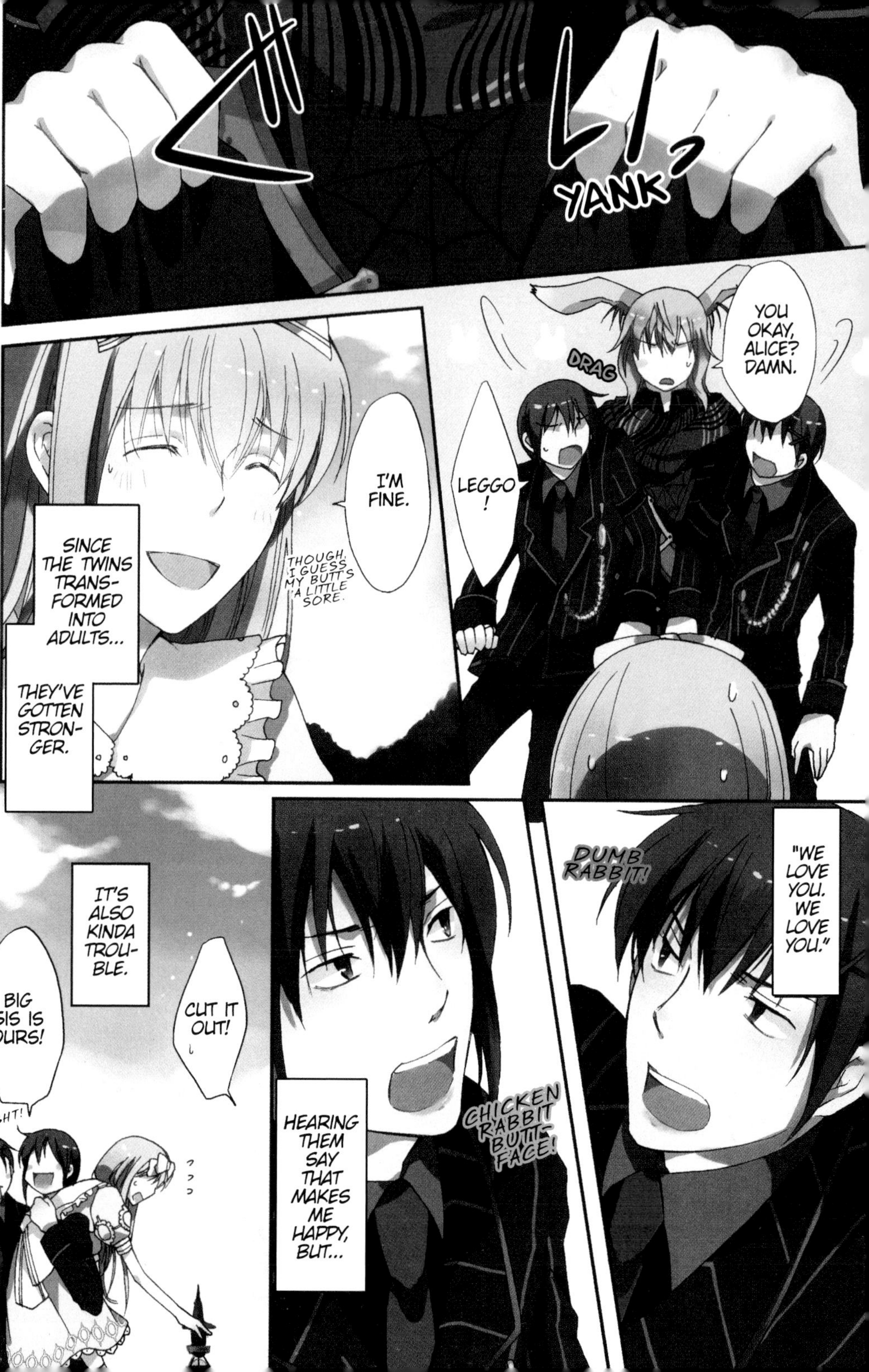
YANK
YOU OKAY, ALICE? DAMN.
DRAG
LEGGO!
I'M FINE.
THOUGH, I GUESS MY BUTT'S A LITTLE SORE.
SINCE THE TWINS TRANSFORMED INTO ADULTS...
THEY'VE GOTTEN STRONGER.
"WE LOVE YOU. WE LOVE YOU."
DUMB RABBIT!
CHICKEN RABBIT BUTT-FACE!
HEARING THEM SAY THAT MAKES ME HAPPY, BUT...
IT'S ALSO KINDA TROUBLE.
CUT IT OUT!
BIG SIS IS OURS!
RIGHT!

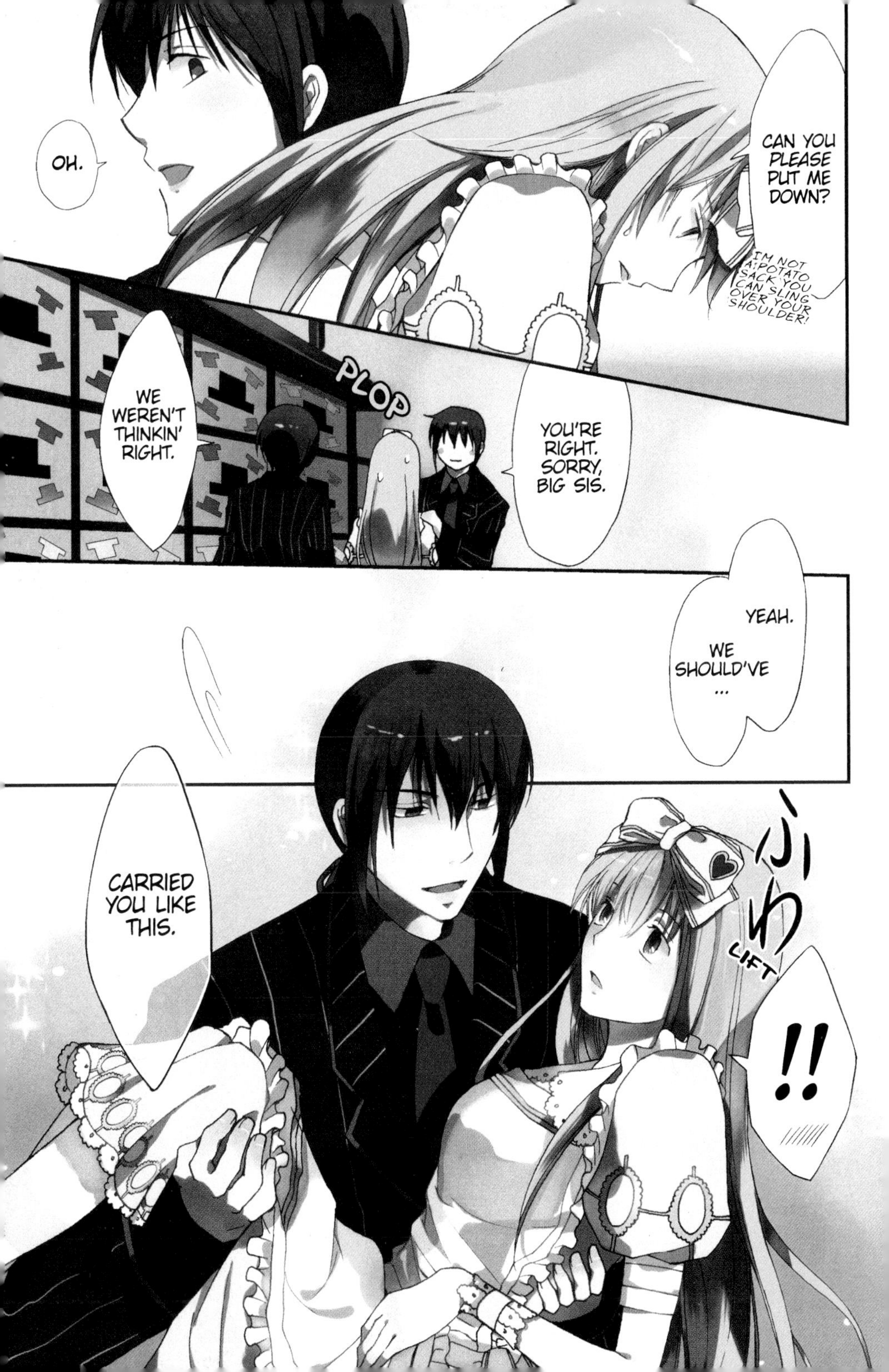
CAN YOU PLEASE PUT ME DOWN?
I'M NOT A POTATO SACK YOU CAN SLING OVER YOUR SHOULDER!
OH.
PLOP
YOU'RE RIGHT. SORRY, BIG SIS.
WE WEREN'T THINKIN' RIGHT.
YEAH.
WE SHOULD'VE ...
ふわ
LIFT
CARRIED YOU LIKE THIS.
!!

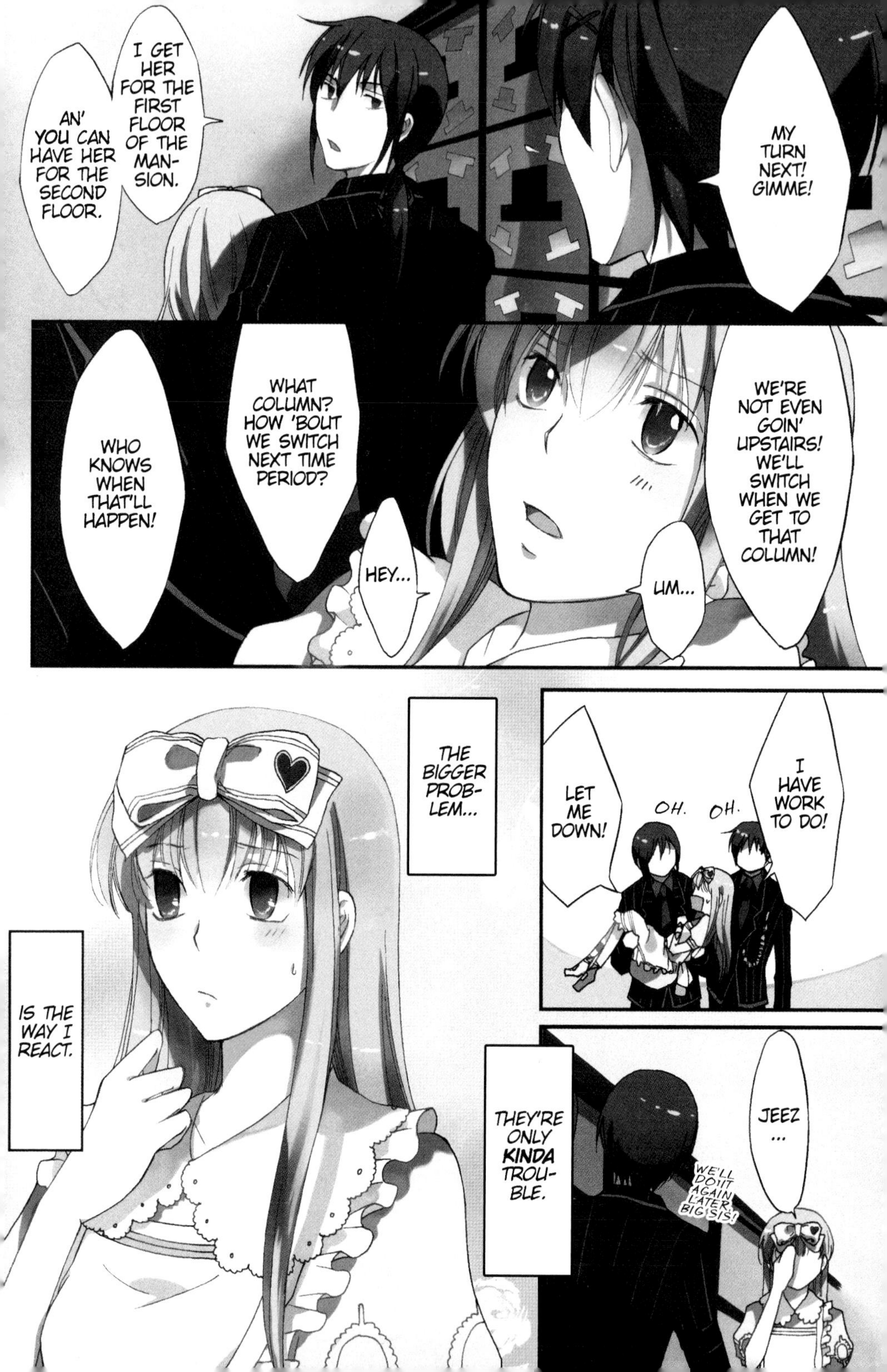
MY TURN NEXT! GIMME!
I GET HER FOR THE FIRST FLOOR OF THE MANSION.
AN' YOU CAN HAVE HER FOR THE SECOND FLOOR.
WE'RE NOT EVEN GOIN' UPSTAIRS! WE'LL SWITCH WHEN WE GET TO THAT COLUMN!
UM...
HEY...
WHAT COLUMN? HOW 'BOUT WE SWITCH NEXT TIME PERIOD?
WHO KNOWS WHEN THAT'LL HAPPEN!
I HAVE WORK TO DO!
OH. OH.
LET ME DOWN!
JEEZ ...
WE'LL DO IT AGAIN LATER, BIG SIS!
THEY'RE ONLY **KINDA** TROUBLE.
THE BIGGER PROBLEM...
IS THE WAY I REACT.

ALICE IN THE COUNTRY OF CLOVER
~Twin Lovers~

Kei Shichiri

七里 慧

SEVEN SEAS ENTERTAINMENT PRESENTS

Alice IN THE COUNTRY OF Clover

TWIN LOVERS

art by KEI SHICHIRI / story by QUINROSE

TRANSLATION
Angela Liu

ADAPTATION
Lianne Sentar

LETTERING AND LAYOUT
Laura Scoville

LOGO DESIGN
Courtney Williams

COVER DESIGN
Nicky Lim

PROOFREADER
Rebecca Scoble
Lee Otter

MANAGING EDITOR
Adam Arnold

PUBLISHER
Jason DeAngelis

ALICE IN THE COUNTRY OF CLOVER: TWIN LOVERS

First published in Japan in 2011 by ICHIJINSHA Inc., Tokyo.
English translation rights arranged with ICHIJINSHA Inc., Tokyo, Japan.

ISBN: 978-1-626921-27-6

Printed in Canada

First Printing: May 2015

10 9 8 7 6 5 4 3 2 1

FOLLOW US ONLINE: ***www.gomanga.com***

READING DIRECTIONS

This book reads from ***right to left***, Japanese style. If this is your first time reading manga, you start reading from the top right panel on each page and take it from there. If you get lost, just follow the numbered diagram here. It may seem backwards at first, but you□ll get the hang of it! Have fun!!

1
2
3
4
5
6
7
8
9

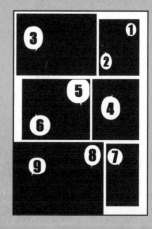

Alice in the Country of Clover

クローバーの国の

アリス

~Wonderful Wonder World~

- STORY -

In *Alice in the Country of Clover*, the game starts with Alice having not fallen in love, but still deciding to stay in Wonderland.

She's acquainted with all the characters from the previous game, *Alice in the Country of Hearts*.

Since love would now start from a place of friendship rather than passion with a new stranger, she can experience a different type of romance from that in the previous game. Her dynamic with the characters is different through this friendship—characters can't always be forceful with her, and in many ways it's more comfortable to grow intimate. The relationships *between* the Ones With Duties have also become more of a factor.

In this game, the story focuses on the mafia. Alice attends the suited meetings (forcefully) and gets involved in various gunfights (forcefully), among other things.

Land fluctuations, sea creatures in the forest, and whispering doors—it's a game more fantastic and more eerie than the first.

Will our everywoman Alice be able to have a romantic relationship in a world devoid of common sense?

Alice in the Country of Clover
Character Information

Elliot March
VA: Tsuguo Mogami

Blood's right-hand man has a criminal past... and a temperamental present. But he's not as bad as he used to be, so that's something. Joining Blood has been good(?) for him.

Blood Dupre
VA: Katsuyuki Konishi

The head of the mafia Hatter Family, Blood is a cunning yet moody puppet-master. Alice now has the pleasure of having him for a landlord.

Alice Liddell
VA: Rie Kugimiya

A normal girl with a bit of a chip on her shoulder. Deciding to stay in the Wonderland she was carried to, she's adapted to her strange new lifestyle.

Vivaldi
VA: Yuuko Kaida

The beautiful Queen of Hearts has an unrivaled temper—which is really saying something in Wonderland. Although a picture-perfect Mad Queen, she cares for Alice as if Alice were her little sister...or a very interesting plaything.

Tweedle Dum
VA: Jun Fukuyama

The second "Bloody Twin" is equally cute and equally scary. In *Clover*, Dum can also turn into an adult.

Tweedle Dee
VA: Jun Fukuyama

One of the "Bloody Twin" gatekeepers of the Hatter territory, Dee can be cute when he's not being terrifying. In *Clover*, he sometimes turns into an adult.

Boris Airay
VA: Noriaki Sugiyama

This riddle-loving cat has a signature smirk—and in *Clover*, a new toy. One of his favorite pastimes is giving the Sleepy Mouse a hard time.

Ace
VA: Daisuke Hirakawa

The unlucky knight of Hearts was a former subordinate of Vivaldi and is perpetually lost. Even though he's depressed to be separated from his friend and boss Julius, he stays positive and tries to overcome it with a smile. He seems like a classic nice guy... or is he?

Peter White
VA: Kouki Miyata

The Prime Minister of Heart Castle—who has rabbit ears growing out of his head—invited (kidnapped) Alice to Wonderland. He loves Alice and hates everything else. His cruel, irrational actions are disturbing, but he acts like a completely different person (rabbit?) when in the throes of his love for Alice.

Gray Ringmarc
VA: Kazuya Nakai

Nightmare's subordinate in *Clover*. He used to have strong social ambition and considered assassinating Nightmare... but since Nightmare was such a useless boss, Gray couldn't help but feel sorry for him and ended up a dedicated assistant. He's a sound thinker with a strong work ethic. He's also highly skilled with his blades, rivaling even Ace.

Nightmare Gottschalk
VA: Tomokazu Sugita

A sickly nightmare who hates the hospital and needles. He has the power to read people's thoughts and enter dreams. Even though he likes to shut himself away in dreams, Gray drags him out to sulk from time to time. He technically holds a high position and has many subordinates, but since he can't even take care of his own health, he leaves most things to Gray.

Pierce Villiers
VA: Souichirou Hoshi

New to *Clover*, Pierce is an insomniac mouse who drinks too much coffee. He loves Nightmare (who can help him sleep) and hates Boris (who terrifies him). He dislikes Blood and Vivaldi for discarding coffee in favor of tea. He likes Elliot and Peter well enough, since rabbits aren't natural predators of mice.

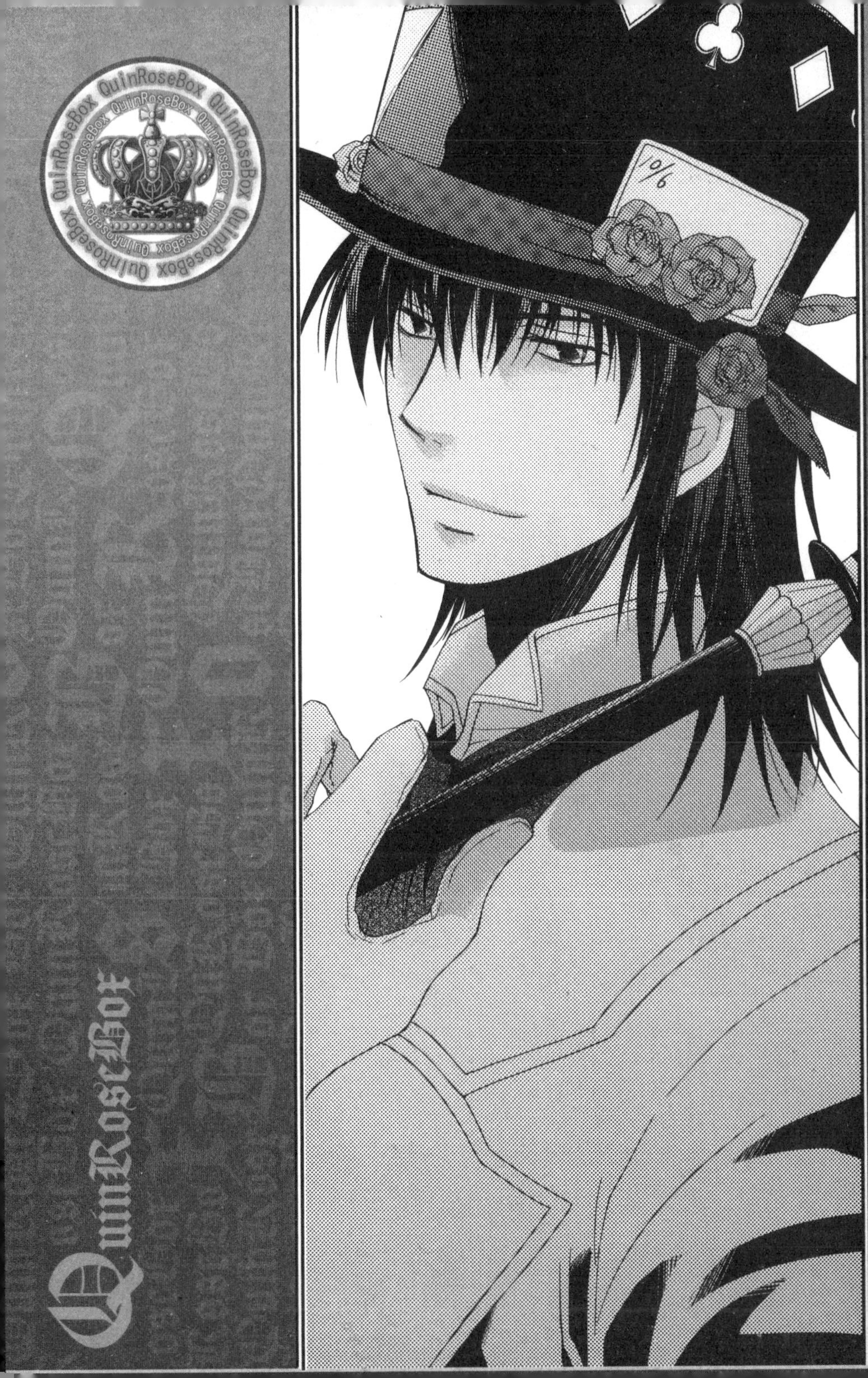
10/6

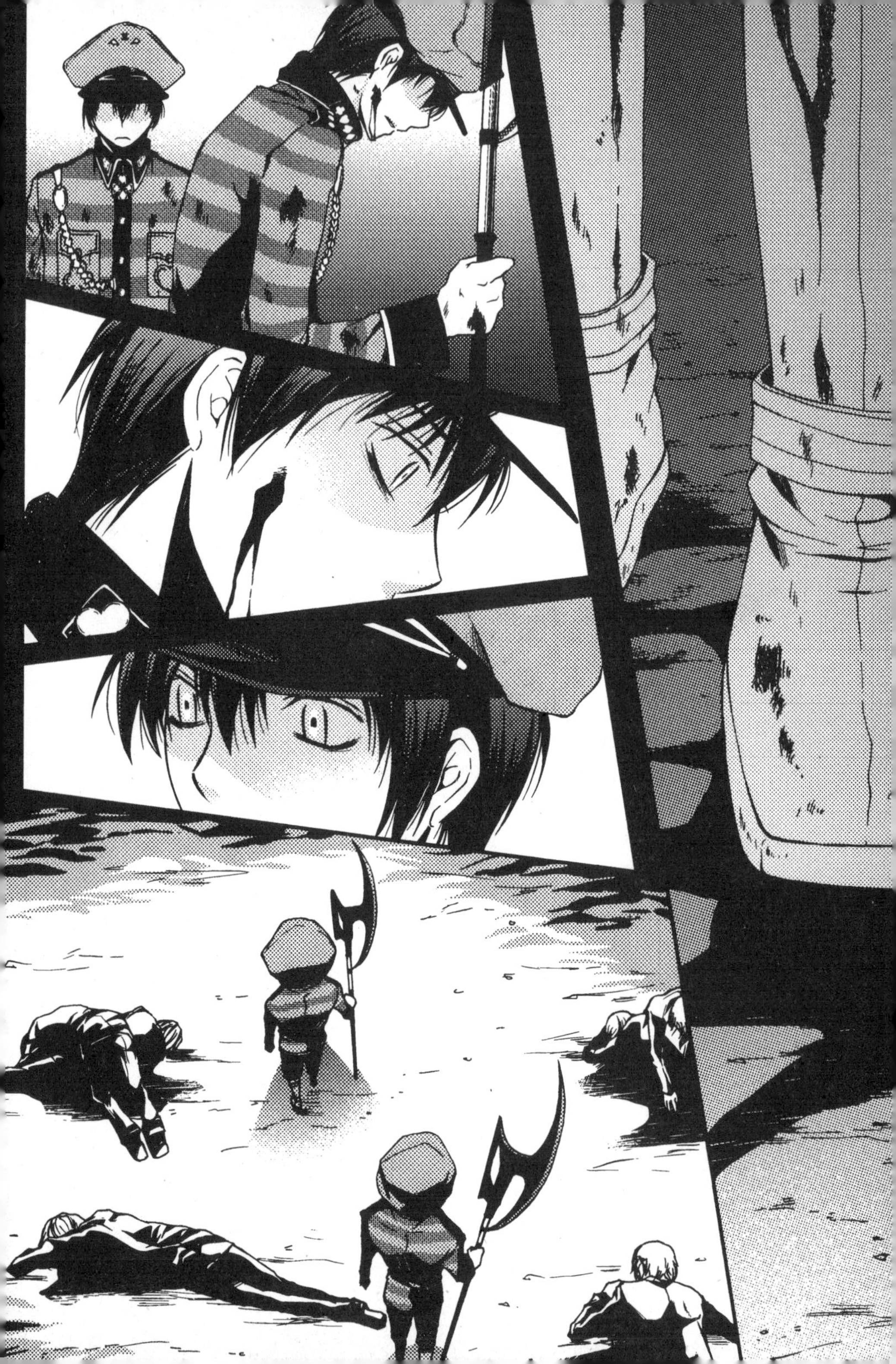

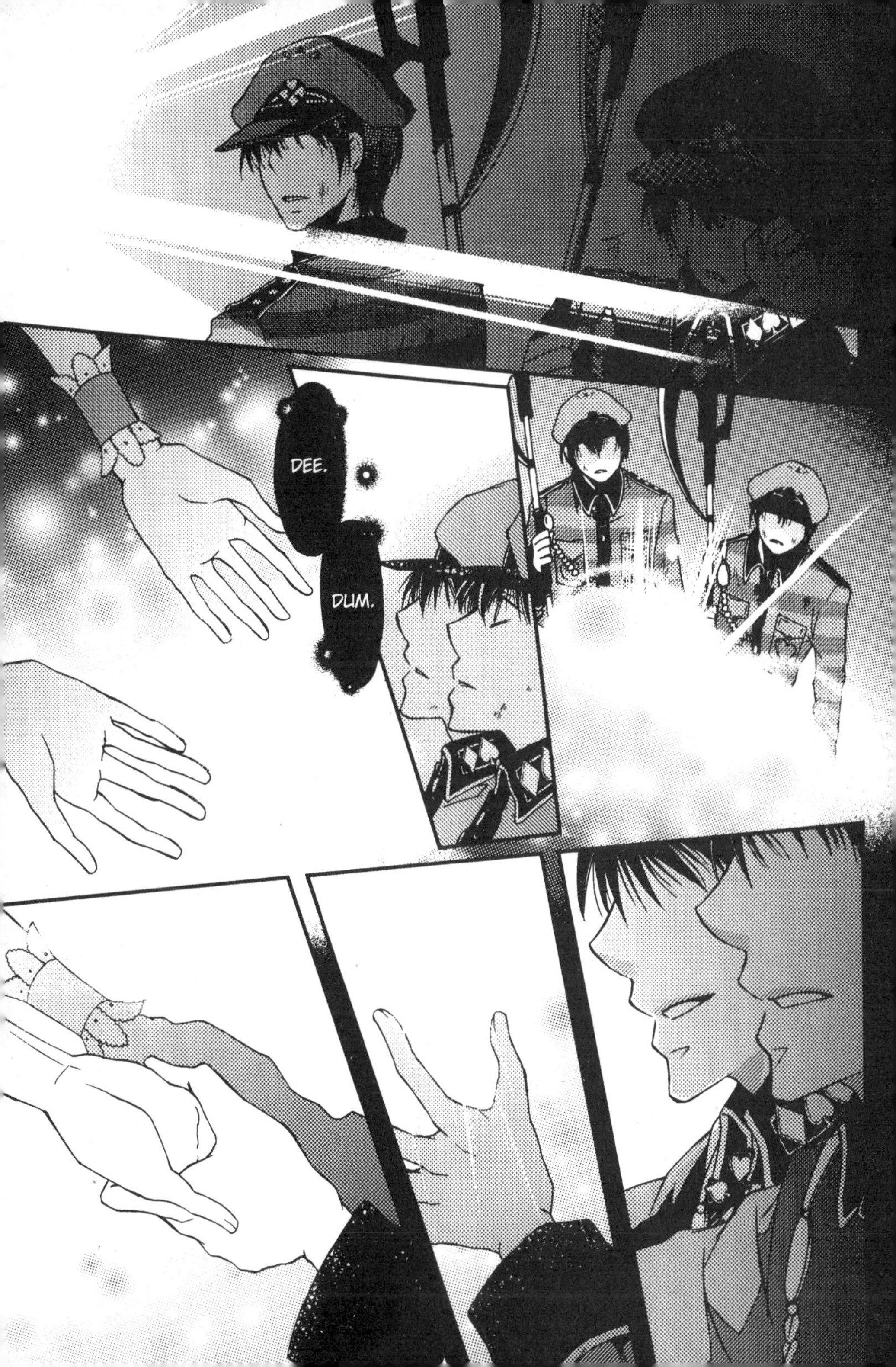
DEE.
DUM.

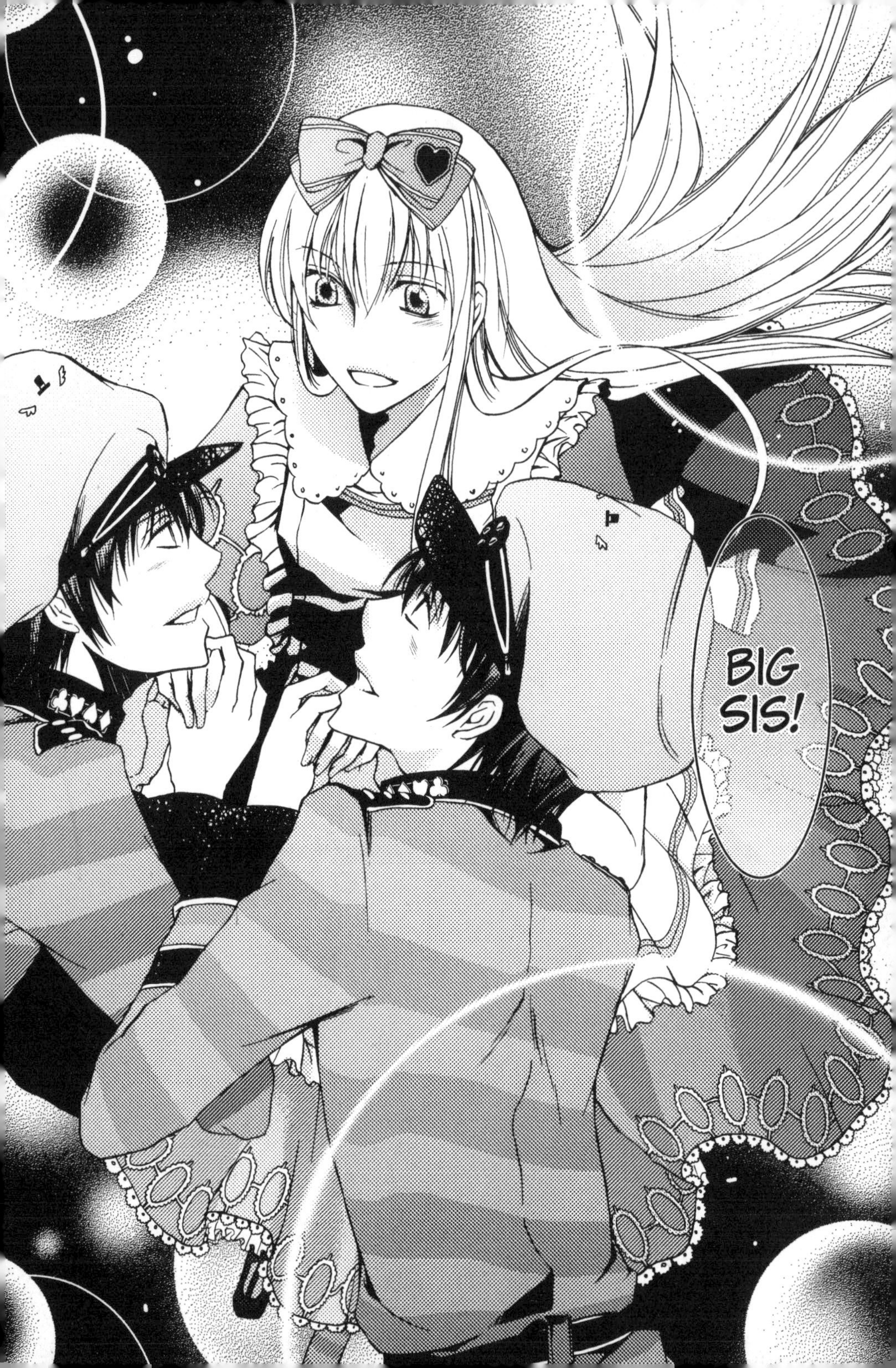
BIG SIS!

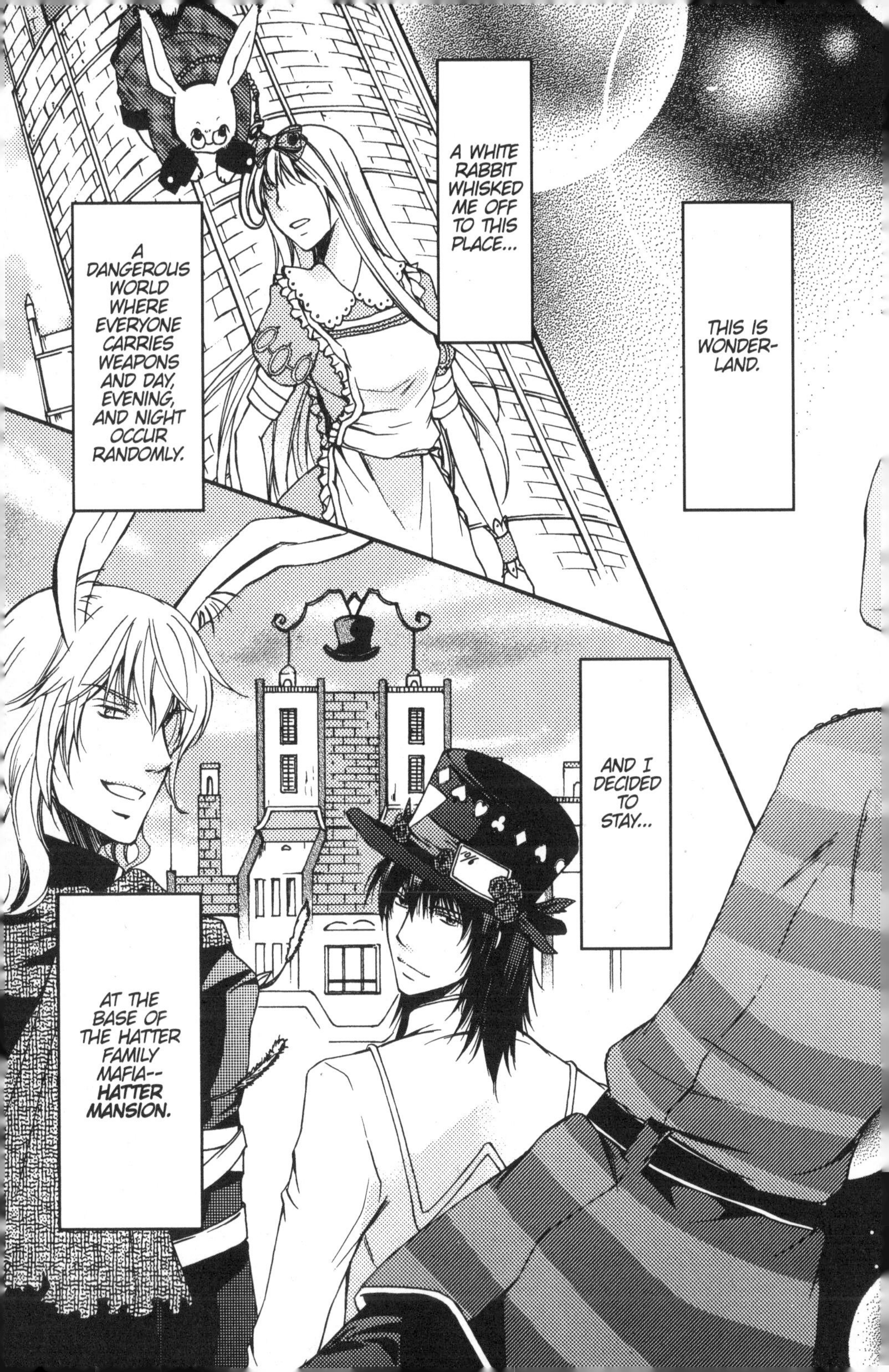
THIS IS WONDER-LAND.
A WHITE RABBIT WHISKED ME OFF TO THIS PLACE...
A DANGEROUS WORLD WHERE EVERYONE CARRIES WEAPONS AND DAY, EVENING, AND NIGHT OCCUR RANDOMLY.
AND I DECIDED TO STAY...
AT THE BASE OF THE HATTER FAMILY MAFIA-- **HATTER MANSION.**

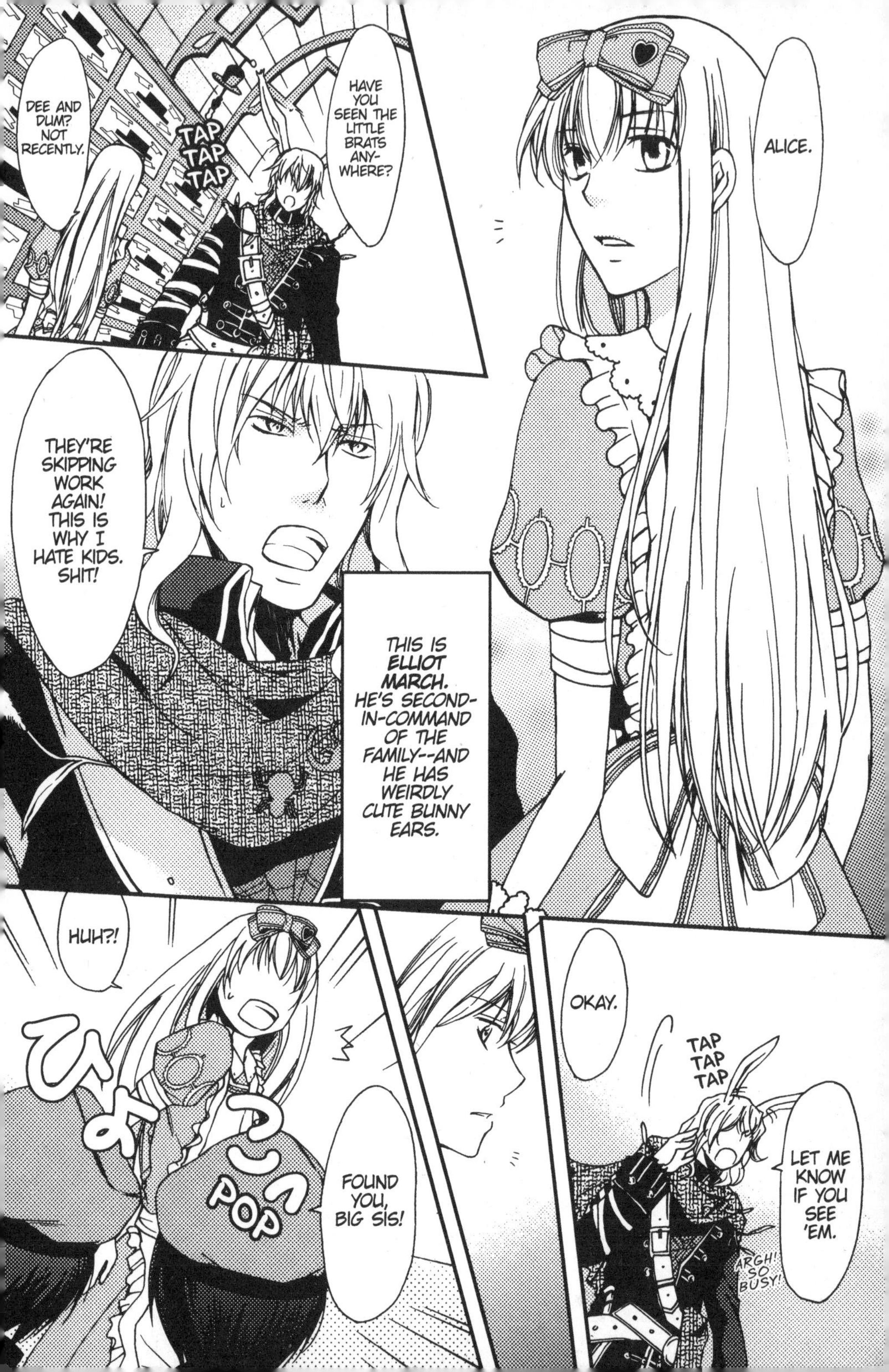
ALICE.
HAVE YOU SEEN THE LITTLE BRATS ANYWHERE?
TAP TAP TAP
DEE AND DUM? NOT RECENTLY.
THEY'RE SKIPPING WORK AGAIN! THIS IS WHY I HATE KIDS. SHIT!
THIS IS ELLIOT MARCH. HE'S SECOND-IN-COMMAND OF THE FAMILY--AND HE HAS WEIRDLY CUTE BUNNY EARS.
OKAY.
TAP TAP TAP
LET ME KNOW IF YOU SEE 'EM.
ARGH! SO BUSY!
FOUND YOU, BIG SIS!
HUH?!
ひょっこ
POP

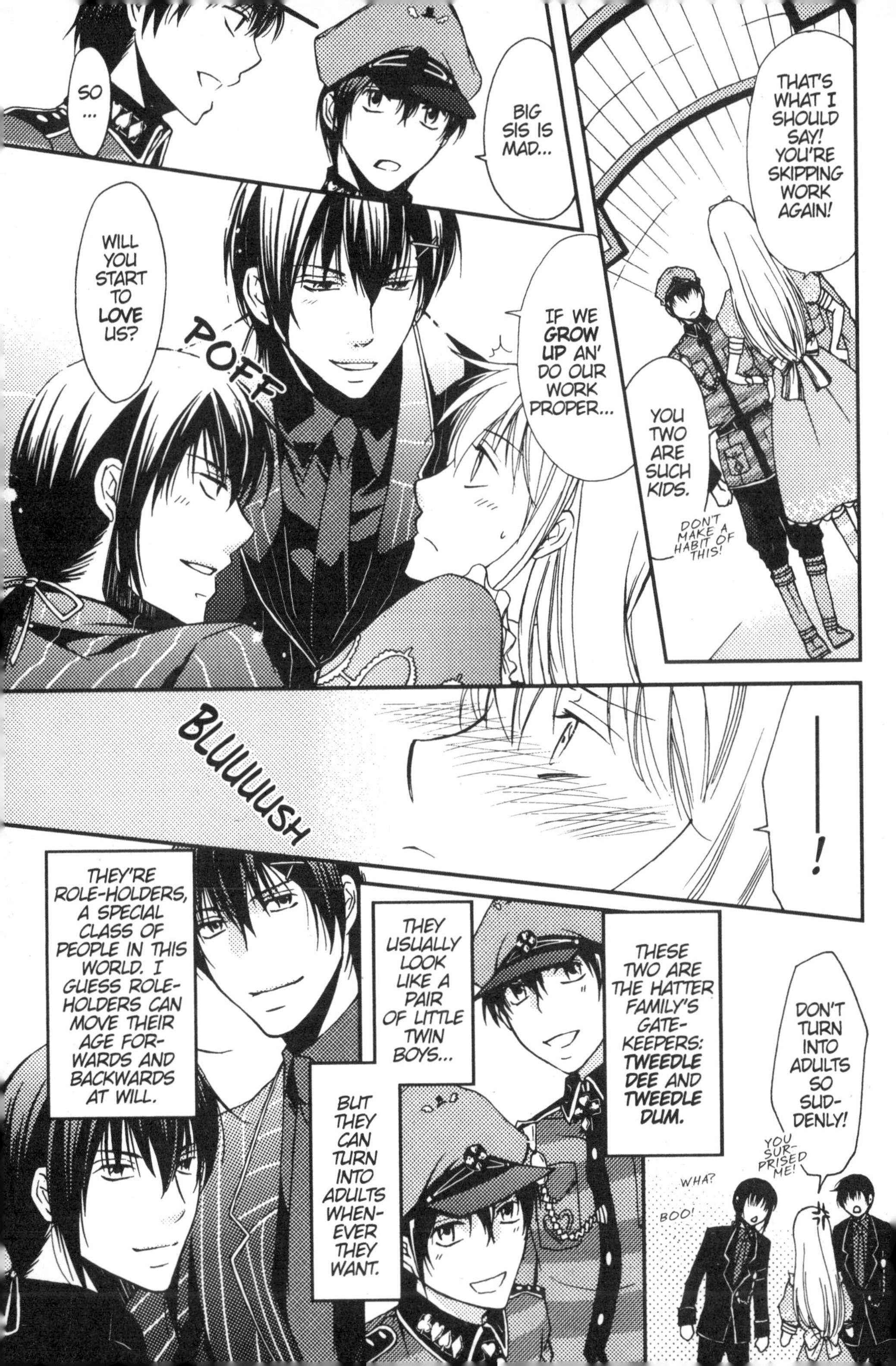
THAT'S WHAT I SHOULD SAY! YOU'RE SKIPPING WORK AGAIN!
YOU TWO ARE SUCH KIDS.
DON'T MAKE A HABIT OF THIS!
BIG SIS IS MAD...
SO ...
IF WE GROW UP AN' DO OUR WORK PROPER...
POFF
WILL YOU START TO LOVE US?
—!
BLUUUUSH
DON'T TURN INTO ADULTS SO SUD-DENLY!
YOU SUR-PRISED ME!
WHA?
BOO!
THESE TWO ARE THE HATTER FAMILY'S GATE-KEEPERS: TWEEDLE DEE AND TWEEDLE DUM.
THEY USUALLY LOOK LIKE A PAIR OF LITTLE TWIN BOYS...
BUT THEY CAN TURN INTO ADULTS WHEN-EVER THEY WANT.
THEY'RE ROLE-HOLDERS, A SPECIAL CLASS OF PEOPLE IN THIS WORLD. I GUESS ROLE-HOLDERS CAN MOVE THEIR AGE FOR-WARDS AND BACKWARDS AT WILL.

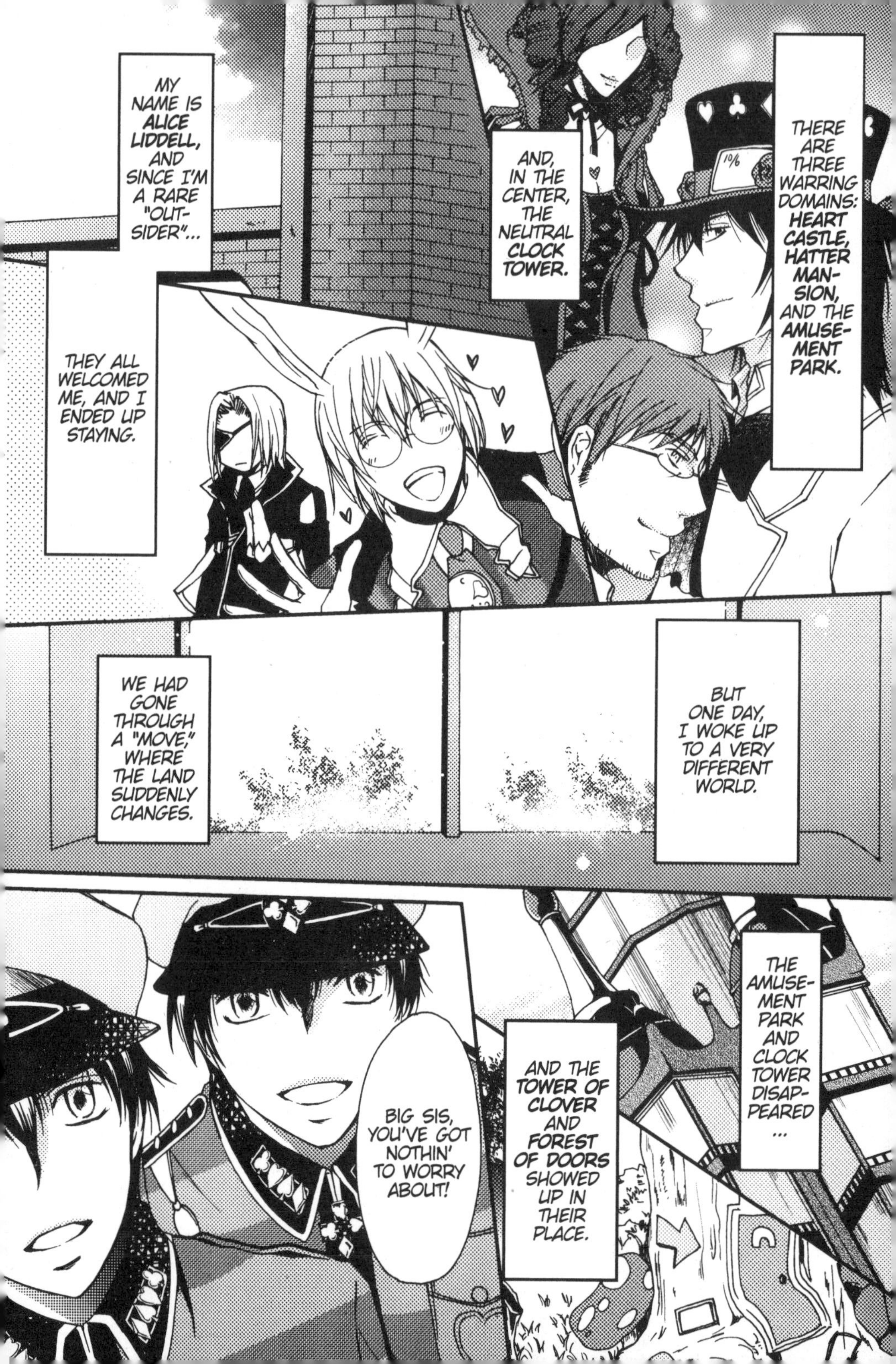
THERE ARE THREE WARRING DOMAINS: HEART CASTLE, HATTER MANSION, AND THE AMUSEMENT PARK.
AND, IN THE CENTER, THE NEUTRAL CLOCK TOWER.
MY NAME IS ALICE LIDDELL, AND SINCE I'M A RARE "OUTSIDER"...
THEY ALL WELCOMED ME, AND I ENDED UP STAYING.
BUT ONE DAY, I WOKE UP TO A VERY DIFFERENT WORLD.
WE HAD GONE THROUGH A "MOVE," WHERE THE LAND SUDDENLY CHANGES.
THE AMUSEMENT PARK AND CLOCK TOWER DISAPPEARED...
AND THE TOWER OF CLOVER AND FOREST OF DOORS SHOWED UP IN THEIR PLACE.
BIG SIS, YOU'VE GOT NOTHIN' TO WORRY ABOUT!

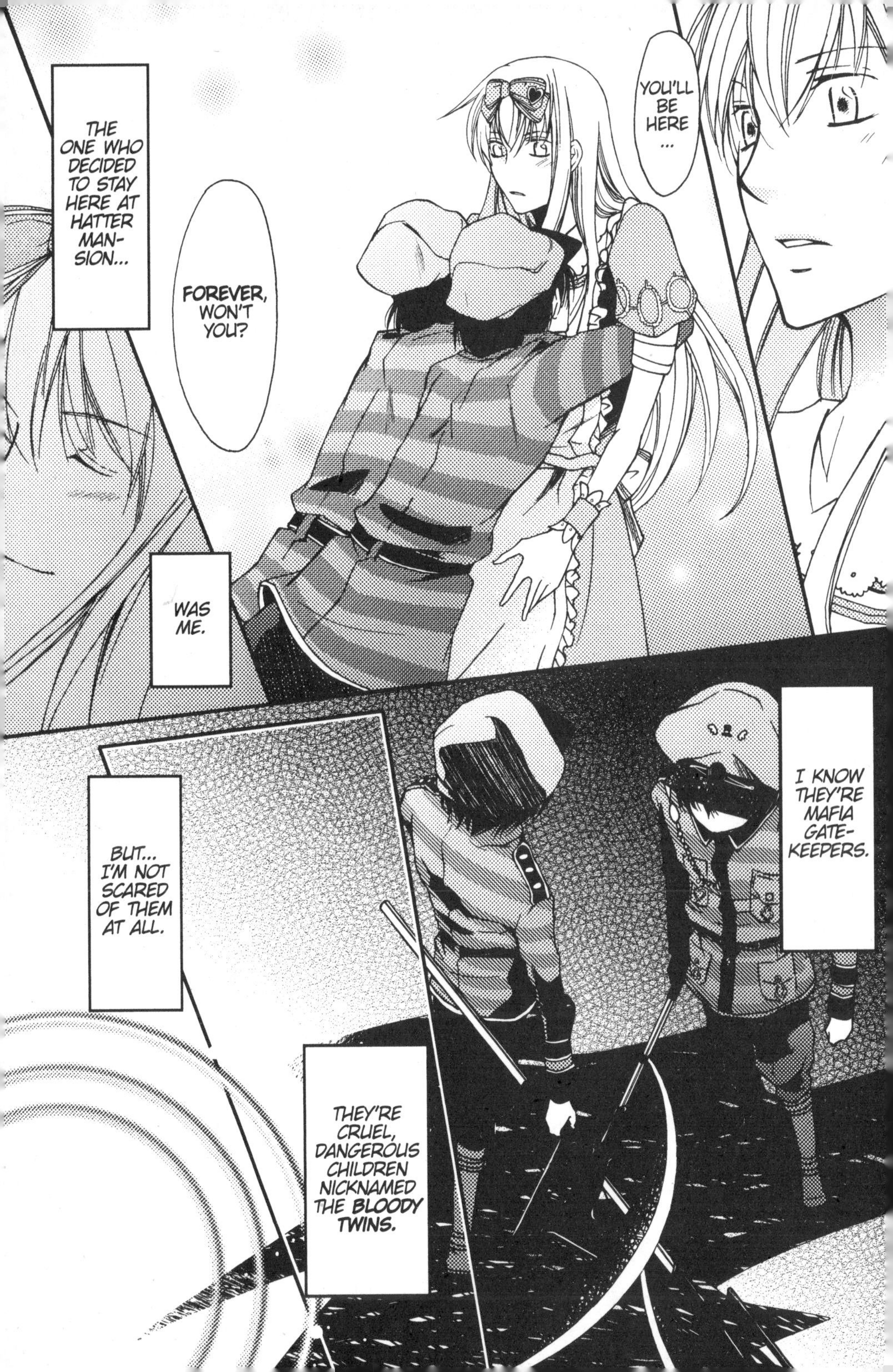
YOU'LL BE HERE...
FOREVER, WON'T YOU?
THE ONE WHO DECIDED TO STAY HERE AT HATTER MAN-SION...
WAS ME.
I KNOW THEY'RE MAFIA GATE-KEEPERS.
BUT... I'M NOT SCARED OF THEM AT ALL.
THEY'RE CRUEL, DANGEROUS CHILDREN NICKNAMED THE BLOODY TWINS.

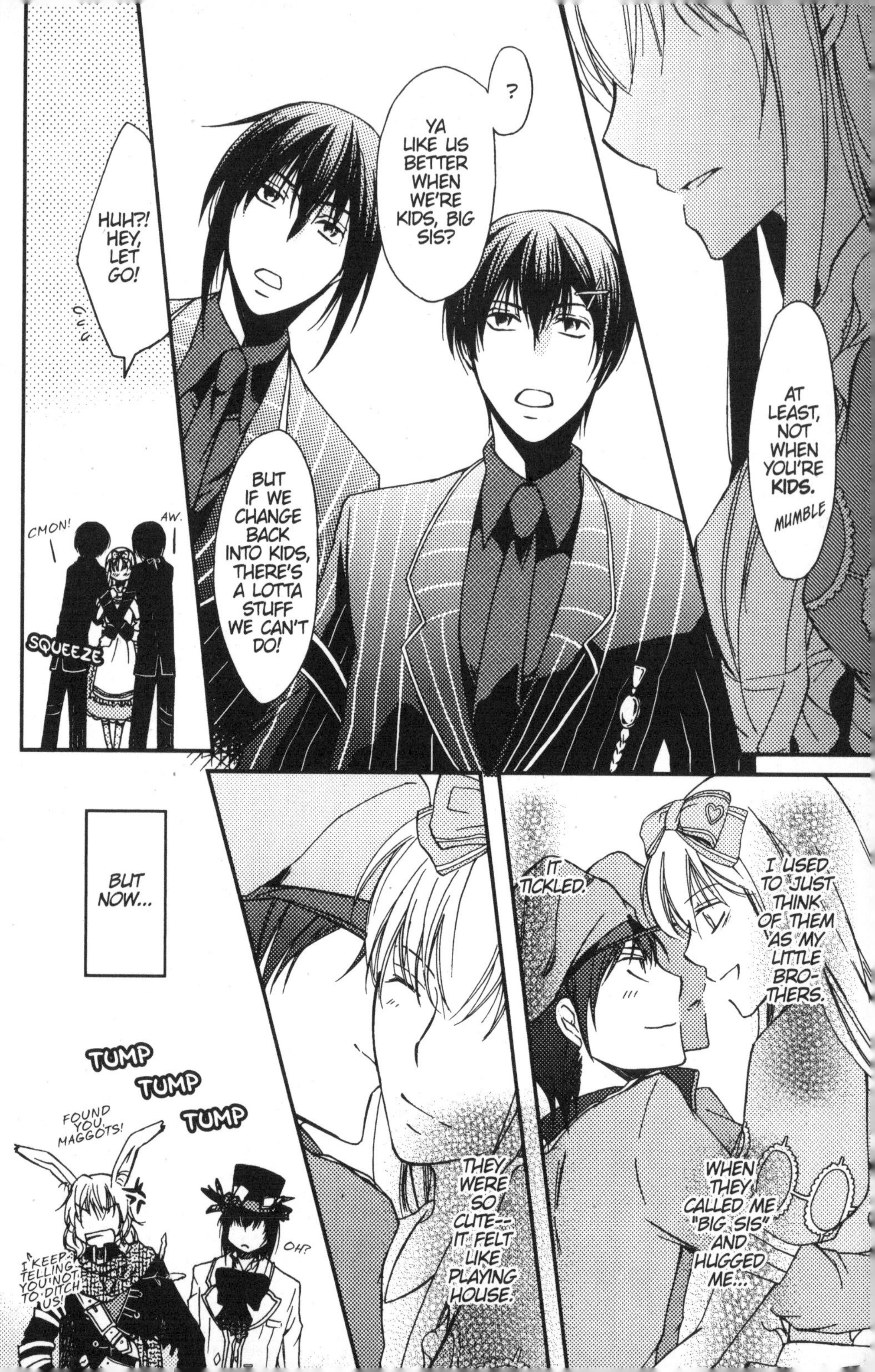
AT LEAST, NOT WHEN YOU'RE KIDS.
MUMBLE
?
YA LIKE US BETTER WHEN WE'RE KIDS, BIG SIS?
HUH?! HEY, LET GO!
BUT IF WE CHANGE BACK INTO KIDS, THERE'S A LOTTA STUFF WE CAN'T DO!
AW.
CMON!
SQUEEZE
I USED TO JUST THINK OF THEM AS MY LITTLE BROTHERS.
IT TICKLED.
WHEN THEY CALLED ME "BIG SIS" AND HUGGED ME...
THEY WERE SO CUTE-- IT FELT LIKE PLAYING HOUSE.
BUT NOW...
TUMP
TUMP
TUMP
FOUND YOU, MAGGOTS!
OH?
I KEEP TELLING YOU NOT TO DITCH US!

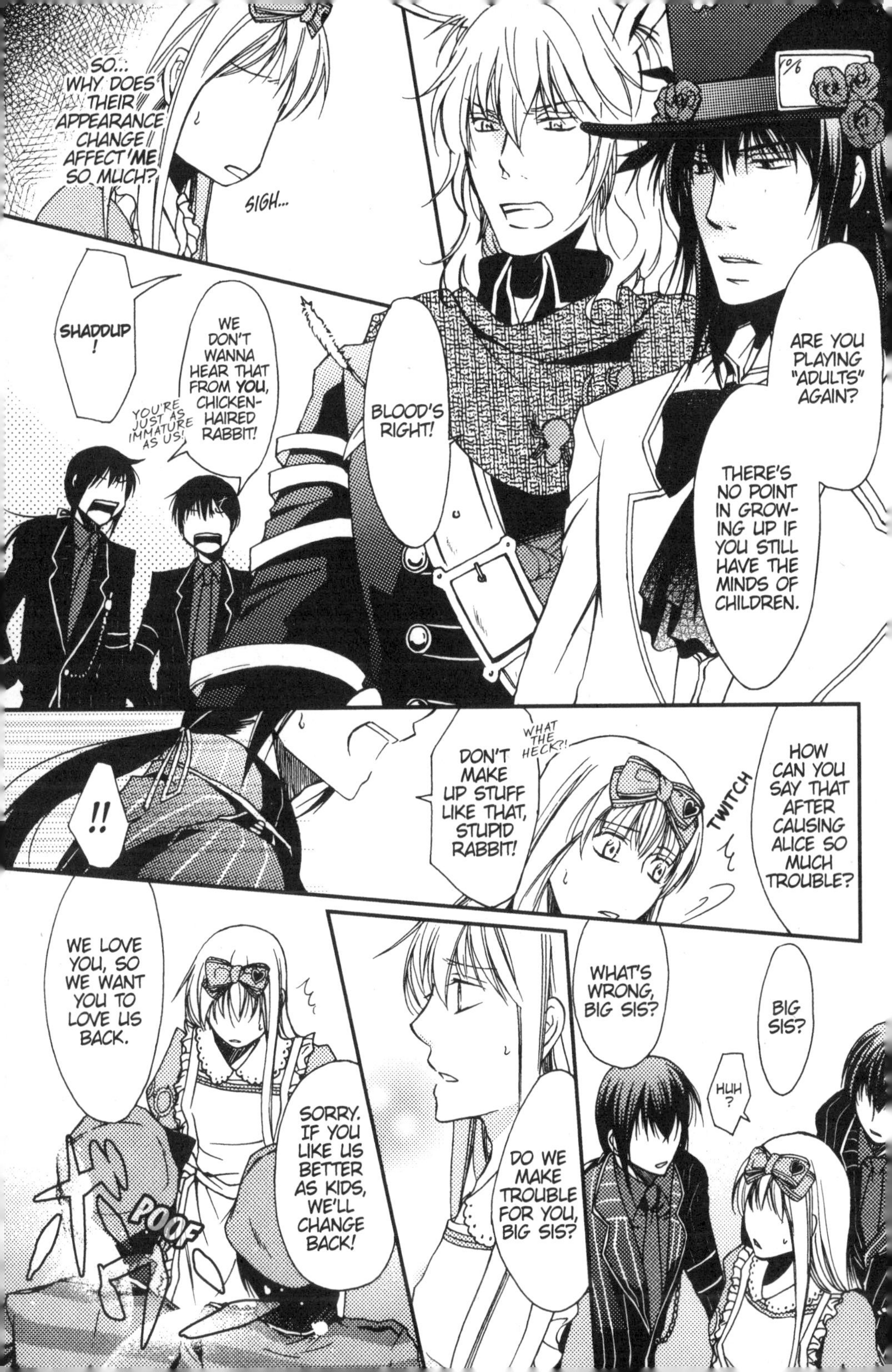
ARE YOU PLAYING "ADULTS" AGAIN?
THERE'S NO POINT IN GROWING UP IF YOU STILL HAVE THE MINDS OF CHILDREN.
BLOOD'S RIGHT!
SO... WHY DOES THEIR APPEARANCE CHANGE AFFECT ME SO MUCH?
SIGH...
WE DON'T WANNA HEAR THAT FROM YOU, CHICKEN-HAIRED RABBIT!
YOU'RE JUST AS IMMATURE AS US!
SHADDUP!
HOW CAN YOU SAY THAT AFTER CAUSING ALICE SO MUCH TROUBLE?
TWITCH
WHAT THE HECK?!
DON'T MAKE UP STUFF LIKE THAT, STUPID RABBIT!
!!
BIG SIS?
HUH?
WHAT'S WRONG, BIG SIS?
DO WE MAKE TROUBLE FOR YOU, BIG SIS?
WE LOVE YOU, SO WE WANT YOU TO LOVE US BACK.
SORRY. IF YOU LIKE US BETTER AS KIDS, WE'LL CHANGE BACK!
POOF

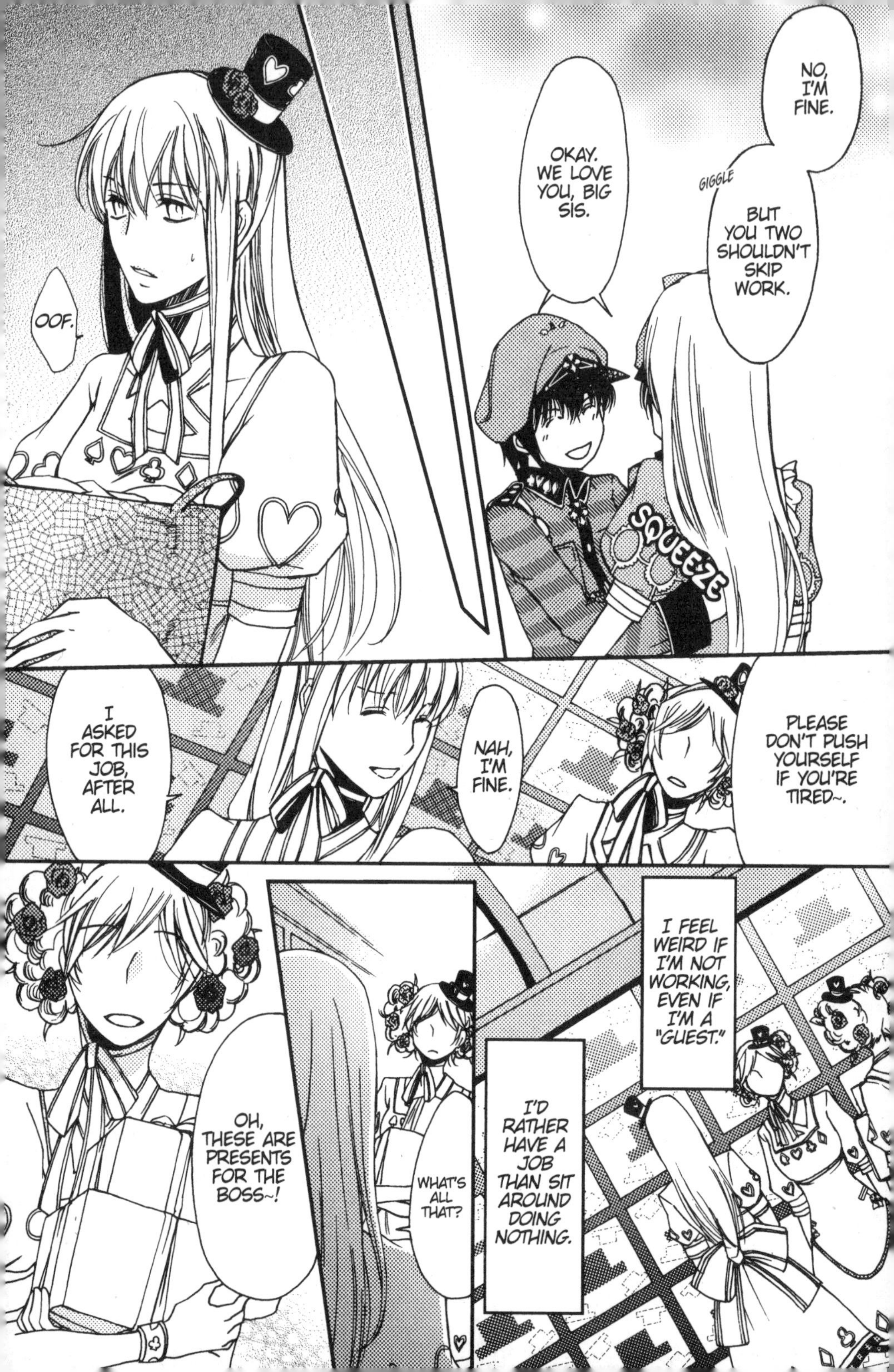
NO, I'M FINE.
GIGGLE
BUT YOU TWO SHOULDN'T SKIP WORK.
OKAY. WE LOVE YOU, BIG SIS.
SQUEEZE
OOF.
PLEASE DON'T PUSH YOURSELF IF YOU'RE TIRED~.
NAH, I'M FINE.
I ASKED FOR THIS JOB, AFTER ALL.
I FEEL WEIRD IF I'M NOT WORKING, EVEN IF I'M A "GUEST."
I'D RATHER HAVE A JOB THAN SIT AROUND DOING NOTHING.
WHAT'S ALL THAT?
OH, THESE ARE PRESENTS FOR THE BOSS~!

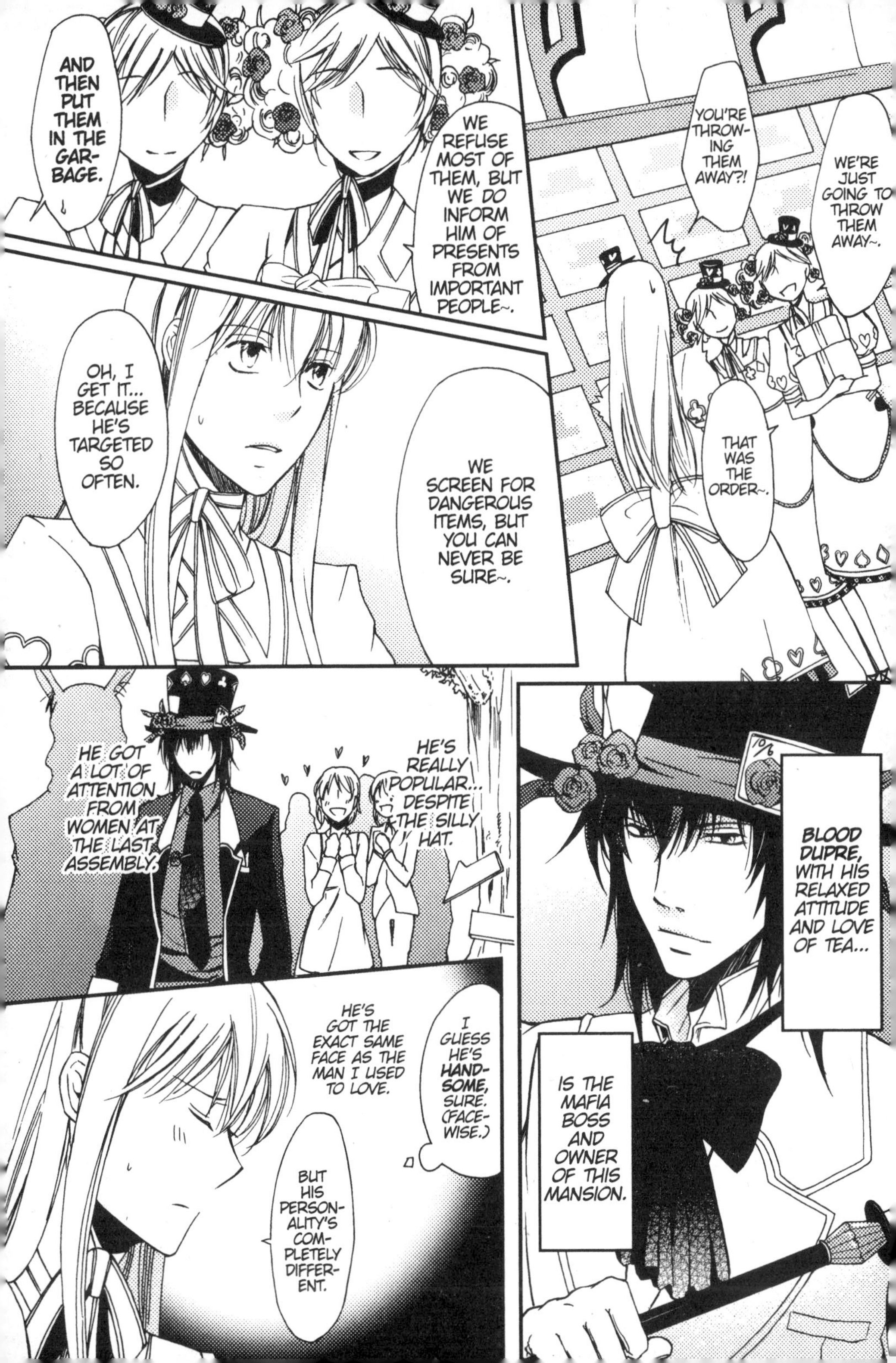
WE'RE JUST GOING TO THROW THEM AWAY~.
YOU'RE THROWING THEM AWAY?!
THAT WAS THE ORDER~.
WE REFUSE MOST OF THEM, BUT WE DO INFORM HIM OF PRESENTS FROM IMPORTANT PEOPLE~.
AND THEN PUT THEM IN THE GARBAGE.
WE SCREEN FOR DANGEROUS ITEMS, BUT YOU CAN NEVER BE SURE~.
OH, I GET IT... BECAUSE HE'S TARGETED SO OFTEN.
BLOOD DUPRE, WITH HIS RELAXED ATTITUDE AND LOVE OF TEA...
IS THE MAFIA BOSS AND OWNER OF THIS MANSION.
HE'S REALLY POPULAR... DESPITE THE SILLY HAT.
HE GOT A LOT OF ATTENTION FROM WOMEN AT THE LAST ASSEMBLY.
I GUESS HE'S HANDSOME, SURE. (FACE-WISE.)
HE'S GOT THE EXACT SAME FACE AS THE MAN I USED TO LOVE.
BUT HIS PERSONALITY'S COMPLETELY DIFFERENT.

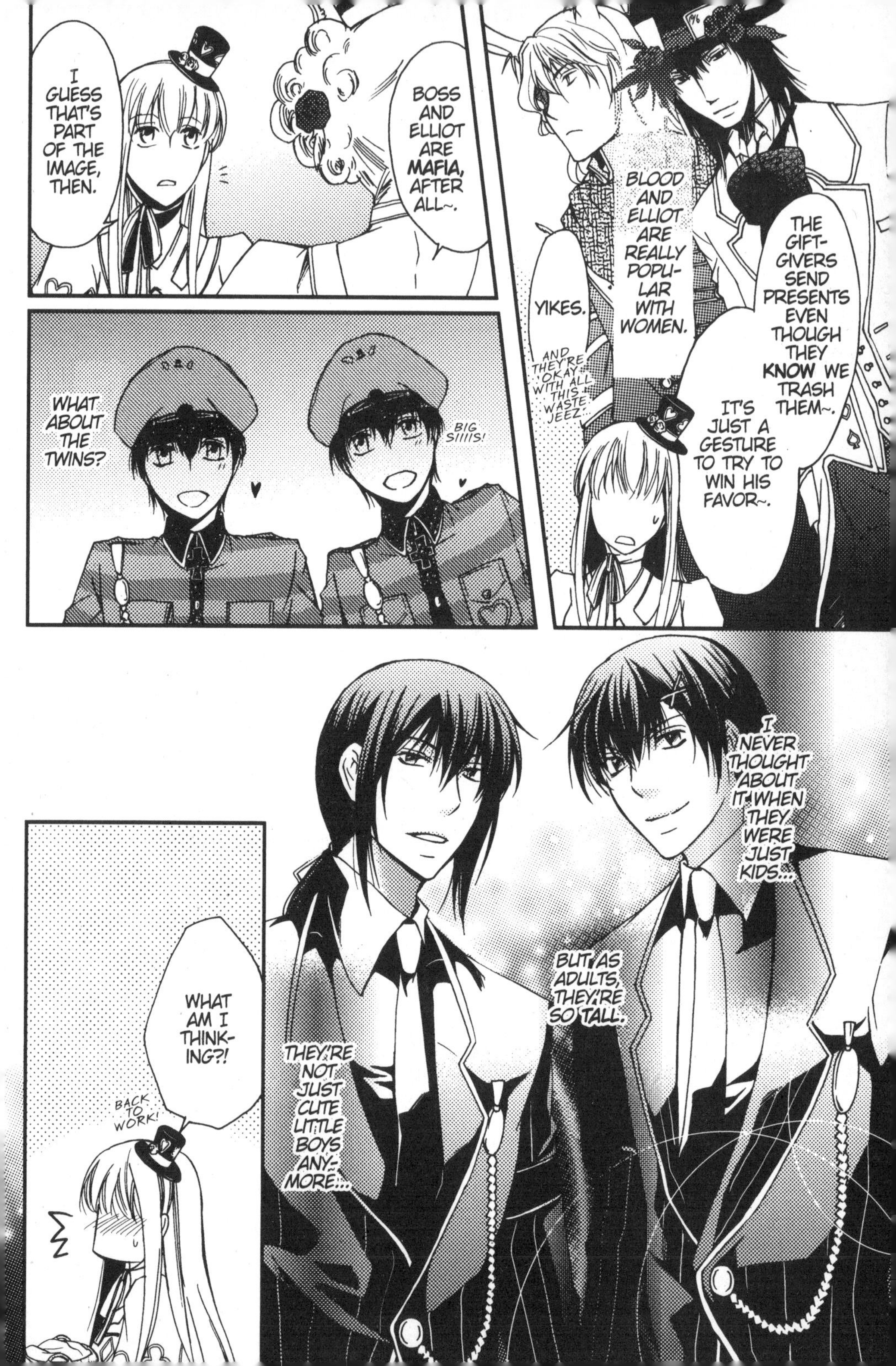
THE GIFT-GIVERS SEND PRESENTS EVEN THOUGH THEY **KNOW** WE TRASH THEM~.
BLOOD AND ELLIOT ARE REALLY POPULAR WITH WOMEN.
YIKES.
AND THEY'RE OKAY WITH ALL THIS WASTE. JEEZ...
IT'S JUST A GESTURE TO TRY TO WIN HIS FAVOR~.
BOSS AND ELLIOT ARE **MAFIA**, AFTER ALL~.
I GUESS THAT'S PART OF THE IMAGE, THEN.
BIG SIIIIS!
WHAT ABOUT THE TWINS?
I NEVER THOUGHT ABOUT IT WHEN THEY WERE JUST KIDS...
BUT AS ADULTS, THEY'RE SO TALL.
THEY'RE NOT JUST CUTE LITTLE BOYS ANYMORE...
WHAT AM I THINKING?!
BACK TO WORK!

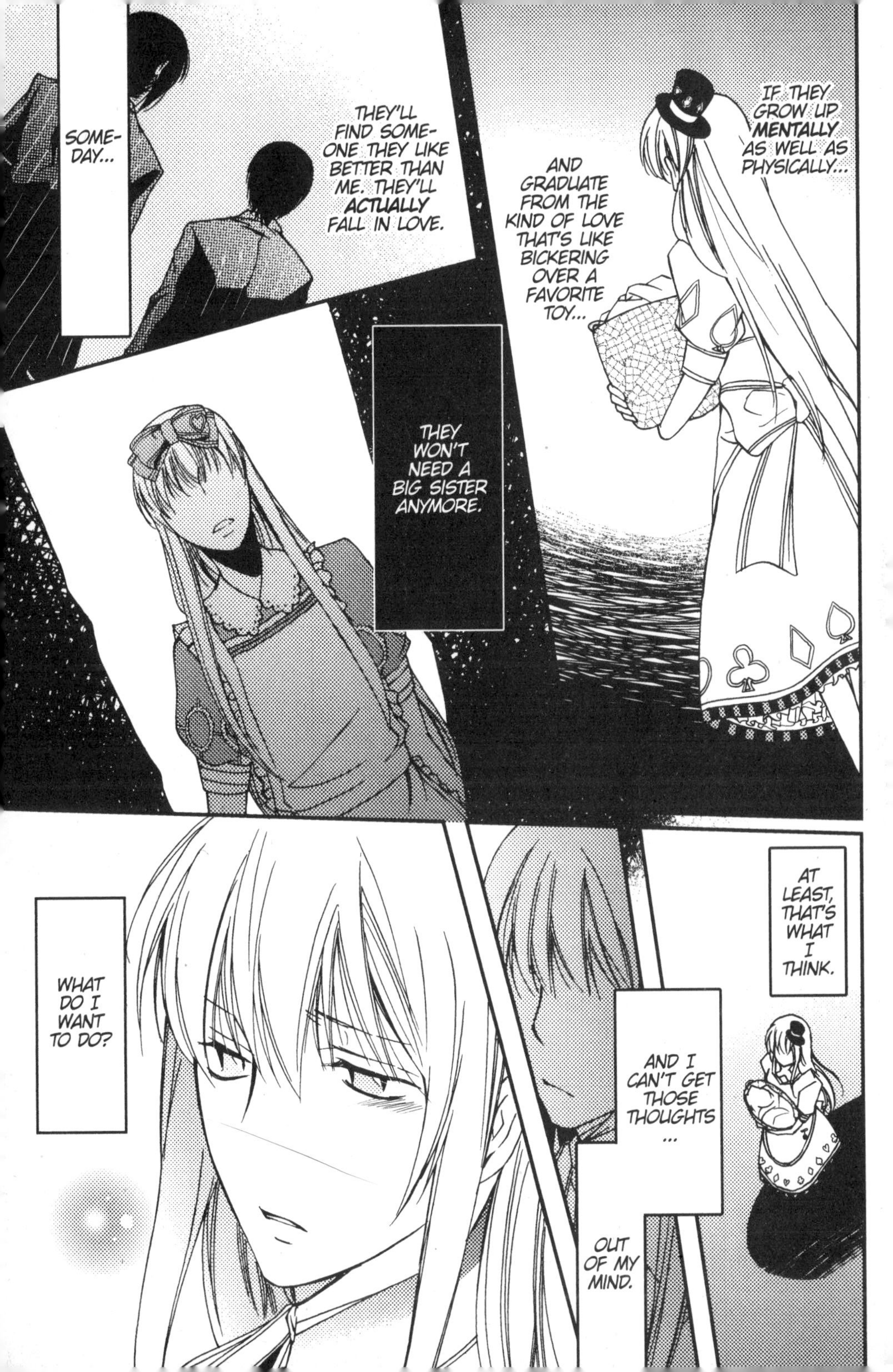
IF THEY GROW UP MENTALLY AS WELL AS PHYSICALLY...
AND GRADUATE FROM THE KIND OF LOVE THAT'S LIKE BICKERING OVER A FAVORITE TOY...
THEY'LL FIND SOME-ONE THEY LIKE BETTER THAN ME. THEY'LL ACTUALLY FALL IN LOVE.
SOME-DAY...
THEY WON'T NEED A BIG SISTER ANYMORE.
AT LEAST, THAT'S WHAT I THINK.
AND I CAN'T GET THOSE THOUGHTS ...
OUT OF MY MIND.
WHAT DO I WANT TO DO?

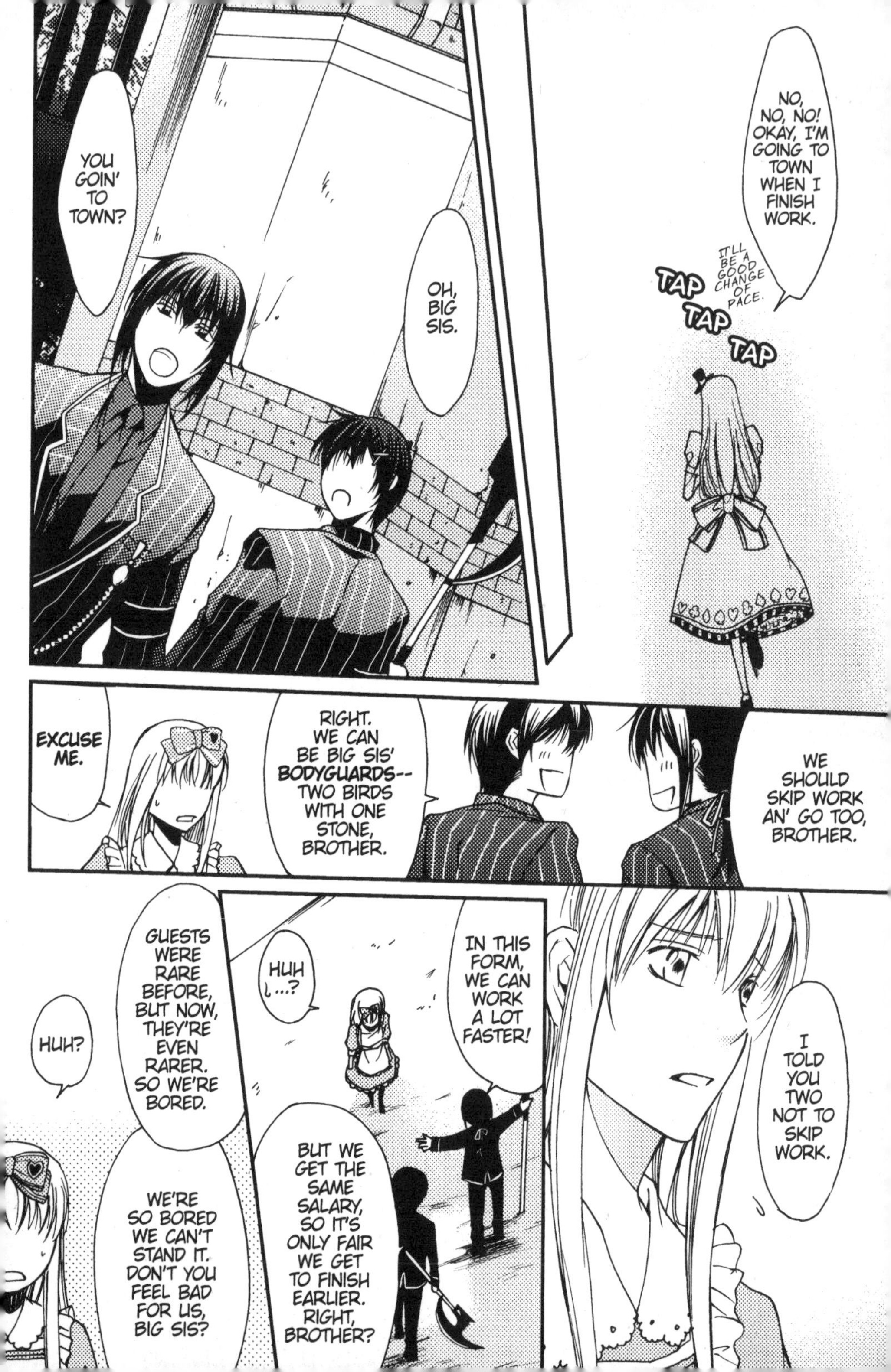
NO, NO, NO! OKAY, I'M GOING TO TOWN WHEN I FINISH WORK.
IT'LL BE A GOOD CHANGE OF PACE.
TAP TAP TAP
OH, BIG SIS.
YOU GOIN' TO TOWN?
WE SHOULD SKIP WORK AN' GO TOO, BROTHER.
RIGHT. WE CAN BE BIG SIS' BODYGUARDS-- TWO BIRDS WITH ONE STONE, BROTHER.
EXCUSE ME.
I TOLD YOU TWO NOT TO SKIP WORK.
IN THIS FORM, WE CAN WORK A LOT FASTER!
HUH...?
BUT WE GET THE SAME SALARY, SO IT'S ONLY FAIR WE GET TO FINISH EARLIER. RIGHT, BROTHER?
GUESTS WERE RARE BEFORE, BUT NOW, THEY'RE EVEN RARER. SO WE'RE BORED.
HUH?
WE'RE SO BORED WE CAN'T STAND IT. DON'T YOU FEEL BAD FOR US, BIG SIS?

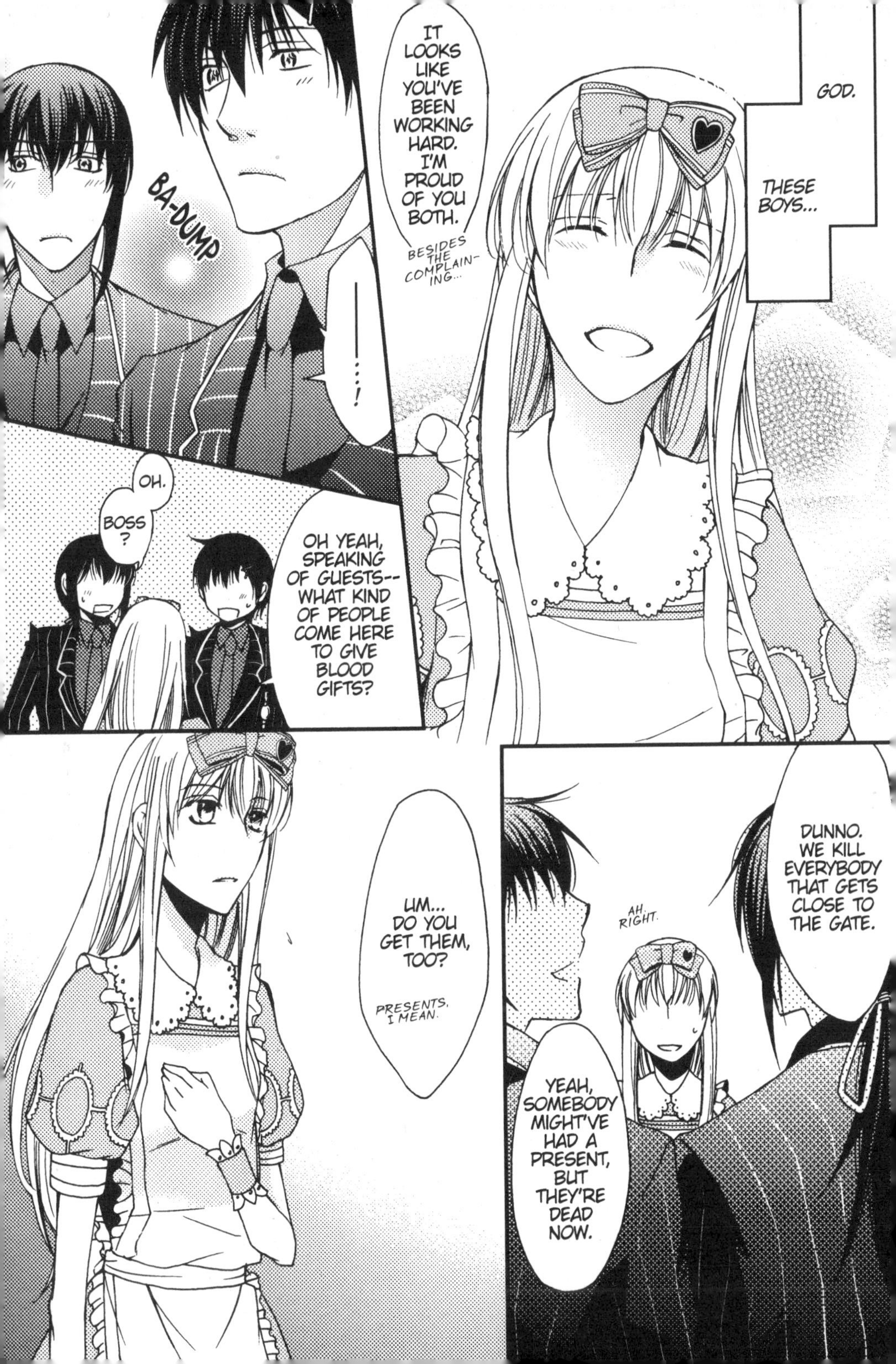
GOD.
THESE BOYS...
IT LOOKS LIKE YOU'VE BEEN WORKING HARD. I'M PROUD OF YOU BOTH.
BESIDES THE COMPLAIN-ING...
...!
BA-DUMP
OH YEAH, SPEAKING OF GUESTS-- WHAT KIND OF PEOPLE COME HERE TO GIVE BLOOD GIFTS?
OH.
BOSS?
DUNNO. WE KILL EVERYBODY THAT GETS CLOSE TO THE GATE.
AH. RIGHT.
YEAH, SOMEBODY MIGHT'VE HAD A PRESENT, BUT THEY'RE DEAD NOW.
UM... DO YOU GET THEM, TOO?
PRESENTS, I MEAN.

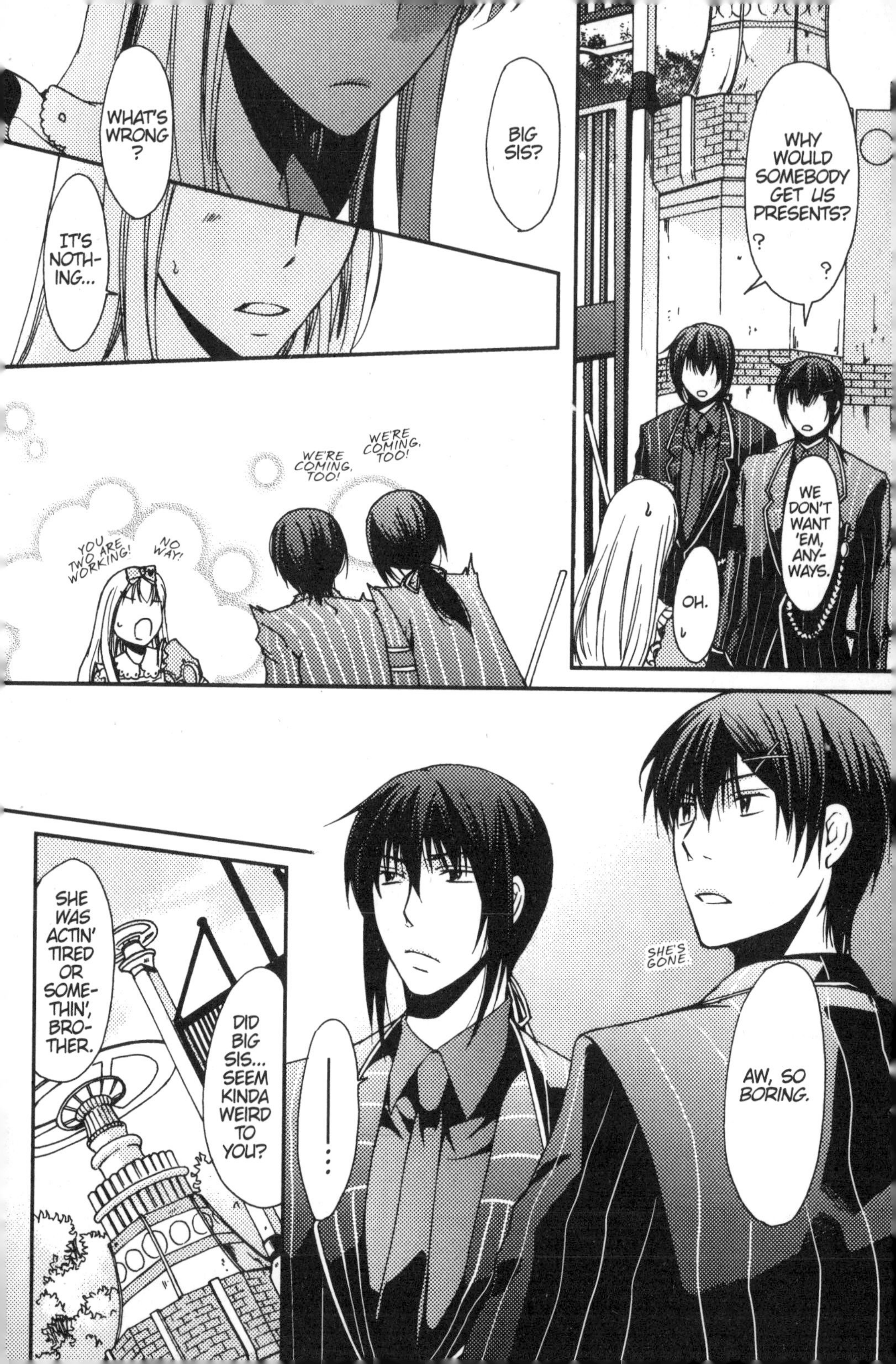
WHY WOULD SOMEBODY GET US PRESENTS?
? ?
WE DON'T WANT 'EM, ANYWAYS.
OH.
BIG SIS?
WHAT'S WRONG?
IT'S NOTHING...
WE'RE COMING, TOO!
WE'RE COMING, TOO!
NO WAY!
YOU TWO ARE WORKING!
SHE'S GONE.
AW, SO BORING.
DID BIG SIS... SEEM KINDA WEIRD TO YOU?
......
SHE WAS ACTIN' TIRED OR SOMETHIN', BROTHER.

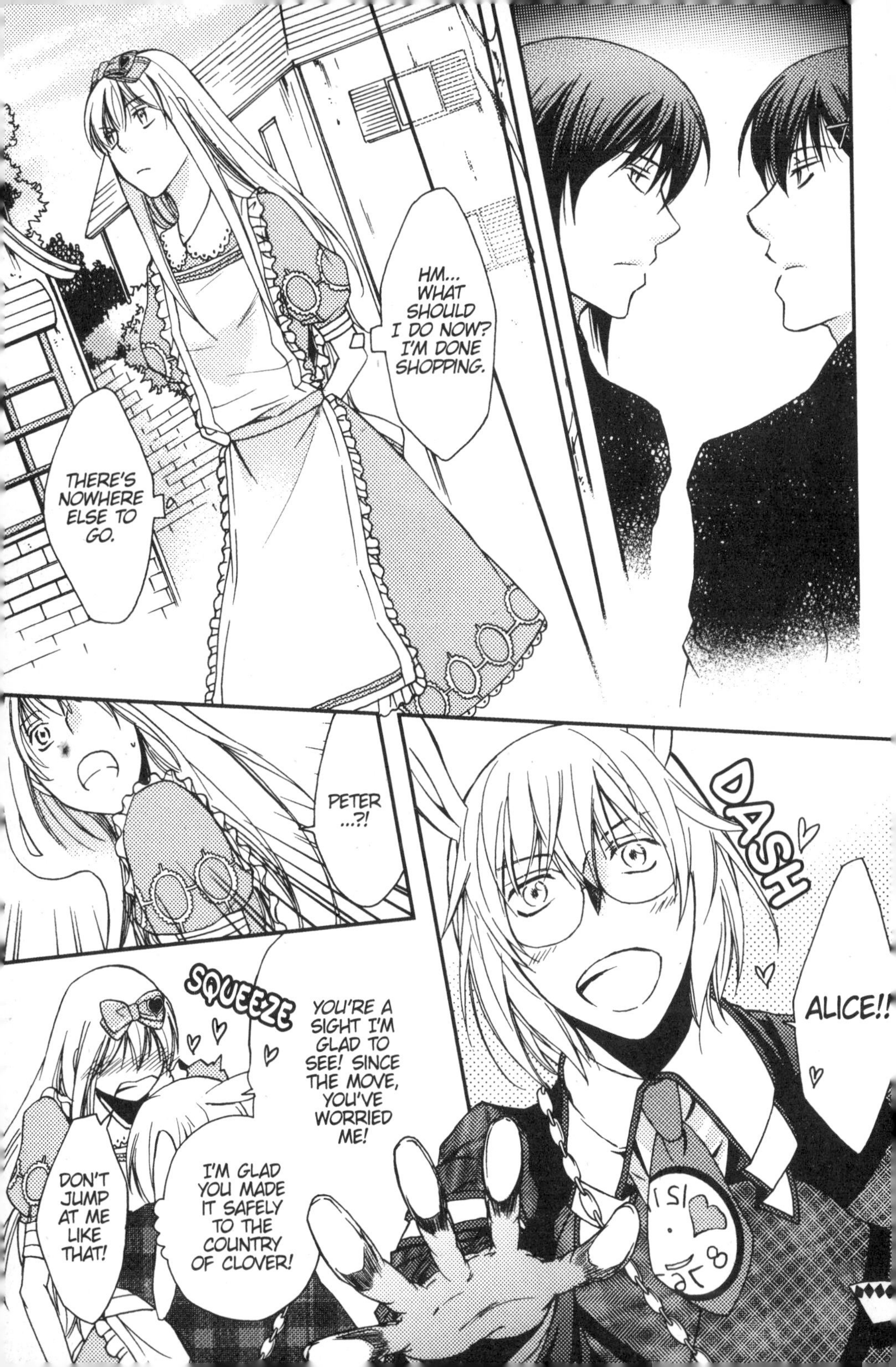
HM... WHAT SHOULD I DO NOW? I'M DONE SHOPPING.
THERE'S NOWHERE ELSE TO GO.
DASH
ALICE!!
PETER ...?!
YOU'RE A SIGHT I'M GLAD TO SEE! SINCE THE MOVE, YOU'VE WORRIED ME!
SQUEEZE
I'M GLAD YOU MADE IT SAFELY TO THE COUNTRY OF CLOVER!
DON'T JUMP AT ME LIKE THAT!

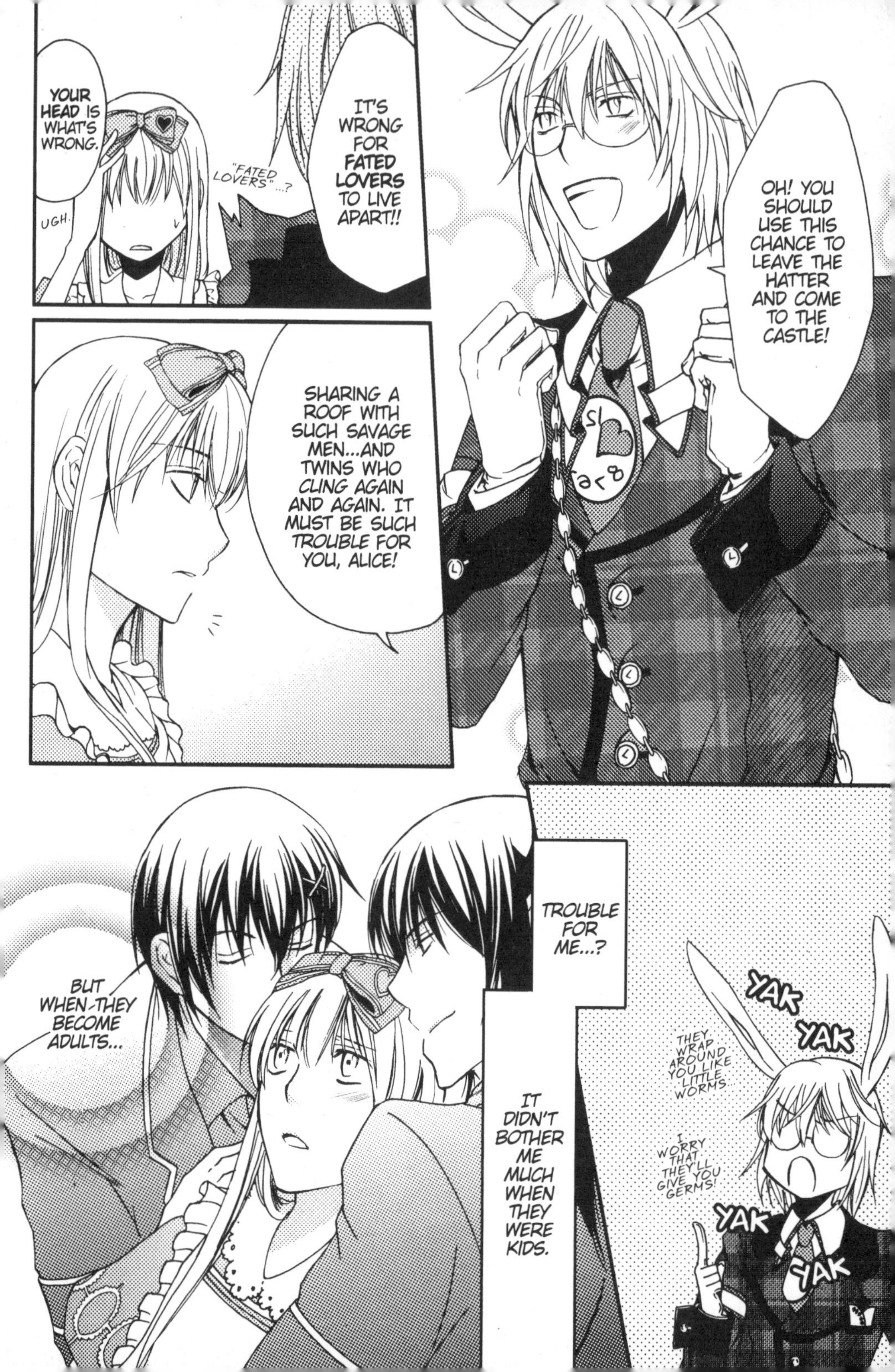
OH! YOU SHOULD USE THIS CHANCE TO LEAVE THE HATTER AND COME TO THE CASTLE!
IT'S WRONG FOR FATED LOVERS TO LIVE APART!!
"FATED LOVERS"...?
YOUR HEAD IS WHAT'S WRONG.
UGH.
SHARING A ROOF WITH SUCH SAVAGE MEN...AND TWINS WHO CLING AGAIN AND AGAIN. IT MUST BE SUCH TROUBLE FOR YOU, ALICE!
YAK
YAK
THEY WRAP AROUND YOU LIKE LITTLE WORMS.
I WORRY THAT THEY'LL GIVE YOU GERMS!
YAK
YAK
TROUBLE FOR ME...?
IT DIDN'T BOTHER ME MUCH WHEN THEY WERE KIDS.
BUT WHEN THEY BECOME ADULTS...

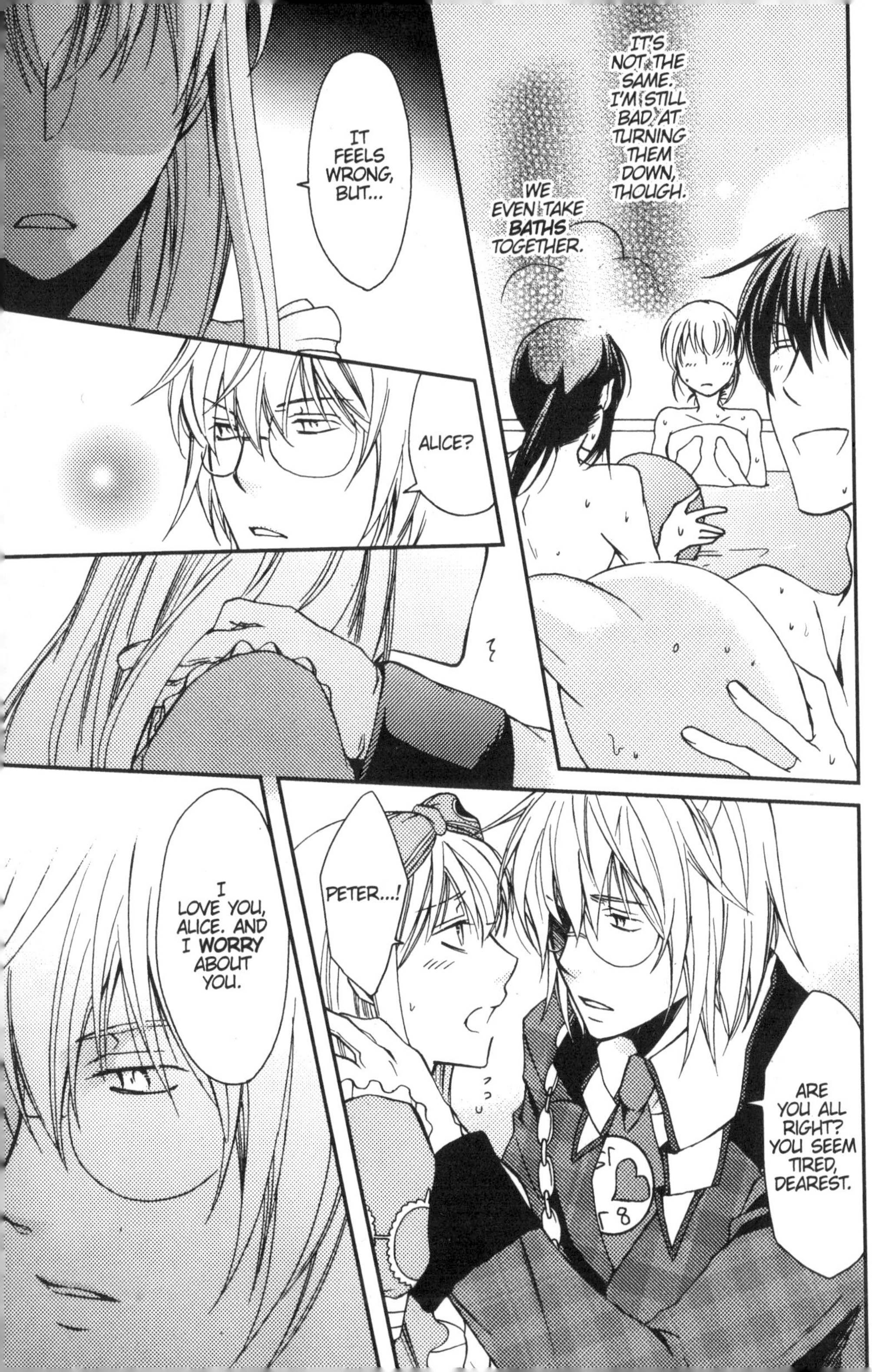
IT'S NOT THE SAME. I'M STILL BAD AT TURNING THEM DOWN, THOUGH.
WE EVEN TAKE **BATHS** TOGETHER.
IT FEELS WRONG, BUT...
ALICE?
ARE YOU ALL RIGHT? YOU SEEM TIRED, DEAREST.
PETER...!
I LOVE YOU, ALICE. AND I **WORRY** ABOUT YOU.

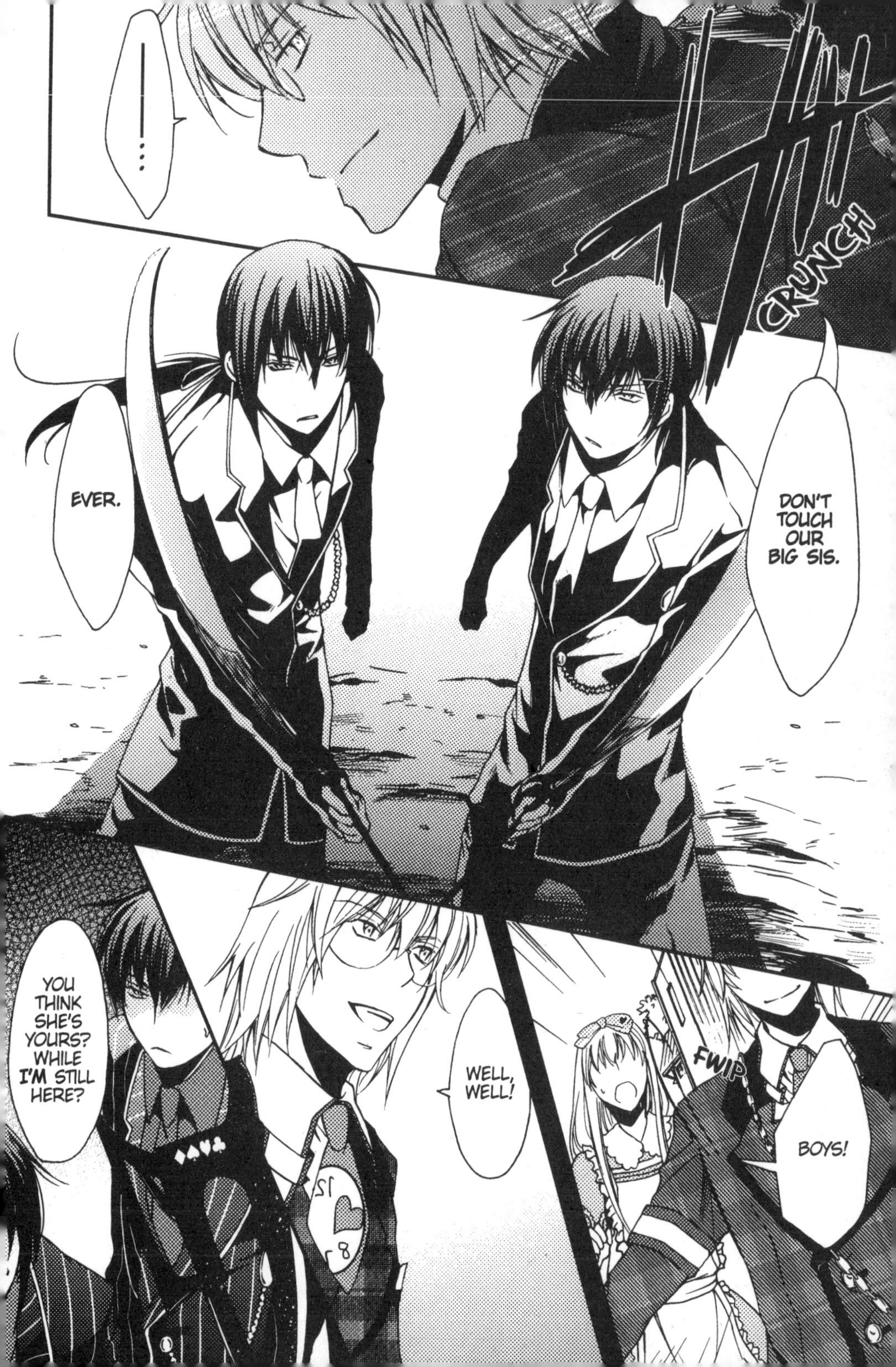
CRUNCH
!…
DON'T TOUCH OUR BIG SIS.
EVER.
FWIP
BOYS!
WELL, WELL!
YOU THINK SHE'S YOURS? WHILE I'M STILL HERE?

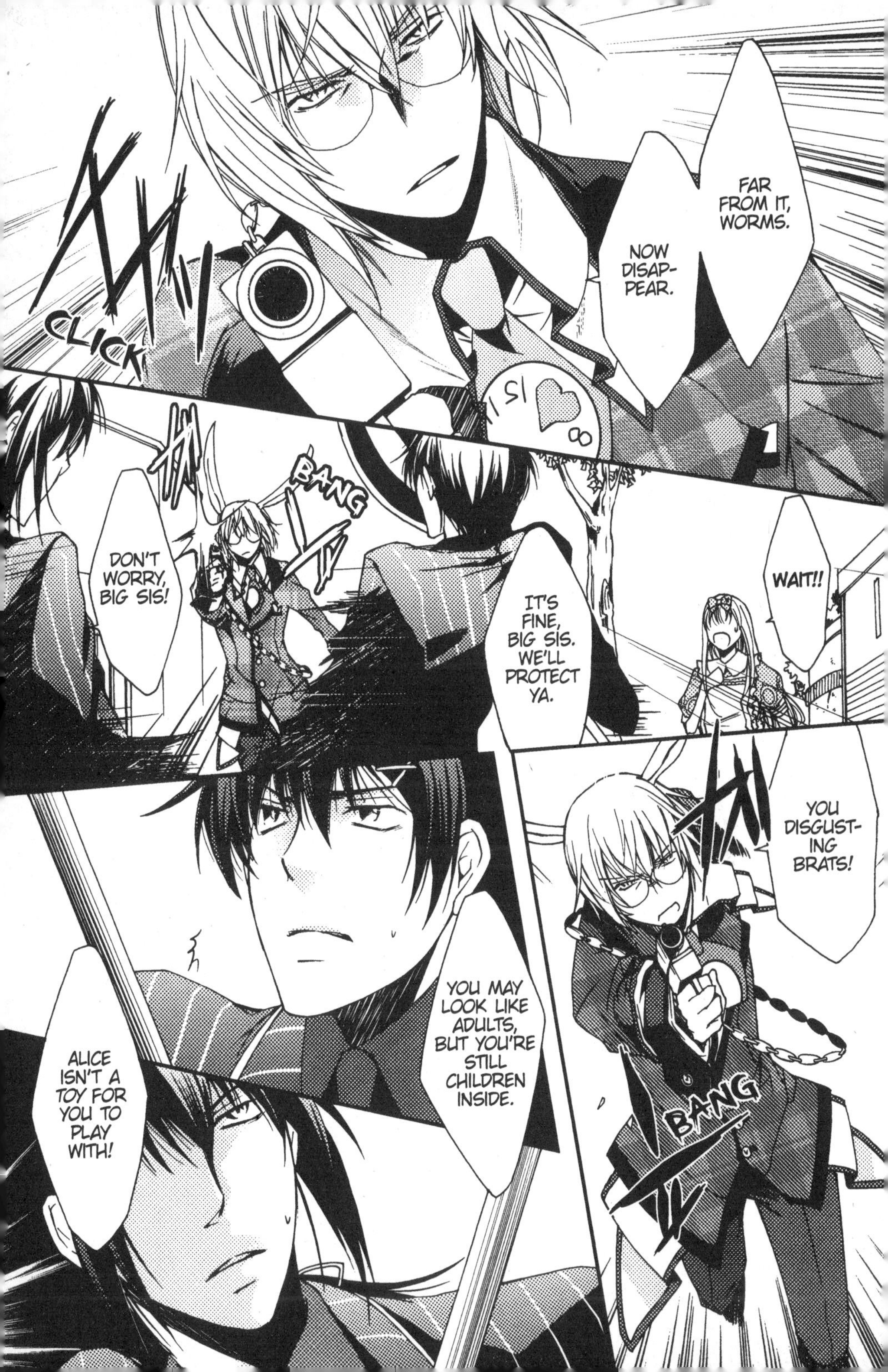
FAR FROM IT, WORMS.
NOW DISAP-PEAR.
CLICK
WAIT!!
IT'S FINE, BIG SIS. WE'LL PROTECT YA.
BANG
DON'T WORRY, BIG SIS!
YOU DISGUST-ING BRATS!
BANG
YOU MAY LOOK LIKE ADULTS, BUT YOU'RE STILL CHILDREN INSIDE.
ALICE ISN'T A TOY FOR YOU TO PLAY WITH!

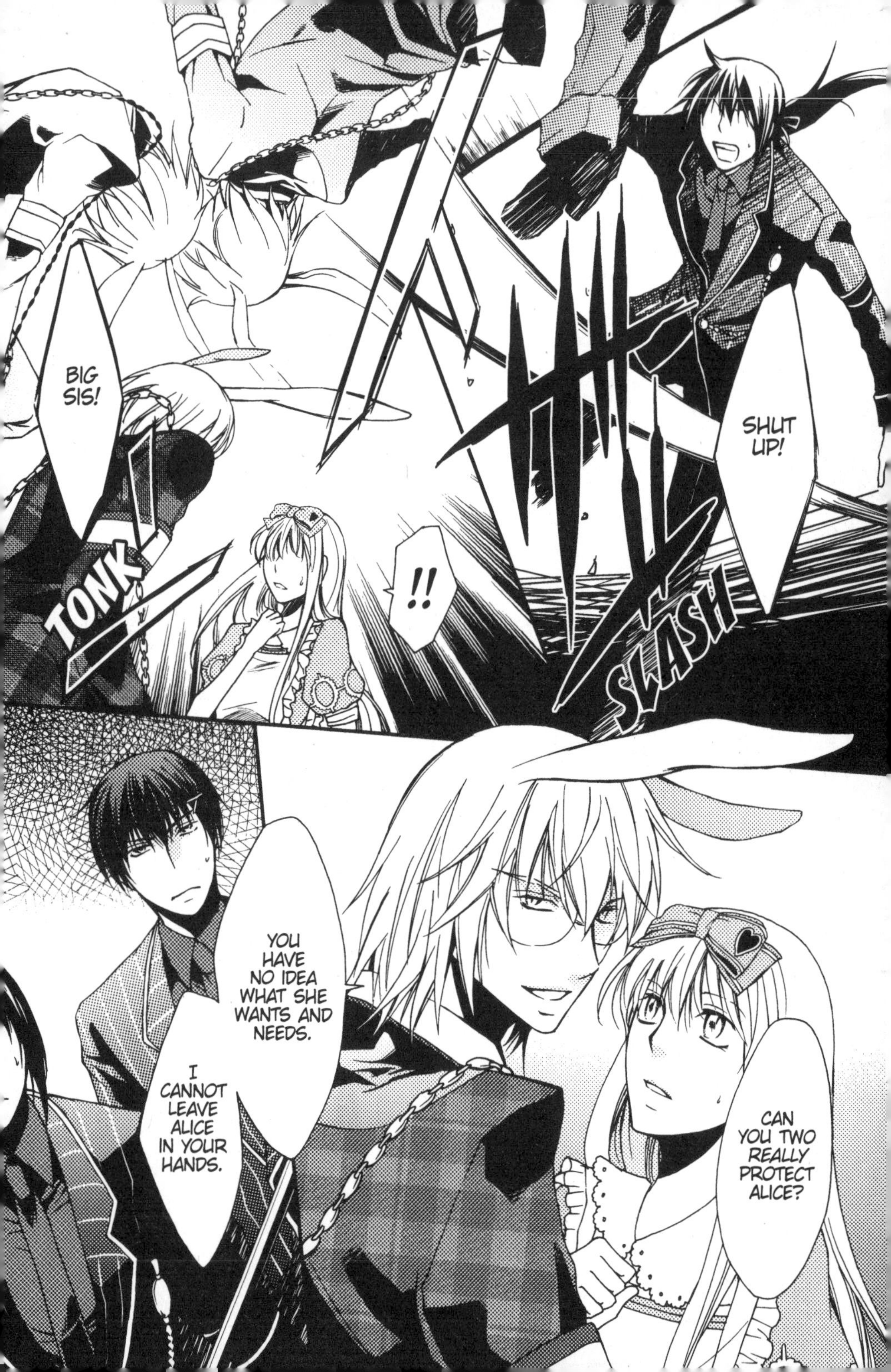
SHUT UP!
SLASH
!!
BIG SIS!
TONK
CAN YOU TWO REALLY PROTECT ALICE?
YOU HAVE NO IDEA WHAT SHE WANTS AND NEEDS.
I CANNOT LEAVE ALICE IN YOUR HANDS.

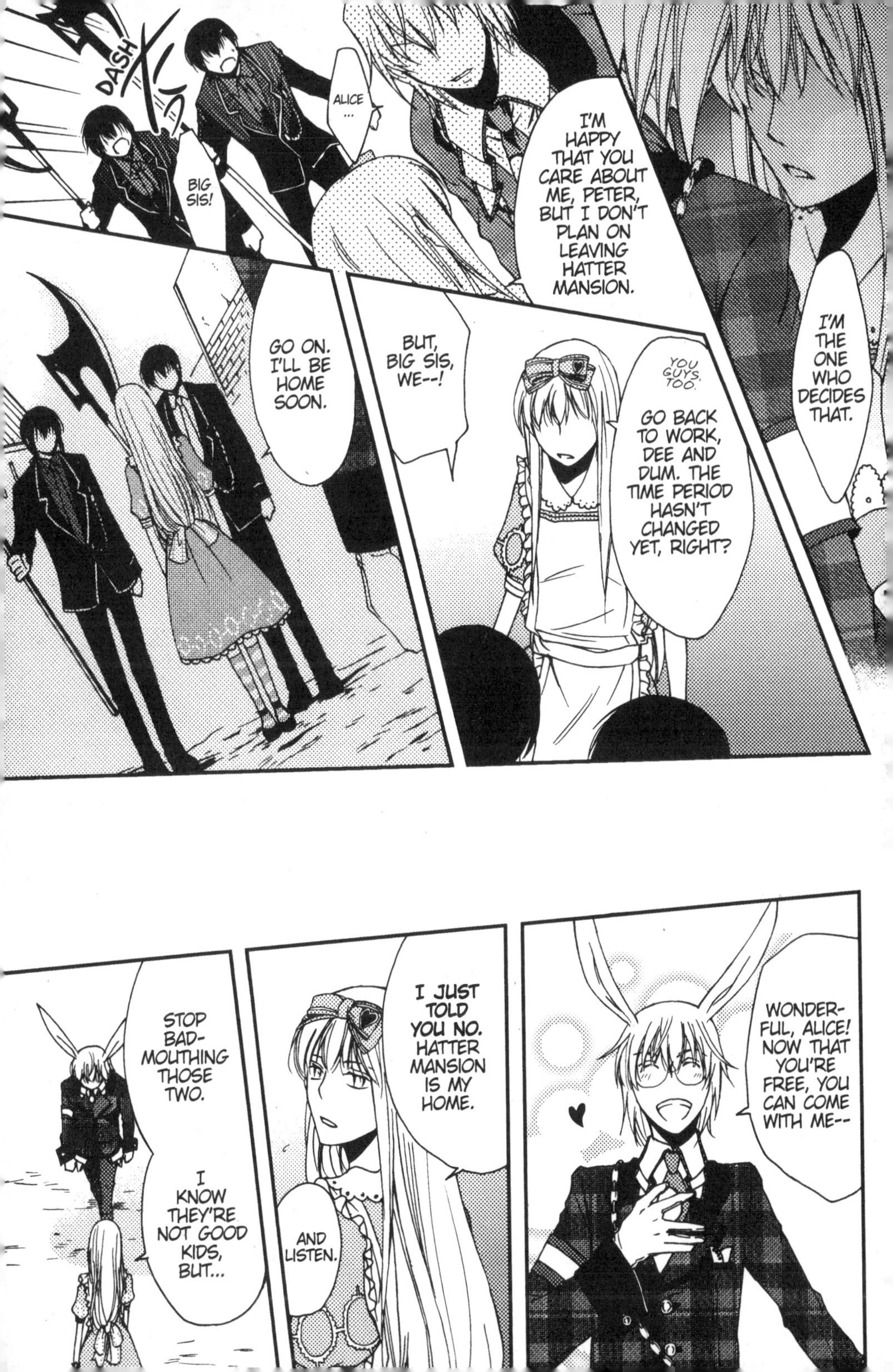
I'M HAPPY THAT YOU CARE ABOUT ME, PETER, BUT I DON'T PLAN ON LEAVING HATTER MANSION.
I'M THE ONE WHO DECIDES THAT.
ALICE ...
DASH
BIG SIS!
YOU GUYS, TOO.
GO BACK TO WORK, DEE AND DUM. THE TIME PERIOD HASN'T CHANGED YET, RIGHT?
BUT, BIG SIS, WE--!
GO ON. I'LL BE HOME SOON.
WONDER-FUL, ALICE! NOW THAT YOU'RE FREE, YOU CAN COME WITH ME--
I JUST TOLD YOU NO. HATTER MANSION IS MY HOME.
AND LISTEN.
STOP BAD-MOUTHING THOSE TWO.
I KNOW THEY'RE NOT GOOD KIDS, BUT...

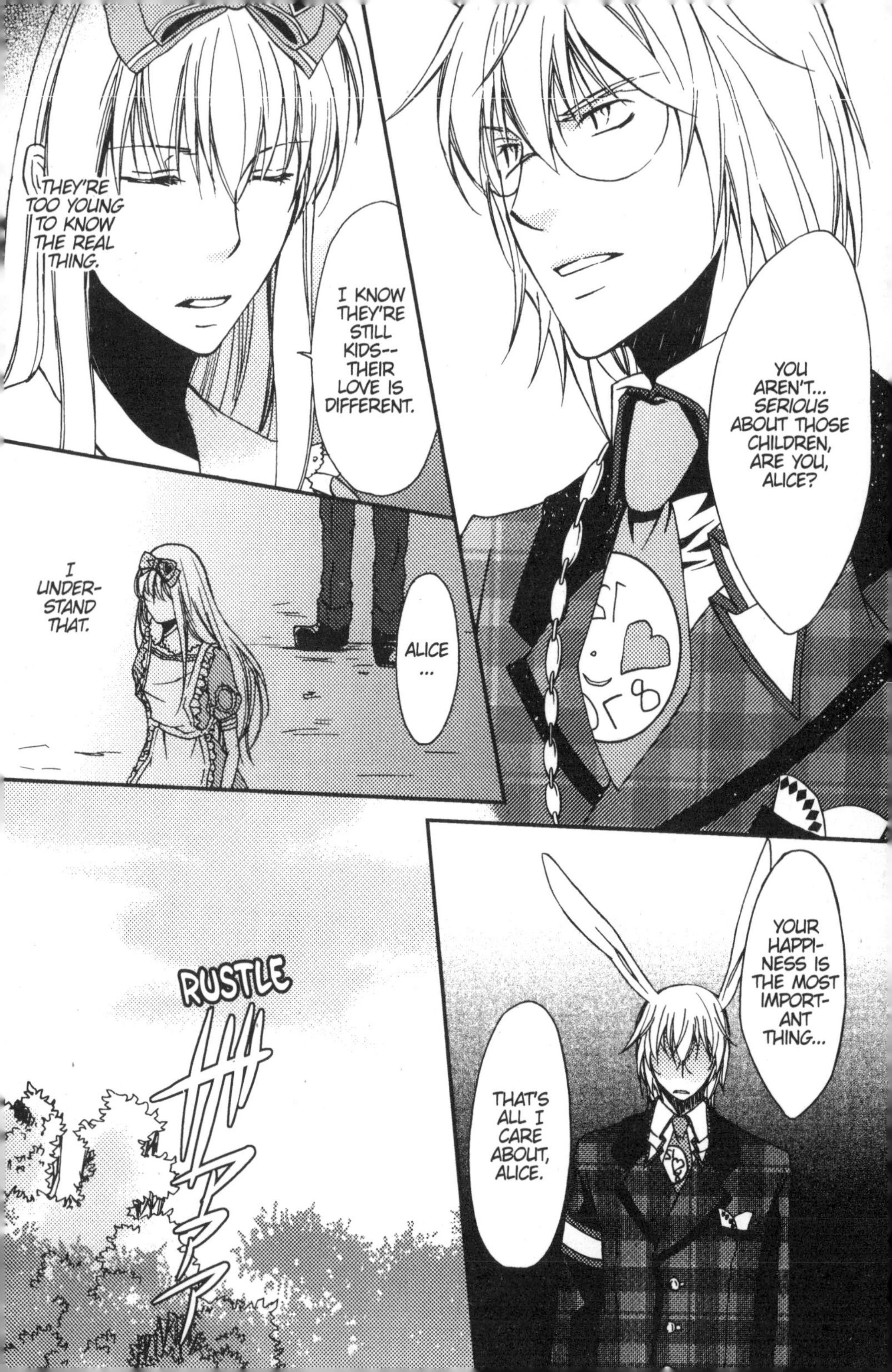
YOU AREN'T... SERIOUS ABOUT THOSE CHILDREN, ARE YOU, ALICE?
I KNOW THEY'RE STILL KIDS-- THEIR LOVE IS DIFFERENT.
THEY'RE TOO YOUNG TO KNOW THE REAL THING.
ALICE ...
I UNDER-STAND THAT.
YOUR HAPPI-NESS IS THE MOST IMPORT-ANT THING...
THAT'S ALL I CARE ABOUT, ALICE.
RUSTLE

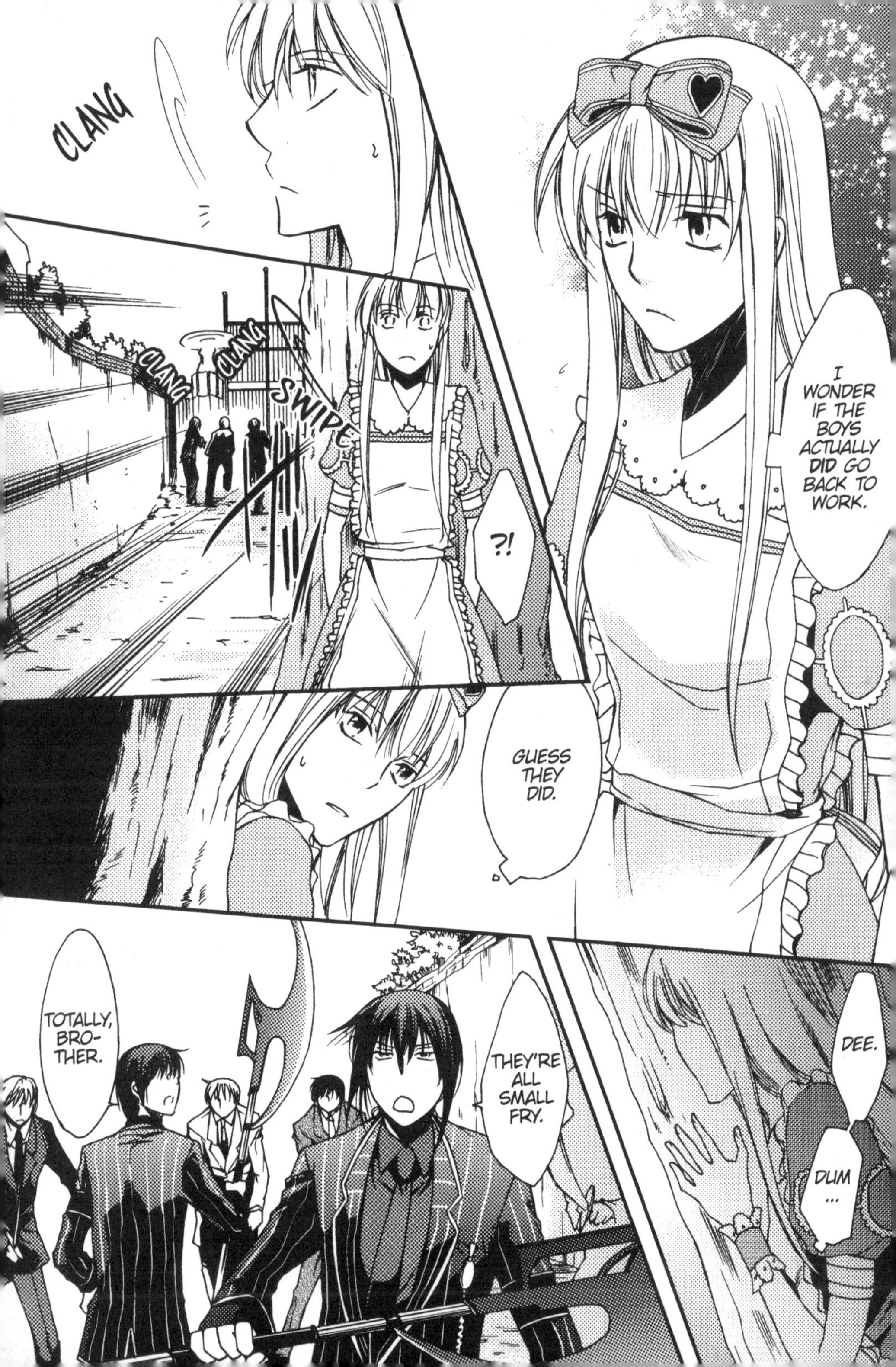
I WONDER IF THE BOYS ACTUALLY DID GO BACK TO WORK.
CLANG
CLANG
CLANG
SWIPE
?!
GUESS THEY DID.
DEE.
DUM ...
THEY'RE ALL SMALL FRY.
TOTALLY, BRO-THER.

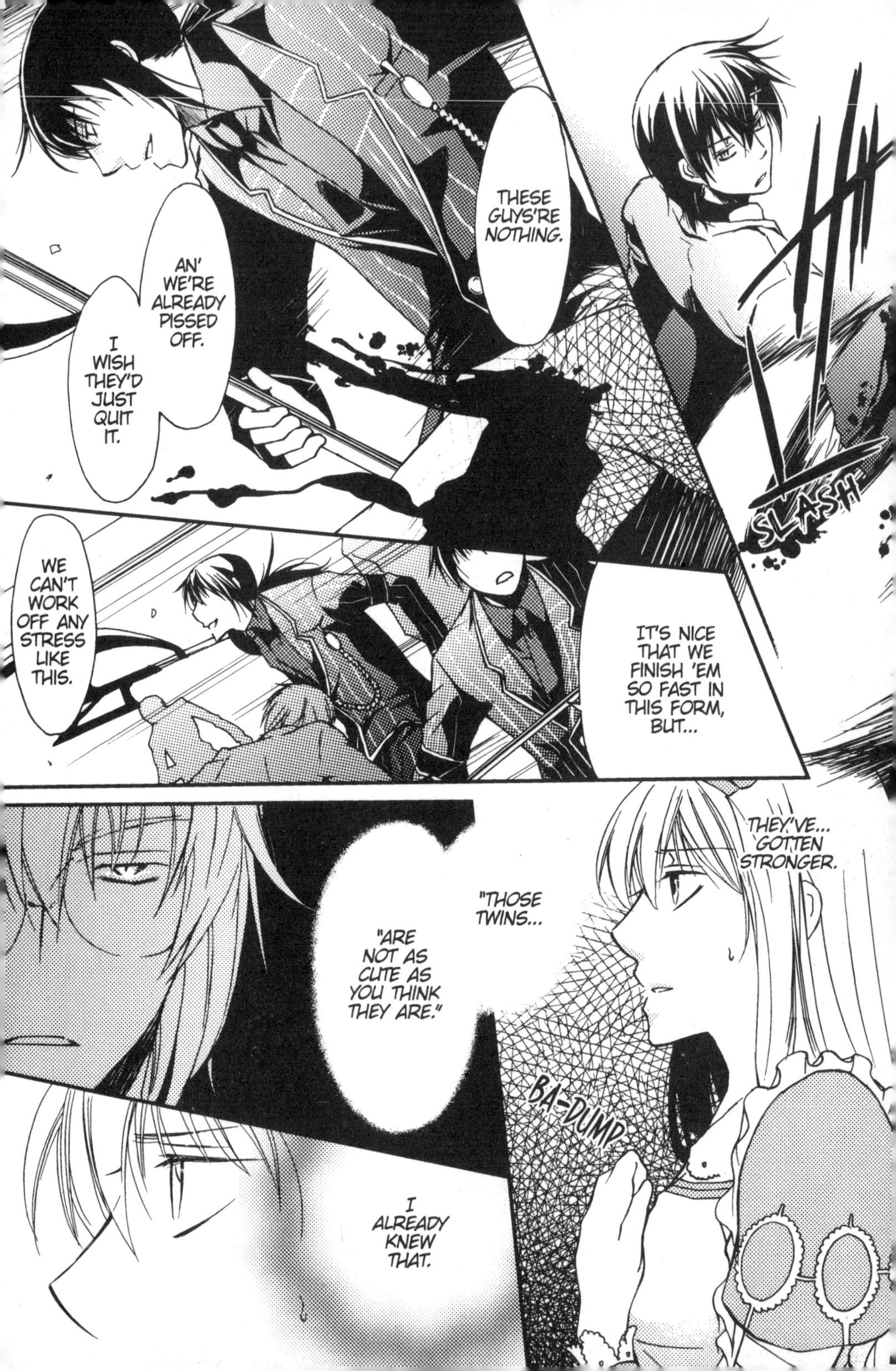
THESE GUYS'RE NOTHING.
AN' WE'RE ALREADY PISSED OFF.
I WISH THEY'D JUST QUIT IT.
SLASH
IT'S NICE THAT WE FINISH 'EM SO FAST IN THIS FORM, BUT...
WE CAN'T WORK OFF ANY STRESS LIKE THIS.
THEY'VE... GOTTEN STRONGER.
"THOSE TWINS...
"ARE NOT AS CUTE AS YOU THINK THEY ARE."
BA-DUMP
I ALREADY KNEW THAT.

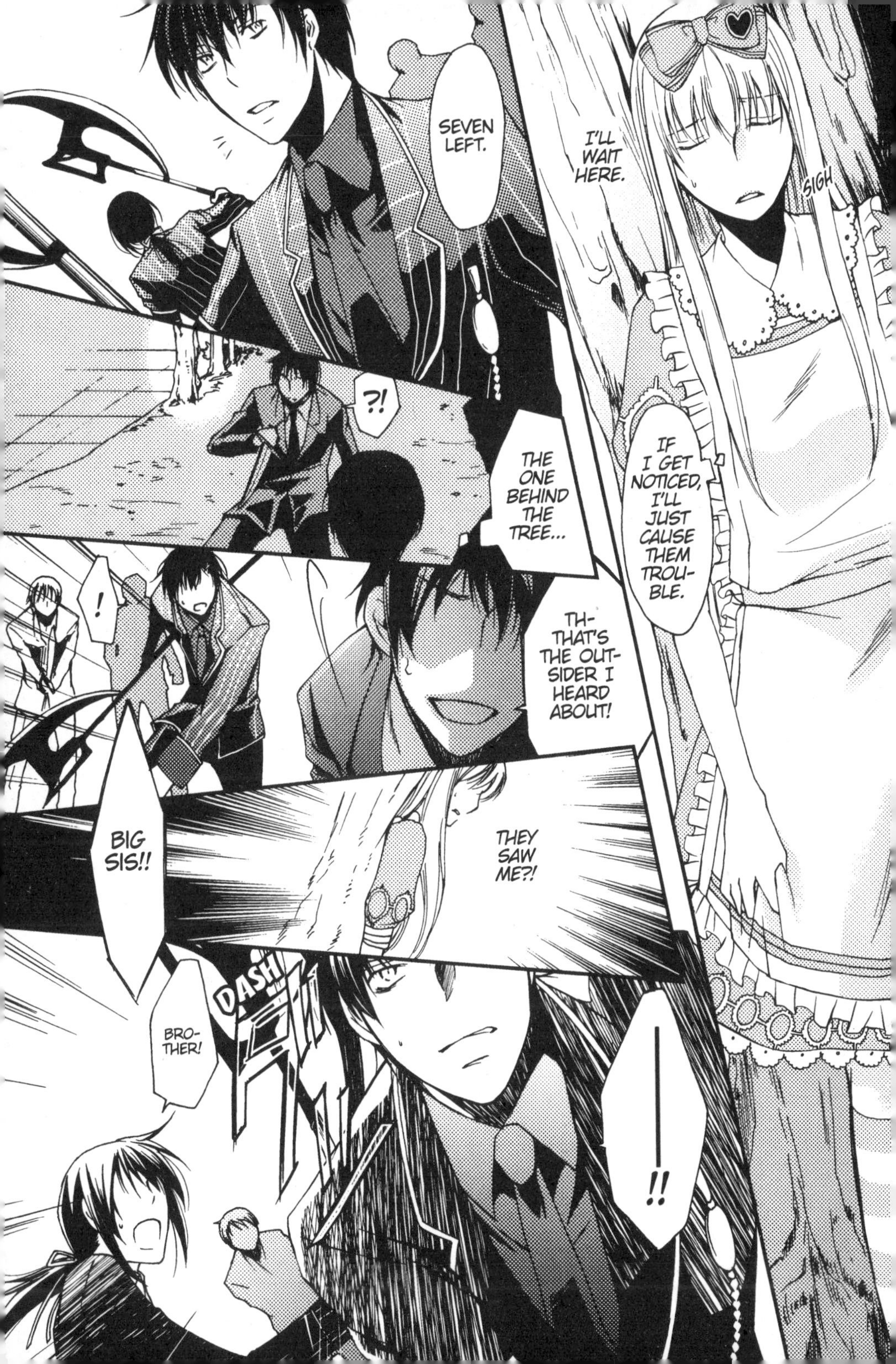

I'LL WAIT HERE.
SIGH
IF I GET NOTICED, I'LL JUST CAUSE THEM TROUBLE.
SEVEN LEFT.
THE ONE BEHIND THE TREE...
?!
TH-THAT'S THE OUTSIDER I HEARD ABOUT!
!
THEY SAW ME?!
BIG SIS!!
—!!
DASH
BROTHER!

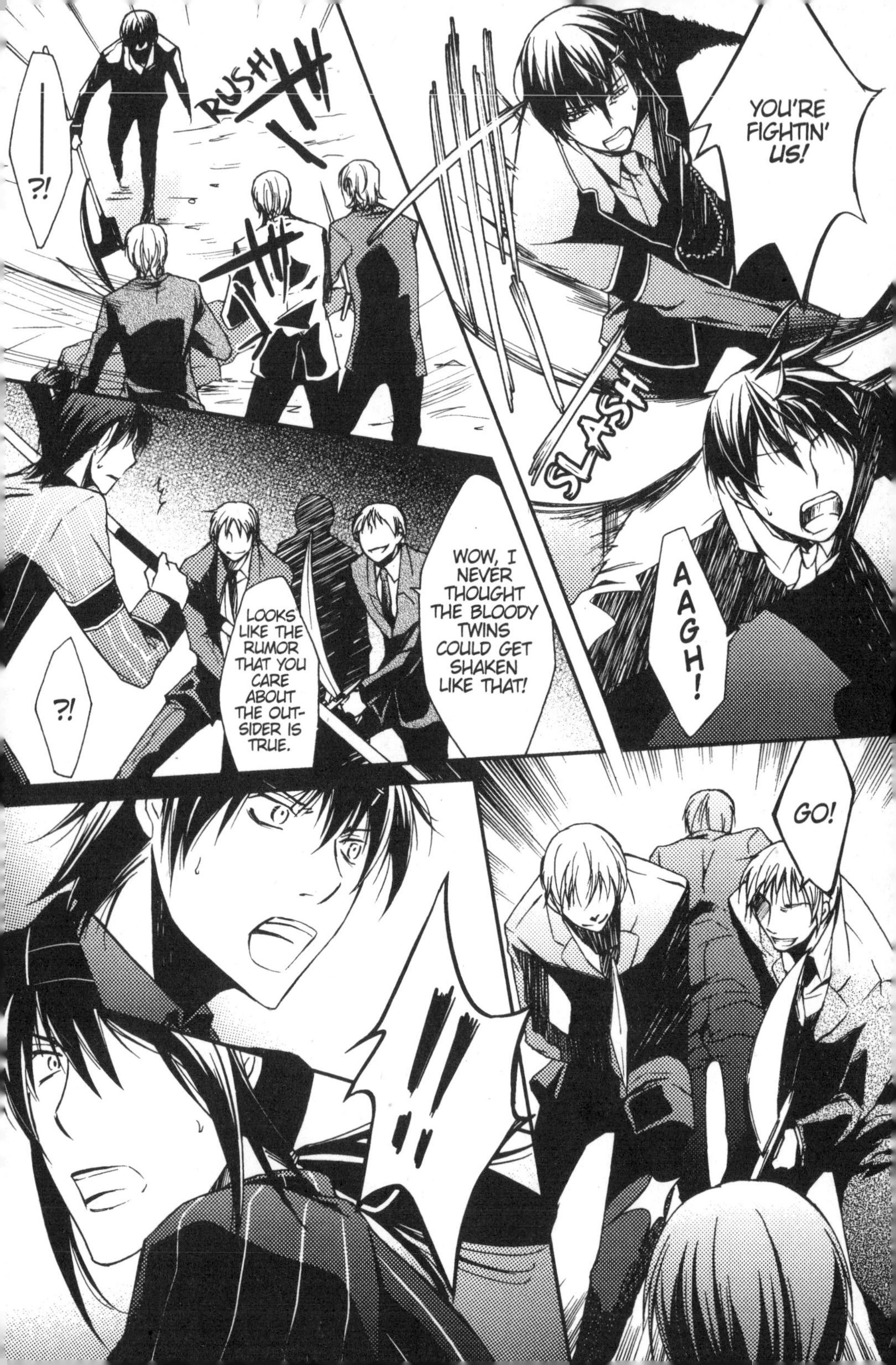

YOU'RE FIGHTIN' US!
SLASH
AAGH!
RUSH
?!
WOW, I NEVER THOUGHT THE BLOODY TWINS COULD GET SHAKEN LIKE THAT!
LOOKS LIKE THE RUMOR THAT YOU CARE ABOUT THE OUT-SIDER IS TRUE.
?!
GO!

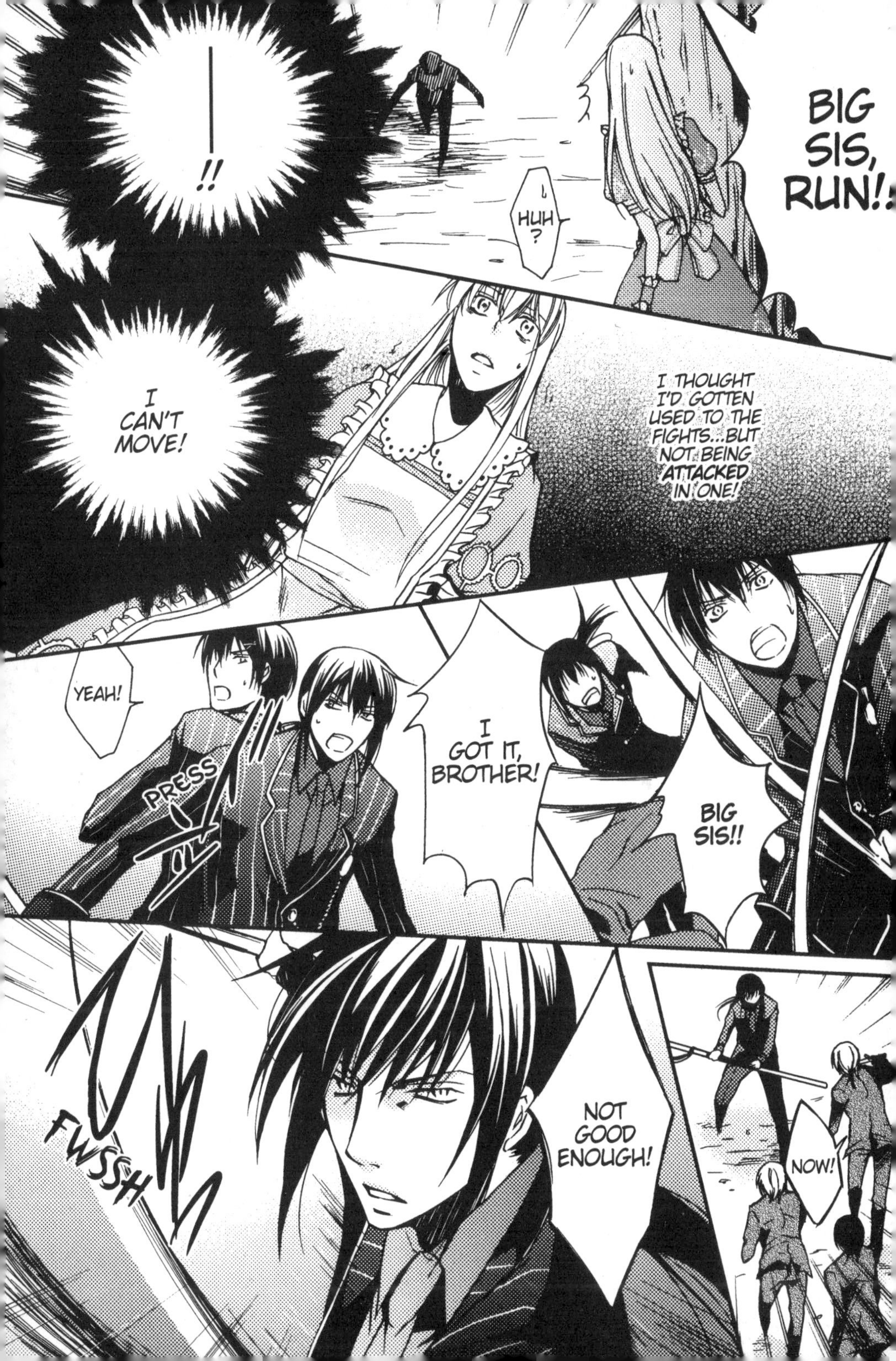
BIG SIS, RUN!!
HUH?
—!!
I THOUGHT I'D GOTTEN USED TO THE FIGHTS...BUT NOT BEING ATTACKED IN ONE!
I CAN'T MOVE!
BIG SIS!!
I GOT IT, BROTHER!
YEAH!
PRESS
NOW!
NOT GOOD ENOUGH!
FWSSH

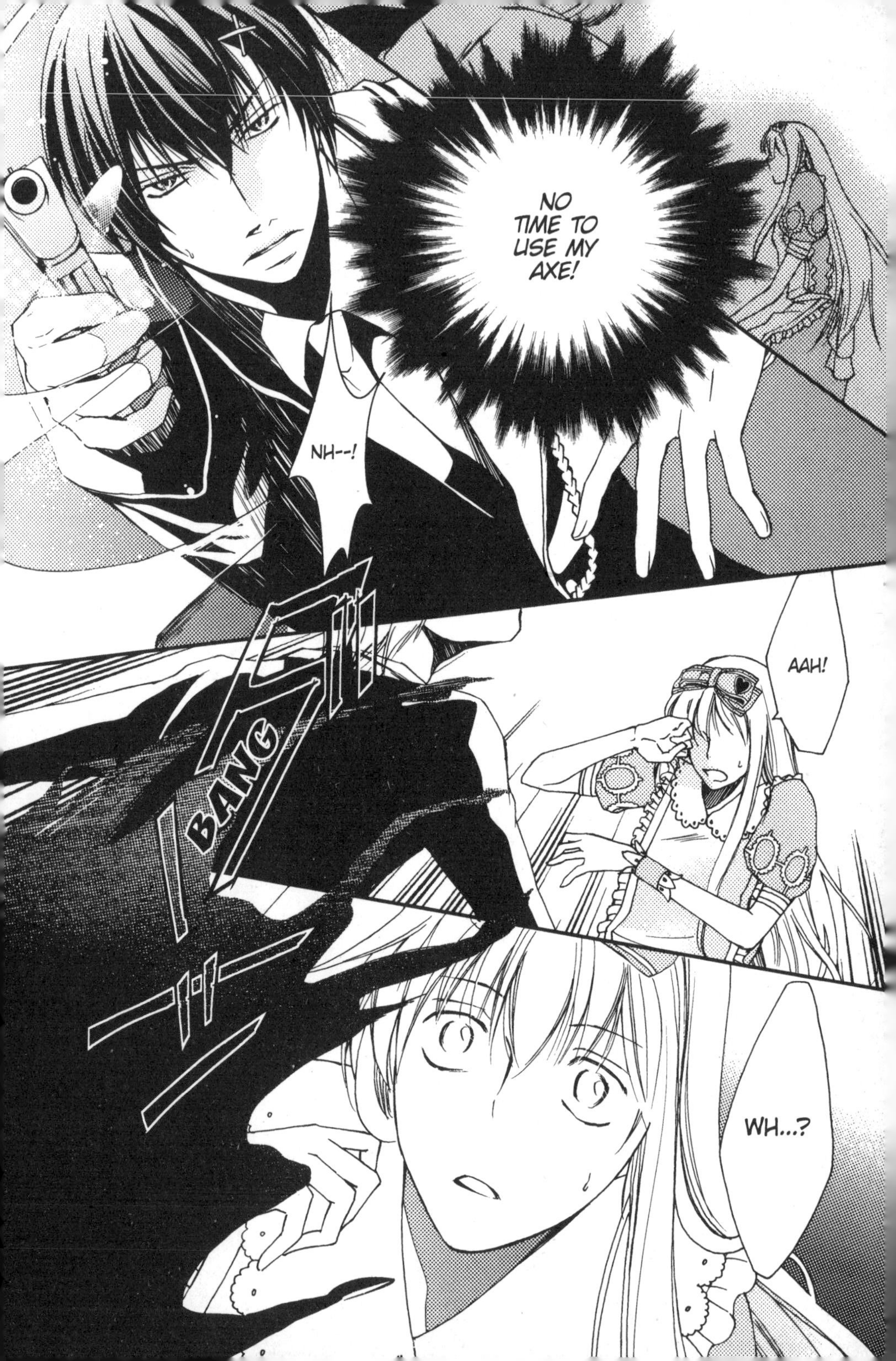
NO TIME TO USE MY AXE!
NH--!
AAH!
BANG
WH...?

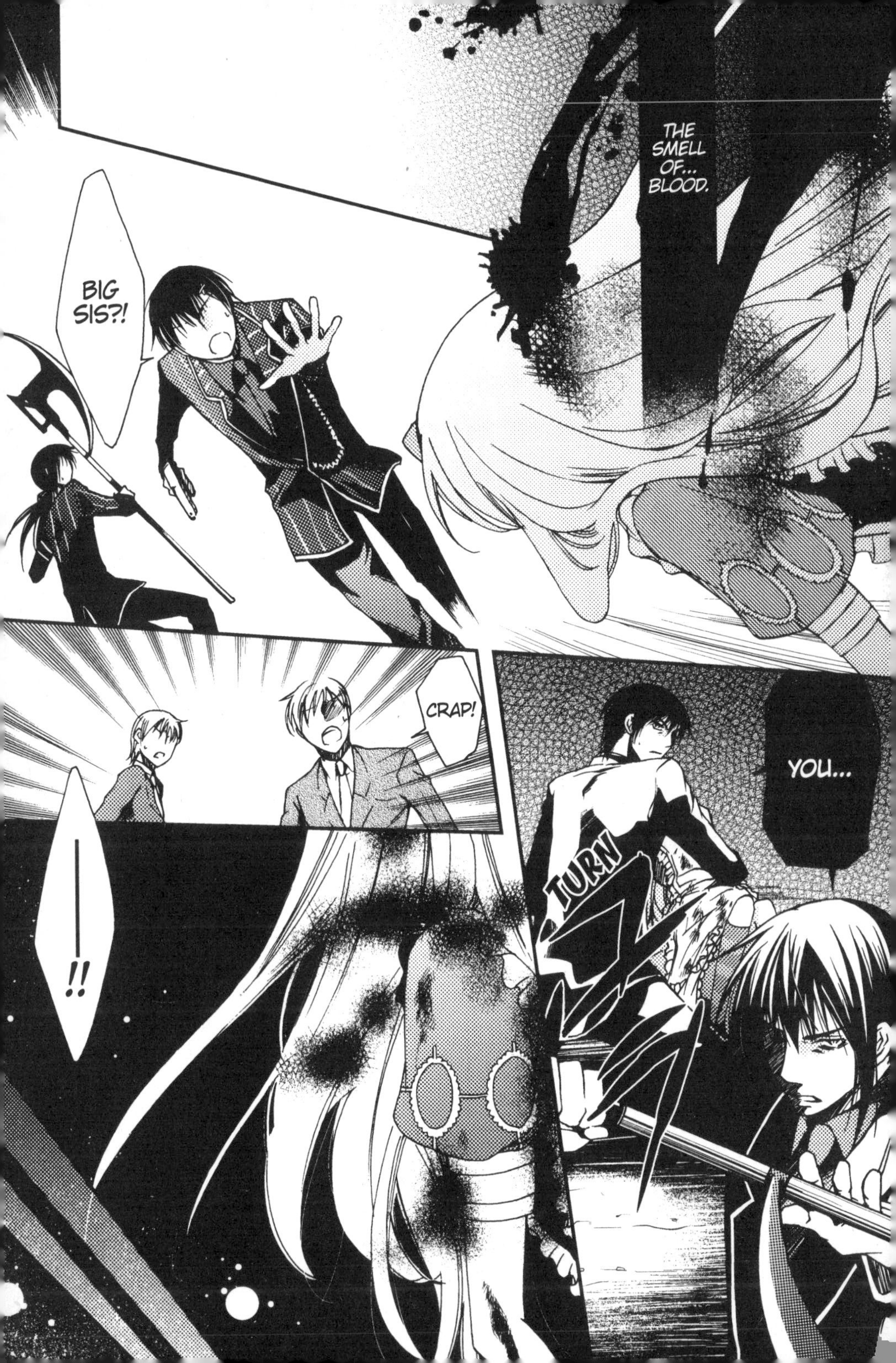
THE SMELL OF... BLOOD.
BIG SIS?!
YOU...
CRAP!
TURN
——!!

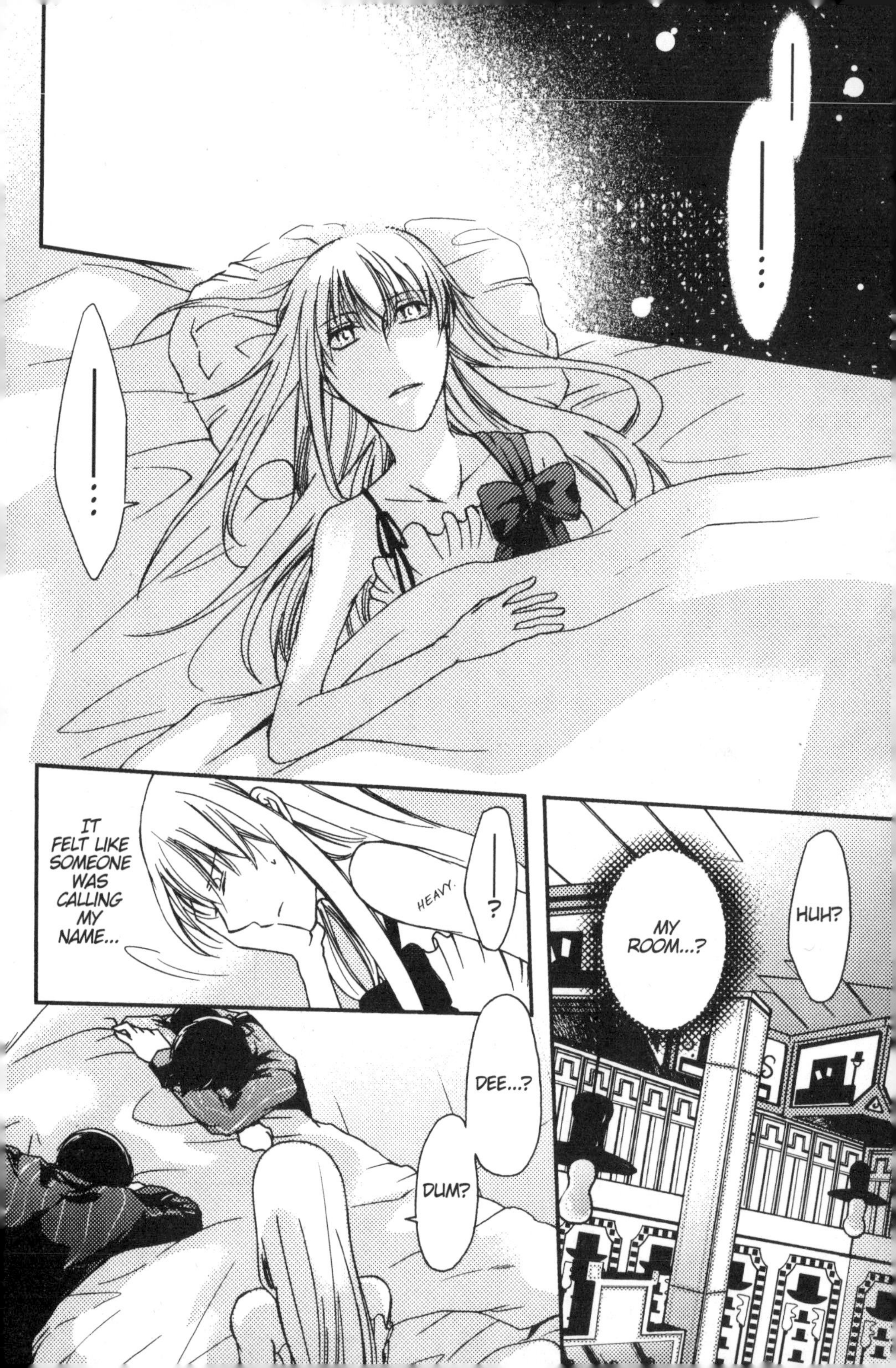
―――…
―――…
HUH?
MY ROOM...?
――?
HEAVY.
IT FELT LIKE SOMEONE WAS CALLING MY NAME...
DEE...?
DUM?

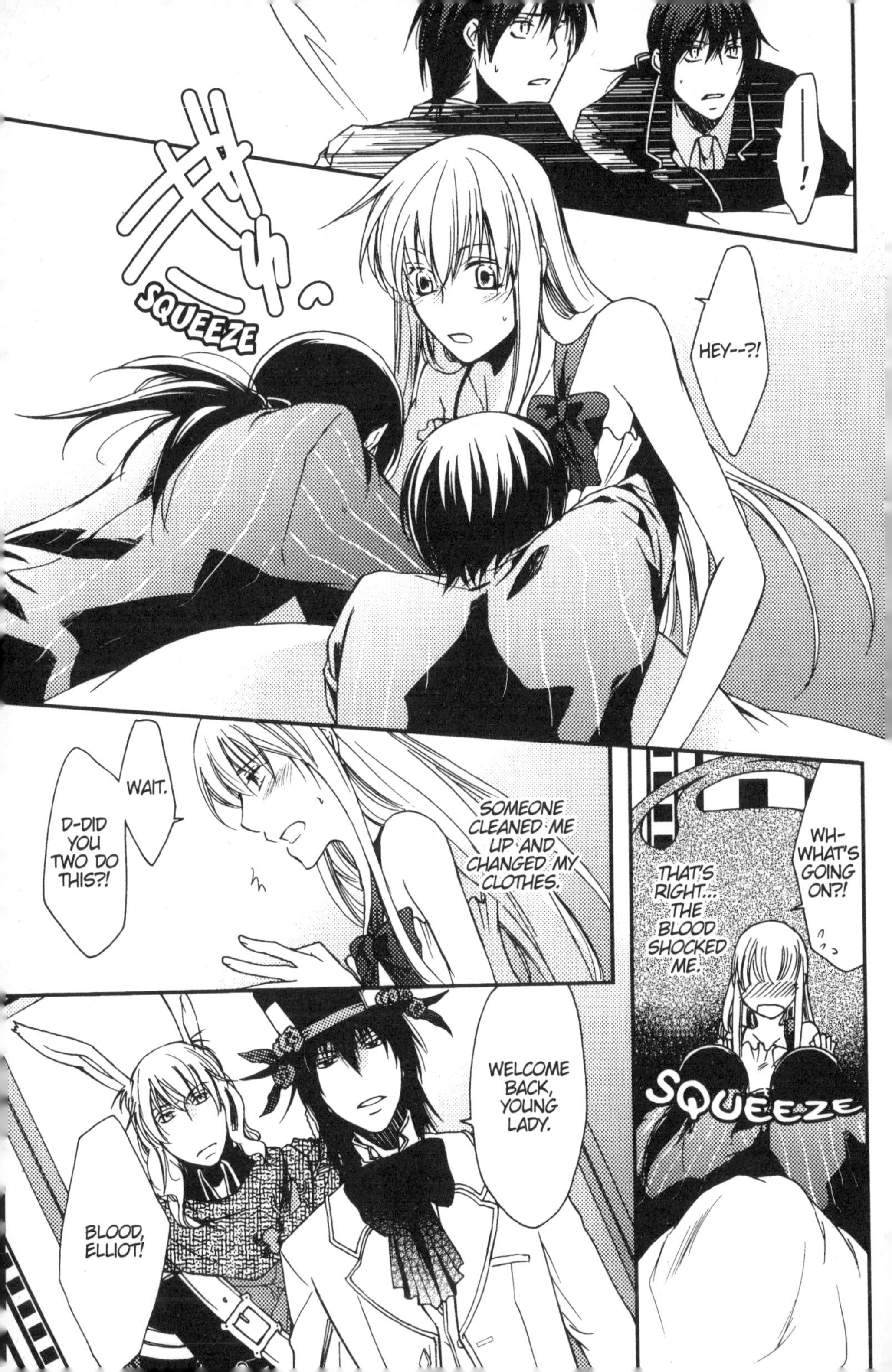
!
SQUEEZE
HEY--?!
WH- WHAT'S GOING ON?!
THAT'S RIGHT... THE BLOOD SHOCKED ME.
SQUEEZE
SOMEONE CLEANED ME UP AND CHANGED MY CLOTHES.
WAIT.
D-DID YOU TWO DO THIS?!
WELCOME BACK, YOUNG LADY.
BLOOD, ELLIOT!

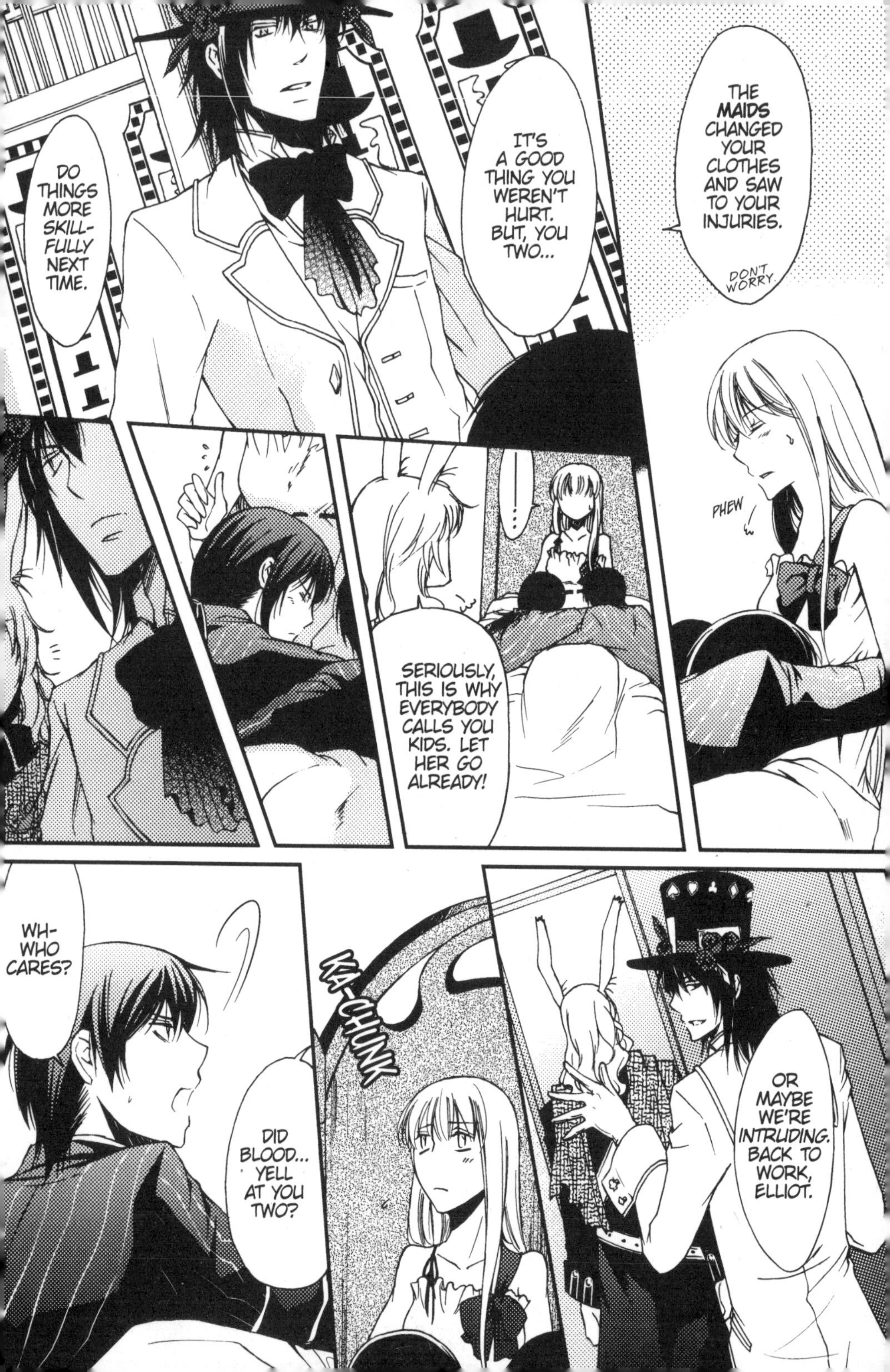
THE MAIDS CHANGED YOUR CLOTHES AND SAW TO YOUR INJURIES.
DON'T WORRY.
IT'S A GOOD THING YOU WEREN'T HURT. BUT, YOU TWO...
DO THINGS MORE SKILL-FULLY NEXT TIME.
PHEW
...!
SERIOUSLY, THIS IS WHY EVERYBODY CALLS YOU KIDS. LET HER GO ALREADY!
OR MAYBE WE'RE INTRUDING. BACK TO WORK, ELLIOT.
KA-CHUNK
DID BLOOD... YELL AT YOU TWO?
WH-WHO CARES?

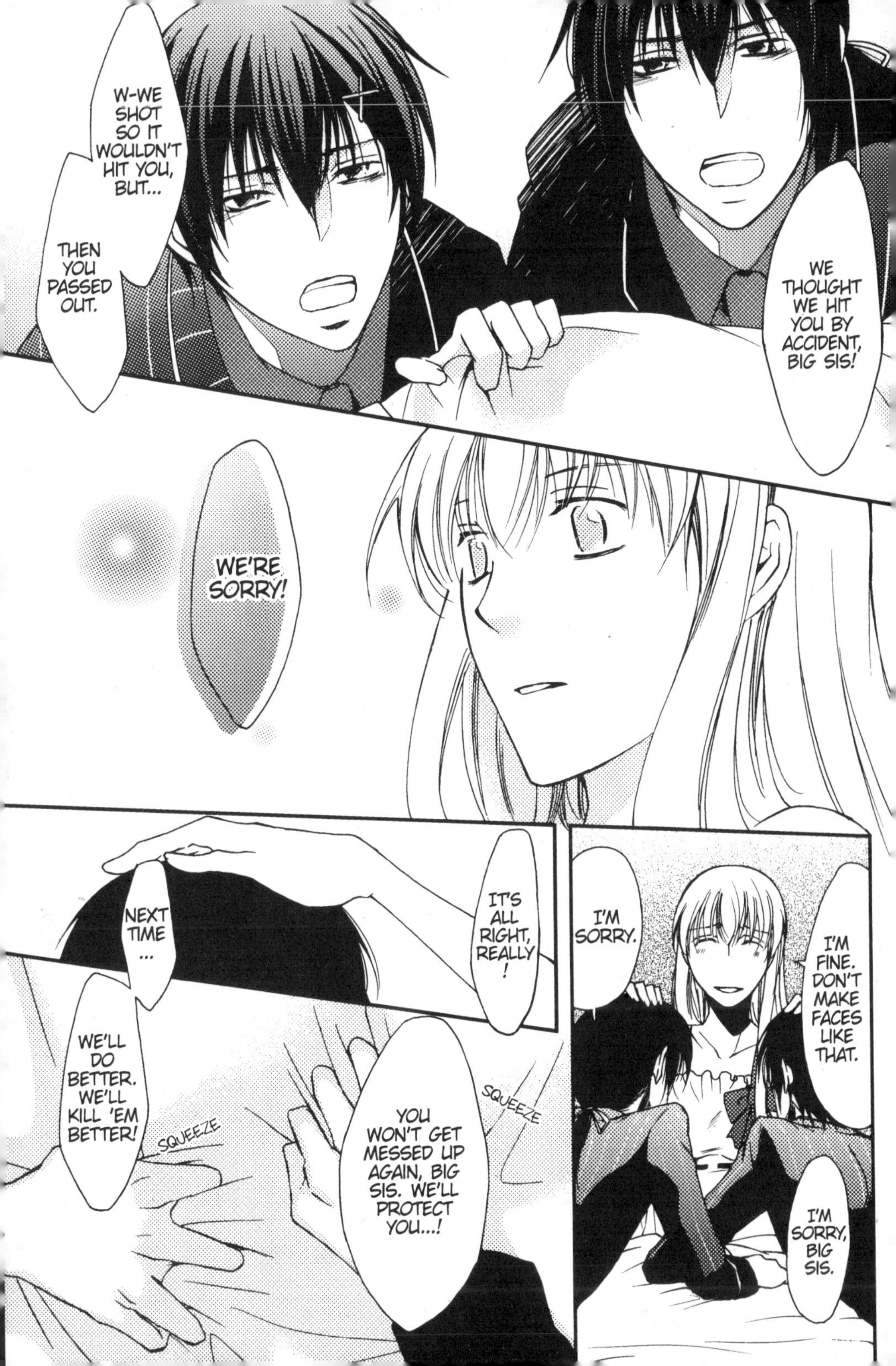
WE THOUGHT WE HIT YOU BY ACCIDENT, BIG SIS!
W-WE SHOT SO IT WOULDN'T HIT YOU, BUT...
THEN YOU PASSED OUT.
WE'RE SORRY!
I'M FINE. DON'T MAKE FACES LIKE THAT.
I'M SORRY.
I'M SORRY, BIG SIS.
IT'S ALL RIGHT, REALLY!
NEXT TIME...
SQUEEZE
YOU WON'T GET MESSED UP AGAIN, BIG SIS. WE'LL PROTECT YOU...!
WE'LL DO BETTER. WE'LL KILL 'EM BETTER!
SQUEEZE

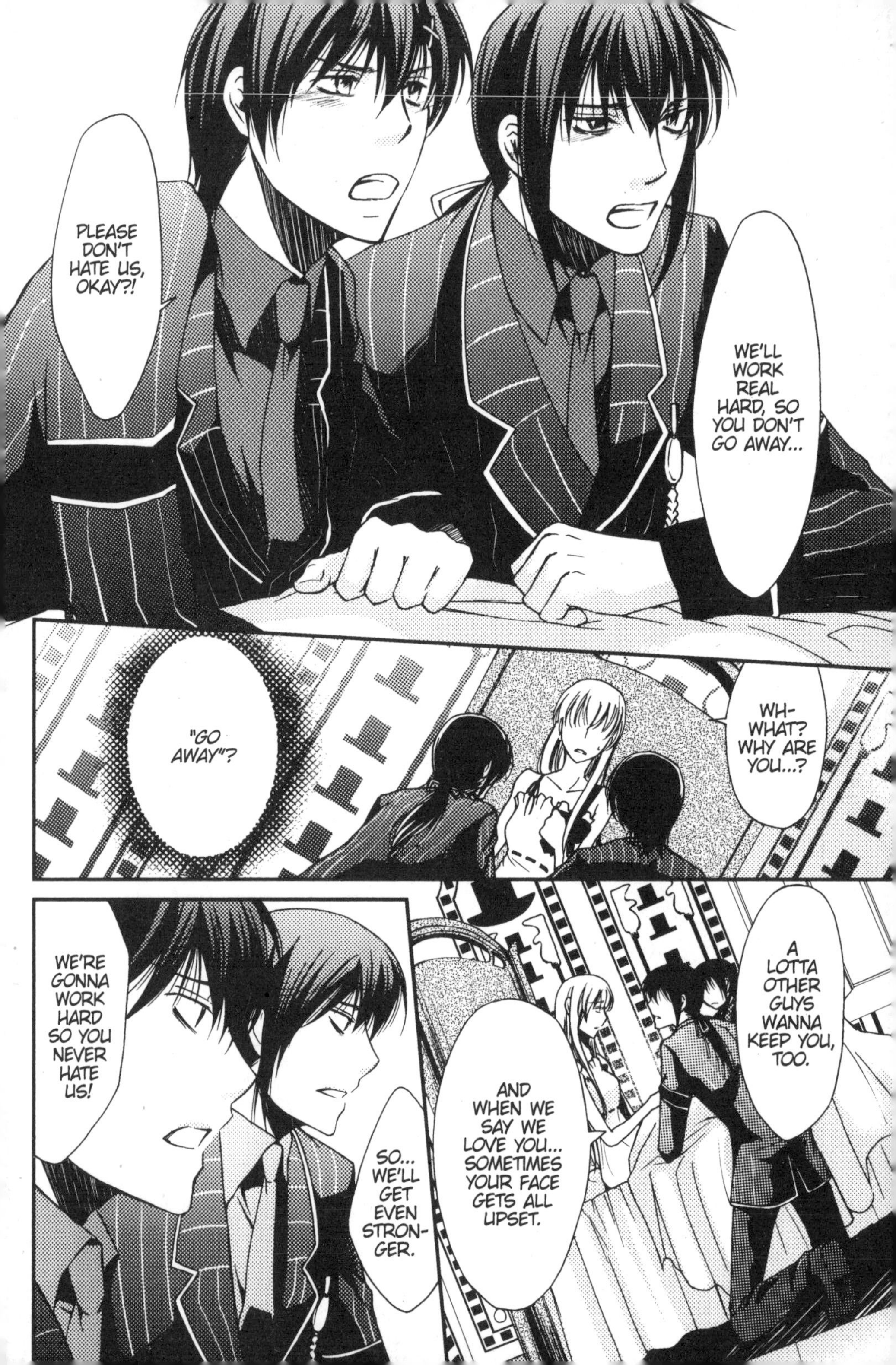
WE'LL WORK REAL HARD, SO YOU DON'T GO AWAY...
PLEASE DON'T HATE US, OKAY?!
WH-WHAT? WHY ARE YOU...?
"GO AWAY"?
A LOTTA OTHER GUYS WANNA KEEP YOU, TOO.
AND WHEN WE SAY WE LOVE YOU... SOMETIMES YOUR FACE GETS ALL UPSET.
SO... WE'LL GET EVEN STRONGER.
WE'RE GONNA WORK HARD SO YOU NEVER HATE US!

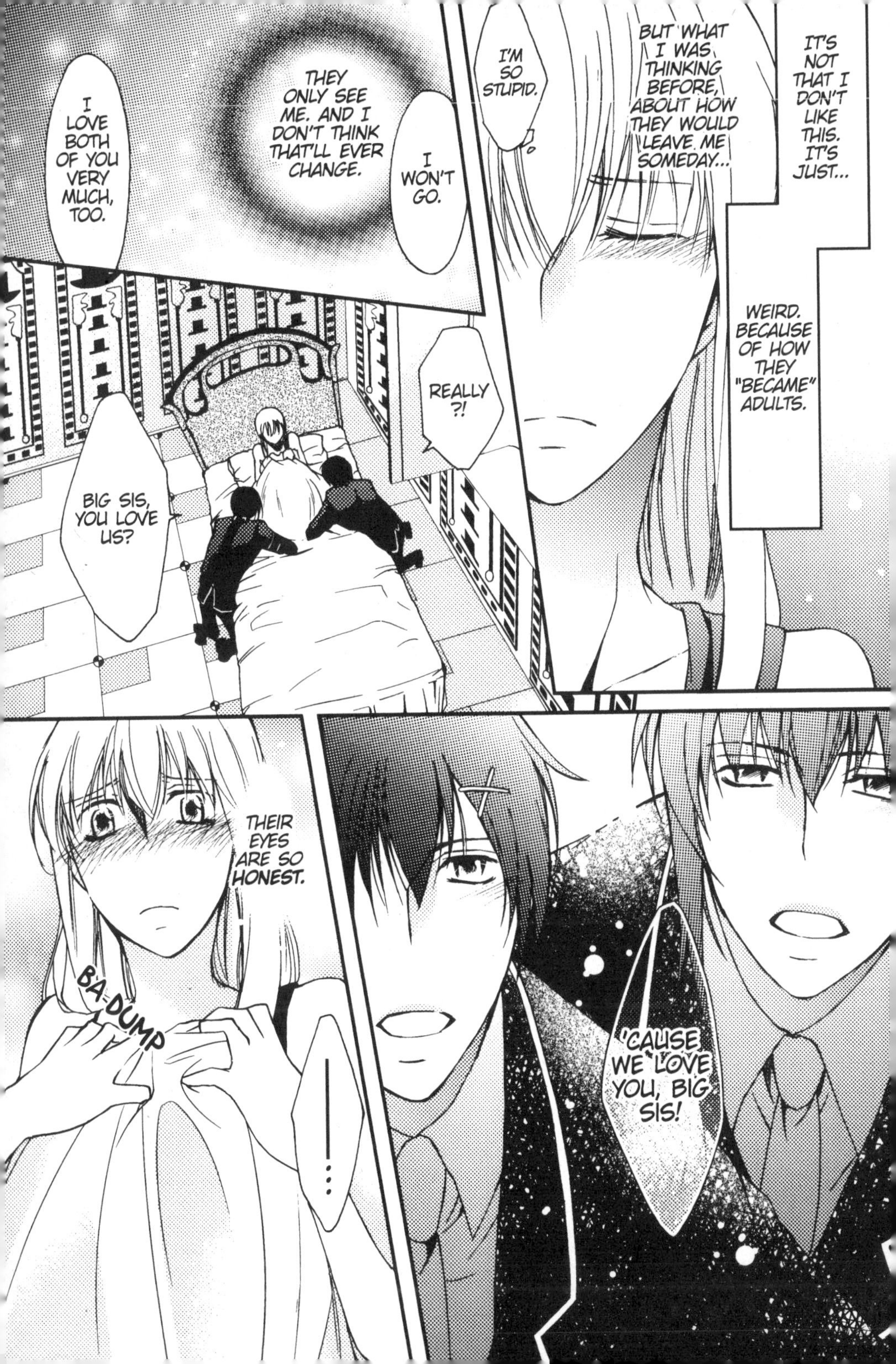
IT'S NOT THAT I DON'T LIKE THIS. IT'S JUST...
WEIRD. BECAUSE OF HOW THEY "BECAME" ADULTS.
BUT WHAT I WAS THINKING BEFORE, ABOUT HOW THEY WOULD LEAVE ME SOMEDAY...
I'M SO STUPID.
I WON'T GO.
THEY ONLY SEE ME. AND I DON'T THINK THAT'LL EVER CHANGE.
I LOVE BOTH OF YOU VERY MUCH, TOO.
REALLY?!
BIG SIS, YOU LOVE US?
'CAUSE WE LOVE YOU, BIG SIS!
...!
THEIR EYES ARE SO HONEST.
BA-DUMP

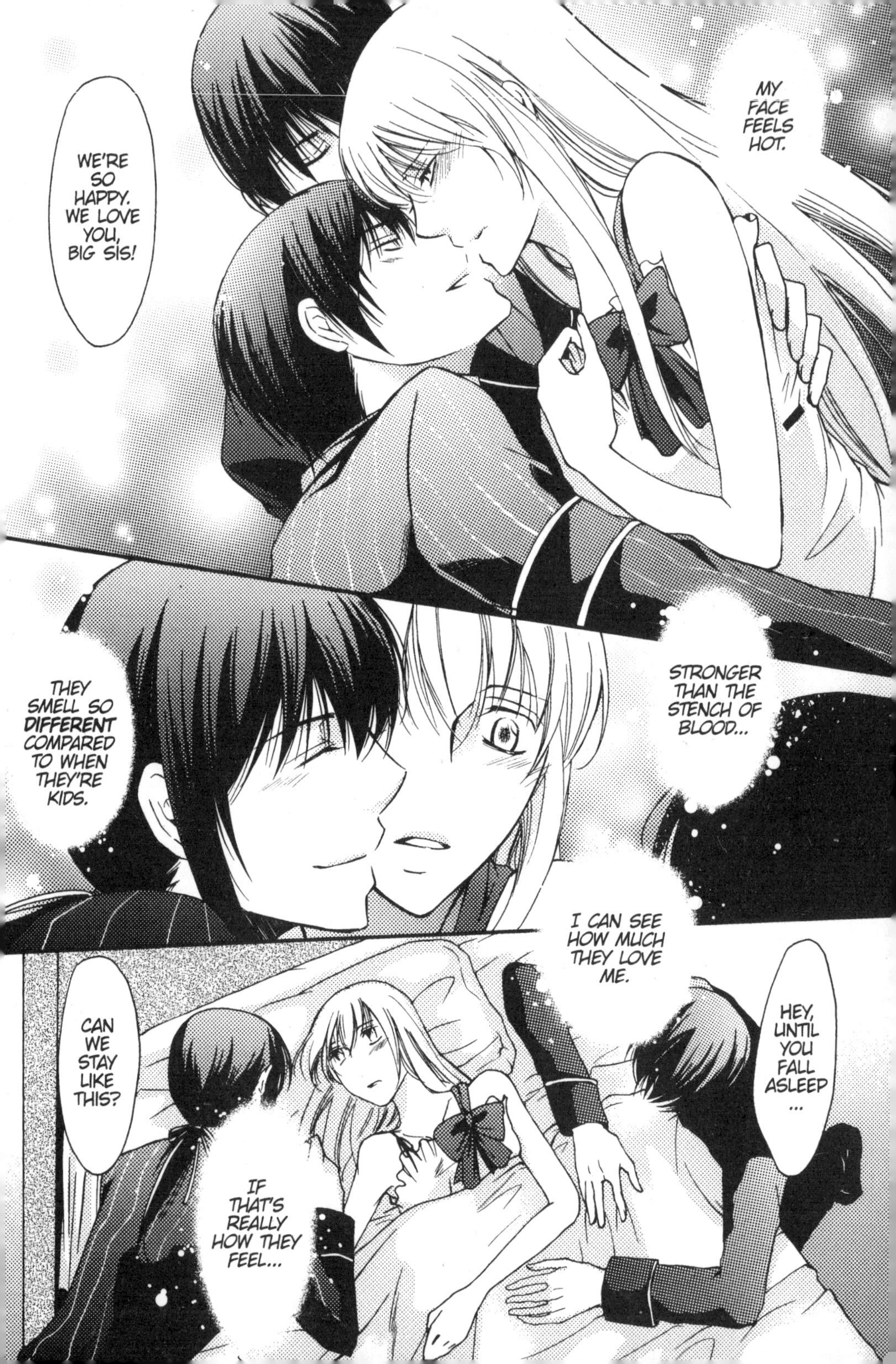

MY FACE FEELS HOT.
WE'RE SO HAPPY. WE LOVE YOU, BIG SIS!
STRONGER THAN THE STENCH OF BLOOD...
THEY SMELL SO **DIFFERENT** COMPARED TO WHEN THEY'RE KIDS.
HEY, UNTIL YOU FALL ASLEEP...
I CAN SEE HOW MUCH THEY LOVE ME.
CAN WE STAY LIKE THIS?
IF THAT'S REALLY HOW THEY FEEL...

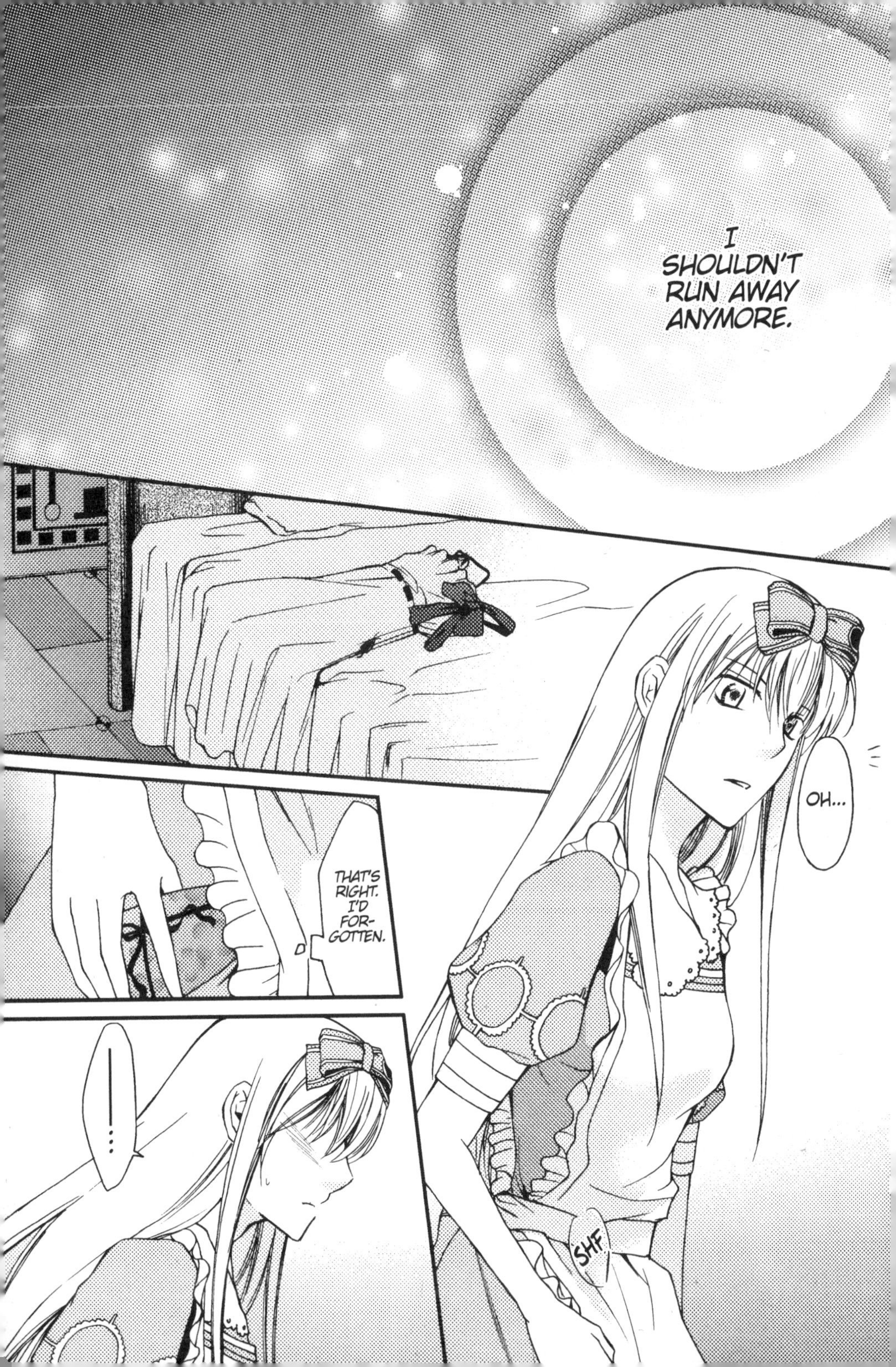
I SHOULDN'T RUN AWAY ANYMORE.
OH...
THAT'S RIGHT. I'D FOR-GOTTEN.
SHF
!.....

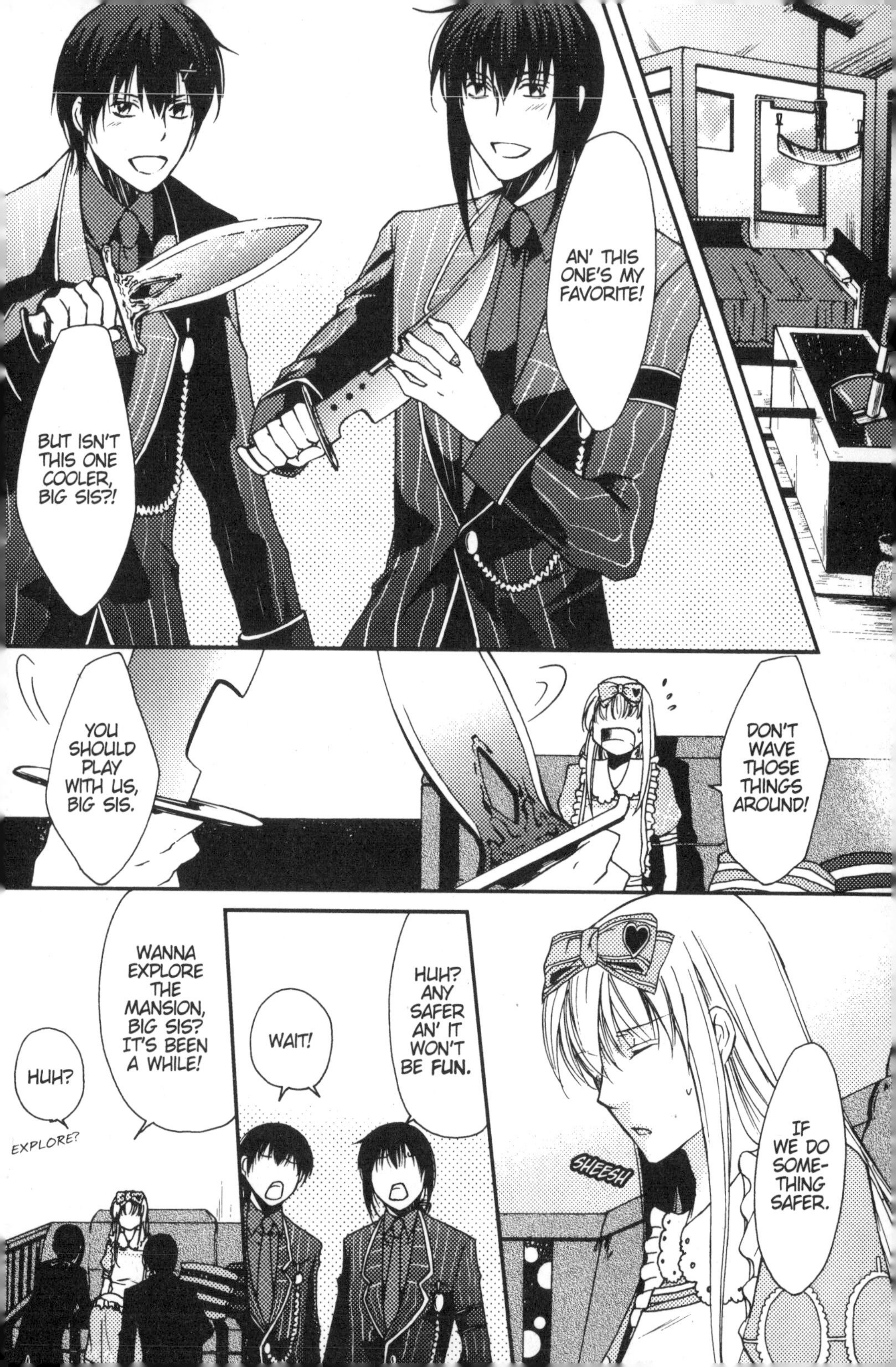
AN' THIS ONE'S MY FAVORITE!
BUT ISN'T THIS ONE COOLER, BIG SIS?!
DON'T WAVE THOSE THINGS AROUND!
YOU SHOULD PLAY WITH US, BIG SIS.
SHEESH
IF WE DO SOME-THING SAFER.
HUH? ANY SAFER AN' IT WON'T BE FUN.
WAIT!
WANNA EXPLORE THE MANSION, BIG SIS? IT'S BEEN A WHILE!
HUH?
EXPLORE?

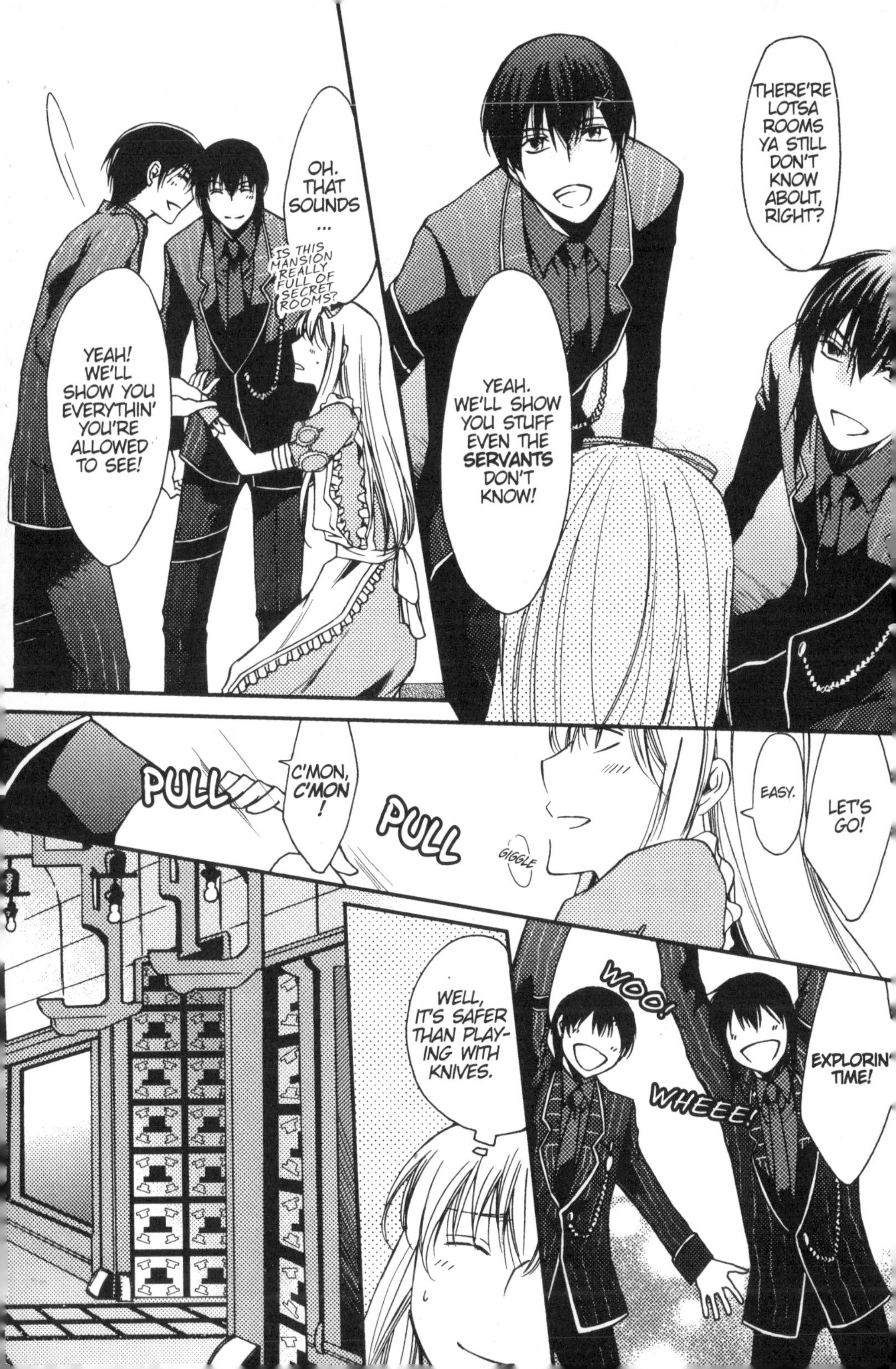
THERE'RE LOTSA ROOMS YA STILL DON'T KNOW ABOUT, RIGHT?
YEAH. WE'LL SHOW YOU STUFF EVEN THE **SERVANTS** DON'T KNOW!
OH. THAT SOUNDS ...
IS THIS MANSION REALLY FULL OF SECRET ROOMS?
YEAH! WE'LL SHOW YOU EVERYTHIN' YOU'RE ALLOWED TO SEE!
LET'S GO!
EASY.
GIGGLE
PULL
C'MON, C'MON!
PULL
EXPLORIN' TIME!
WHEEEE!
WOO!
WELL, IT'S SAFER THAN PLAY-ING WITH KNIVES.

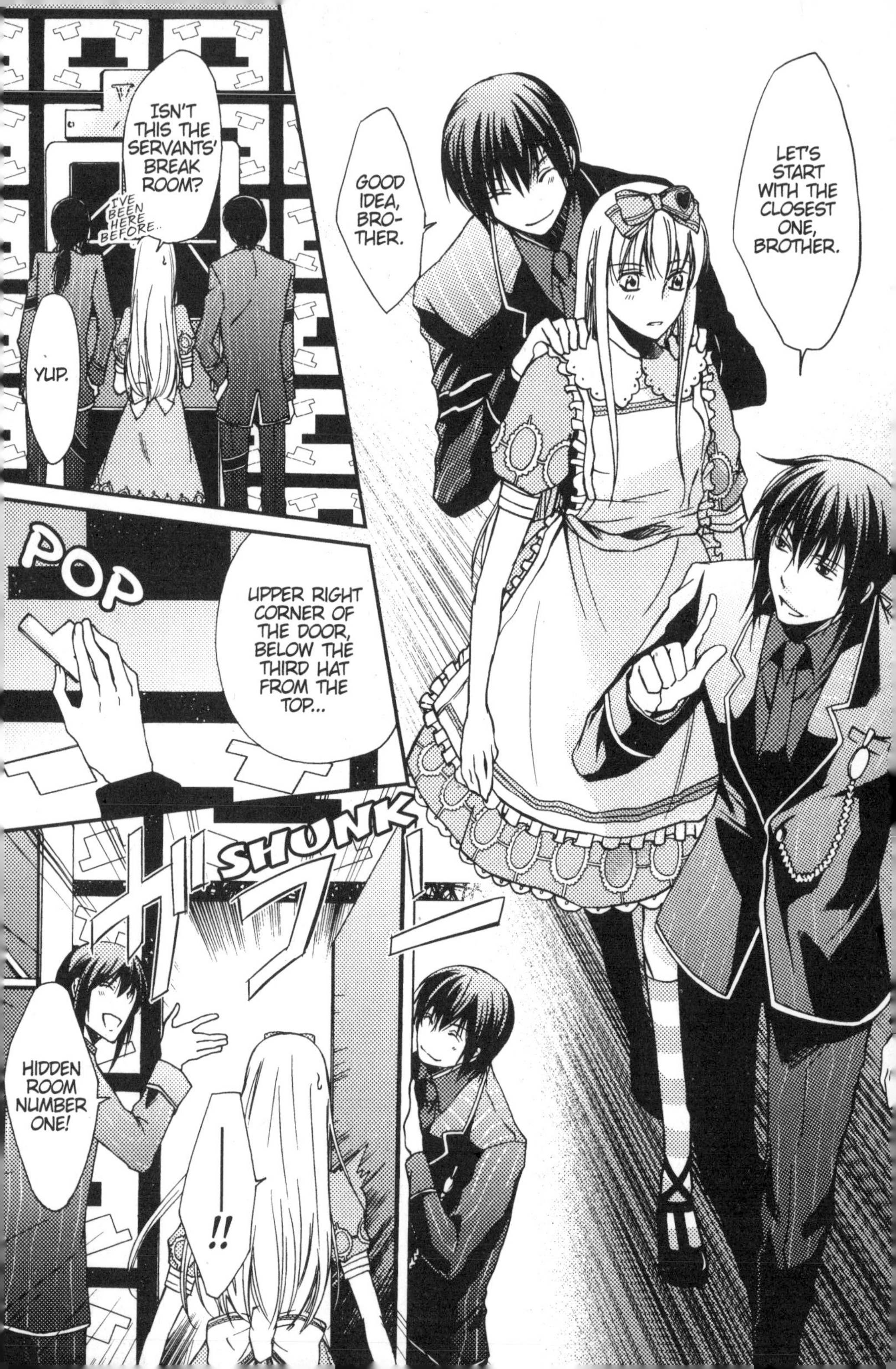

LET'S START WITH THE CLOSEST ONE, BROTHER.
GOOD IDEA, BROTHER.
ISN'T THIS THE SERVANTS' BREAK ROOM?
I'VE BEEN HERE BEFORE..
YUP.
UPPER RIGHT CORNER OF THE DOOR, BELOW THE THIRD HAT FROM THE TOP...
POP
SHUNK
—!!
HIDDEN ROOM NUMBER ONE!

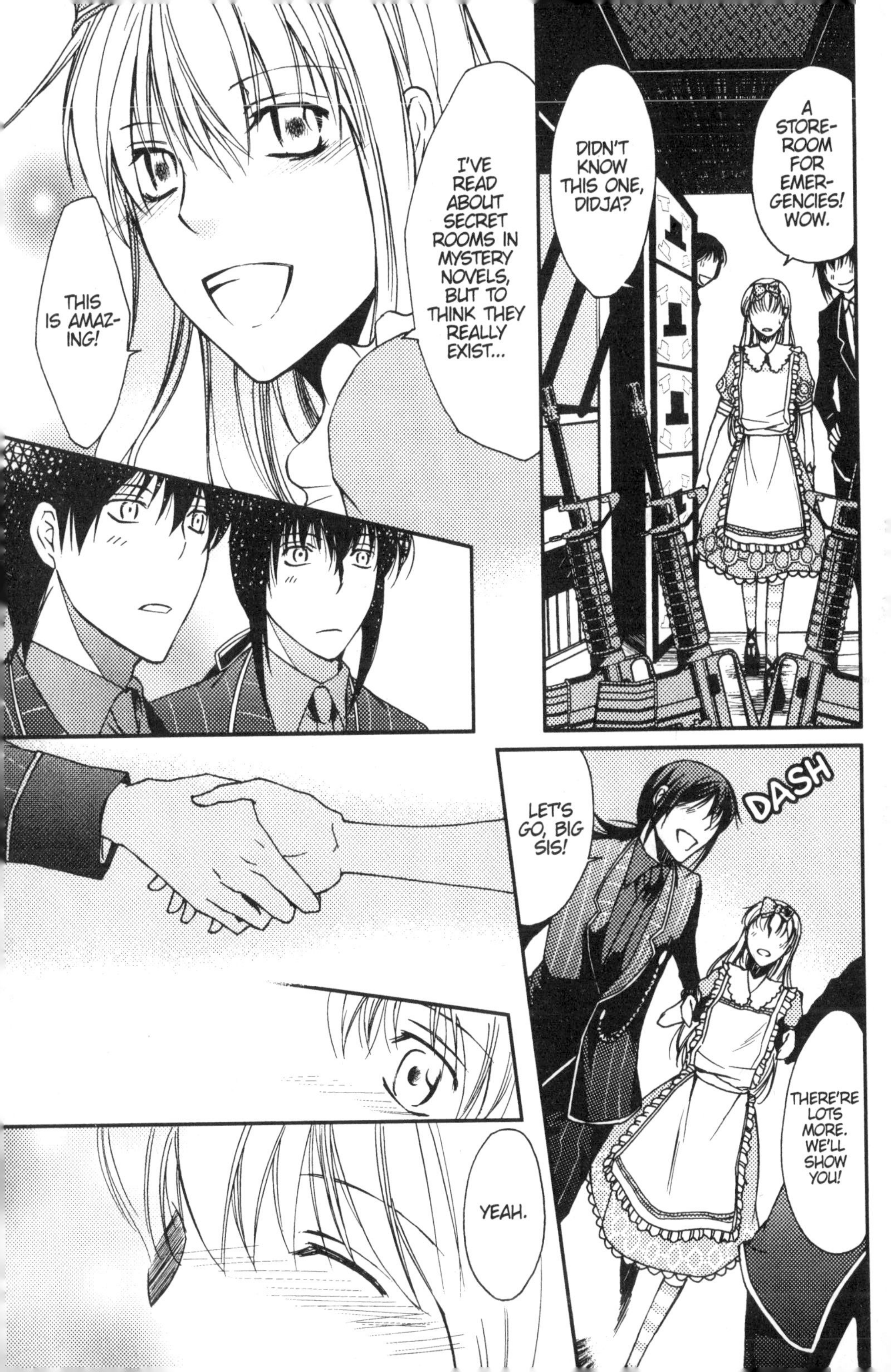
A STORE-ROOM FOR EMERGENCIES! WOW.
DIDN'T KNOW THIS ONE, DIDJA?
I'VE READ ABOUT SECRET ROOMS IN MYSTERY NOVELS, BUT TO THINK THEY REALLY EXIST...
THIS IS AMAZ-ING!
DASH
LET'S GO, BIG SIS!
THERE'RE LOTS MORE. WE'LL SHOW YOU!
YEAH.

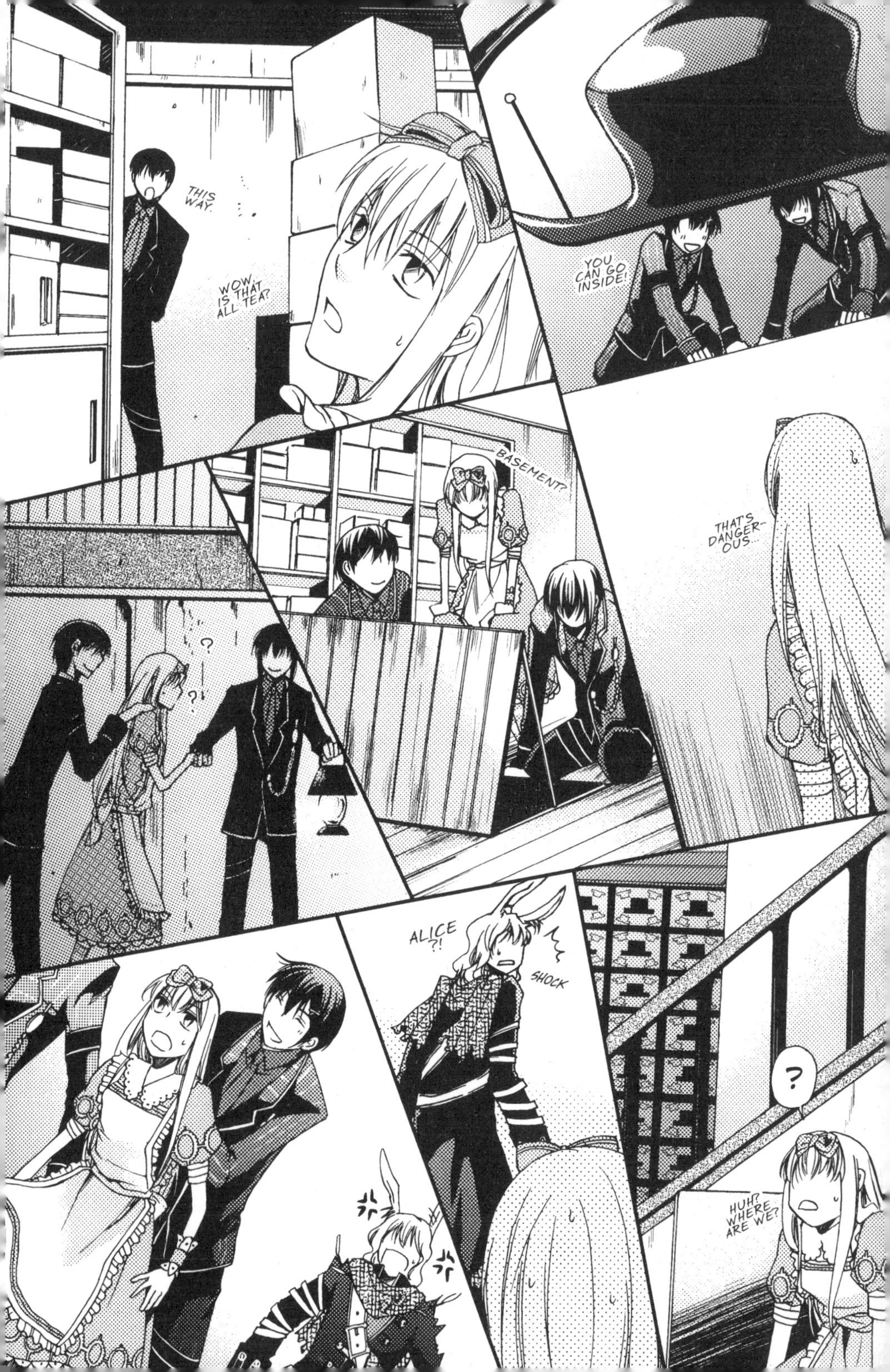
YOU CAN GO INSIDE!
THIS WAY.
WOW, IS THAT ALL TEA?
THAT'S DANGER-OUS...
BASEMENT?
?
?!
?
HUH? WHERE ARE WE?
ALICE ?!
SHOCK

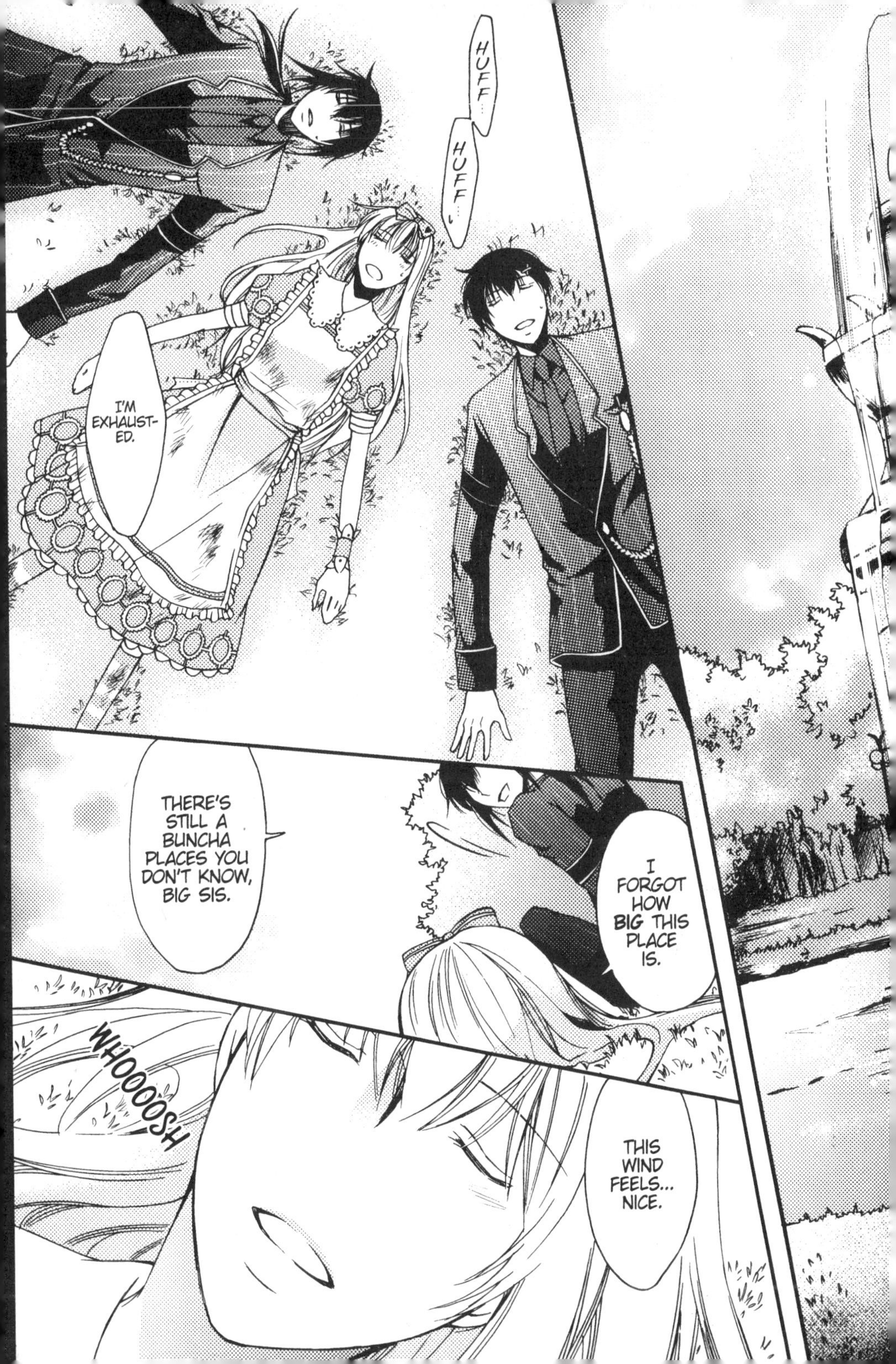
HUFF...
HUFF...
I'M EXHAUST-ED.
I FORGOT HOW BIG THIS PLACE IS.
THERE'S STILL A BUNCHA PLACES YOU DON'T KNOW, BIG SIS.
THIS WIND FEELS... NICE.
WHOOOOSH

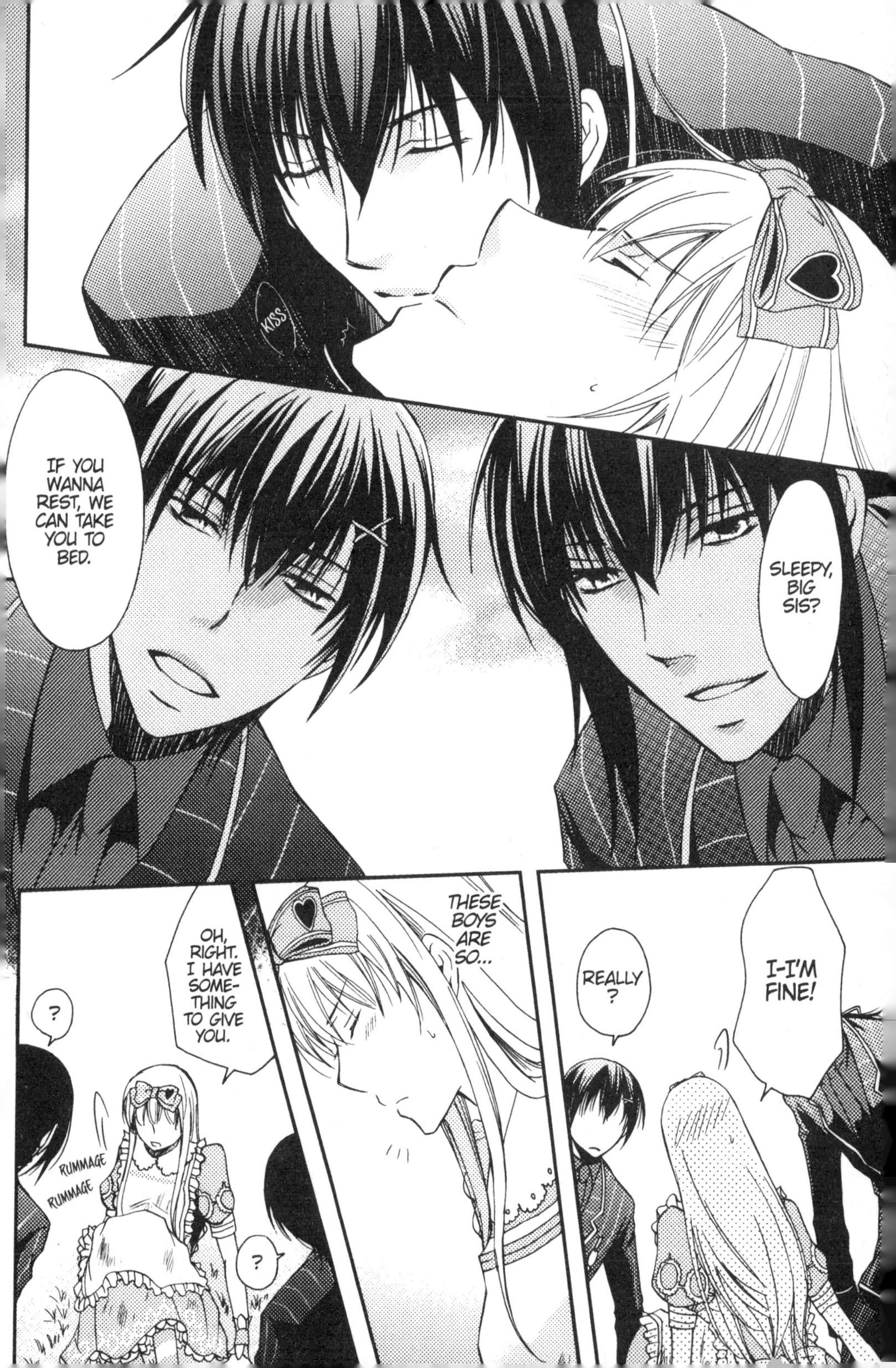
KISS
SLEEPY, BIG SIS?
IF YOU WANNA REST, WE CAN TAKE YOU TO BED.
I-I'M FINE!
REALLY?
THESE BOYS ARE SO...
OH, RIGHT. I HAVE SOME-THING TO GIVE YOU.
?
RUMMAGE
RUMMAGE
?

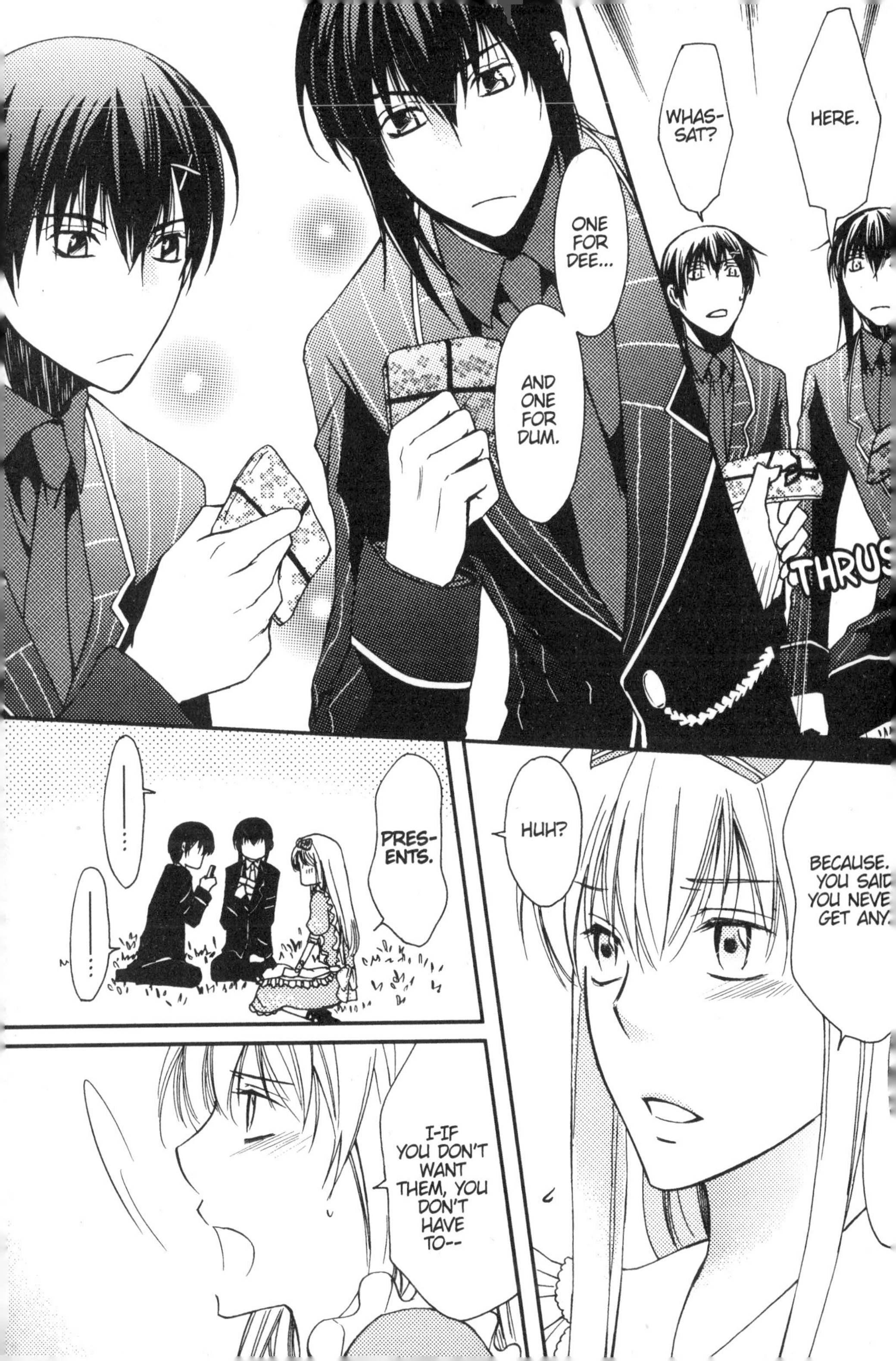
HERE.
WHAS-SAT?
THRUS
ONE FOR DEE...
AND ONE FOR DUM.
HUH?
BECAUSE. YOU SAID YOU NEVE GET ANY.
......
......
PRES-ENTS.
I-IF YOU DON'T WANT THEM, YOU DON'T HAVE TO--

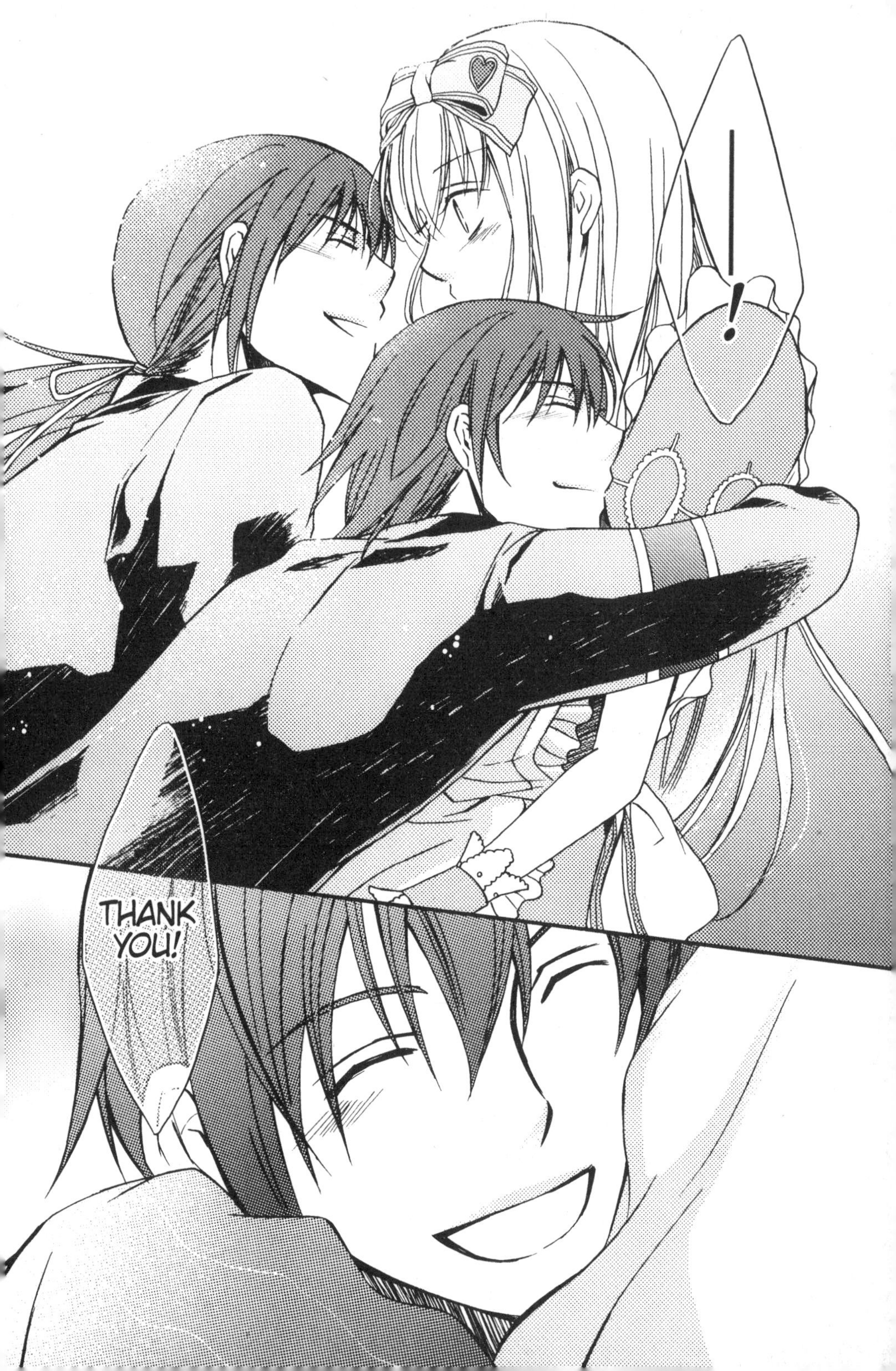
!
THANK YOU!

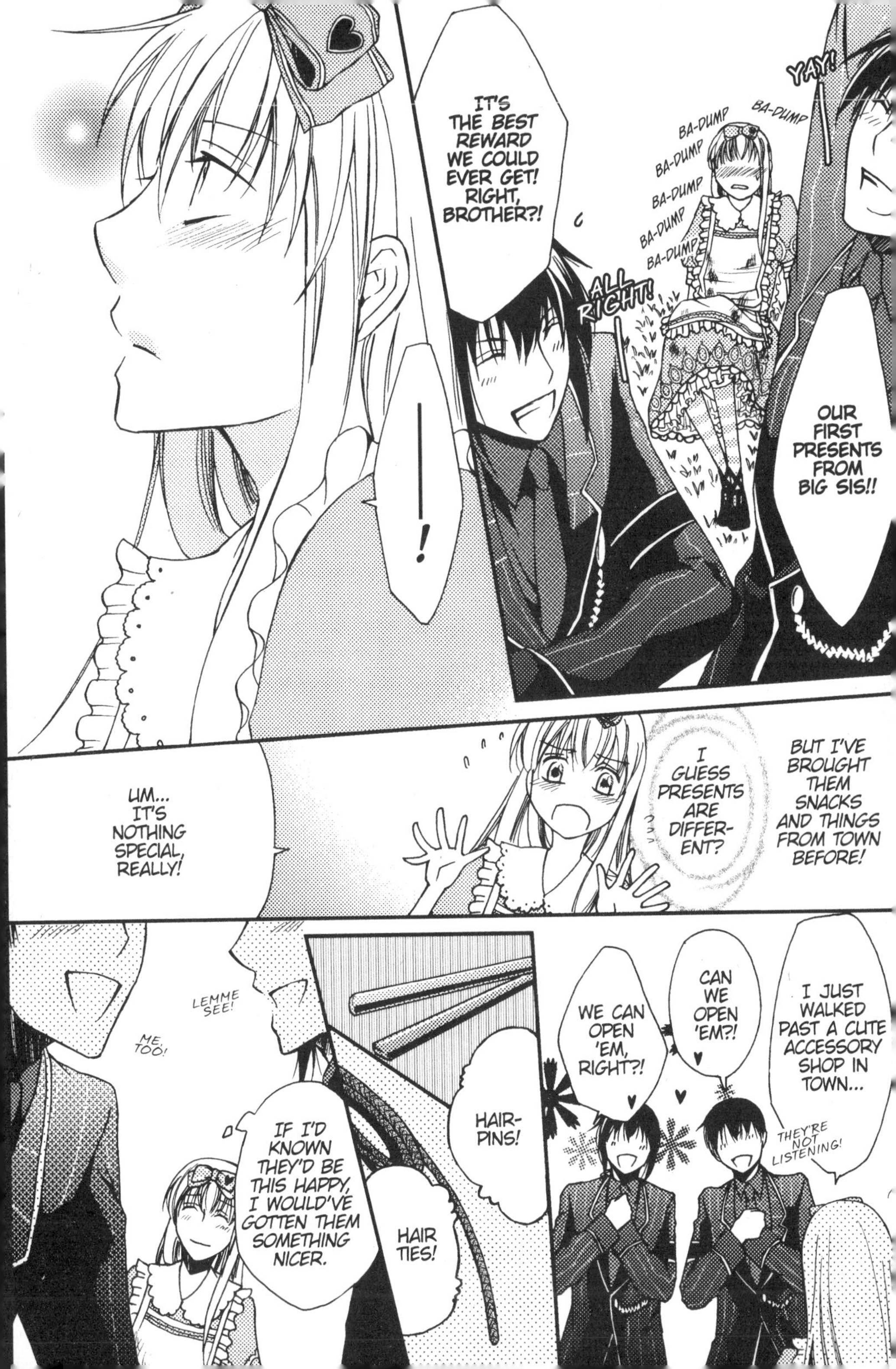
YAY!
BA-DUMP
BA-DUMP
BA-DUMP
BA-DUMP
BA-DUMP
BA-DUMP
OUR FIRST PRESENTS FROM BIG SIS!!
IT'S THE BEST REWARD WE COULD EVER GET! RIGHT, BROTHER?!
ALL RIGHT!
—!
BUT I'VE BROUGHT THEM SNACKS AND THINGS FROM TOWN BEFORE!
I GUESS PRESENTS ARE DIFFER-ENT?
UM... IT'S NOTHING SPECIAL, REALLY!
I JUST WALKED PAST A CUTE ACCESSORY SHOP IN TOWN...
THEY'RE NOT LISTENING!
CAN WE OPEN 'EM?!
WE CAN OPEN 'EM, RIGHT?!
HAIR-PINS!
HAIR TIES!
IF I'D KNOWN THEY'D BE THIS HAPPY, I WOULD'VE GOTTEN THEM SOMETHING NICER.
LEMME SEE!
ME, TOO!

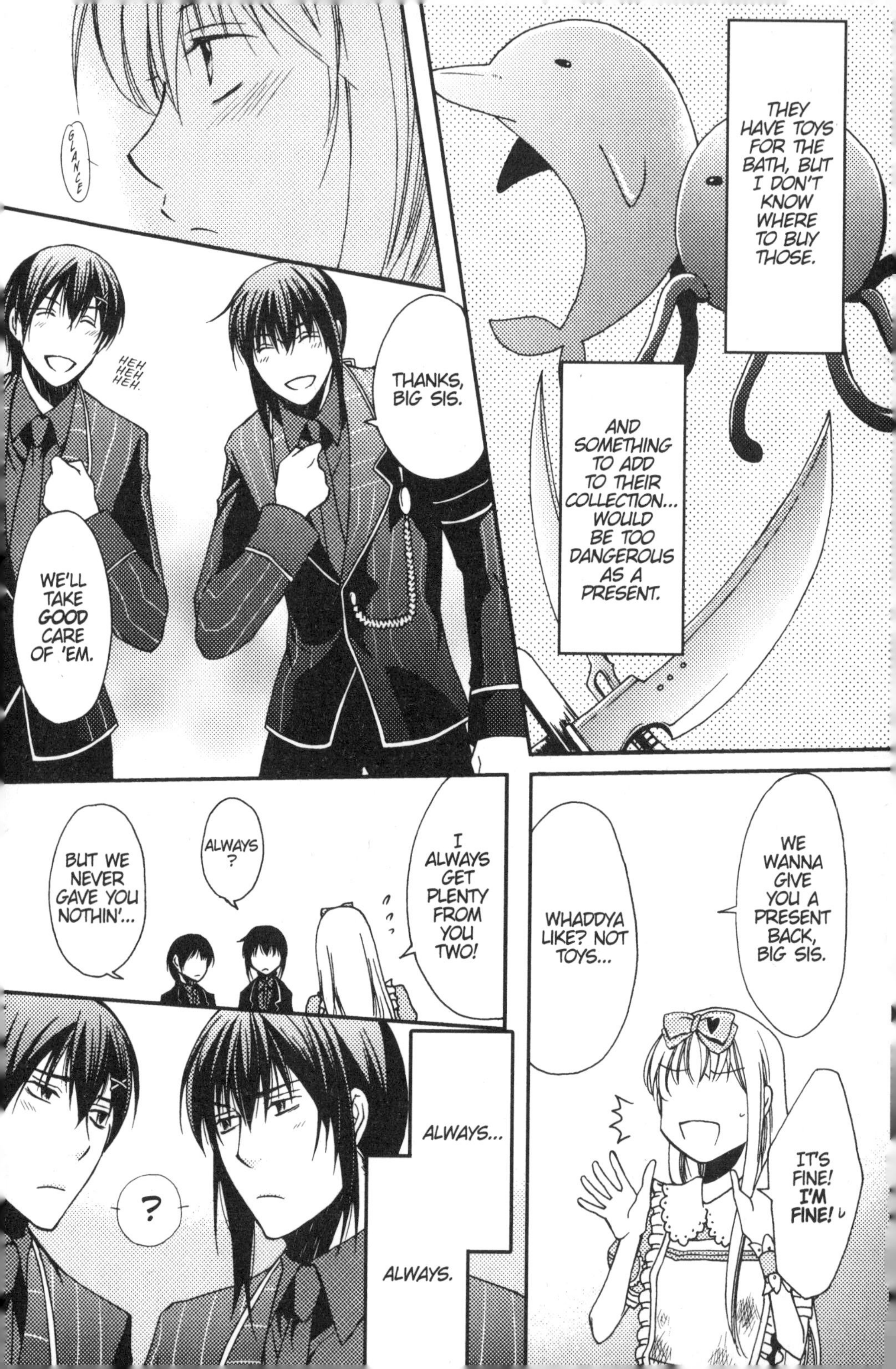
THEY HAVE TOYS FOR THE BATH, BUT I DON'T KNOW WHERE TO BUY THOSE.
AND SOMETHING TO ADD TO THEIR COLLECTION... WOULD BE TOO DANGEROUS AS A PRESENT.
GLANCE
THANKS, BIG SIS.
HEH HEH HEH.
WE'LL TAKE **GOOD** CARE OF 'EM.
WE WANNA GIVE YOU A PRESENT BACK, BIG SIS.
WHADDYA LIKE? NOT TOYS...
IT'S FINE! **I'M FINE!**
I ALWAYS GET PLENTY FROM YOU TWO!
ALWAYS?
BUT WE NEVER GAVE YOU NOTHIN'...
ALWAYS...
?
ALWAYS.

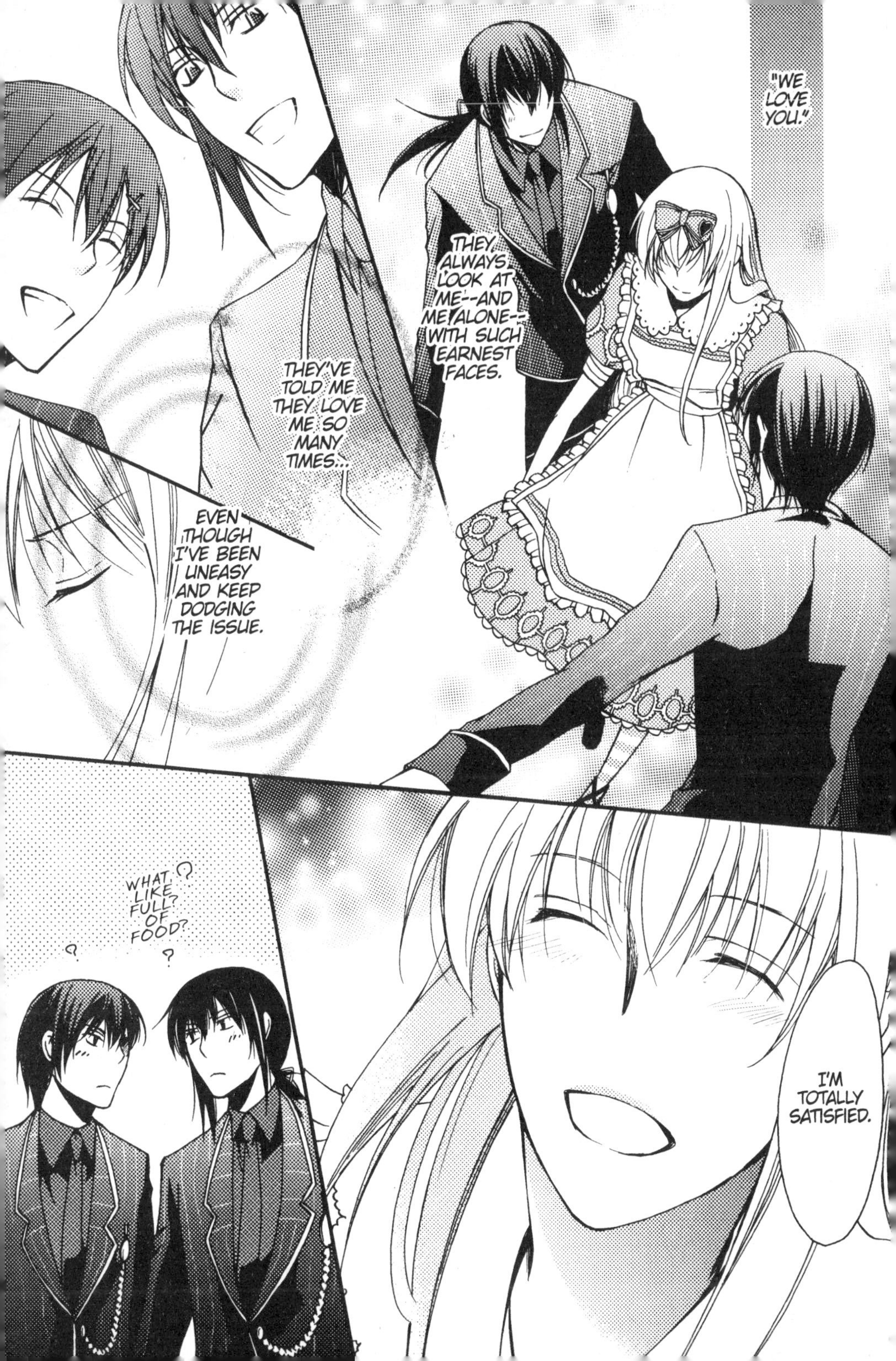
"WE LOVE YOU."
THEY ALWAYS LOOK AT ME--AND ME ALONE--WITH SUCH EARNEST FACES.
THEY'VE TOLD ME THEY LOVE ME SO MANY TIMES...
EVEN THOUGH I'VE BEEN UNEASY AND KEEP DODGING THE ISSUE.
I'M TOTALLY SATISFIED.
WHAT, LIKE FULL? OF FOOD?
?
?
?

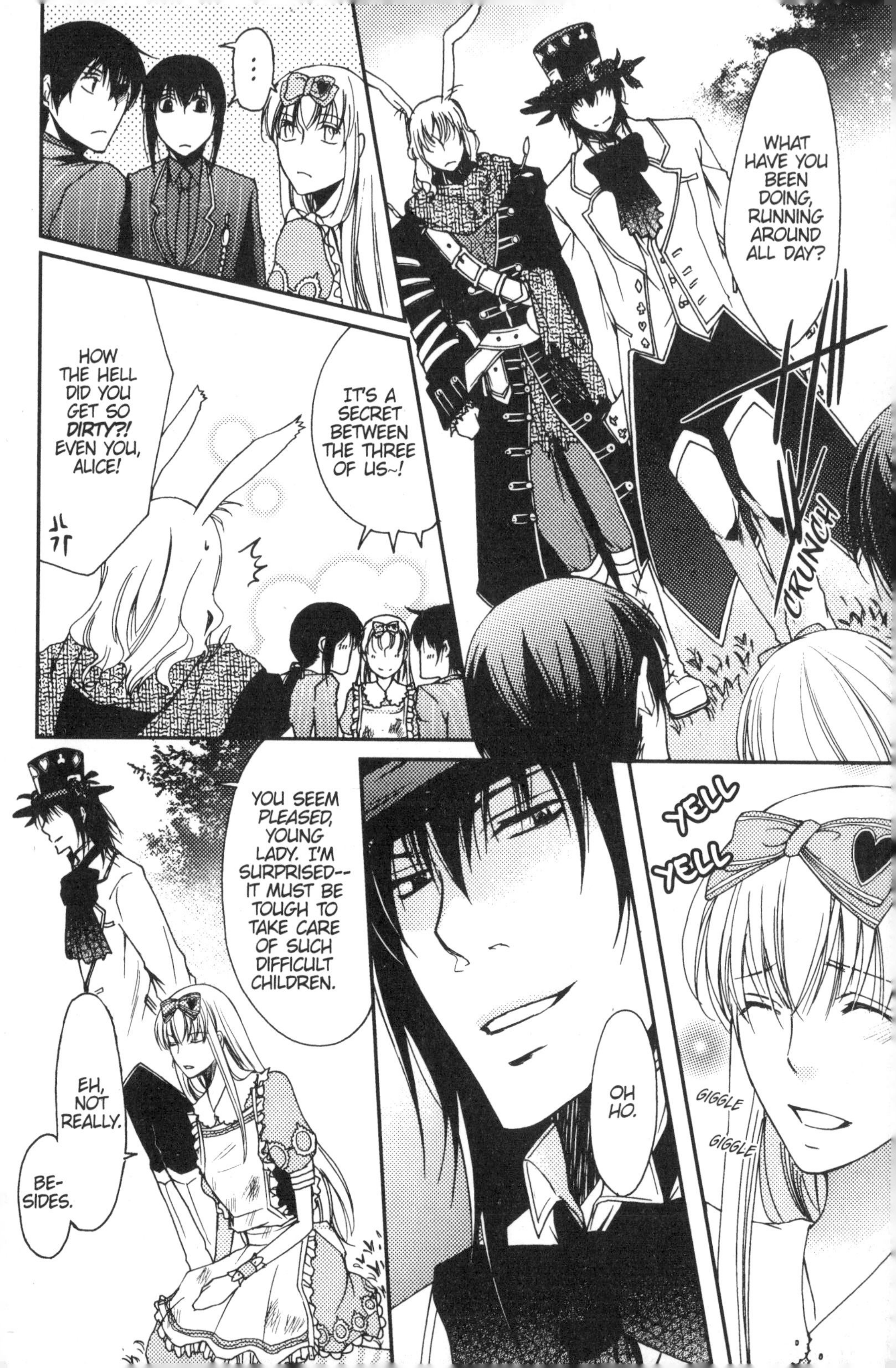
WHAT HAVE YOU BEEN DOING, RUNNING AROUND ALL DAY?
CRUNCH
...
IT'S A SECRET BETWEEN THE THREE OF US~!
HOW THE HELL DID YOU GET SO **DIRTY?!** EVEN YOU, ALICE!
YELL
YELL
GIGGLE
GIGGLE
OH HO.
YOU SEEM PLEASED, YOUNG LADY. I'M SURPRISED-- IT MUST BE TOUGH TO TAKE CARE OF SUCH DIFFICULT CHILDREN.
EH, NOT REALLY.
BE-SIDES.

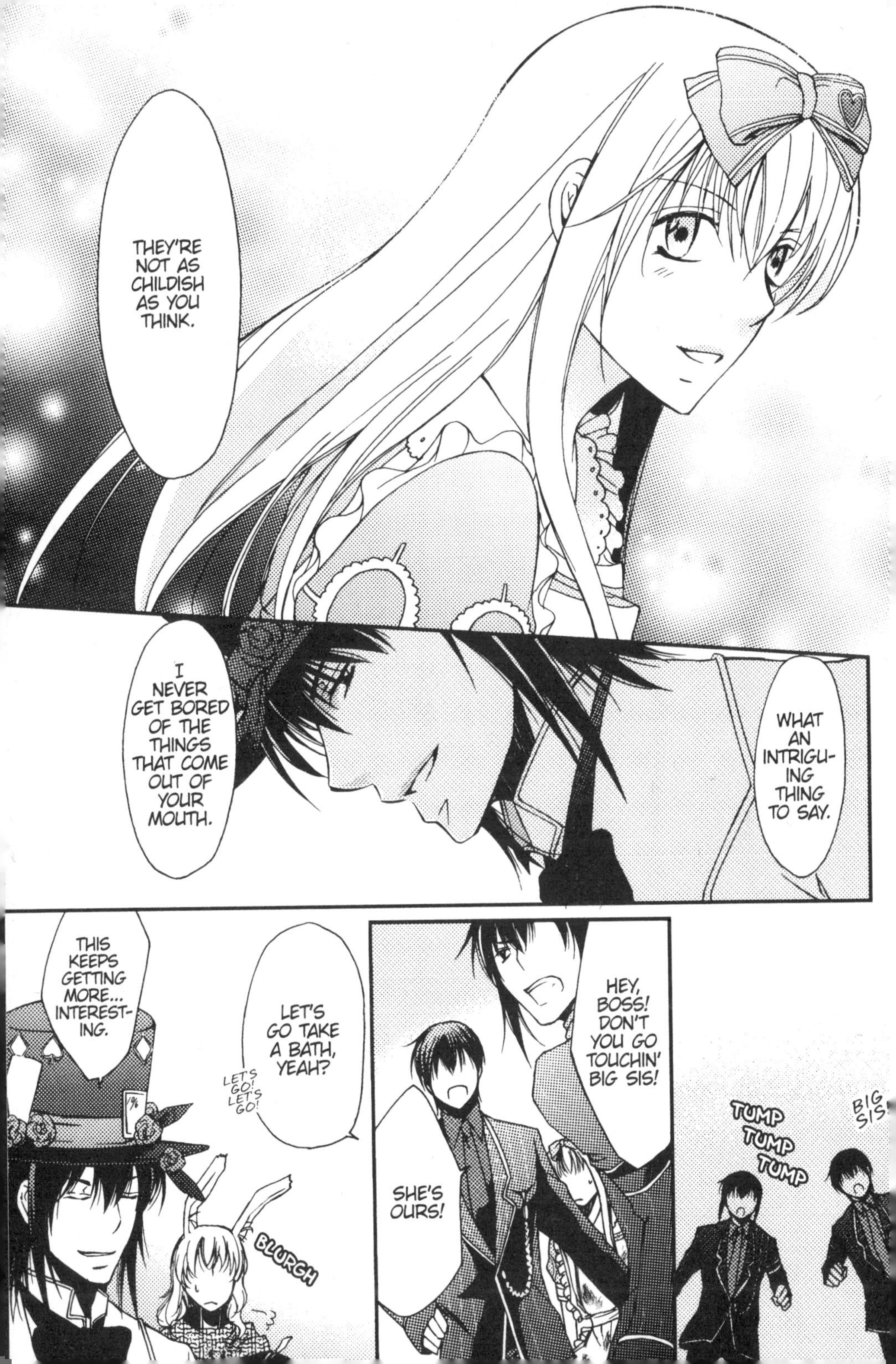
THEY'RE NOT AS CHILDISH AS YOU THINK.
WHAT AN INTRIGUING THING TO SAY.
I NEVER GET BORED OF THE THINGS THAT COME OUT OF YOUR MOUTH.
BIG SIS!
TUMP TUMP TUMP
HEY, BOSS! DON'T YOU GO TOUCHIN' BIG SIS!
SHE'S OURS!
THIS KEEPS GETTING MORE... INTEREST-ING.
LET'S GO TAKE A BATH, YEAH?
LET'S GO! LET'S GO!
BLURGH

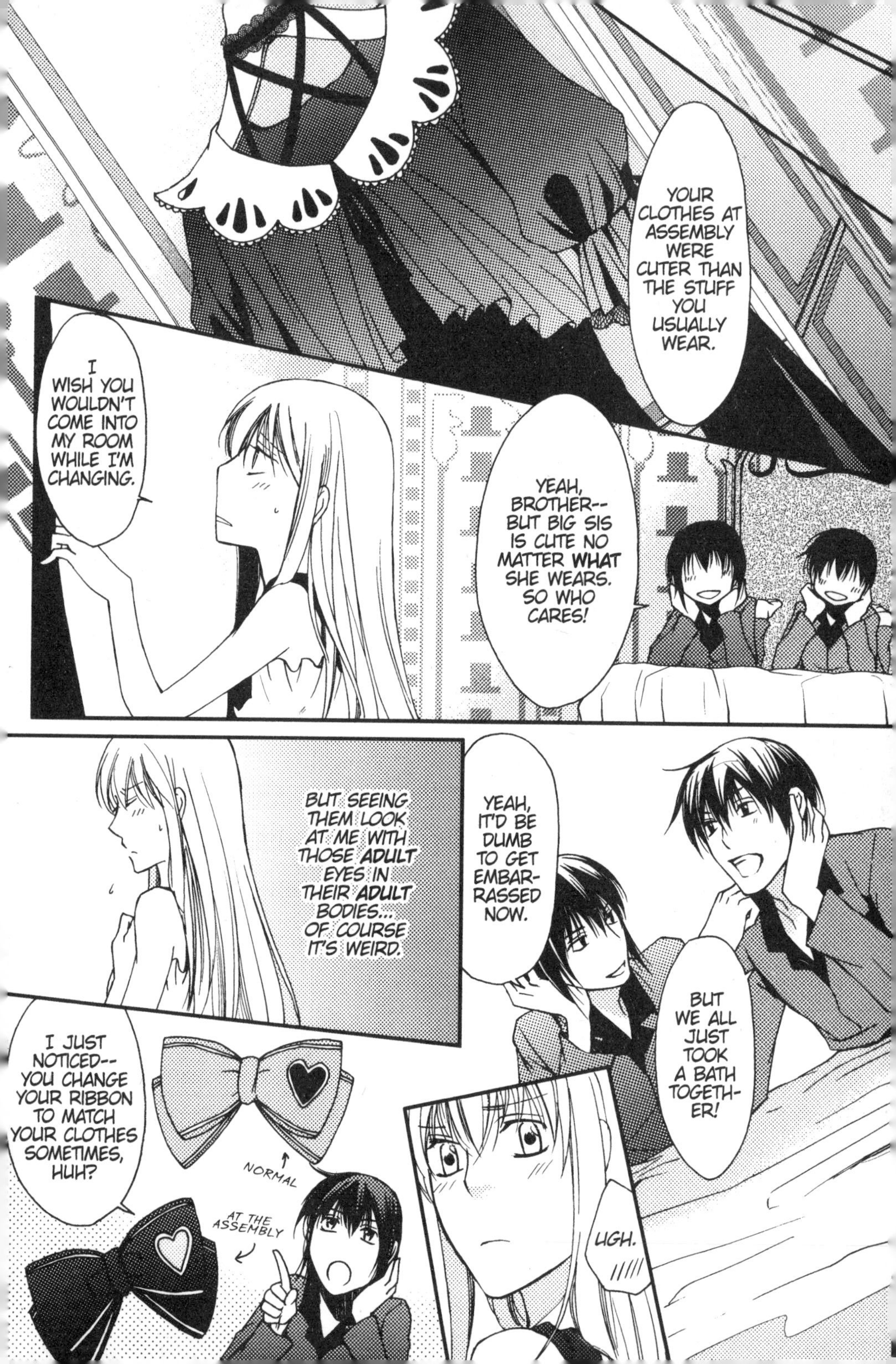
YOUR CLOTHES AT ASSEMBLY WERE CUTER THAN THE STUFF YOU USUALLY WEAR.
I WISH YOU WOULDN'T COME INTO MY ROOM WHILE I'M CHANGING.
YEAH, BROTHER-- BUT BIG SIS IS CUTE NO MATTER **WHAT** SHE WEARS. SO WHO CARES!
YEAH, IT'D BE DUMB TO GET EMBAR-RASSED NOW.
BUT WE ALL JUST TOOK A BATH TOGETH-ER!
UGH.
BUT SEEING THEM LOOK AT ME WITH THOSE **ADULT** EYES IN THEIR **ADULT** BODIES... OF COURSE IT'S WEIRD.
I JUST NOTICED-- YOU CHANGE YOUR RIBBON TO MATCH YOUR CLOTHES SOMETIMES, HUH?
NORMAL
AT THE ASSEMBLY

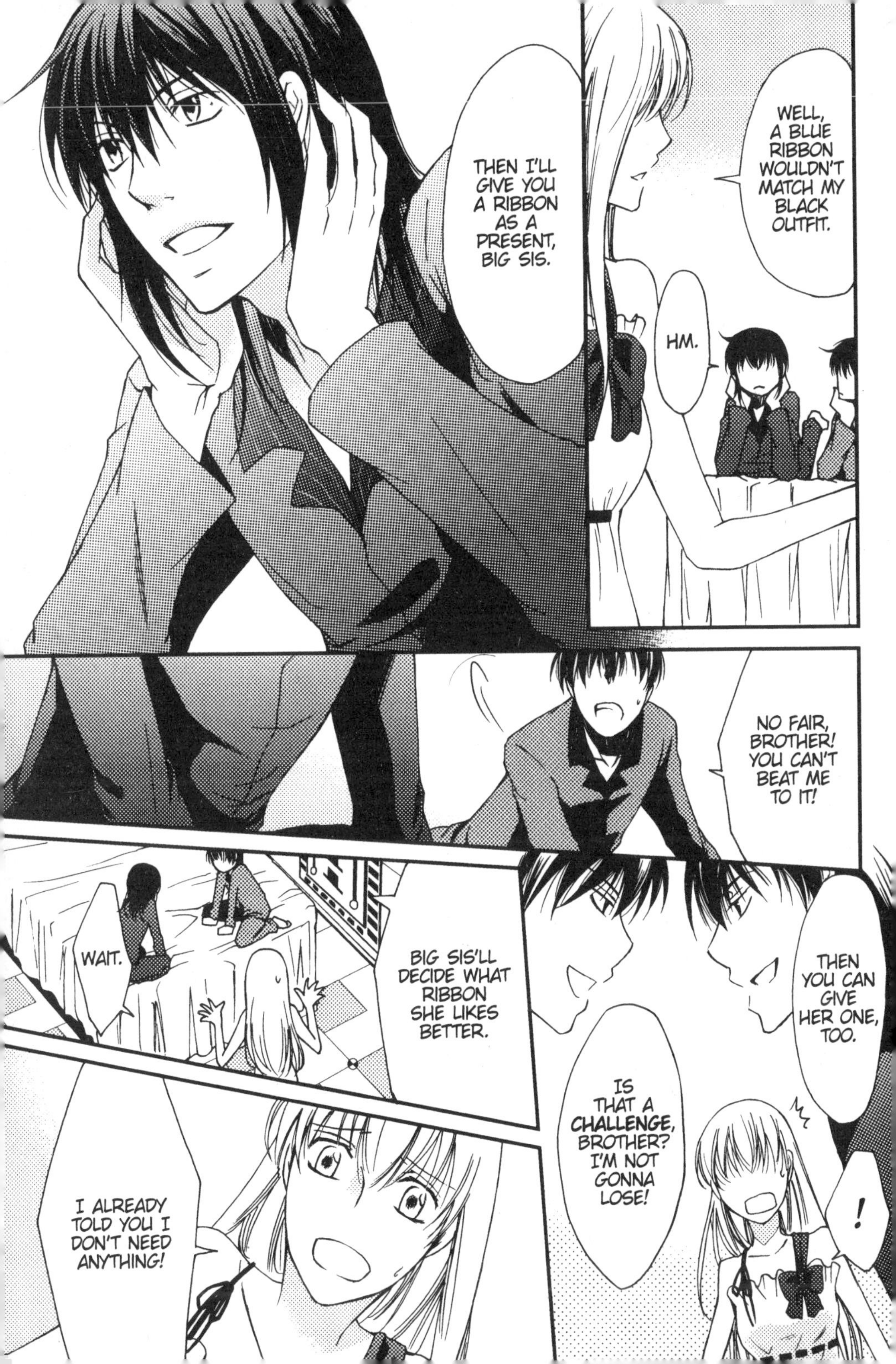
WELL, A BLUE RIBBON WOULDN'T MATCH MY BLACK OUTFIT.
HM.
THEN I'LL GIVE YOU A RIBBON AS A PRESENT, BIG SIS.
NO FAIR, BROTHER! YOU CAN'T BEAT ME TO IT!
THEN YOU CAN GIVE HER ONE, TOO.
IS THAT A CHALLENGE, BROTHER? I'M NOT GONNA LOSE!
!
BIG SIS'LL DECIDE WHAT RIBBON SHE LIKES BETTER.
WAIT.
I ALREADY TOLD YOU I DON'T NEED ANYTHING!

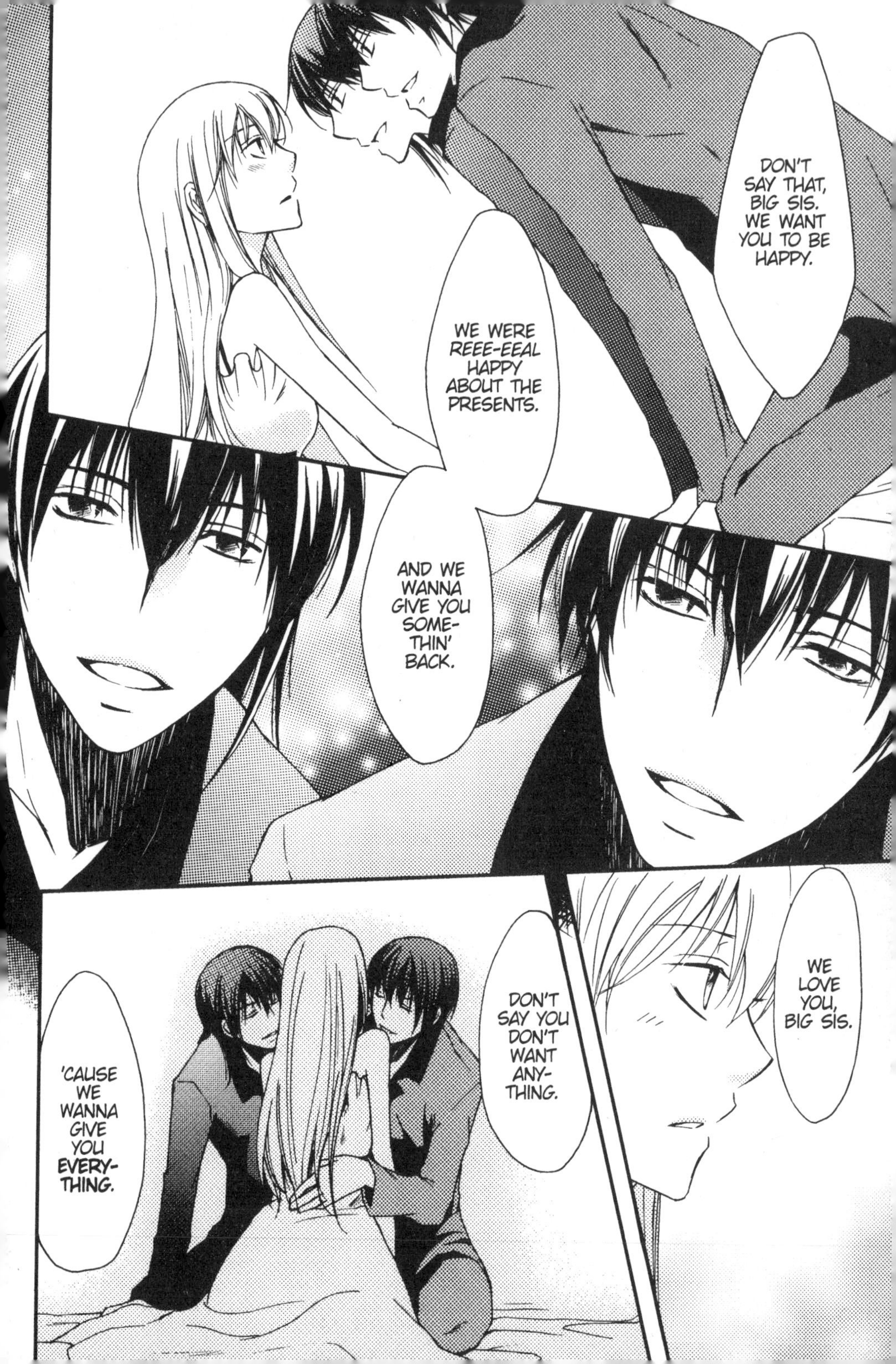
DON'T SAY THAT, BIG SIS. WE WANT YOU TO BE HAPPY.
WE WERE REEE-EEAL HAPPY ABOUT THE PRESENTS.
AND WE WANNA GIVE YOU SOMETHIN' BACK.
WE LOVE YOU, BIG SIS.
DON'T SAY YOU DON'T WANT ANYTHING.
'CAUSE WE WANNA GIVE YOU EVERYTHING.

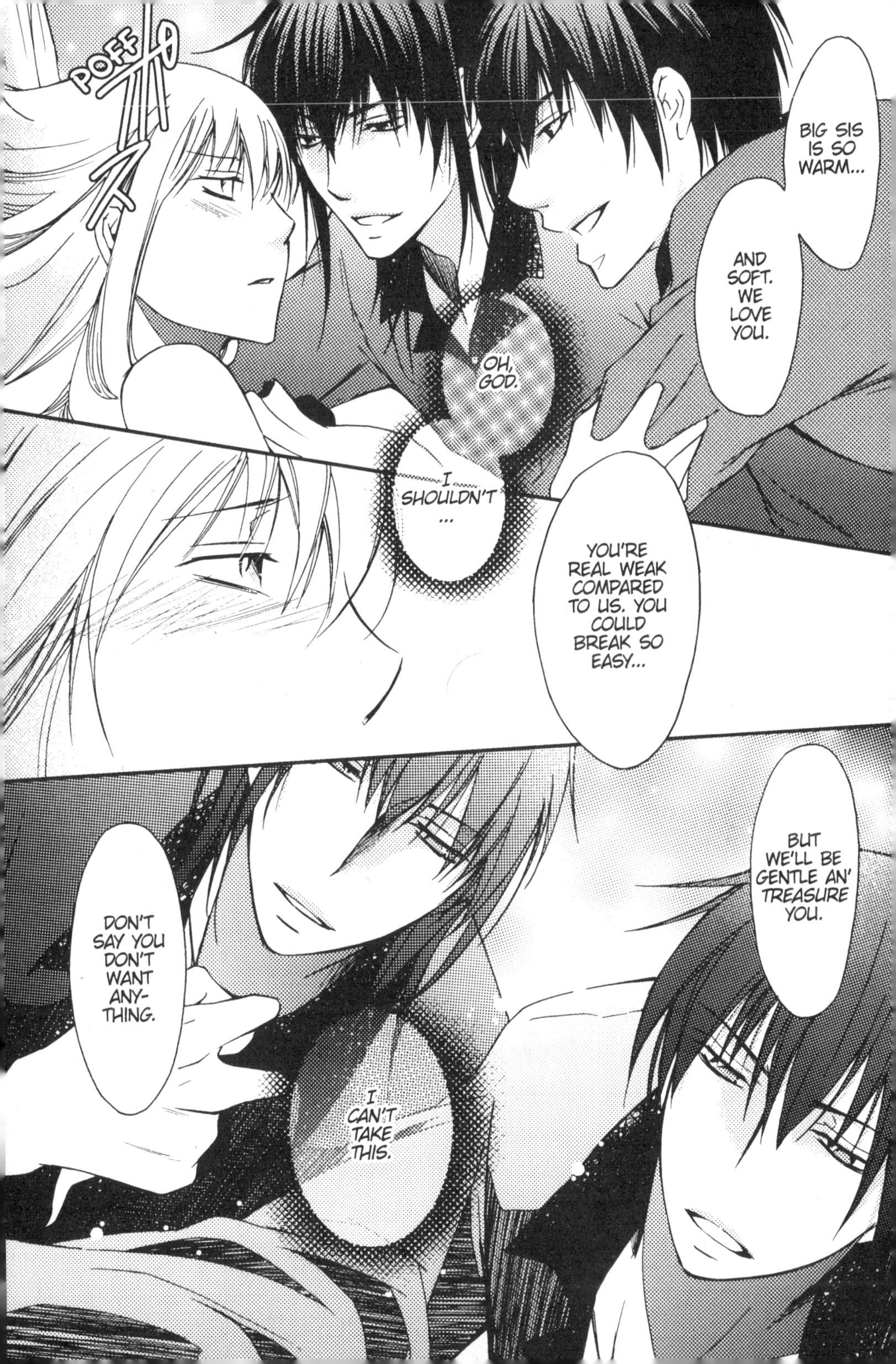
BIG SIS IS SO WARM...
AND SOFT. WE LOVE YOU.
OH, GOD.
POFF
YOU'RE REAL WEAK COMPARED TO US. YOU COULD BREAK SO EASY...
I SHOULDN'T ...
BUT WE'LL BE GENTLE AN' TREASURE YOU.
DON'T SAY YOU DON'T WANT ANY-THING.
I CAN'T TAKE THIS.

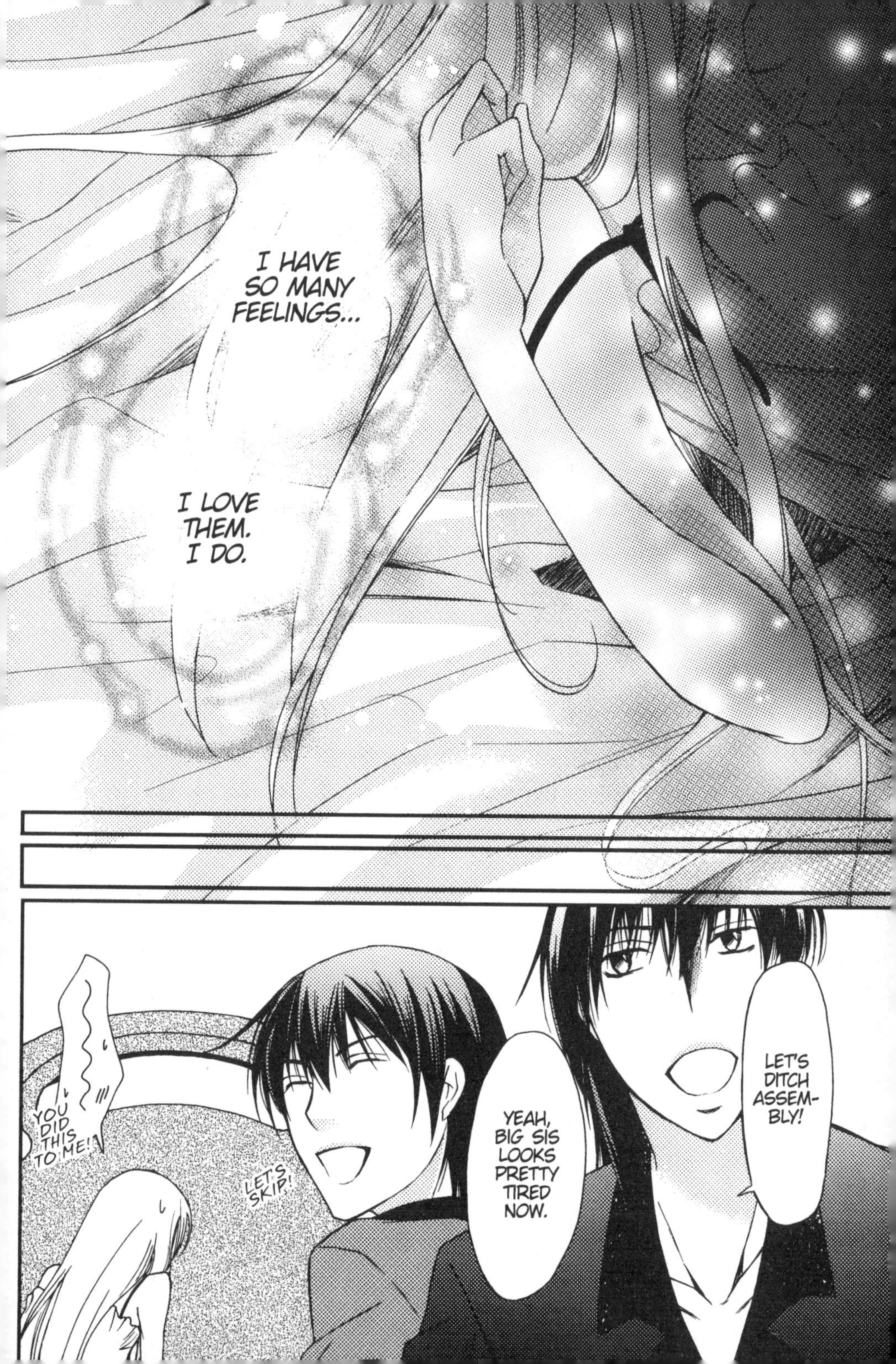
I HAVE SO MANY FEELINGS...
I LOVE THEM. I DO.
LET'S DITCH ASSEM-BLY!
YEAH, BIG SIS LOOKS PRETTY TIRED NOW.
LET'S SKIP!
YOU DID THIS TO ME!

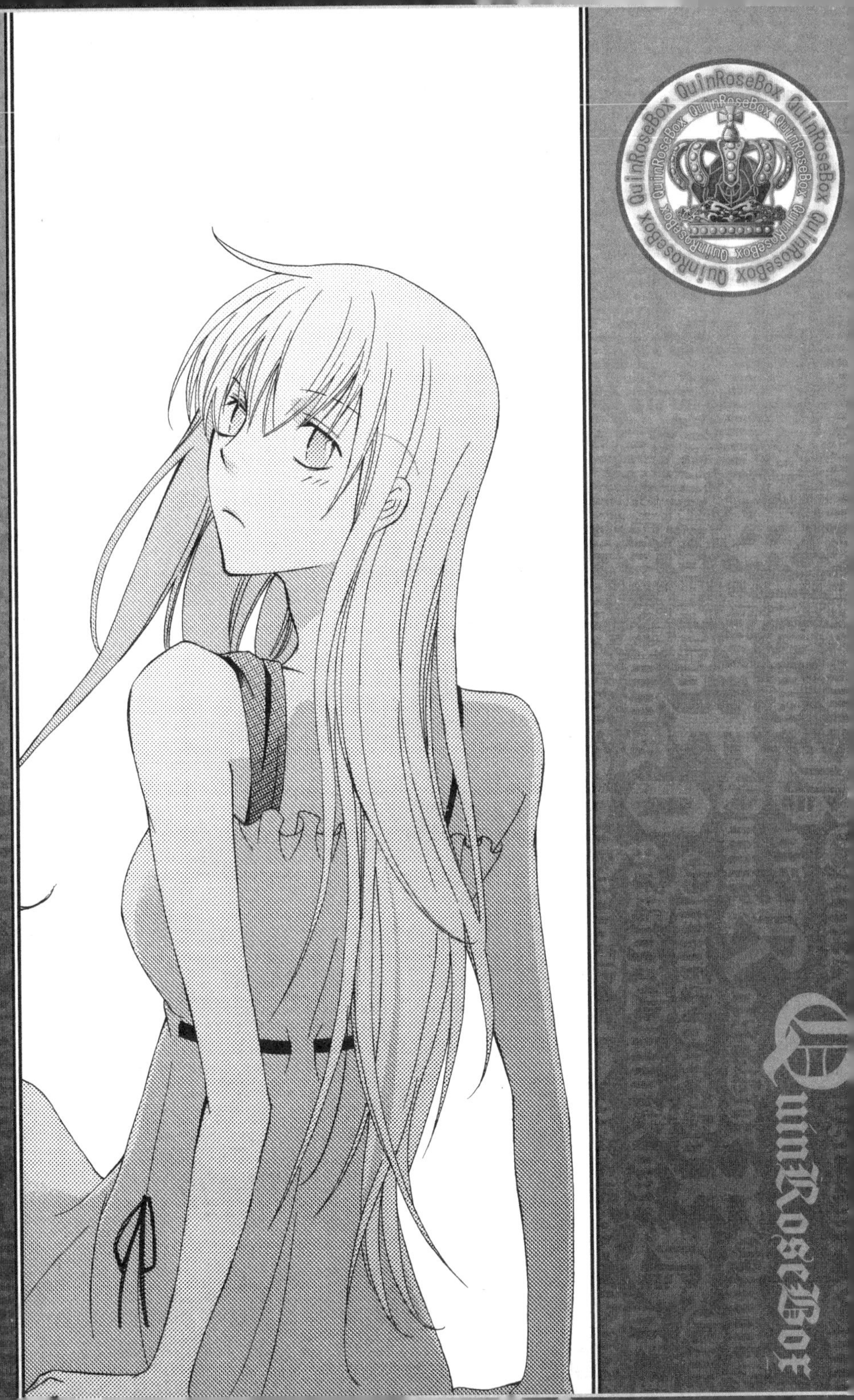

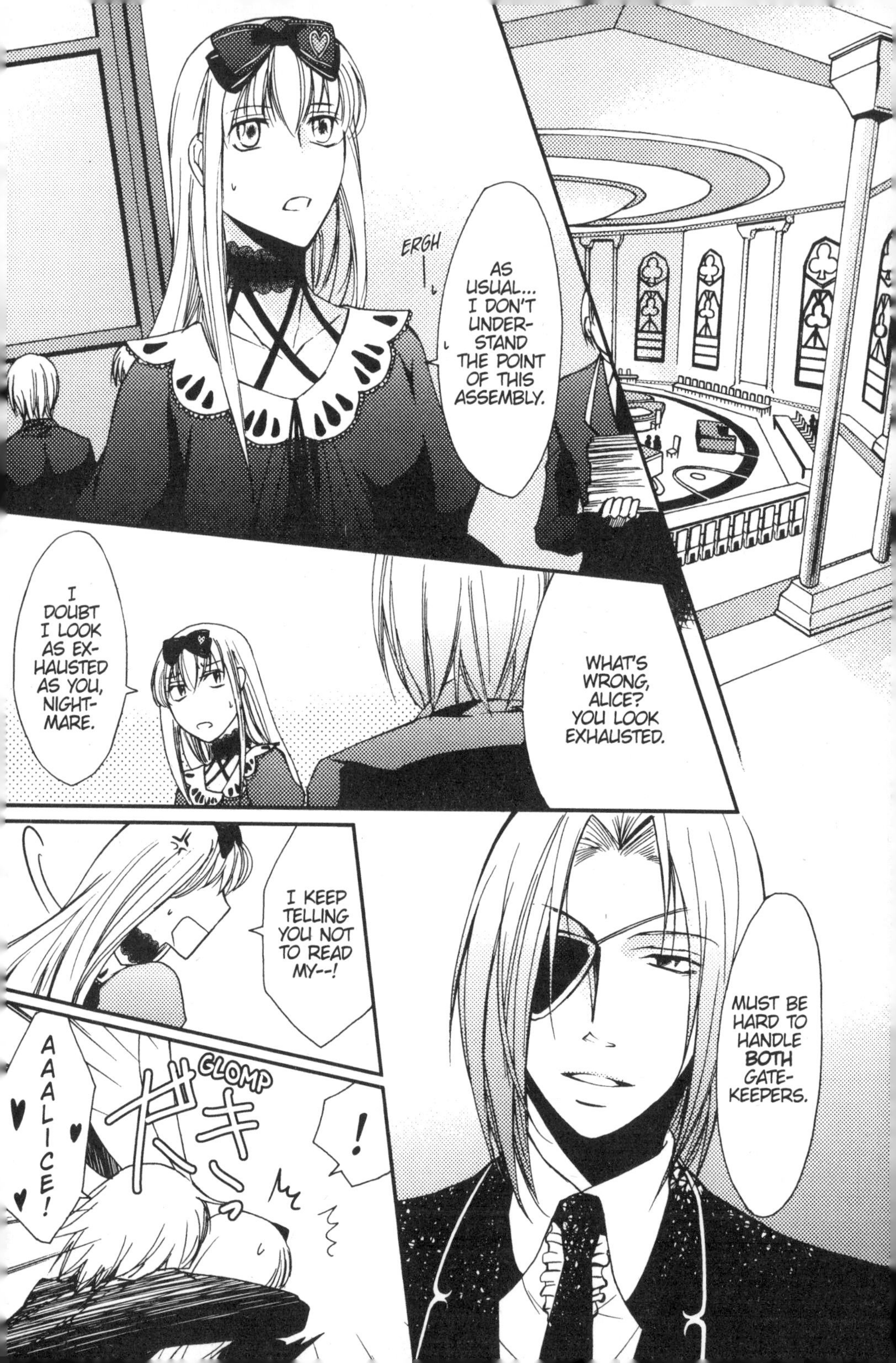
ERGH
AS USUAL... I DON'T UNDERSTAND THE POINT OF THIS ASSEMBLY.
WHAT'S WRONG, ALICE? YOU LOOK EXHAUSTED.
I DOUBT I LOOK AS EXHAUSTED AS YOU, NIGHTMARE.
MUST BE HARD TO HANDLE BOTH GATEKEEPERS.
I KEEP TELLING YOU NOT TO READ MY--!
!
GLOMP
AAALICE!

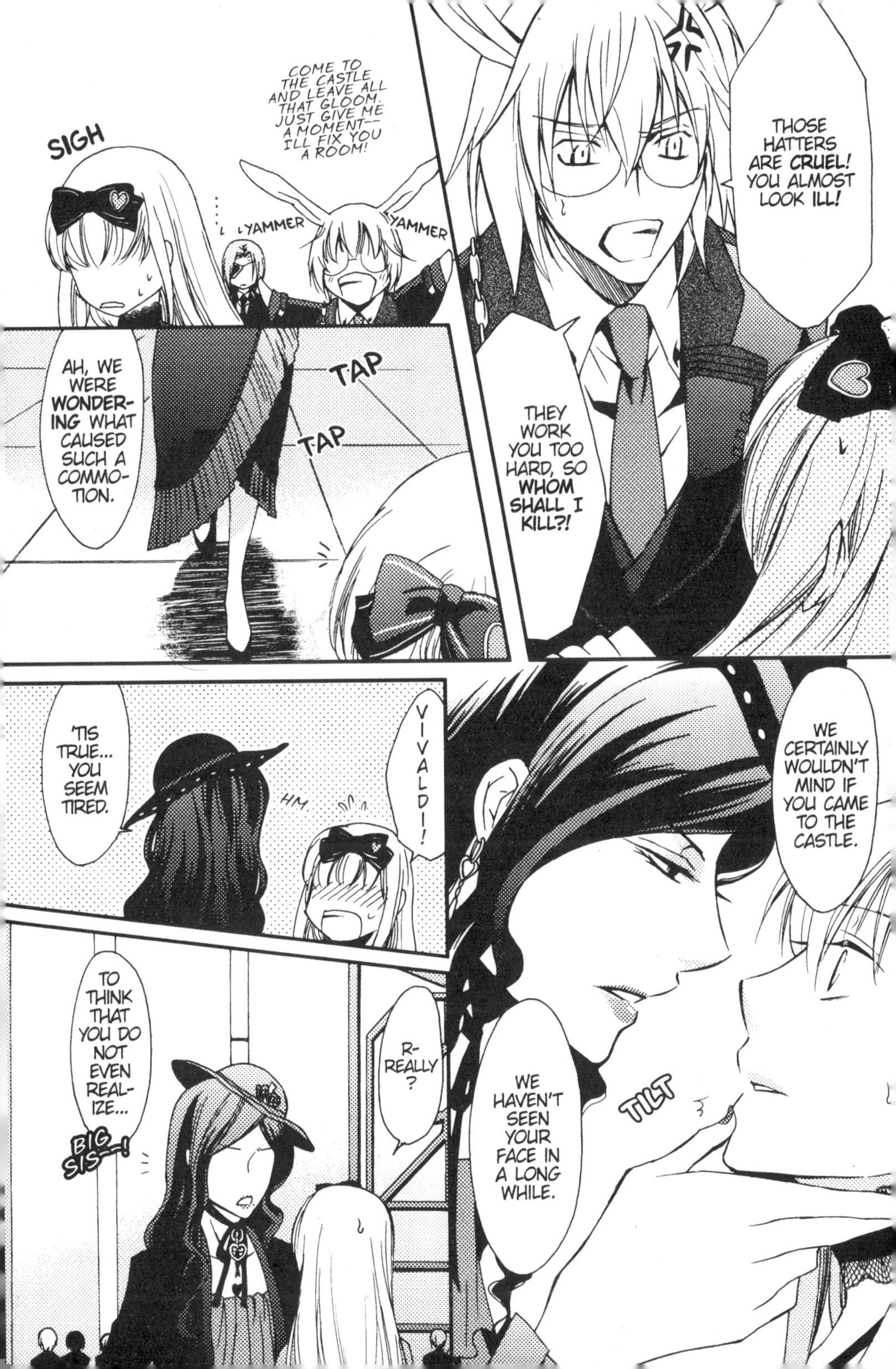
THOSE HATTERS ARE CRUEL! YOU ALMOST LOOK ILL!
THEY WORK YOU TOO HARD, SO WHOM SHALL I KILL?!
COME TO THE CASTLE AND LEAVE ALL THAT GLOOM. JUST GIVE ME A MOMENT-- I'LL FIX YOU A ROOM!
YAMMER
YAMMER
SIGH
TAP
TAP
AH, WE WERE WONDERING WHAT CAUSED SUCH A COMMOTION.
WE CERTAINLY WOULDN'T MIND IF YOU CAME TO THE CASTLE.
TILT
WE HAVEN'T SEEN YOUR FACE IN A LONG WHILE.
VIVALDI!
HM
'TIS TRUE... YOU SEEM TIRED.
R-REALLY?
TO THINK THAT YOU DO NOT EVEN REALIZE...
BIG SIS--!

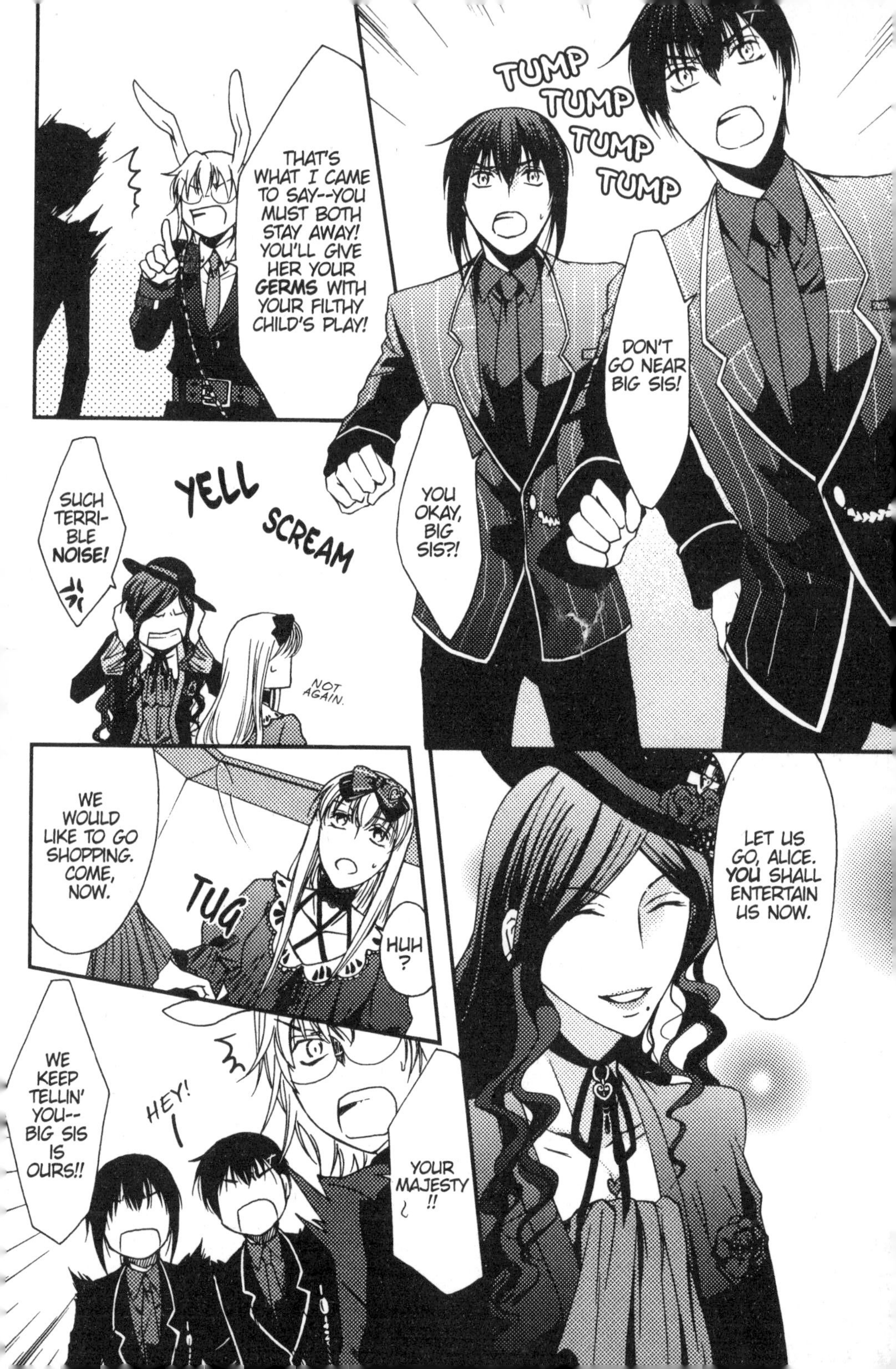
TUMP TUMP TUMP TUMP
DON'T GO NEAR BIG SIS!
YOU OKAY, BIG SIS?!
THAT'S WHAT I CAME TO SAY--YOU MUST BOTH STAY AWAY! YOU'LL GIVE HER YOUR GERMS WITH YOUR FILTHY CHILD'S PLAY!
YELL
SCREAM
SUCH TERRI-BLE NOISE!
NOT AGAIN.
LET US GO, ALICE. YOU SHALL ENTERTAIN US NOW.
WE WOULD LIKE TO GO SHOPPING. COME, NOW.
TUG
HUH?
YOUR MAJESTY!!
HEY!
WE KEEP TELLIN' YOU-- BIG SIS IS OURS!!

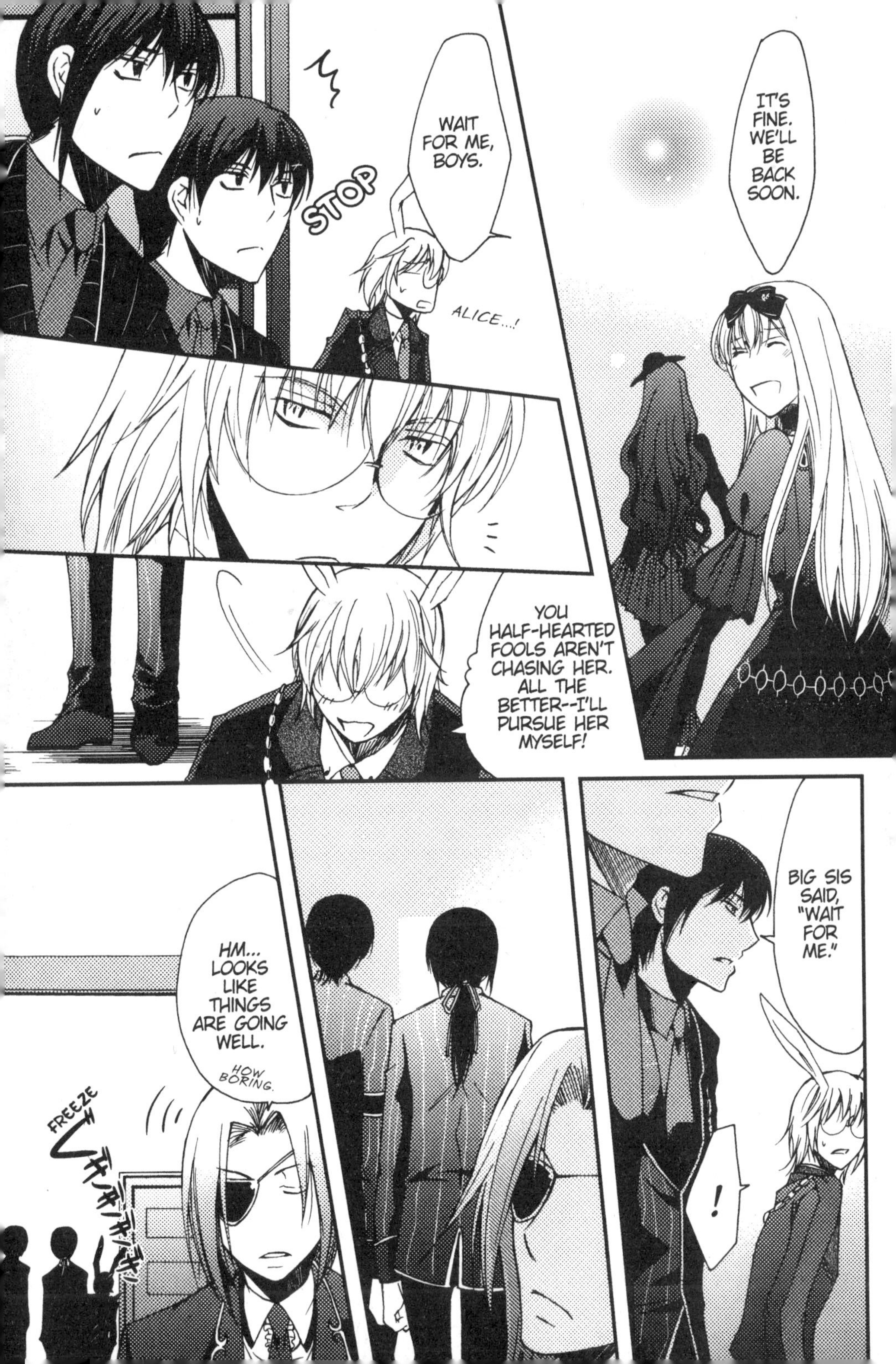
IT'S FINE. WE'LL BE BACK SOON.
WAIT FOR ME, BOYS.
STOP
ALICE...!
YOU HALF-HEARTED FOOLS AREN'T CHASING HER. ALL THE BETTER--I'LL PURSUE HER MYSELF!
BIG SIS SAID, "WAIT FOR ME."
!
HM... LOOKS LIKE THINGS ARE GOING WELL.
HOW BORING.
FREEZE

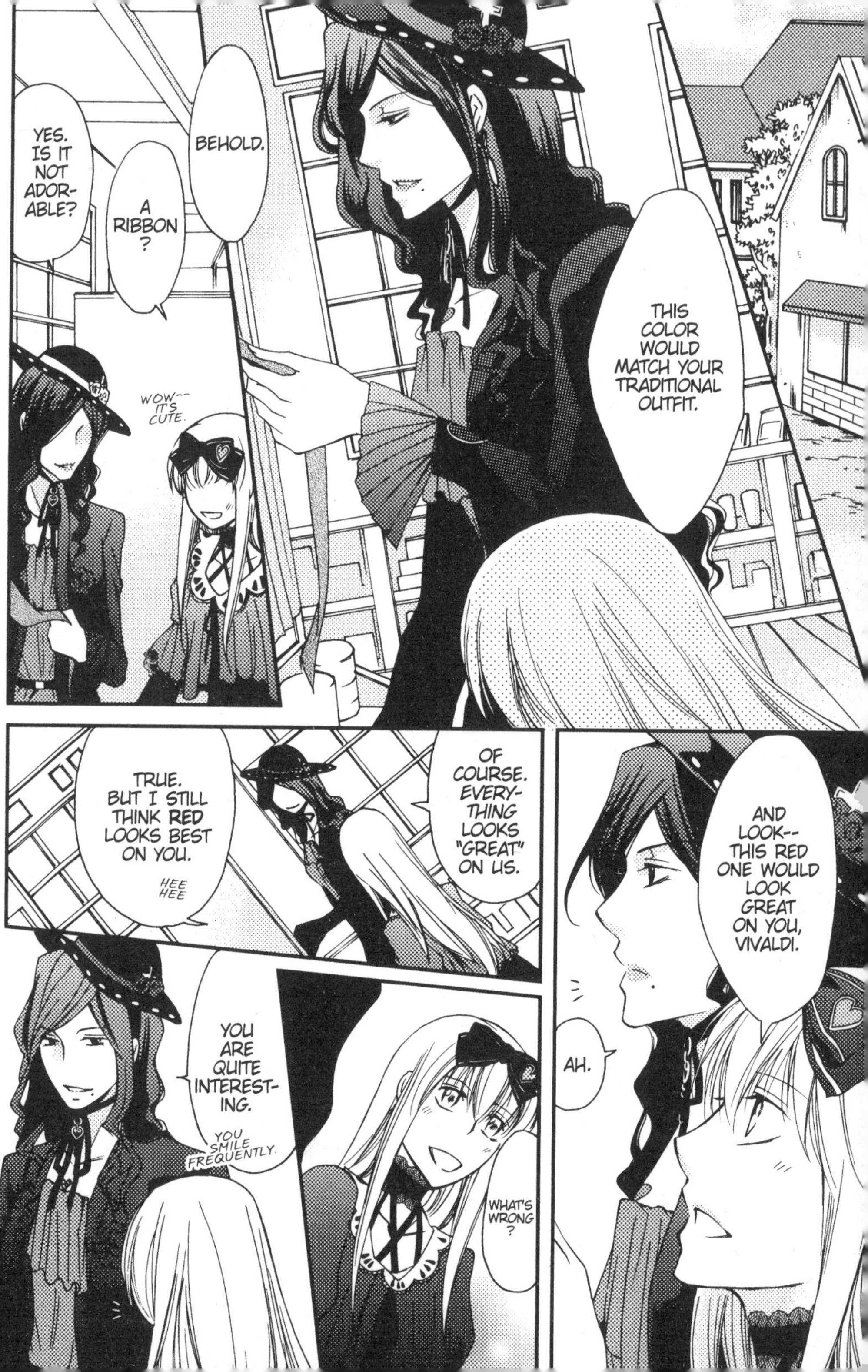
THIS COLOR WOULD MATCH YOUR TRADITIONAL OUTFIT.
BEHOLD.
A RIBBON?
YES. IS IT NOT ADORABLE?
WOW-- IT'S CUTE.
AND LOOK-- THIS RED ONE WOULD LOOK GREAT ON YOU, VIVALDI.
AH.
OF COURSE. EVERYTHING LOOKS "GREAT" ON US.
TRUE. BUT I STILL THINK RED LOOKS BEST ON YOU.
HEE HEE
WHAT'S WRONG?
YOU ARE QUITE INTERESTING.
YOU SMILE FREQUENTLY.

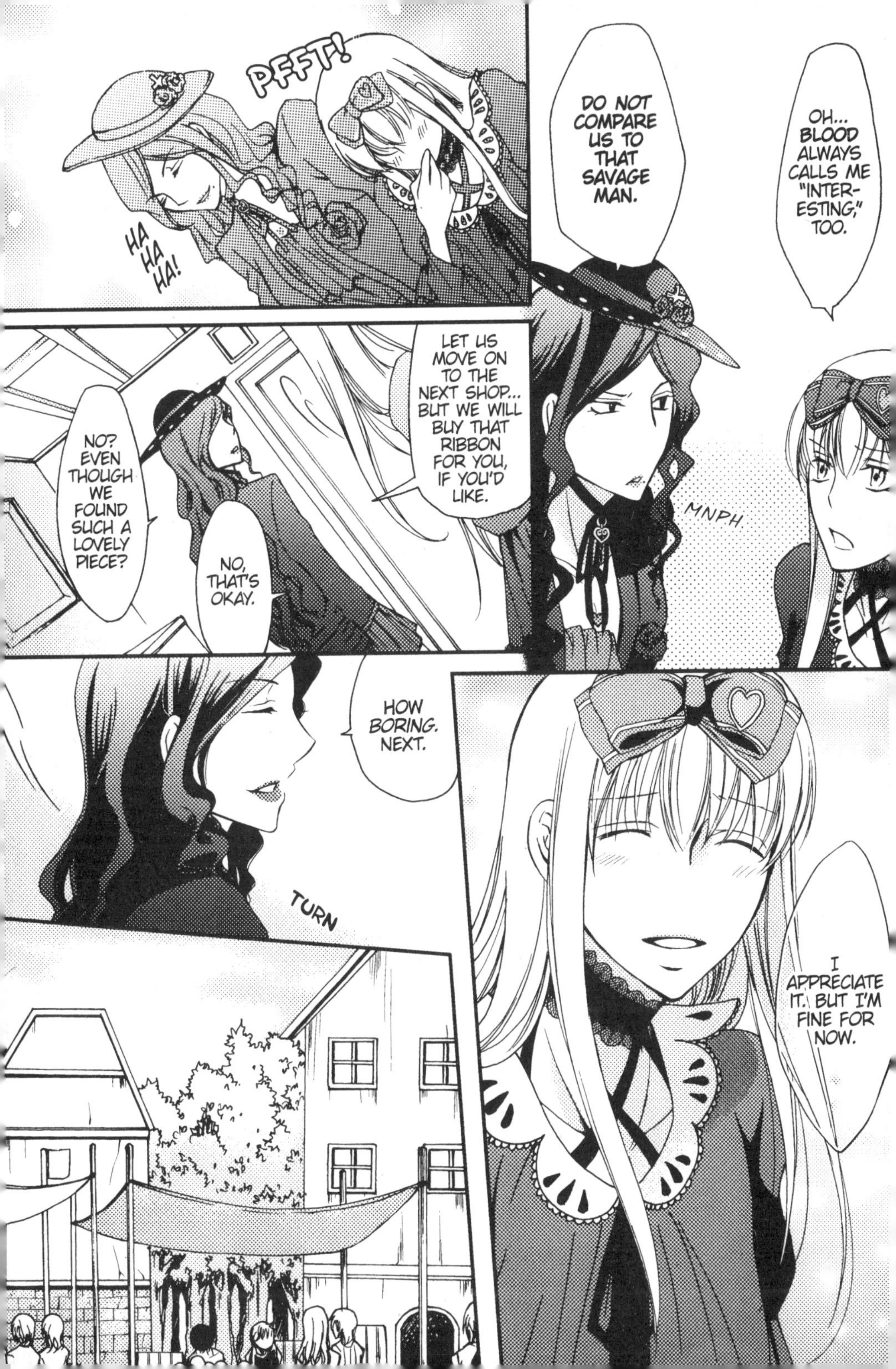
OH... BLOOD ALWAYS CALLS ME "INTER-ESTING," TOO.
DO NOT COMPARE US TO THAT SAVAGE MAN.
MNPH.
PFFT!
HA HA HA!
LET US MOVE ON TO THE NEXT SHOP... BUT WE WILL BUY THAT RIBBON FOR YOU, IF YOU'D LIKE.
NO? EVEN THOUGH WE FOUND SUCH A LOVELY PIECE?
NO, THAT'S OKAY.
I APPRECIATE IT. BUT I'M FINE FOR NOW.
HOW BORING. NEXT.
TURN

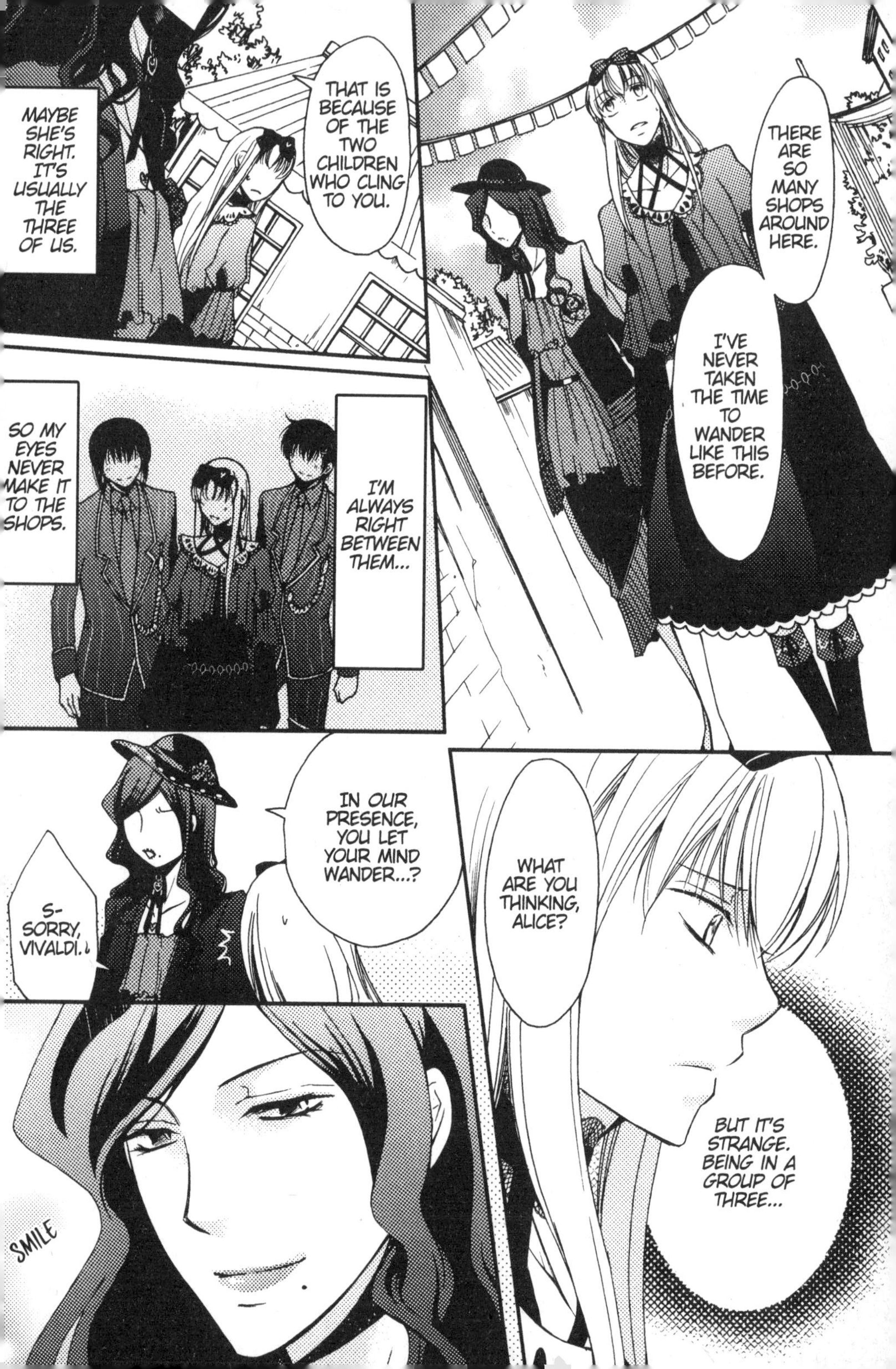
THERE ARE SO MANY SHOPS AROUND HERE.
I'VE NEVER TAKEN THE TIME TO WANDER LIKE THIS BEFORE.
THAT IS BECAUSE OF THE TWO CHILDREN WHO CLING TO YOU.
MAYBE SHE'S RIGHT. IT'S USUALLY THE THREE OF US.
I'M ALWAYS RIGHT BETWEEN THEM...
SO MY EYES NEVER MAKE IT TO THE SHOPS.
WHAT ARE YOU THINKING, ALICE?
BUT IT'S STRANGE. BEING IN A GROUP OF THREE...
IN OUR PRESENCE, YOU LET YOUR MIND WANDER...?
S-SORRY, VIVALDI.
SMILE

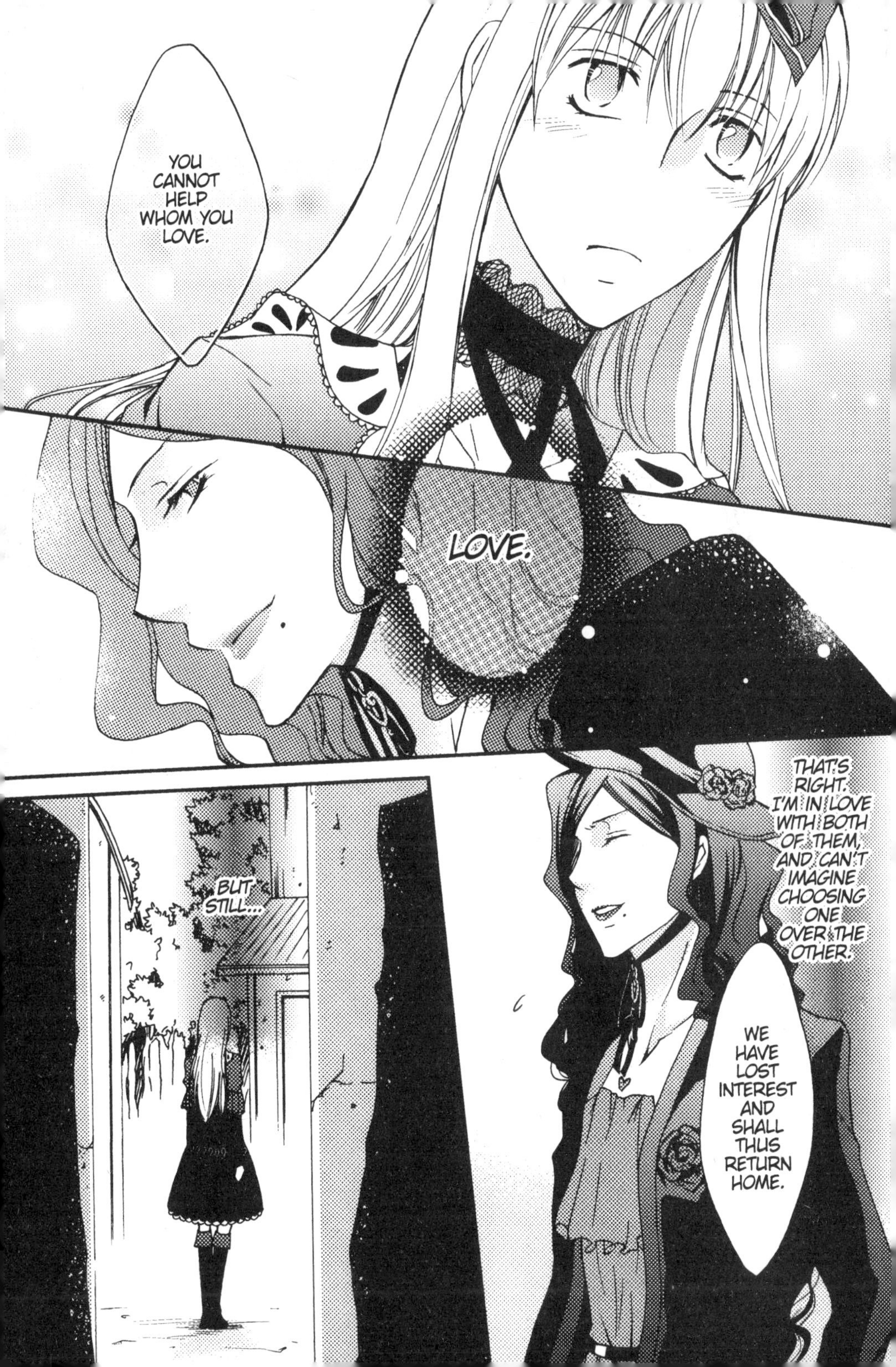
YOU CANNOT HELP WHOM YOU LOVE.
LOVE.
THAT'S RIGHT. I'M IN LOVE WITH BOTH OF THEM, AND CAN'T IMAGINE CHOOSING ONE OVER THE OTHER.
WE HAVE LOST INTEREST AND SHALL THUS RETURN HOME.
BUT STILL...

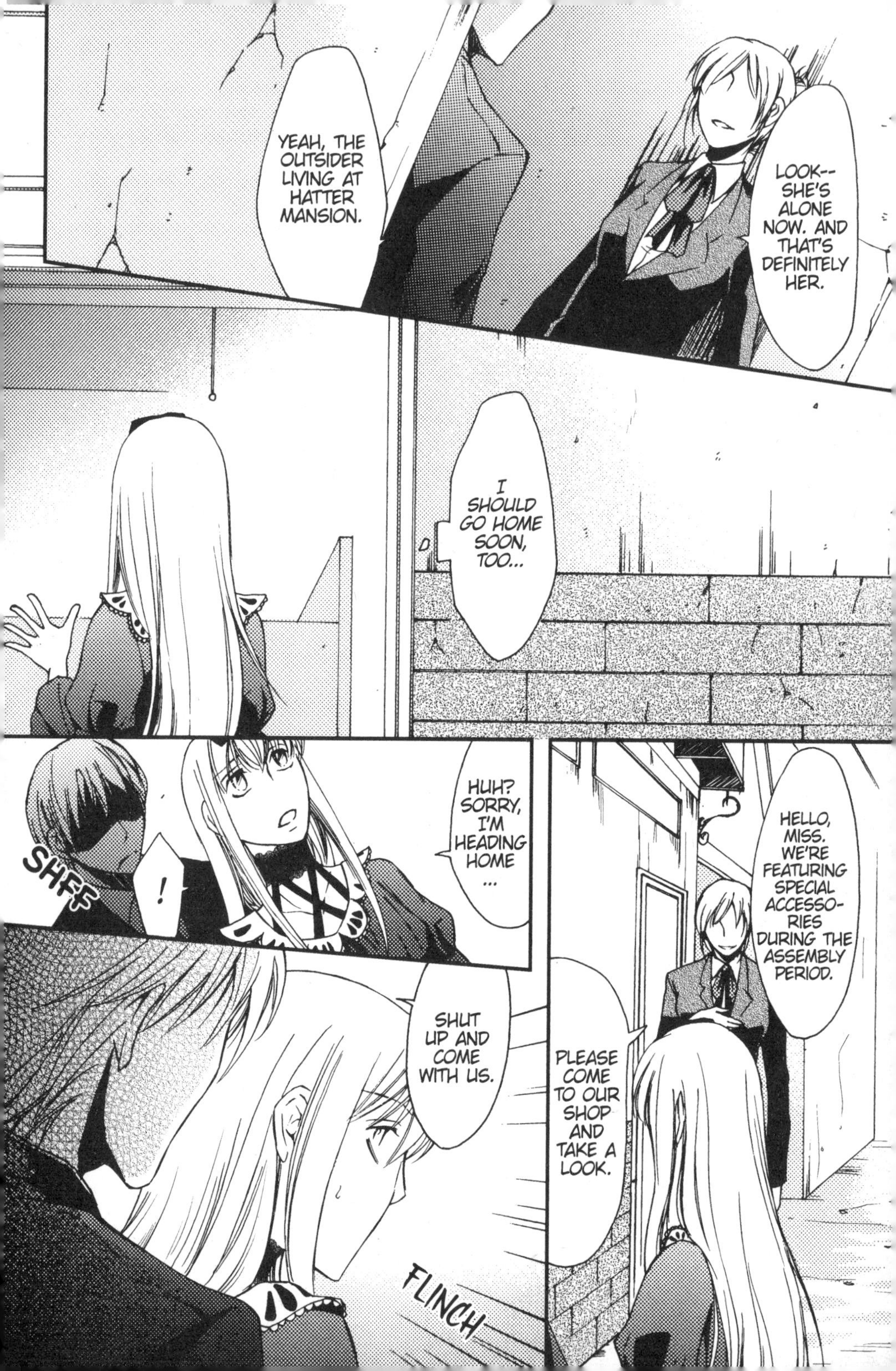
LOOK-- SHE'S ALONE NOW. AND THAT'S DEFINITELY HER.
YEAH, THE OUTSIDER LIVING AT HATTER MANSION.
I SHOULD GO HOME SOON, TOO...
HELLO, MISS. WE'RE FEATURING SPECIAL ACCESSO-RIES DURING THE ASSEMBLY PERIOD.
PLEASE COME TO OUR SHOP AND TAKE A LOOK.
HUH? SORRY, I'M HEADING HOME ...
!
SHFF
SHUT UP AND COME WITH US.
FLINCH

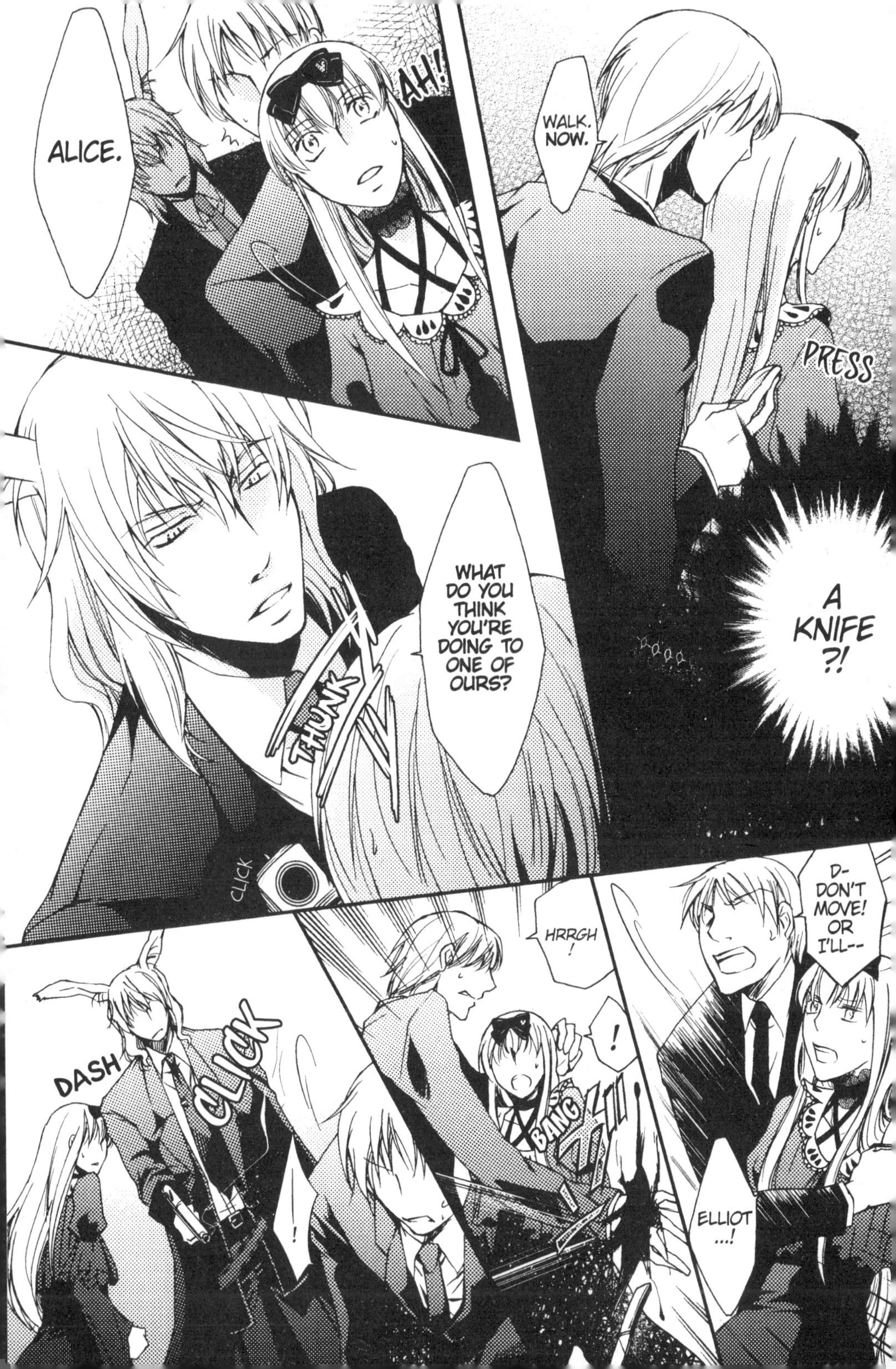
WALK. NOW.
PRESS
A KNIFE?!
ALICE.
AH!
WHAT DO YOU THINK YOU'RE DOING TO ONE OF OURS?
THUNK
CLICK
D-DON'T MOVE! OR I'LL--
ELLIOT...!
HRRGH!
!
BANG
DASH
CLICK
!

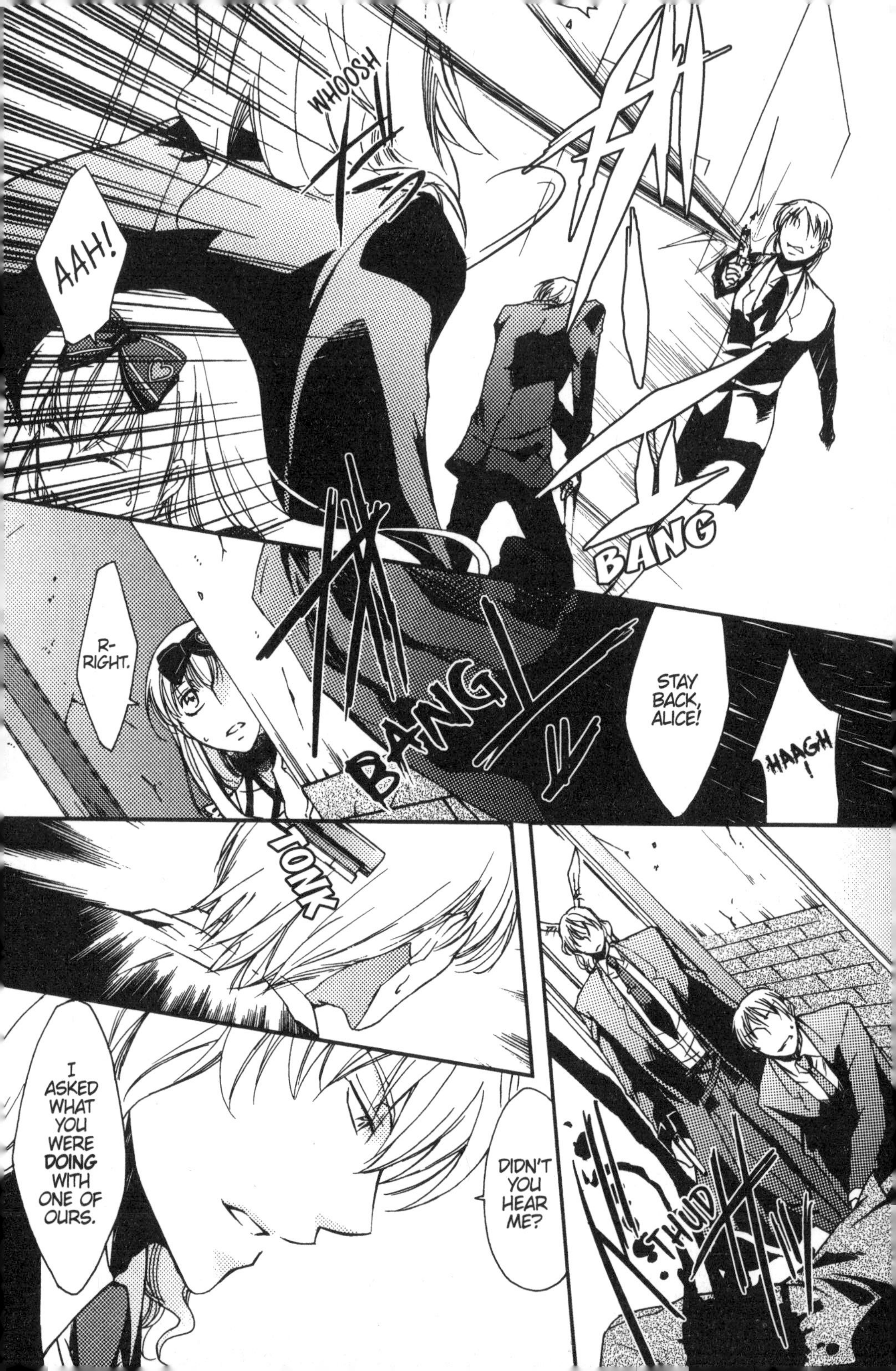
WHOOSH
AAH!
BANG
HAAGH!
STAY BACK, ALICE!
BANG
BANG
R-RIGHT.
THUD
TONK
DIDN'T YOU HEAR ME?
I ASKED WHAT YOU WERE DOING WITH ONE OF OURS.

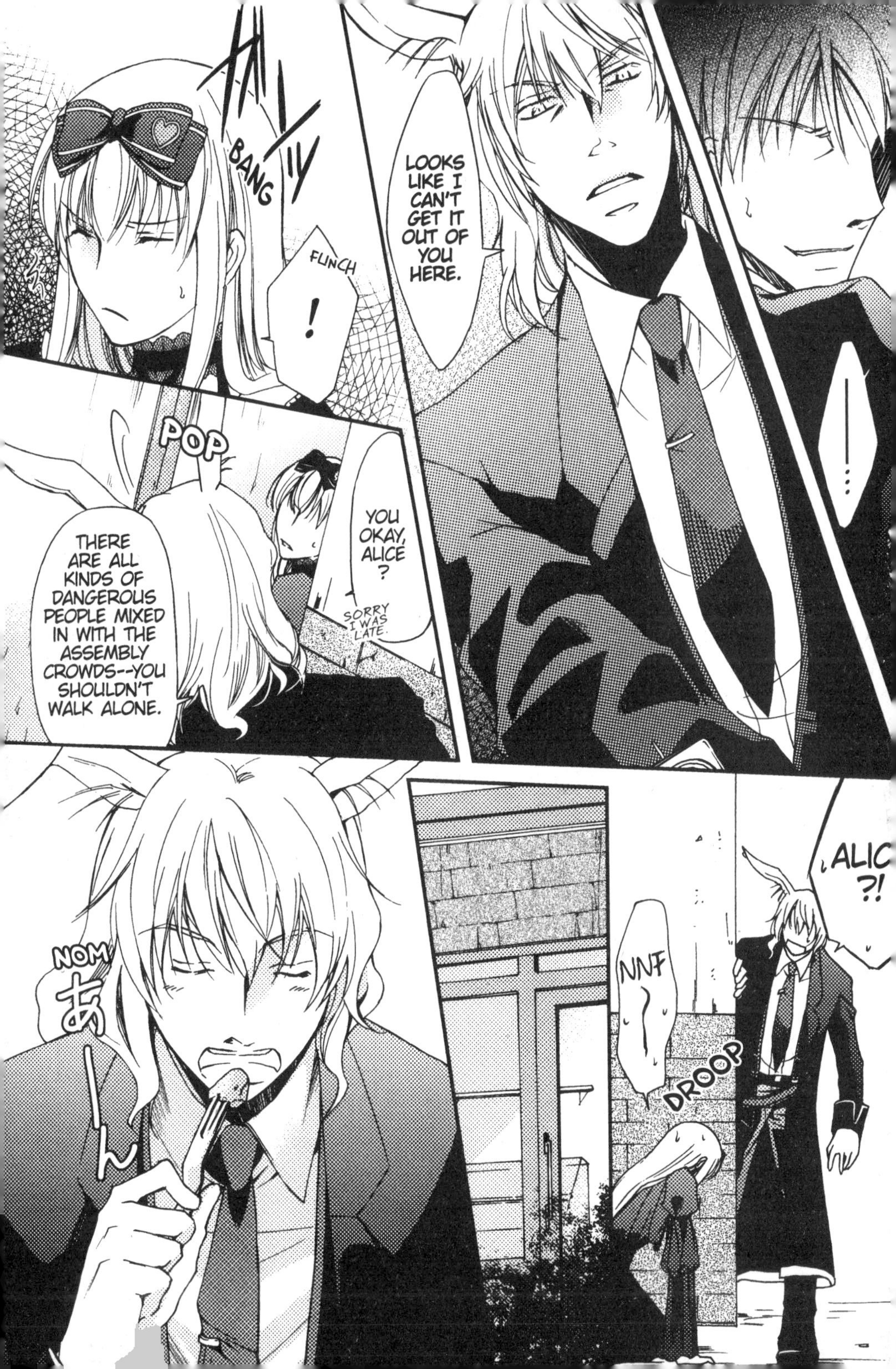

!...
LOOKS LIKE I CAN'T GET IT OUT OF YOU HERE.
BANG
FLINCH
!
POP
YOU OKAY, ALICE?
SORRY I WAS LATE.
THERE ARE ALL KINDS OF DANGEROUS PEOPLE MIXED IN WITH THE ASSEMBLY CROWDS--YOU SHOULDN'T WALK ALONE.
ALIC ?!
DROOP
NNF
NOM
あーん

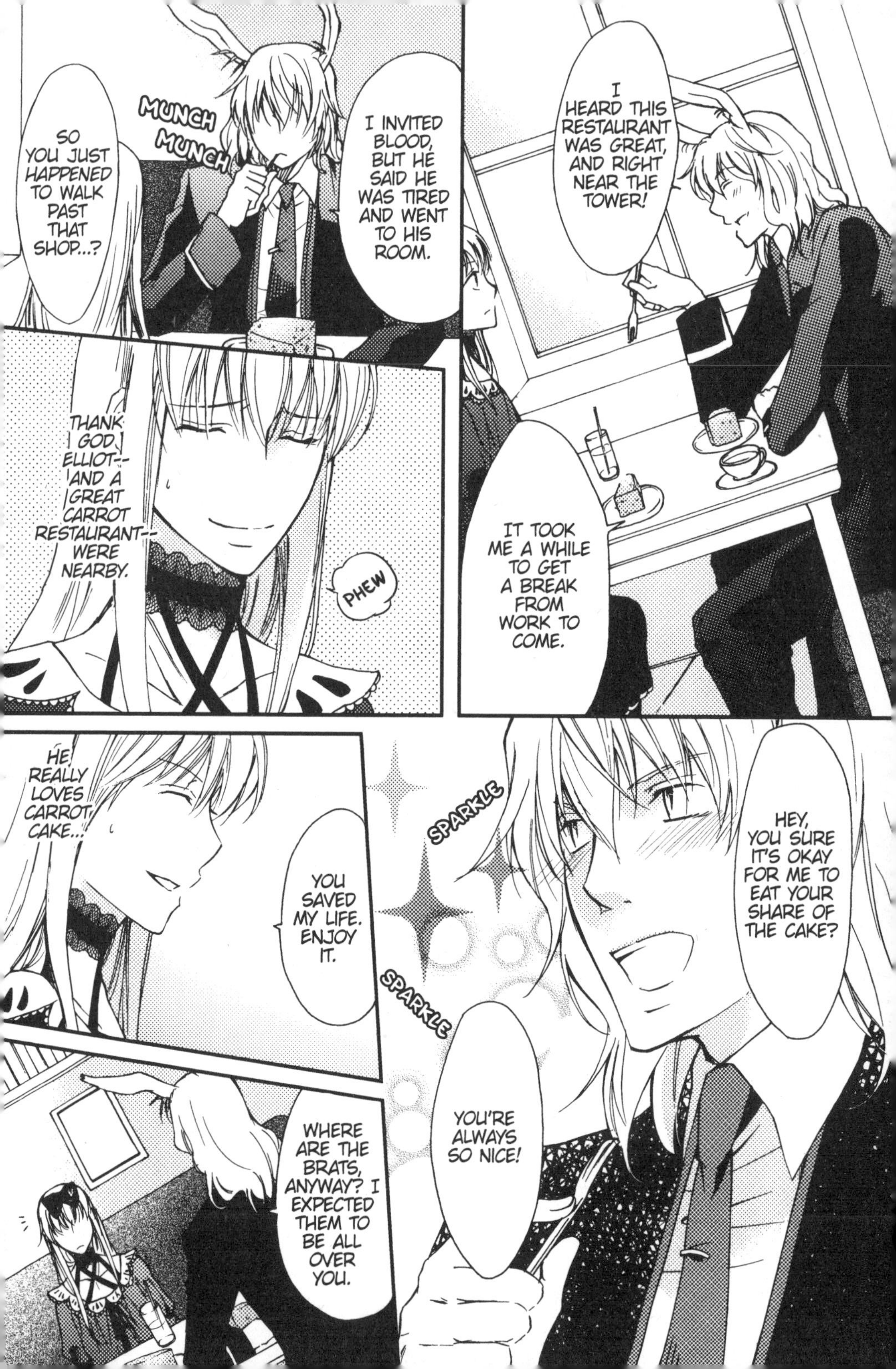
I HEARD THIS RESTAURANT WAS GREAT, AND RIGHT NEAR THE TOWER!
IT TOOK ME A WHILE TO GET A BREAK FROM WORK TO COME.
I INVITED BLOOD, BUT HE SAID HE WAS TIRED AND WENT TO HIS ROOM.
MUNCH MUNCH
SO YOU JUST HAPPENED TO WALK PAST THAT SHOP...?
THANK GOD ELLIOT-- AND A GREAT CARROT RESTAURANT-- WERE NEARBY.
PHEW
HEY, YOU SURE IT'S OKAY FOR ME TO EAT YOUR SHARE OF THE CAKE?
SPARKLE
SPARKLE
YOU'RE ALWAYS SO NICE!
YOU SAVED MY LIFE. ENJOY IT.
HE REALLY LOVES CARROT CAKE...
WHERE ARE THE BRATS, ANYWAY? I EXPECTED THEM TO BE ALL OVER YOU.

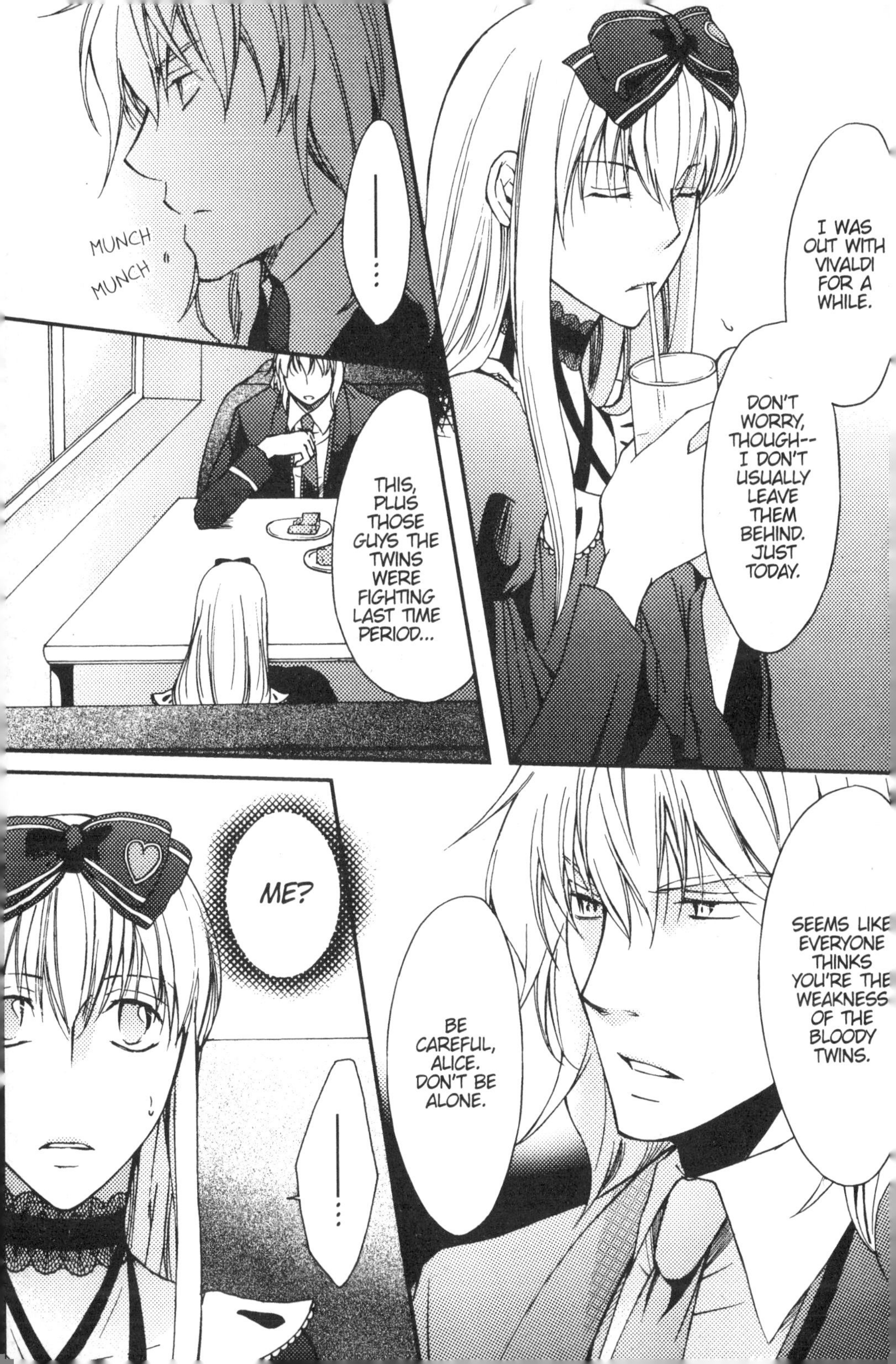
I WAS OUT WITH VIVALDI FOR A WHILE.
DON'T WORRY, THOUGH-- I DON'T USUALLY LEAVE THEM BEHIND. JUST TODAY.
MUNCH MUNCH
......
THIS, PLUS THOSE GUYS THE TWINS WERE FIGHTING LAST TIME PERIOD...
SEEMS LIKE EVERYONE THINKS YOU'RE THE WEAKNESS OF THE BLOODY TWINS.
BE CAREFUL, ALICE. DON'T BE ALONE.
ME?
......

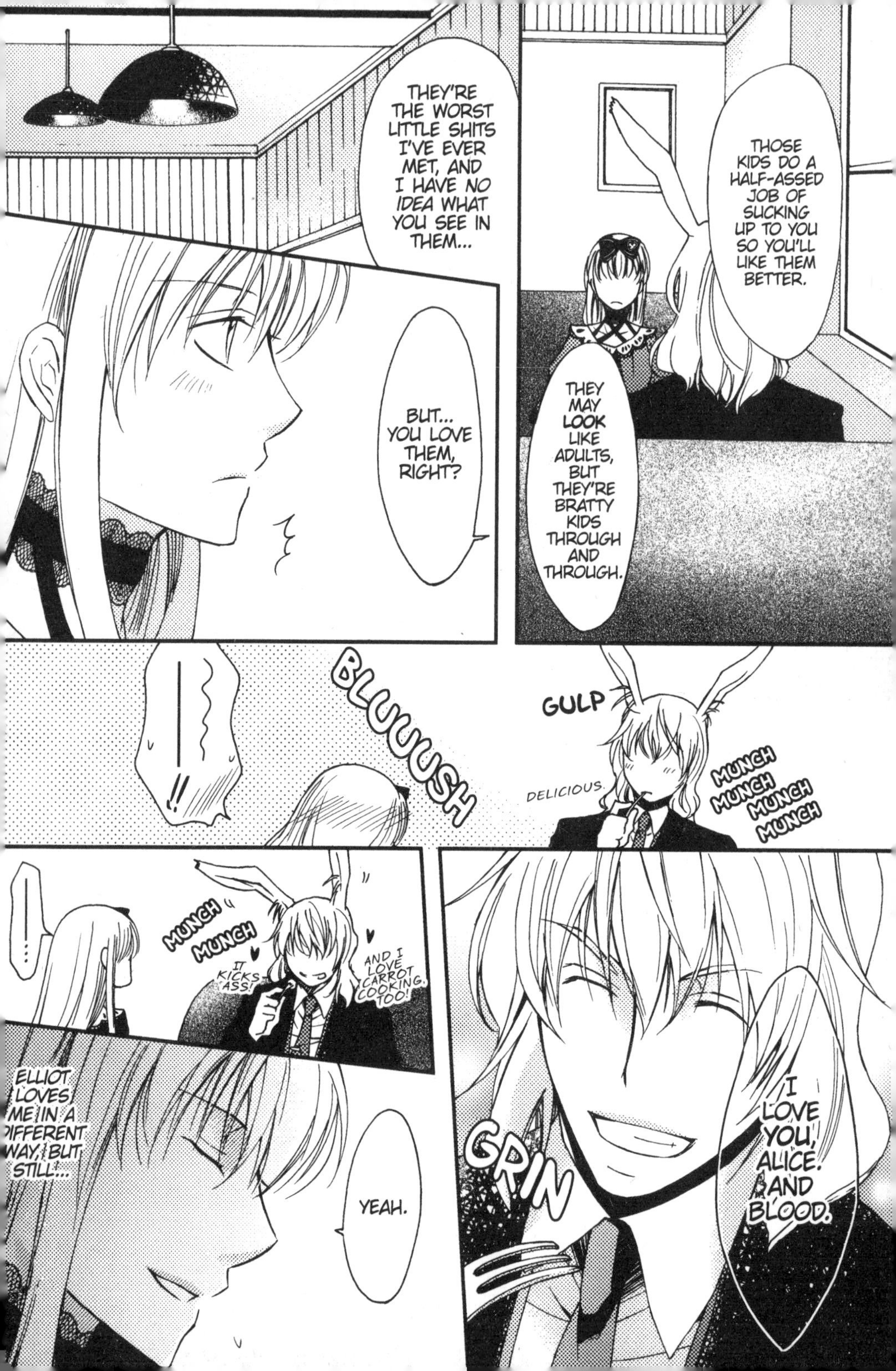
THOSE KIDS DO A HALF-ASSED JOB OF SUCKING UP TO YOU SO YOU'LL LIKE THEM BETTER.
THEY MAY LOOK LIKE ADULTS, BUT THEY'RE BRATTY KIDS THROUGH AND THROUGH.
THEY'RE THE WORST LITTLE SHITS I'VE EVER MET, AND I HAVE NO IDEA WHAT YOU SEE IN THEM...
BUT... YOU LOVE THEM, RIGHT?
GULP
MUNCH MUNCH MUNCH MUNCH
DELICIOUS.
BLUUUSH
—!!
I LOVE YOU, ALICE. AND BLOOD.
GRIN
AND I LOVE CARROT COOKING, TOO!
IT KICKS ASS!
MUNCH MUNCH
!......
ELLIOT LOVES ME IN A DIFFERENT WAY, BUT STILL...
YEAH.

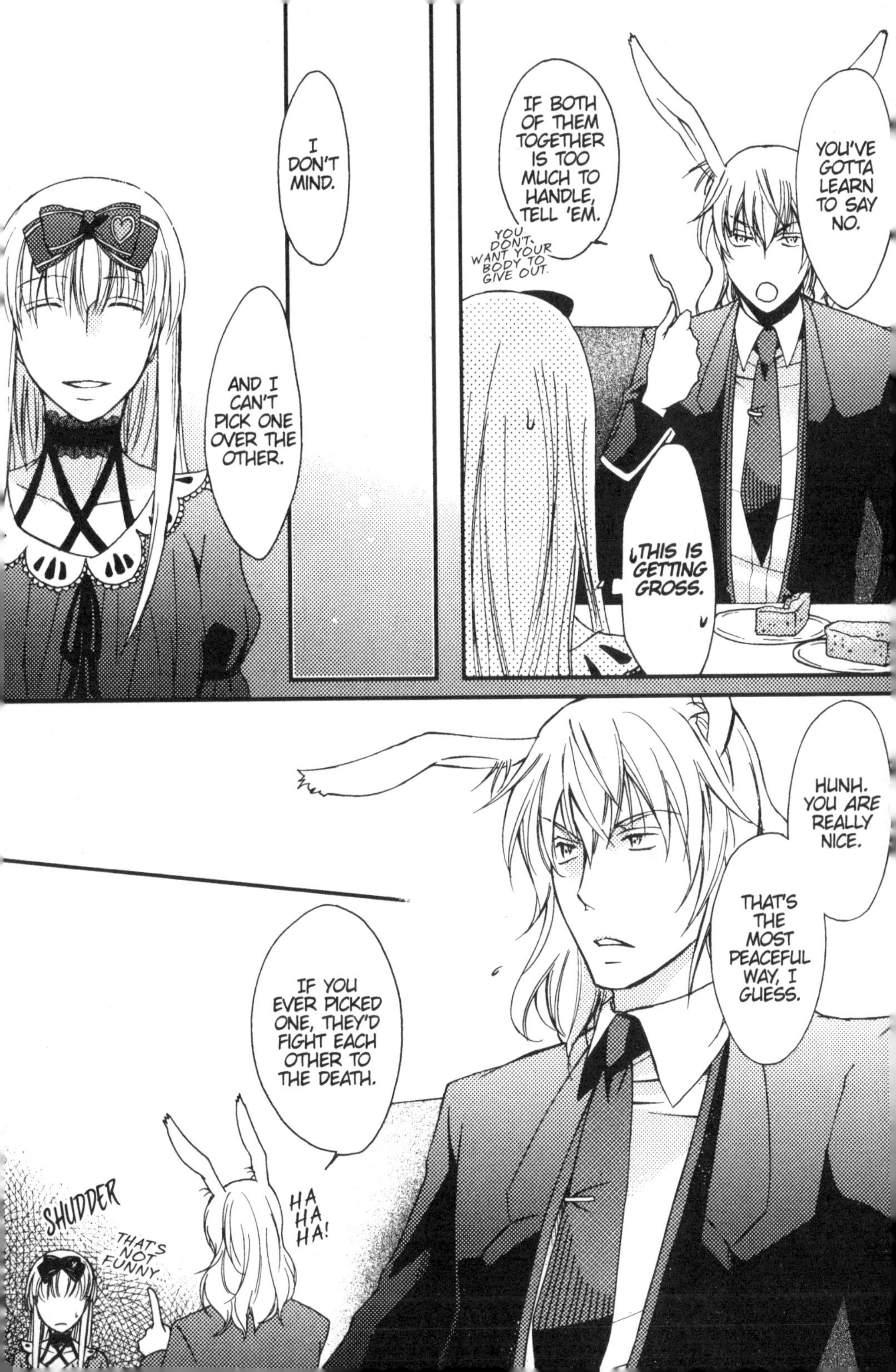
YOU'VE GOTTA LEARN TO SAY NO.
IF BOTH OF THEM TOGETHER IS TOO MUCH TO HANDLE, TELL 'EM.
YOU DON'T WANT YOUR BODY TO GIVE OUT.
THIS IS GETTING GROSS.
I DON'T MIND.
AND I CAN'T PICK ONE OVER THE OTHER.
HUNH. YOU ARE REALLY NICE.
THAT'S THE MOST PEACEFUL WAY, I GUESS.
IF YOU EVER PICKED ONE, THEY'D FIGHT EACH OTHER TO THE DEATH.
HA HA HA!
SHUDDER
THAT'S NOT FUNNY...

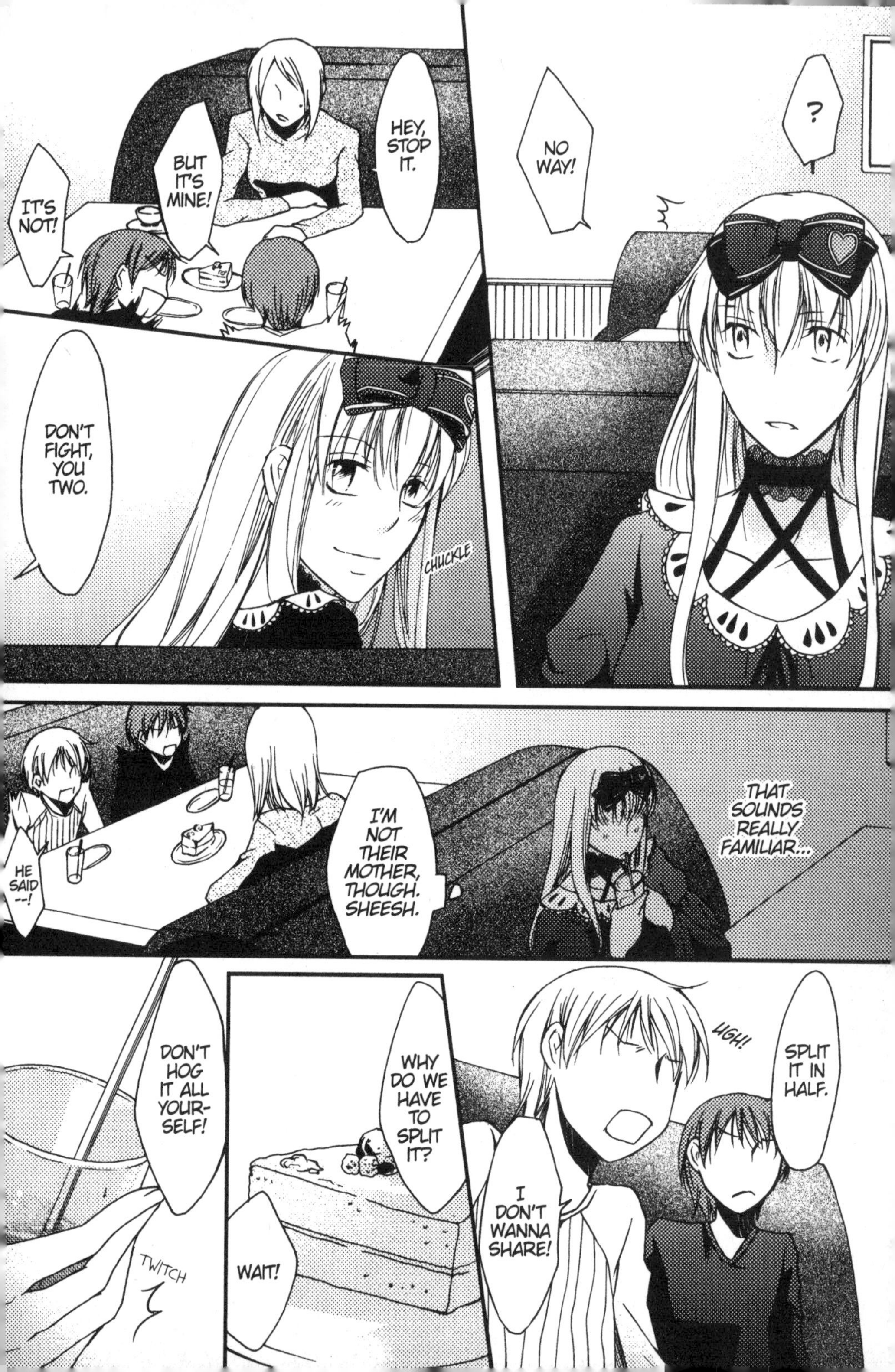
?
NO WAY!
HEY, STOP IT.
BUT IT'S MINE!
IT'S NOT!
DON'T FIGHT, YOU TWO.
CHUCKLE
THAT SOUNDS REALLY FAMILIAR...
I'M NOT THEIR MOTHER, THOUGH. SHEESH.
HE SAID --!
SPLIT IT IN HALF.
UGH!
I DON'T WANNA SHARE!
WHY DO WE HAVE TO SPLIT IT?
WAIT!
DON'T HOG IT ALL YOURSELF!
TWITCH

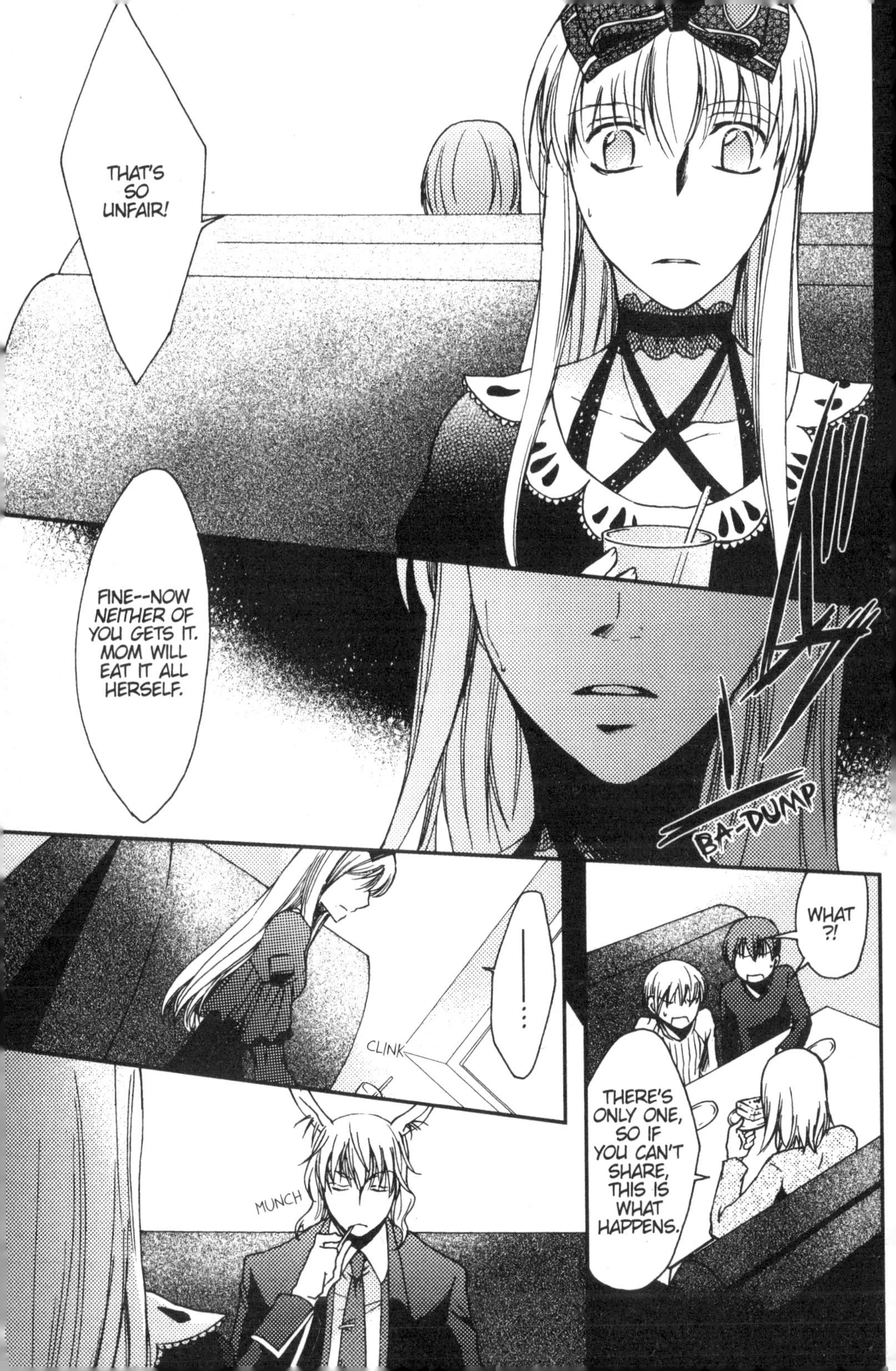
THAT'S SO UNFAIR!
FINE--NOW NEITHER OF YOU GETS IT. MOM WILL EAT IT ALL HERSELF.
BA-DUMP
WHAT?!
THERE'S ONLY ONE, SO IF YOU CAN'T SHARE, THIS IS WHAT HAPPENS.
......
CLINK
MUNCH

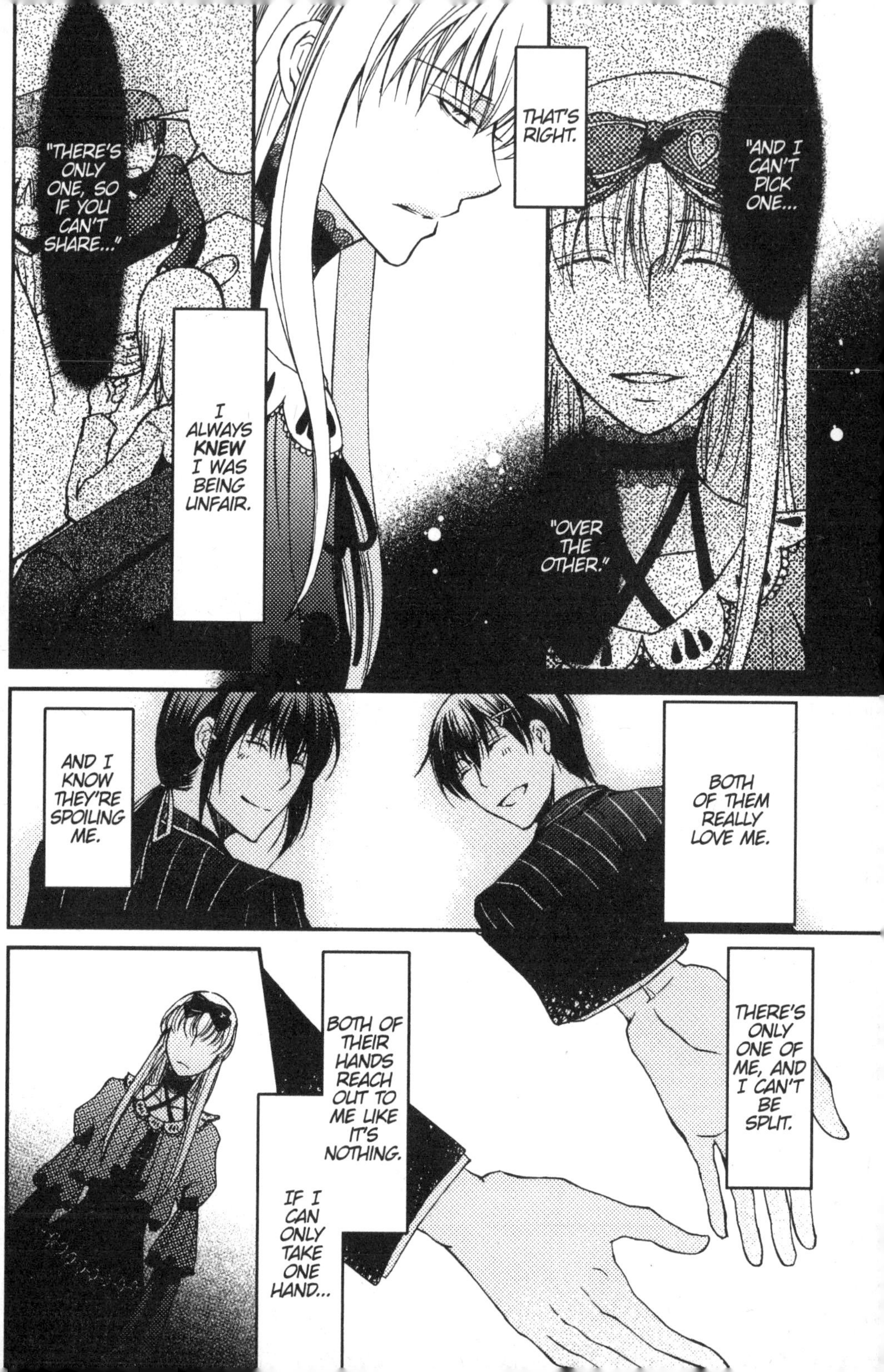
"AND I CAN'T PICK ONE...
"OVER THE OTHER."
THAT'S RIGHT.
"THERE'S ONLY ONE, SO IF YOU CAN'T SHARE..."
I ALWAYS **KNEW** I WAS BEING UNFAIR.
BOTH OF THEM REALLY LOVE ME.
AND I KNOW THEY'RE SPOILING ME.
THERE'S ONLY ONE OF ME, AND I CAN'T BE SPLIT.
BOTH OF THEIR HANDS REACH OUT TO ME LIKE IT'S NOTHING.
IF I CAN ONLY TAKE ONE HAND...

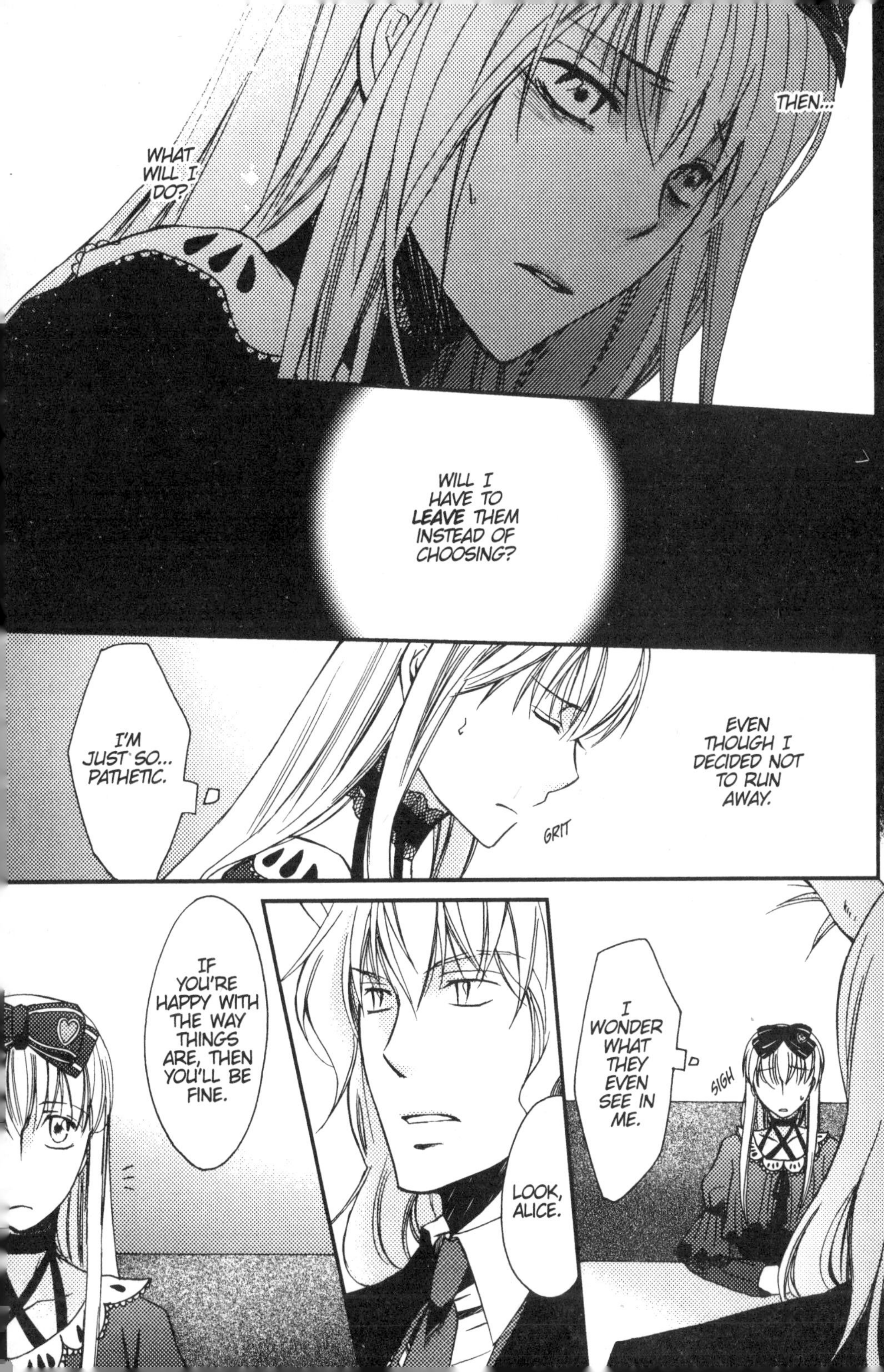
THEN...
WHAT WILL I DO?
WILL I HAVE TO **LEAVE** THEM INSTEAD OF CHOOSING?
EVEN THOUGH I DECIDED NOT TO RUN AWAY.
GRIT
I'M JUST SO... PATHETIC.
I WONDER WHAT THEY EVEN SEE IN ME.
SIGH
LOOK, ALICE.
IF YOU'RE HAPPY WITH THE WAY THINGS ARE, THEN YOU'LL BE FINE.

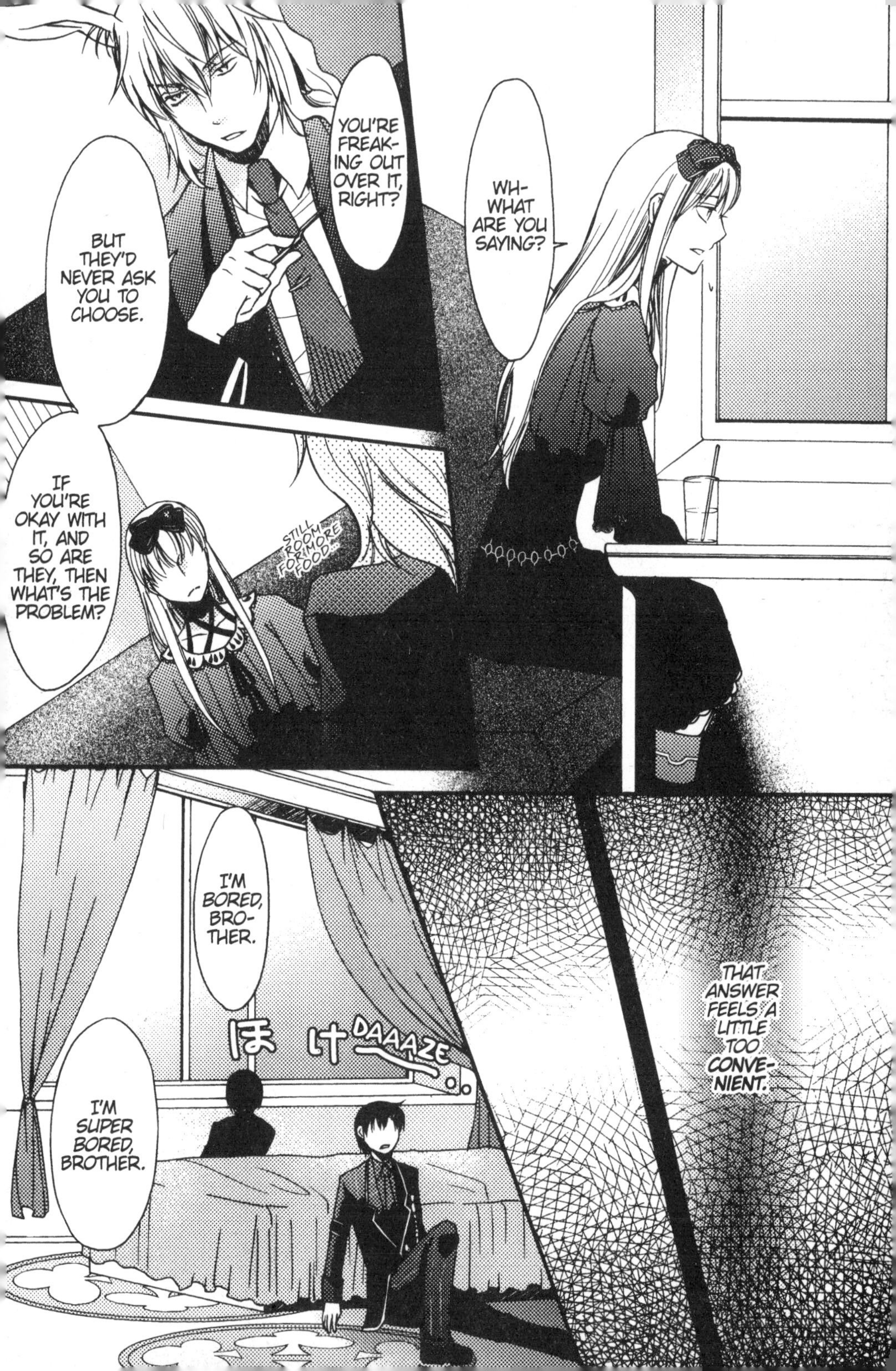
WH- WHAT ARE YOU SAYING?
YOU'RE FREAKING OUT OVER IT, RIGHT?
BUT THEY'D NEVER ASK YOU TO CHOOSE.
IF YOU'RE OKAY WITH IT, AND SO ARE THEY, THEN WHAT'S THE PROBLEM?
STILL ROOM FOR MORE FOOD...
THAT ANSWER FEELS A LITTLE TOO CONVENIENT.
I'M BORED, BROTHER.
ほ け DAAAZE
I'M SUPER BORED, BROTHER.

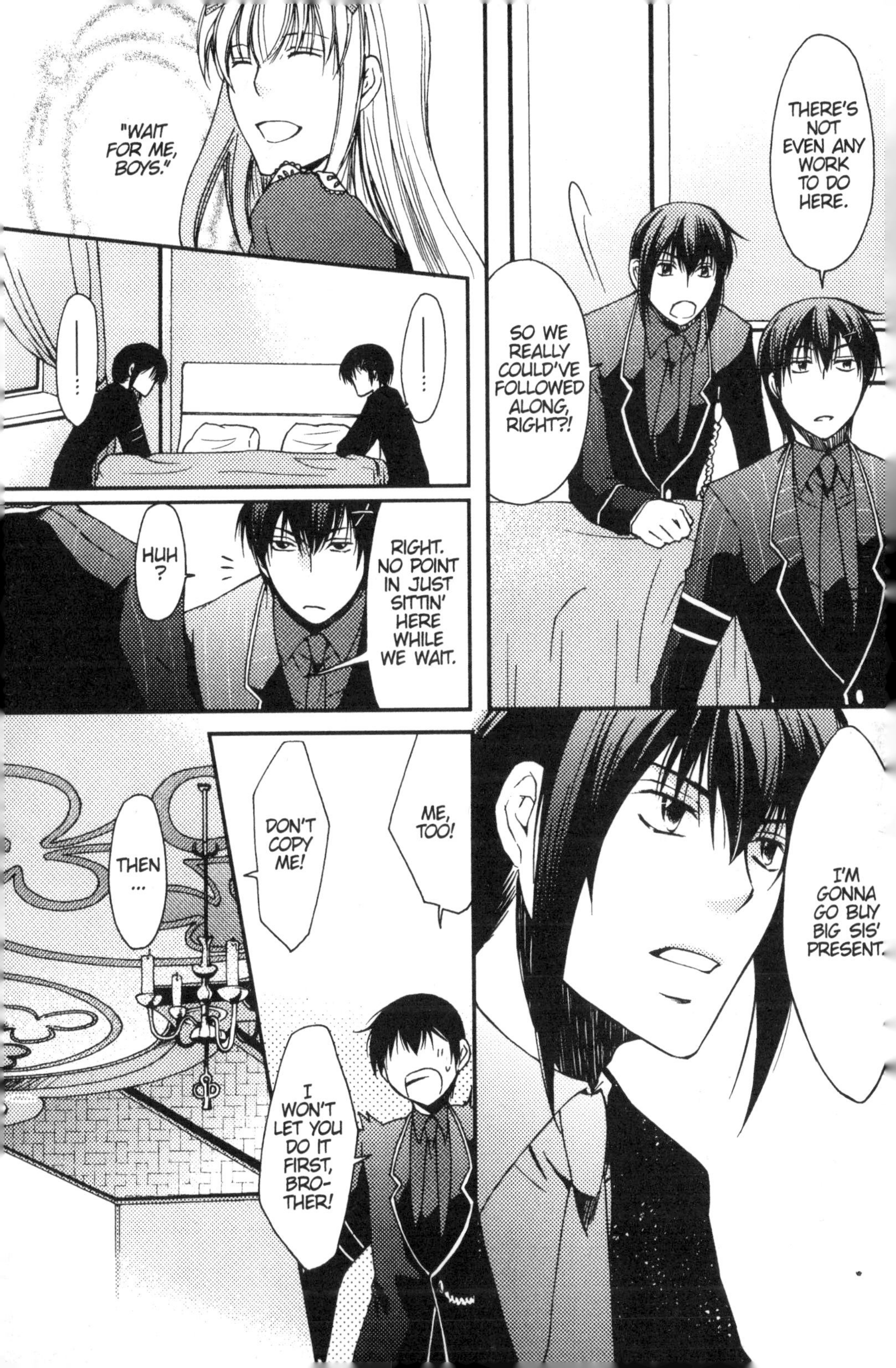
THERE'S NOT EVEN ANY WORK TO DO HERE.
SO WE REALLY COULD'VE FOLLOWED ALONG, RIGHT?!
"WAIT FOR ME, BOYS."
...!
...!
RIGHT. NO POINT IN JUST SITTIN' HERE WHILE WE WAIT.
HUH?
I'M GONNA GO BUY BIG SIS' PRESENT.
ME, TOO!
DON'T COPY ME!
THEN...
I WON'T LET YOU DO IT FIRST, BROTHER!

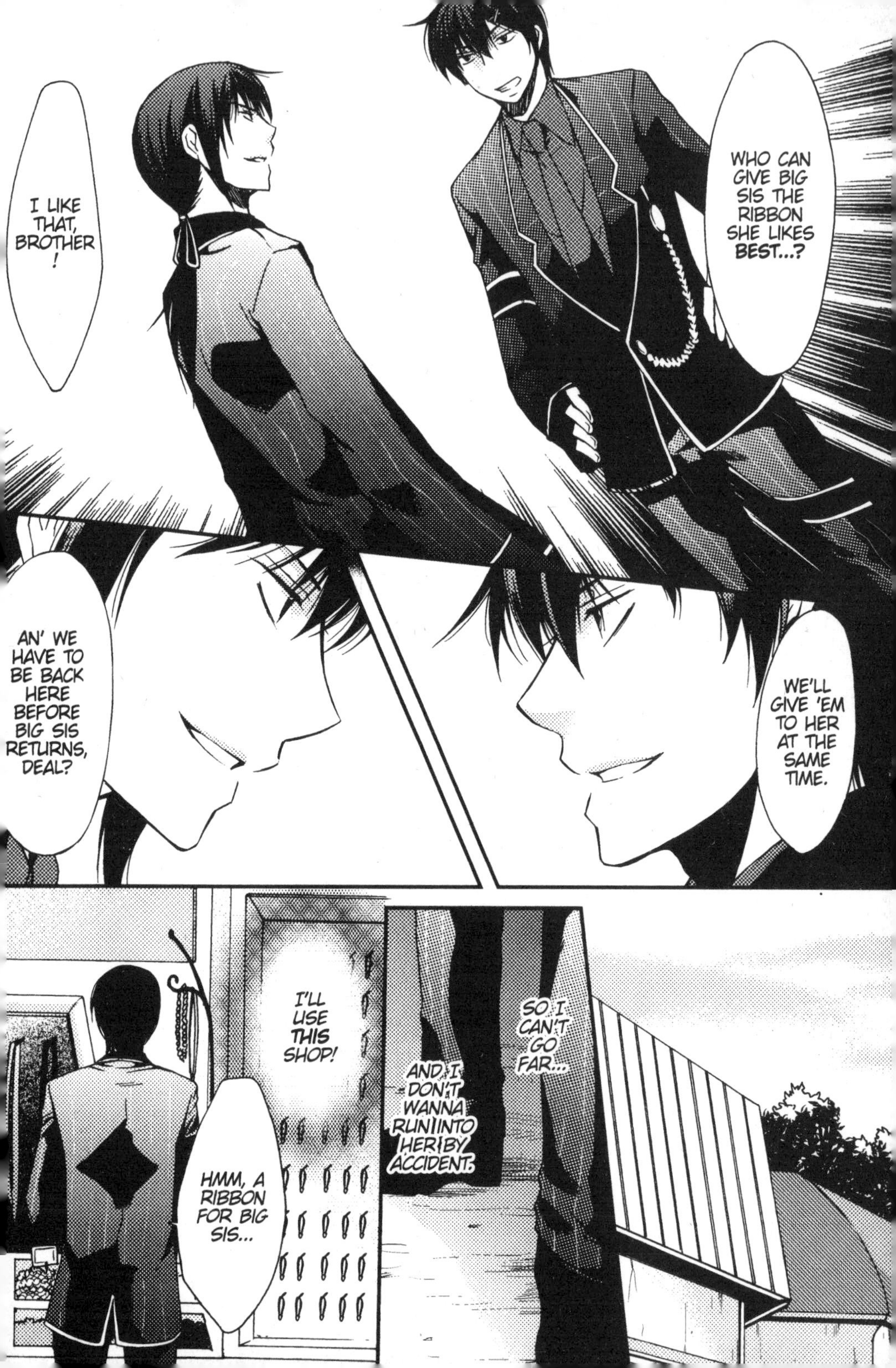
WHO CAN GIVE BIG SIS THE RIBBON SHE LIKES BEST...?
I LIKE THAT, BROTHER!
WE'LL GIVE 'EM TO HER AT THE SAME TIME.
AN' WE HAVE TO BE BACK HERE BEFORE BIG SIS RETURNS, DEAL?
SO I CAN'T GO FAR...
AND I DON'T WANNA RUN INTO HER BY ACCIDENT.
I'LL USE **THIS** SHOP!
HMM, A RIBBON FOR BIG SIS...

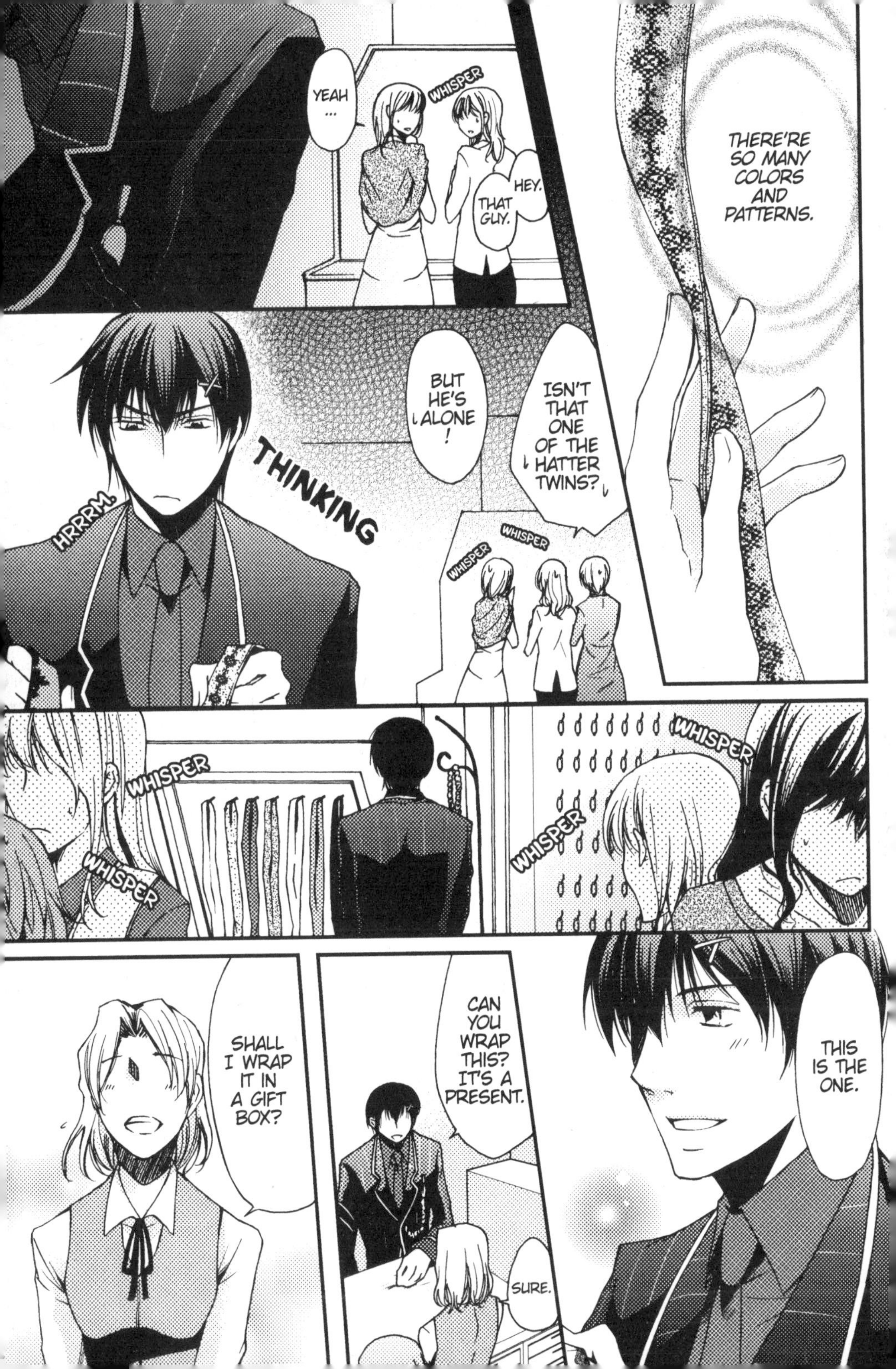
THERE'RE SO MANY COLORS AND PATTERNS.
HEY. THAT GUY.
WHISPER
YEAH ...
ISN'T THAT ONE OF THE HATTER TWINS?
BUT HE'S ALONE!
WHISPER
WHISPER
THINKING
HRRRM.
WHISPER
WHISPER
WHISPER
WHISPER
THIS IS THE ONE.
CAN YOU WRAP THIS? IT'S A PRESENT.
SURE.
SHALL I WRAP IT IN A GIFT BOX?

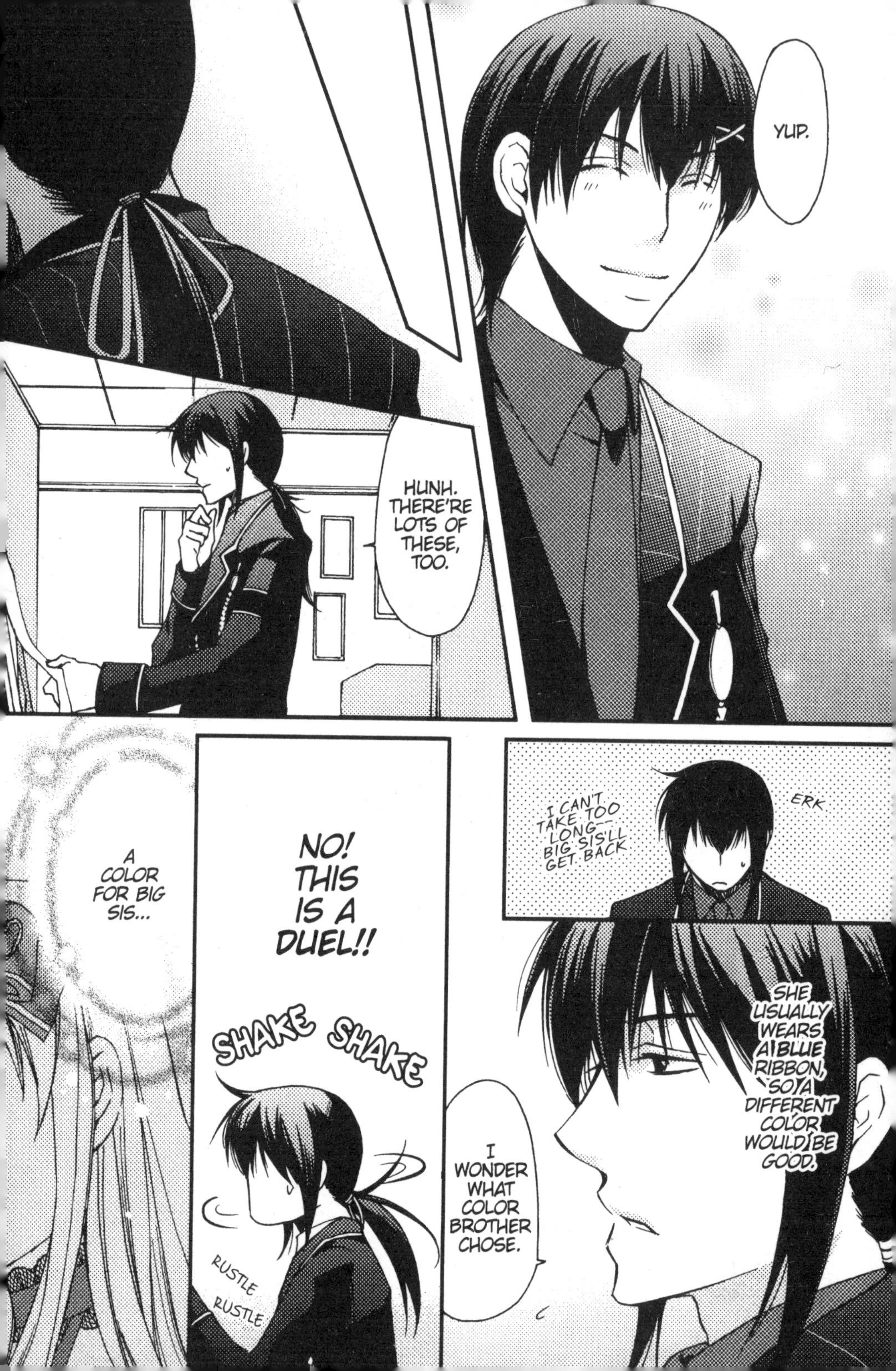
YUP.
HUNH. THERE'RE LOTS OF THESE, TOO.
ERK
I CAN'T TAKE TOO LONG-- BIG SIS'LL GET BACK
SHE USUALLY WEARS A BLUE RIBBON, SO A DIFFERENT COLOR WOULD BE GOOD.
I WONDER WHAT COLOR BROTHER CHOSE.
NO! THIS IS A DUEL!!
SHAKE SHAKE
RUSTLE
RUSTLE
A COLOR FOR BIG SIS...

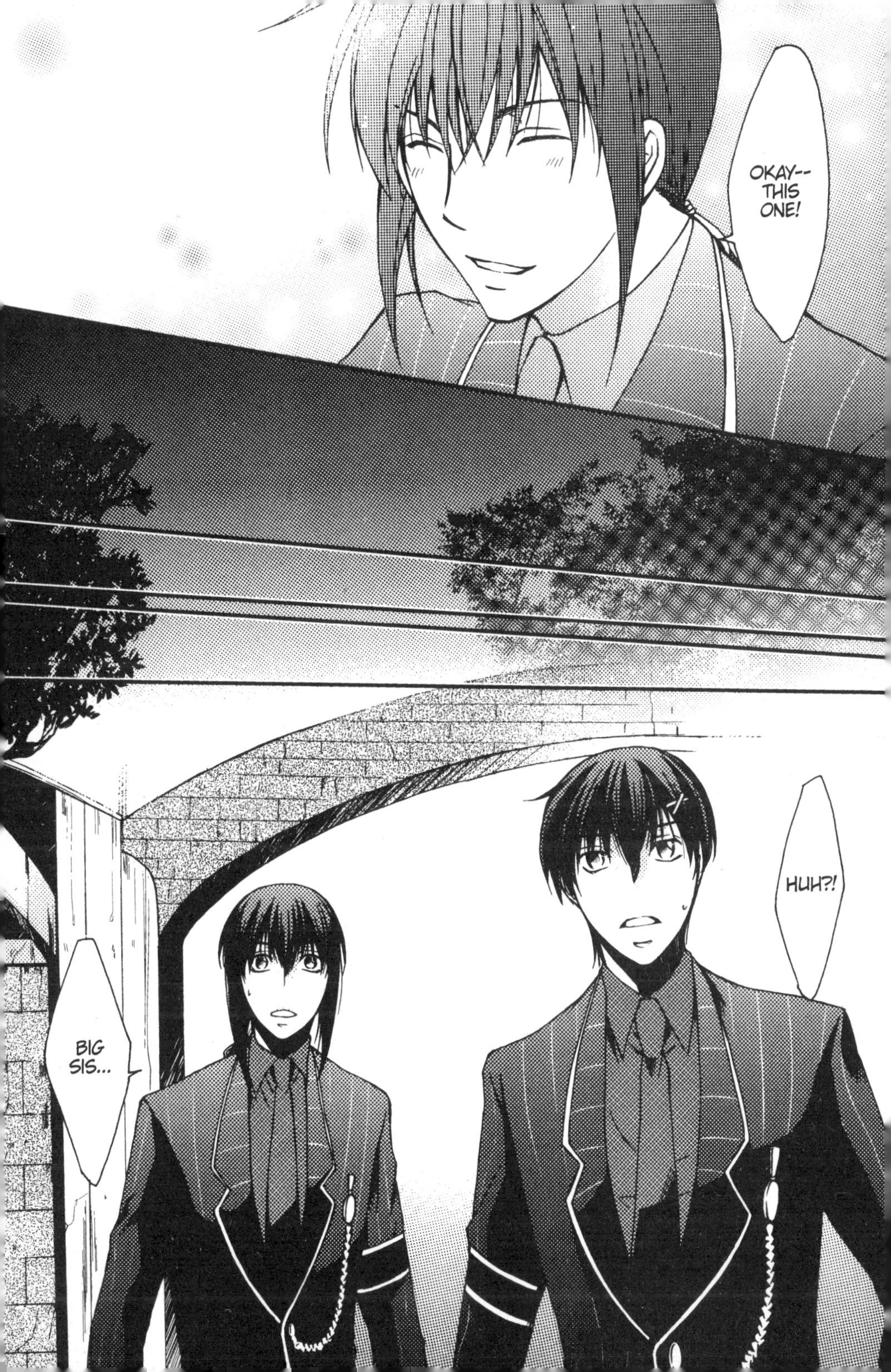
OKAY-- THIS ONE!
HUH?!
BIG SIS...

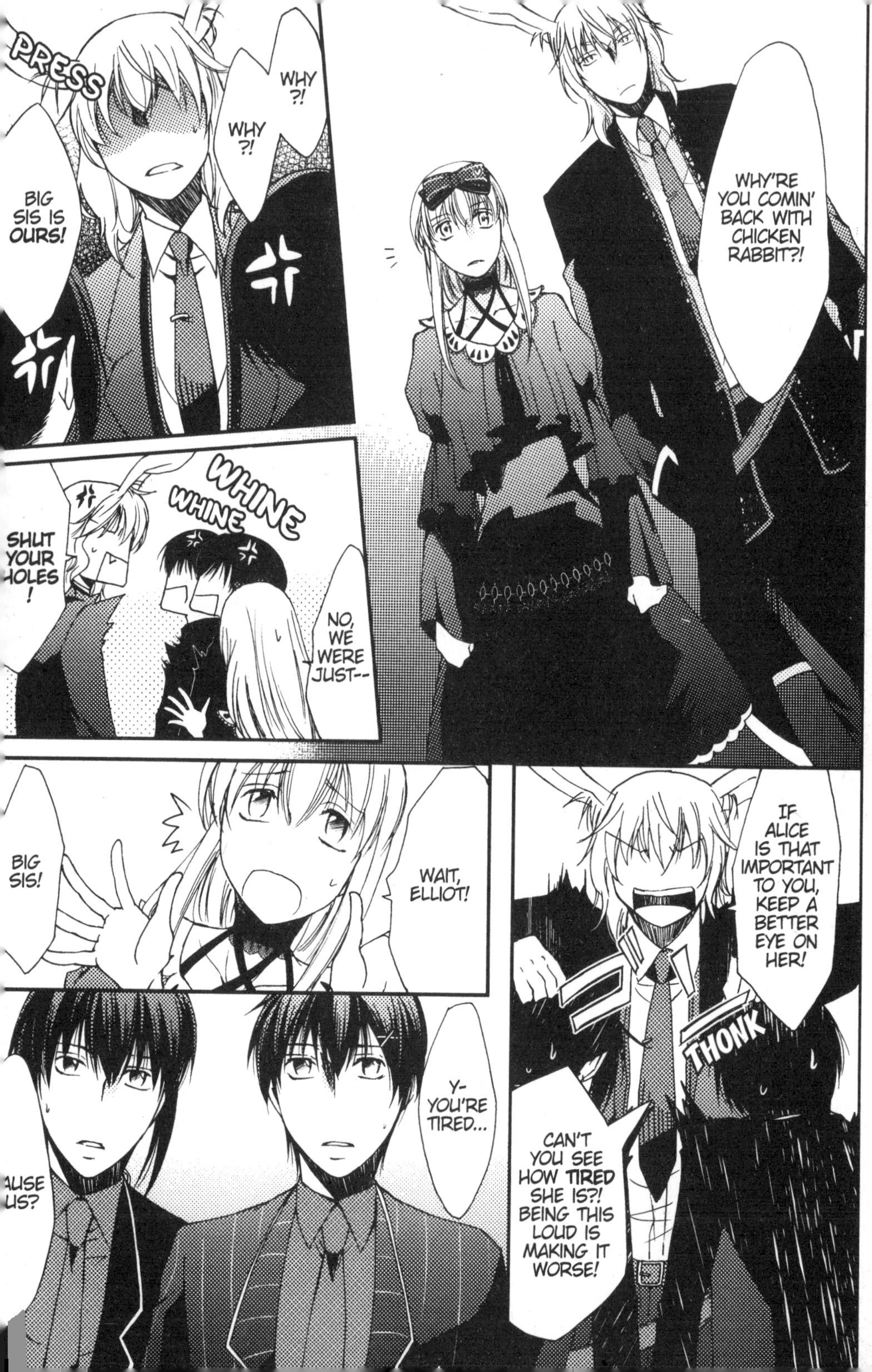
WHY'RE YOU COMIN' BACK WITH CHICKEN RABBIT?!
WHY?!
WHY?!
PRESS
BIG SIS IS OURS!
WHINE
WHINE
SHUT YOUR HOLES!
NO, WE WERE JUST--
IF ALICE IS THAT IMPORTANT TO YOU, KEEP A BETTER EYE ON HER!
THONK
CAN'T YOU SEE HOW TIRED SHE IS?! BEING THIS LOUD IS MAKING IT WORSE!
WAIT, ELLIOT!
BIG SIS!
Y-YOU'RE TIRED...
AUSE US?

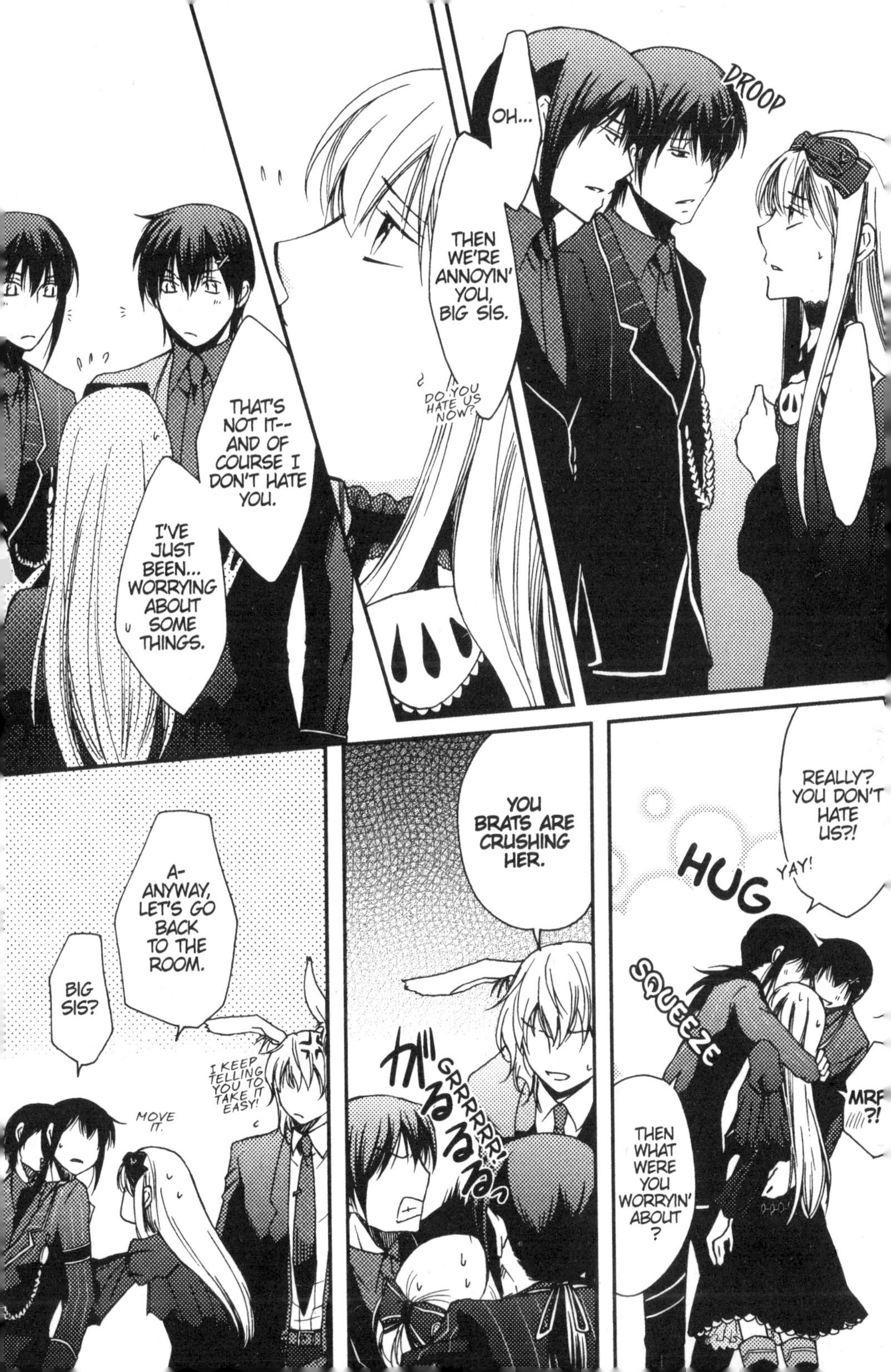
OH...
THEN WE'RE ANNOYIN' YOU, BIG SIS.
DROOP
DO YOU HATE US NOW?
THAT'S NOT IT-- AND OF COURSE I DON'T HATE YOU.
I'VE JUST BEEN... WORRYING ABOUT SOME THINGS.
REALLY? YOU DON'T HATE US?!
YAY!
HUG
SQUEEZE
MRF?!
THEN WHAT WERE YOU WORRYIN' ABOUT?
YOU BRATS ARE CRUSHING HER.
がるるる
GRRRRRR!
A-ANYWAY, LET'S GO BACK TO THE ROOM.
BIG SIS?
I KEEP TELLING YOU TO TAKE IT EASY!
MOVE IT.

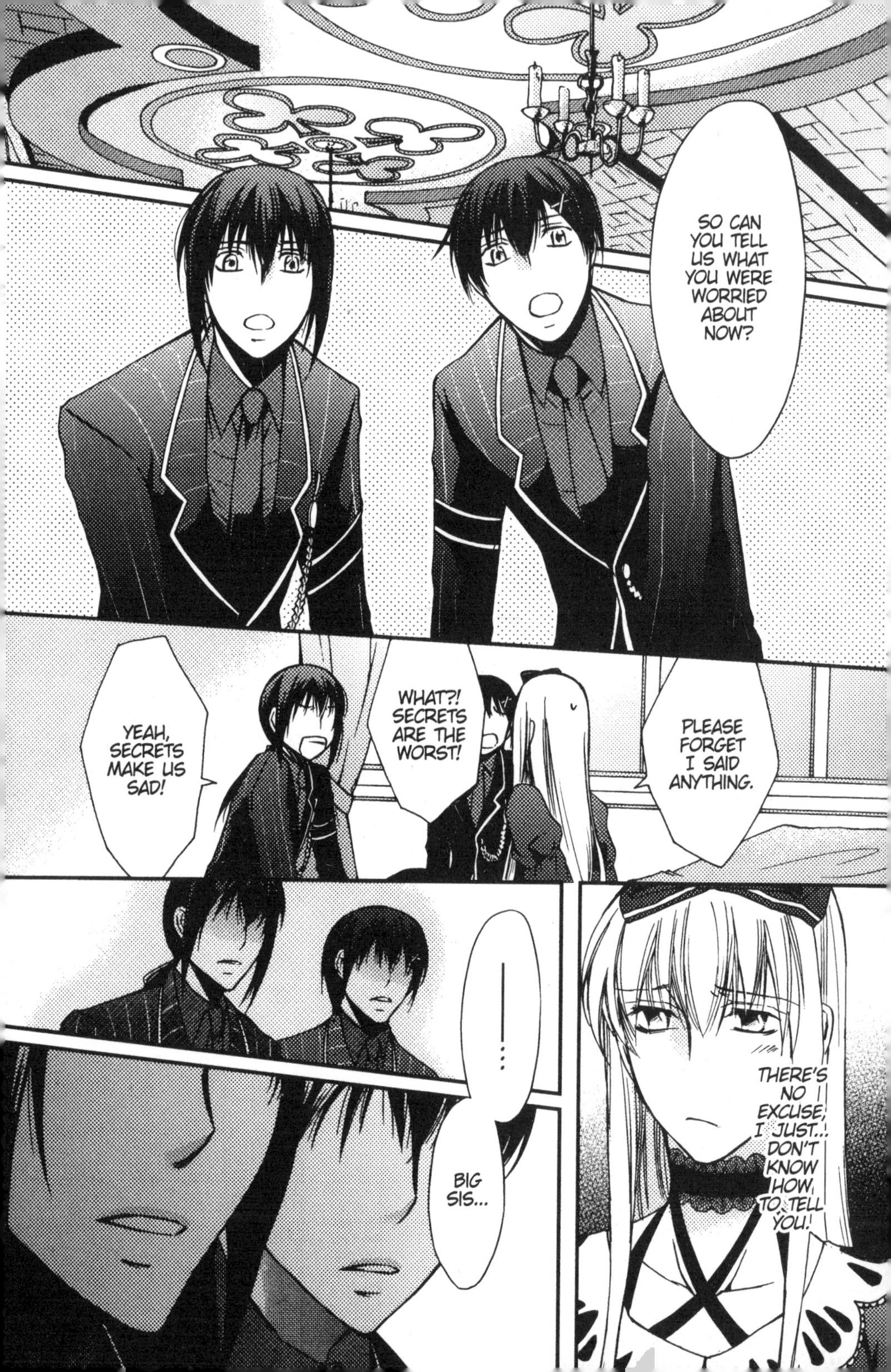
SO CAN YOU TELL US WHAT YOU WERE WORRIED ABOUT NOW?
PLEASE FORGET I SAID ANYTHING.
WHAT?! SECRETS ARE THE WORST!
YEAH, SECRETS MAKE US SAD!
THERE'S NO EXCUSE, I JUST... DON'T KNOW HOW TO TELL YOU.
......
BIG SIS...

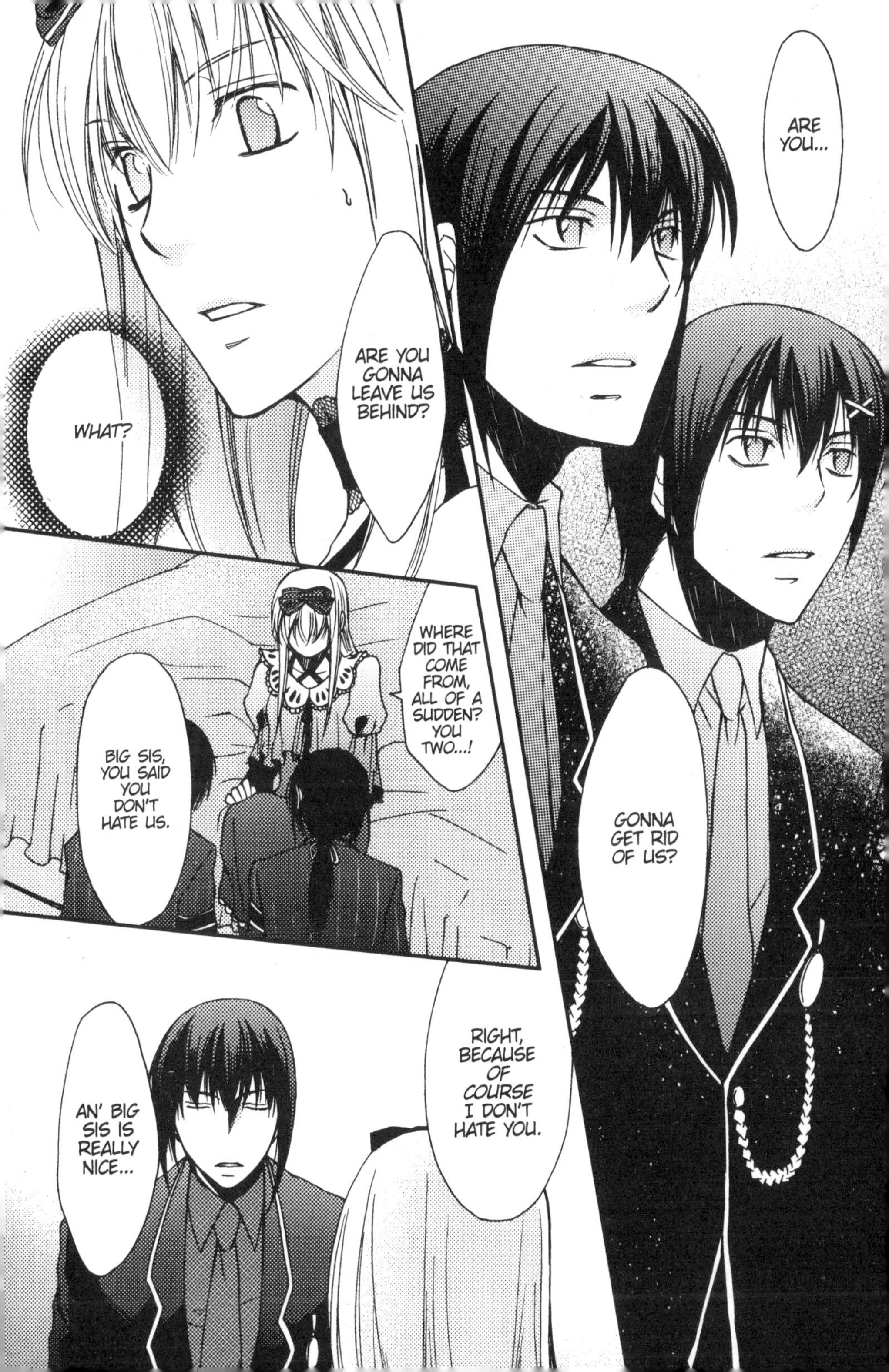
ARE YOU...
GONNA GET RID OF US?
ARE YOU GONNA LEAVE US BEHIND?
WHAT?
WHERE DID THAT COME FROM, ALL OF A SUDDEN? YOU TWO...!
BIG SIS, YOU SAID YOU DON'T HATE US.
RIGHT, BECAUSE OF COURSE I DON'T HATE YOU.
AN' BIG SIS IS REALLY NICE...

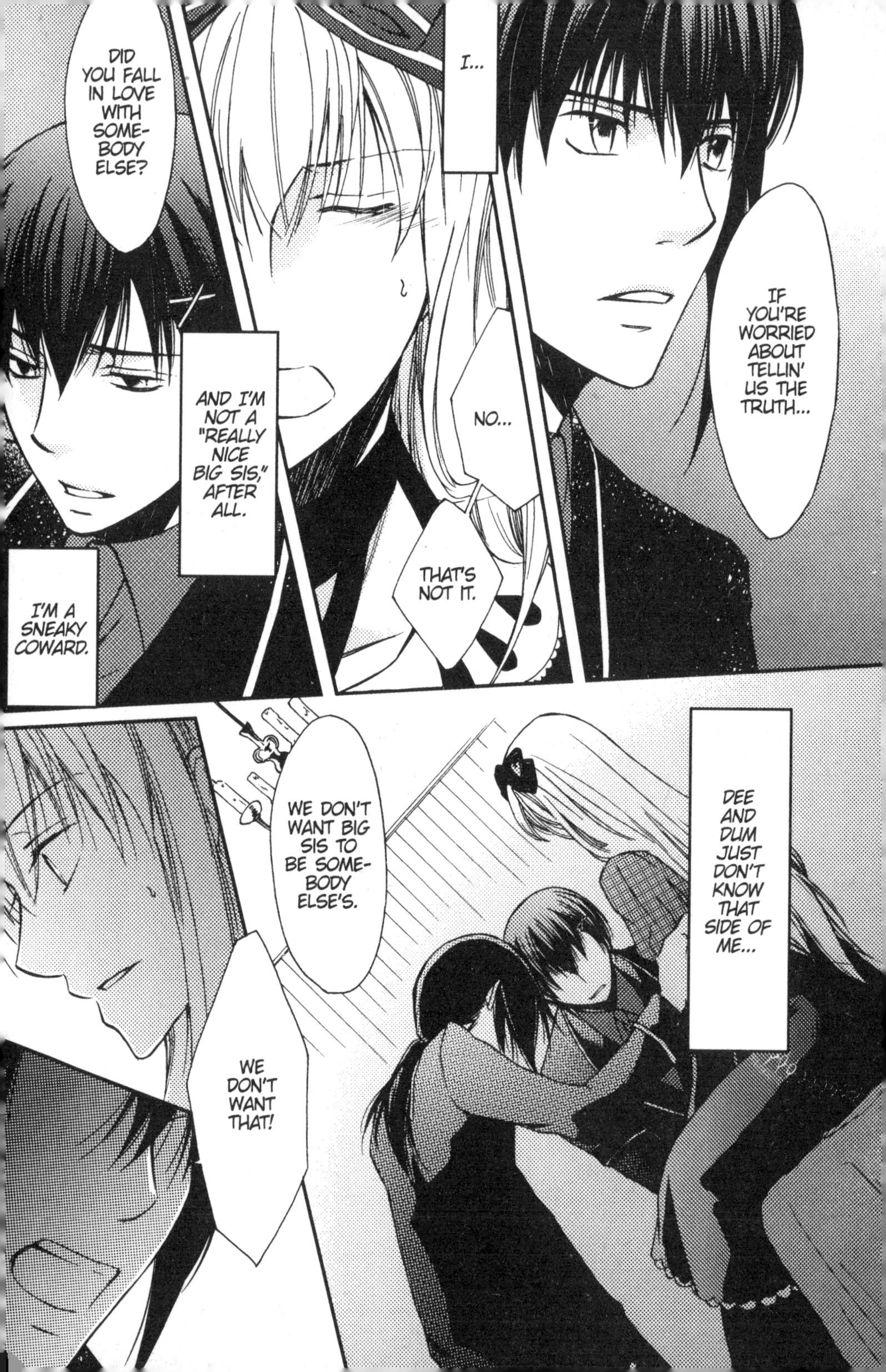
I...
IF YOU'RE WORRIED ABOUT TELLIN' US THE TRUTH...
NO...
THAT'S NOT IT.
DID YOU FALL IN LOVE WITH SOME-BODY ELSE?
AND I'M NOT A "REALLY NICE BIG SIS," AFTER ALL.
I'M A SNEAKY COWARD.
DEE AND DUM JUST DON'T KNOW THAT SIDE OF ME...
WE DON'T WANT BIG SIS TO BE SOME-BODY ELSE'S.
WE DON'T WANT THAT!

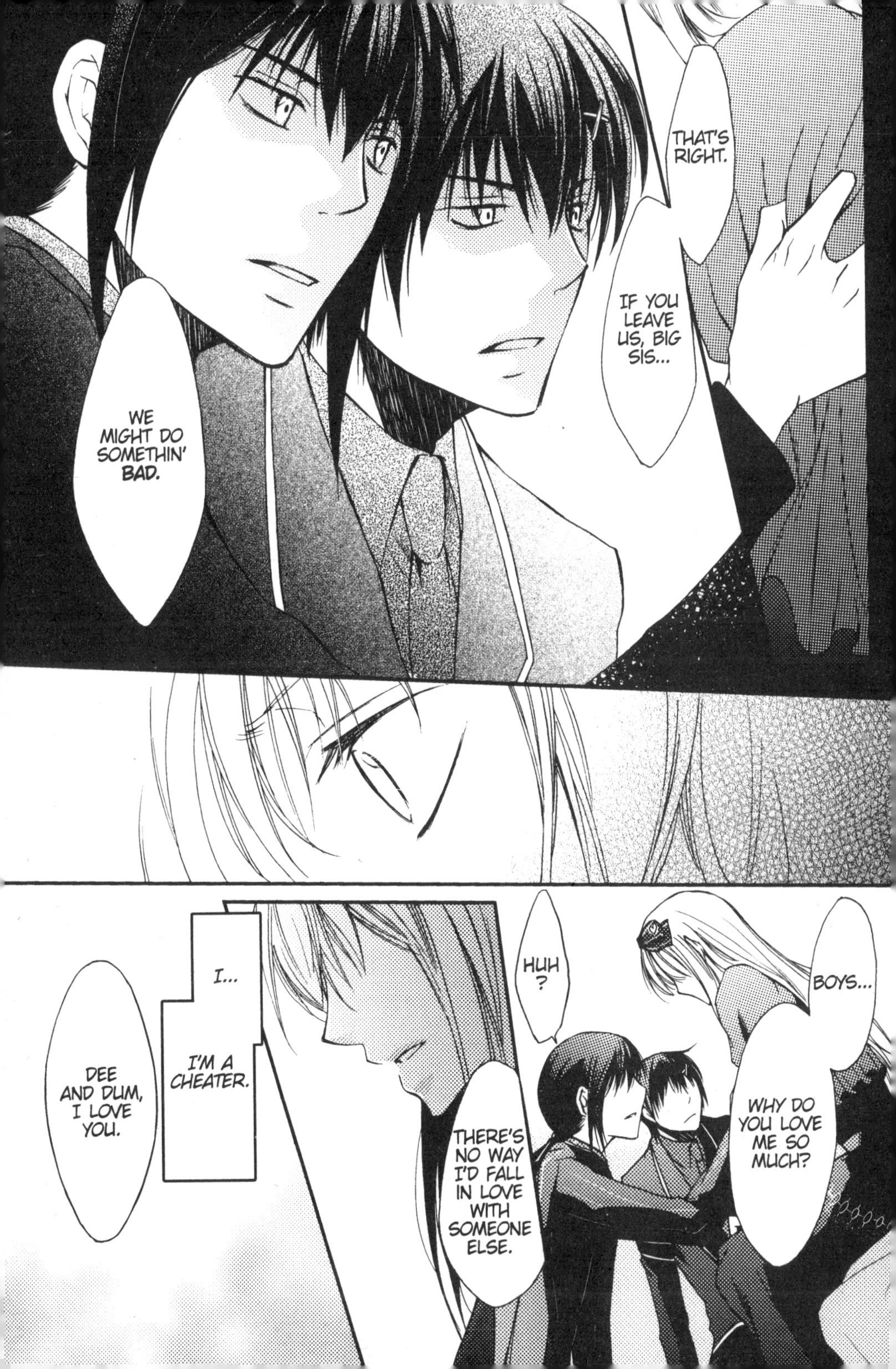
THAT'S RIGHT.
IF YOU LEAVE US, BIG SIS...
WE MIGHT DO SOMETHIN' BAD.
BOYS...
WHY DO YOU LOVE ME SO MUCH?
HUH?
THERE'S NO WAY I'D FALL IN LOVE WITH SOMEONE ELSE.
I...
I'M A CHEATER.
DEE AND DUM, I LOVE YOU.

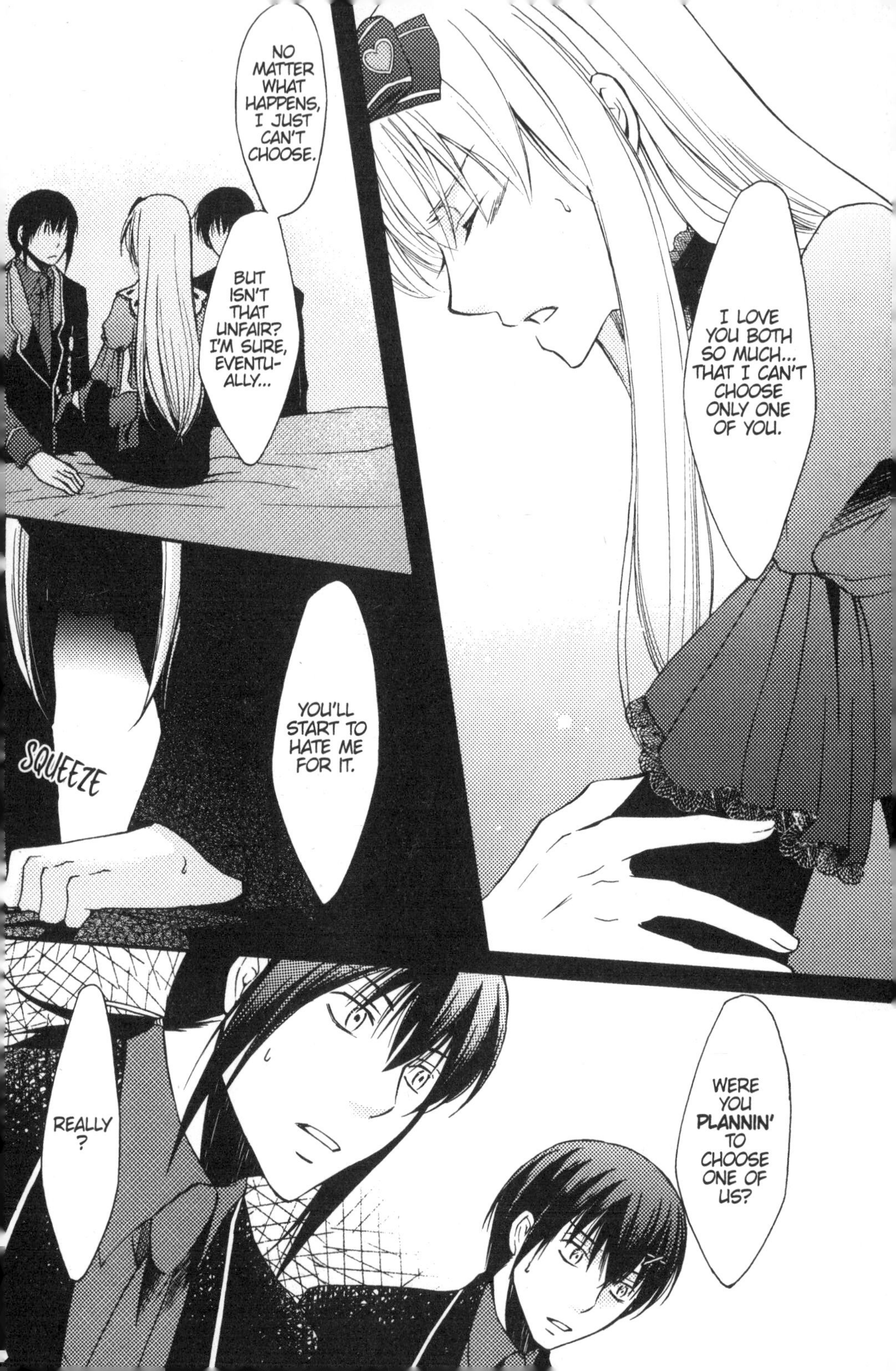
I LOVE YOU BOTH SO MUCH... THAT I CAN'T CHOOSE ONLY ONE OF YOU.
NO MATTER WHAT HAPPENS, I JUST CAN'T CHOOSE.
BUT ISN'T THAT UNFAIR? I'M SURE, EVENTU-ALLY...
YOU'LL START TO HATE ME FOR IT.
SQUEEZE
WERE YOU **PLANNIN'** TO CHOOSE ONE OF US?
REALLY?

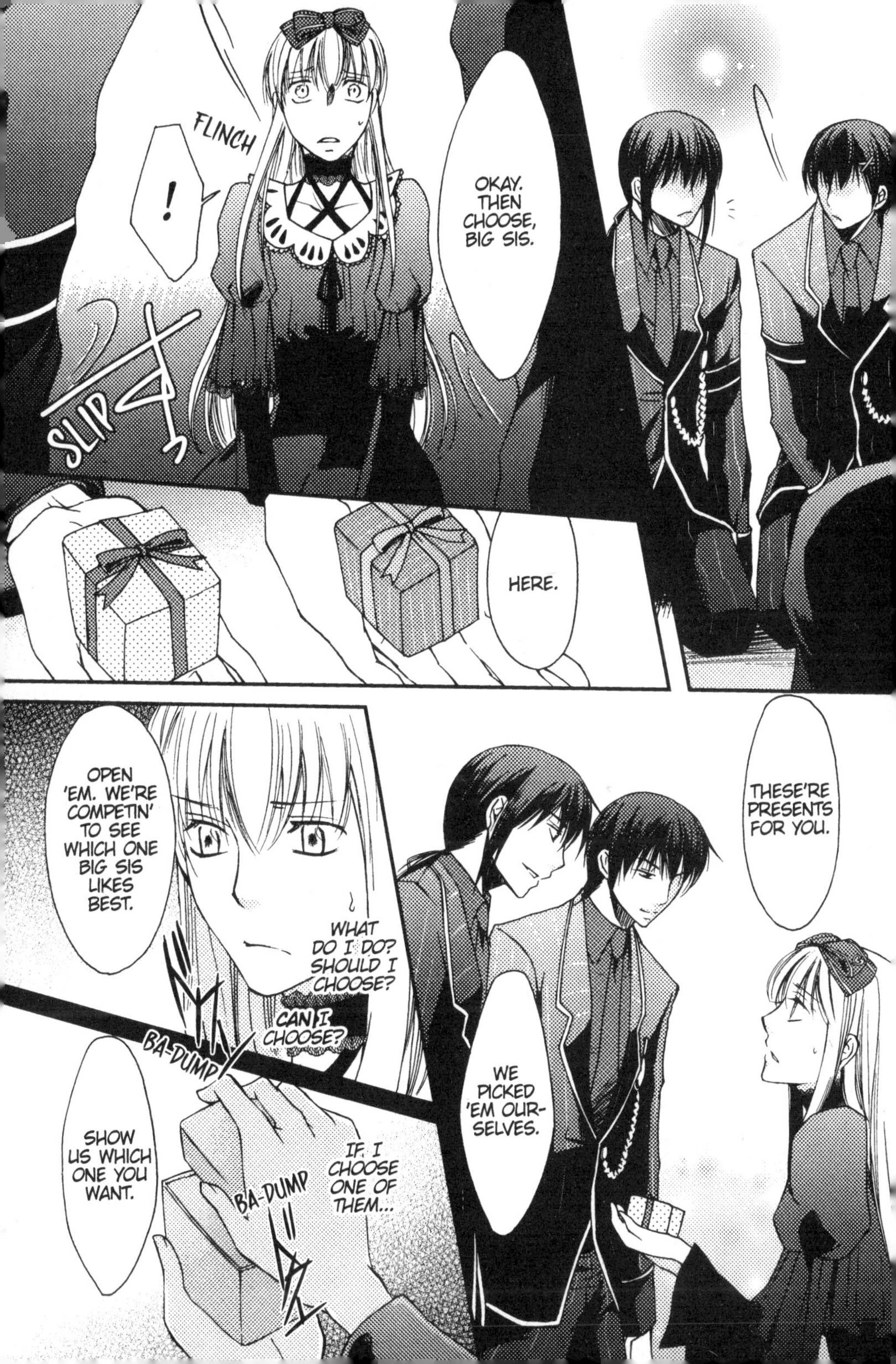
OKAY. THEN CHOOSE, BIG SIS.
FLINCH
!
SLIP
HERE.
THESE'RE PRESENTS FOR YOU.
WE PICKED 'EM OUR-SELVES.
OPEN 'EM. WE'RE COMPETIN' TO SEE WHICH ONE BIG SIS LIKES BEST.
WHAT DO I DO? SHOULD I CHOOSE?
CAN I CHOOSE?
BA-DUMP
SHOW US WHICH ONE YOU WANT.
IF I CHOOSE ONE OF THEM...
BA-DUMP

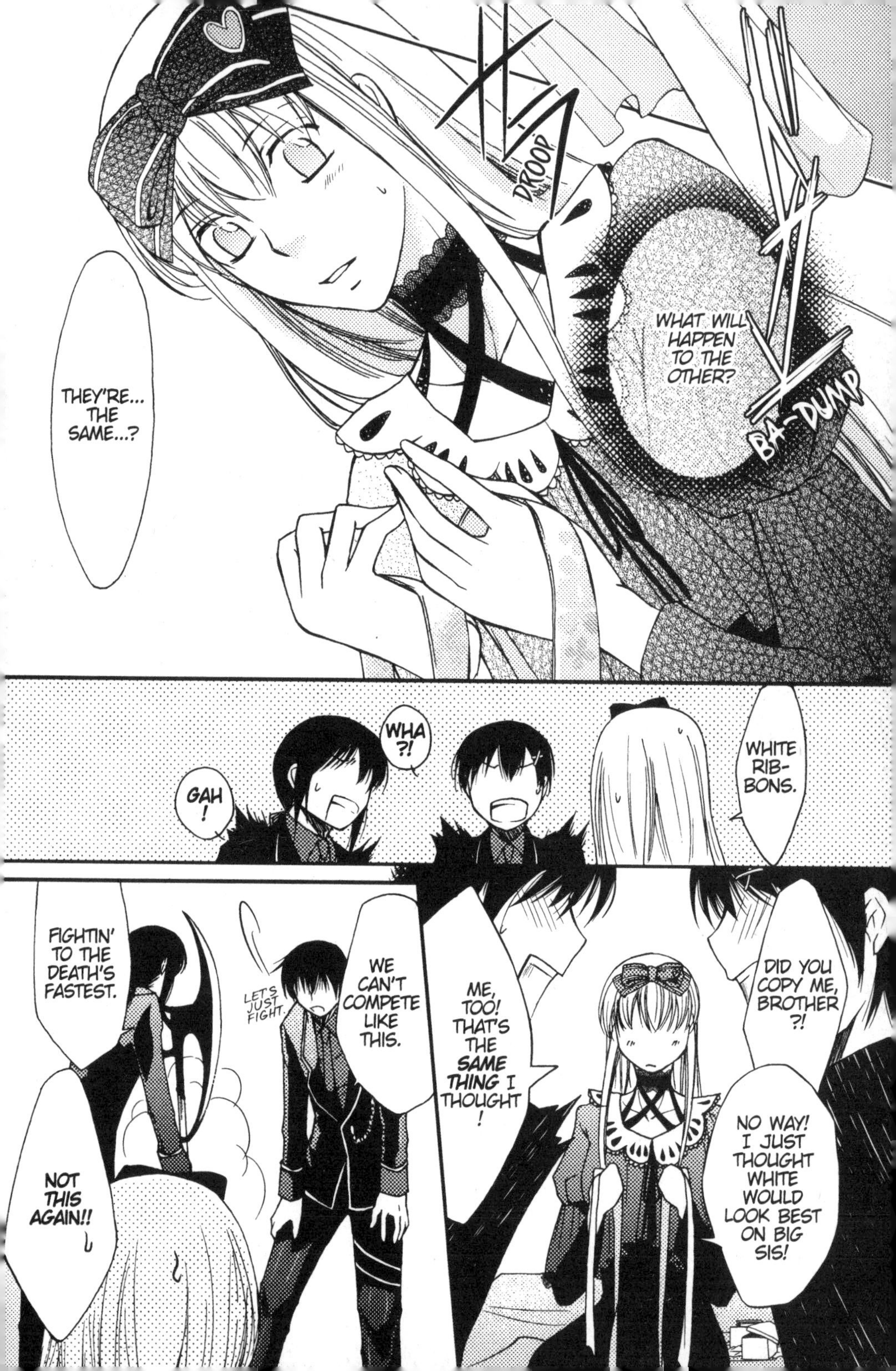
DROOP
WHAT WILL HAPPEN TO THE OTHER?
BA-DUMP
THEY'RE... THE SAME...?
WHITE RIBBONS.
WHA?!
GAH!
DID YOU COPY ME, BROTHER?!
NO WAY! I JUST THOUGHT WHITE WOULD LOOK BEST ON BIG SIS!
ME, TOO! THAT'S THE SAME THING I THOUGHT!
WE CAN'T COMPETE LIKE THIS.
LET'S JUST FIGHT.
FIGHTIN' TO THE DEATH'S FASTEST.
NOT THIS AGAIN!!

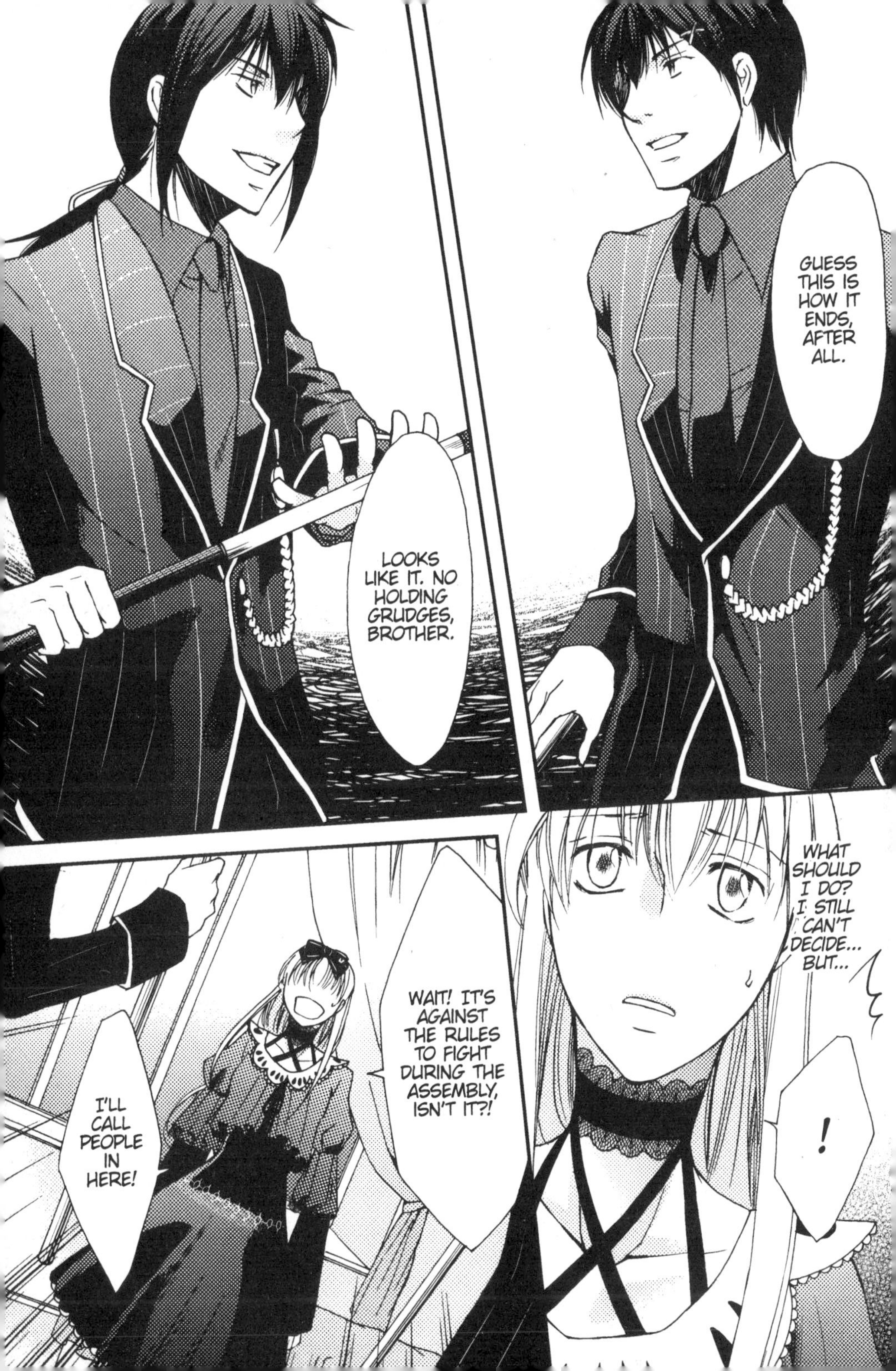
GUESS THIS IS HOW IT ENDS, AFTER ALL.
LOOKS LIKE IT. NO HOLDING GRUDGES, BROTHER.
WHAT SHOULD I DO? I STILL CAN'T DECIDE... BUT...
!
WAIT! IT'S AGAINST THE RULES TO FIGHT DURING THE ASSEMBLY, ISN'T IT?!
I'LL CALL PEOPLE IN HERE!

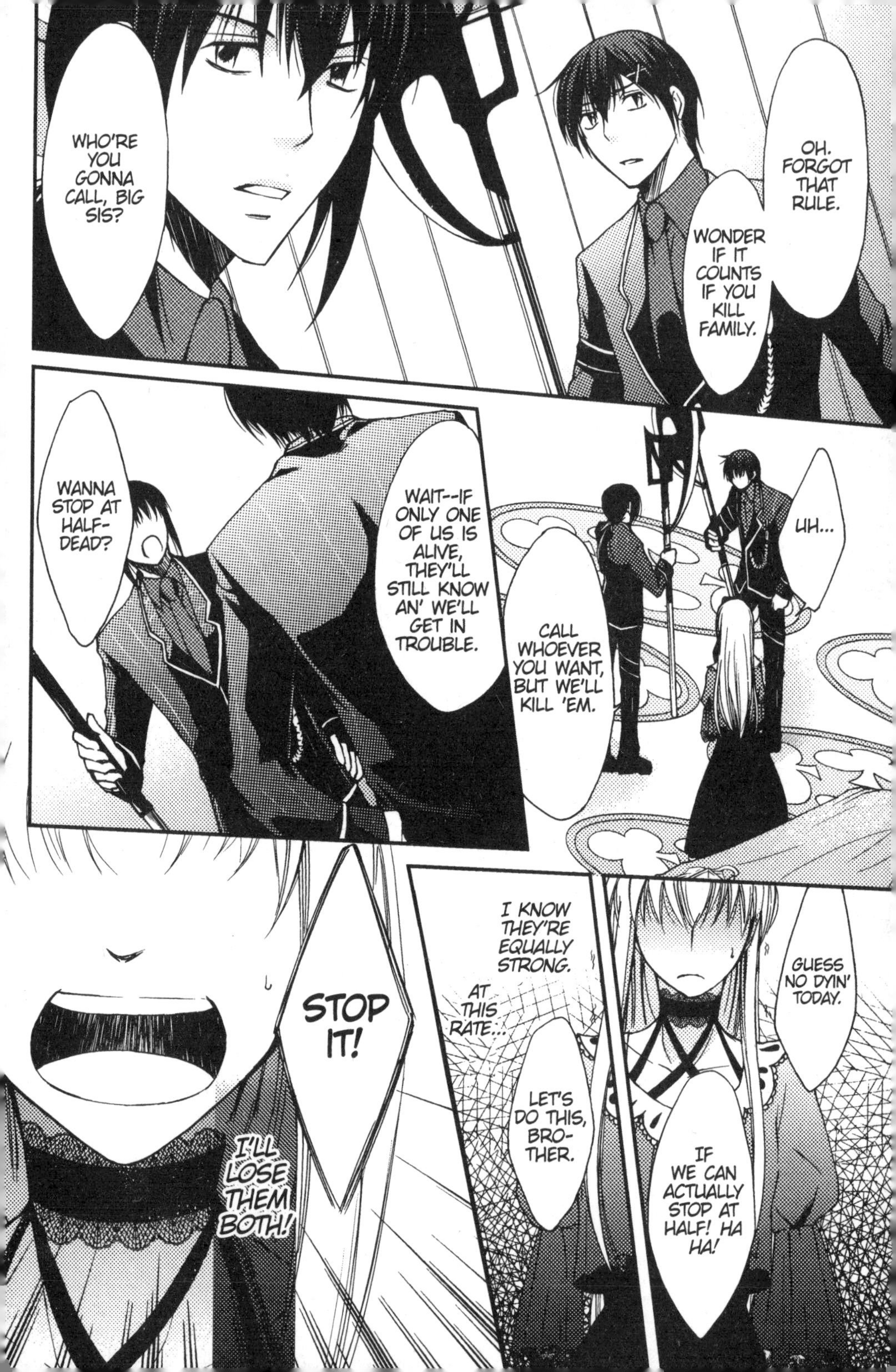
OH. FORGOT THAT RULE.
WONDER IF IT COUNTS IF YOU KILL FAMILY.
WHO'RE YOU GONNA CALL, BIG SIS?
UH...
CALL WHOEVER YOU WANT, BUT WE'LL KILL 'EM.
WAIT--IF ONLY ONE OF US IS ALIVE, THEY'LL STILL KNOW AN' WE'LL GET IN TROUBLE.
WANNA STOP AT HALF-DEAD?
GUESS NO DYIN' TODAY.
IF WE CAN ACTUALLY STOP AT HALF! HA HA!
I KNOW THEY'RE EQUALLY STRONG.
AT THIS RATE...
LET'S DO THIS, BRO-THER.
STOP IT!
I'LL LOSE THEM BOTH!

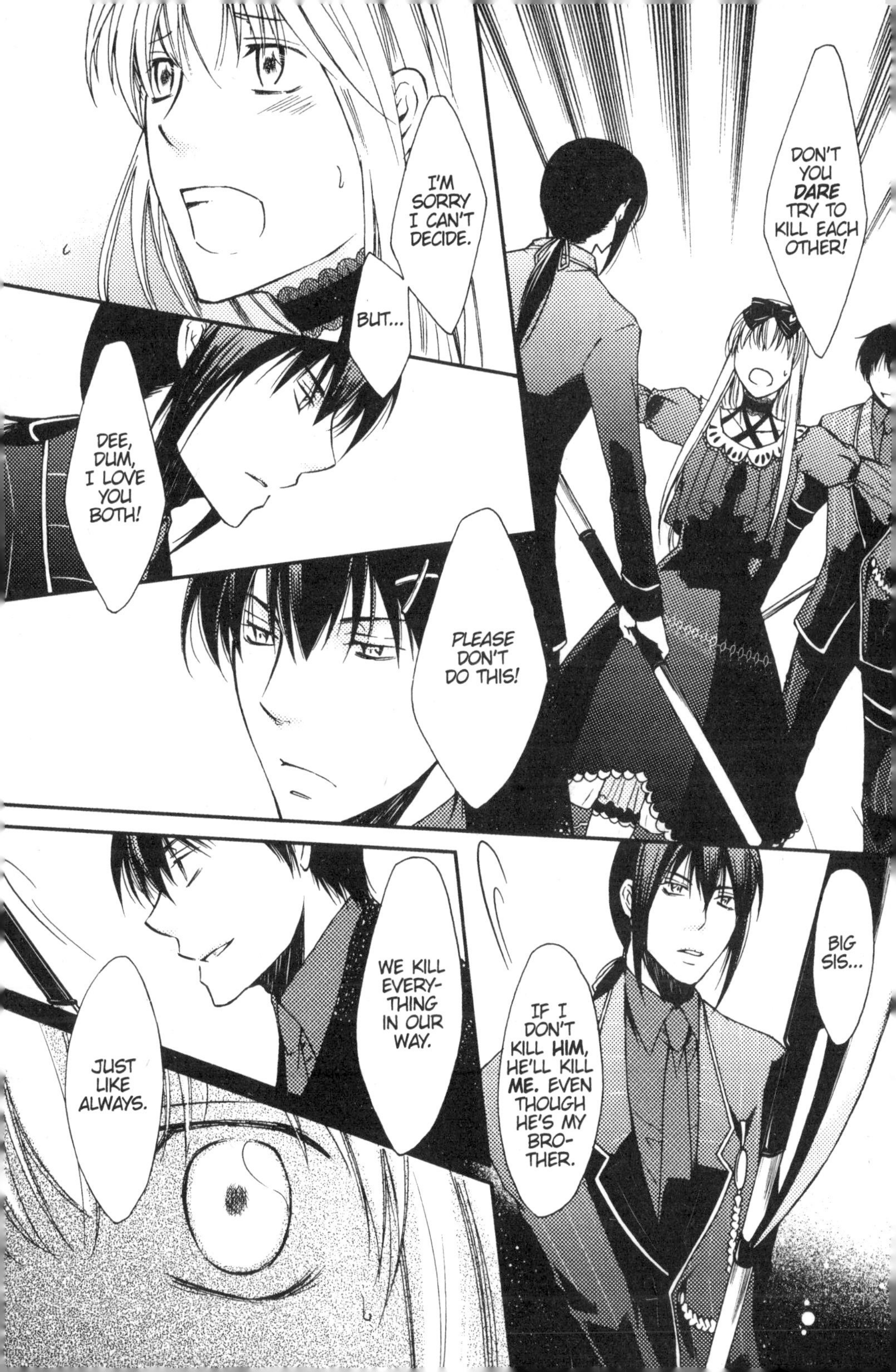
DON'T YOU DARE TRY TO KILL EACH OTHER!
I'M SORRY I CAN'T DECIDE.
BUT...
DEE, DUM, I LOVE YOU BOTH!
PLEASE DON'T DO THIS!
BIG SIS...
IF I DON'T KILL HIM, HE'LL KILL ME. EVEN THOUGH HE'S MY BRO-THER.
WE KILL EVERY-THING IN OUR WAY.
JUST LIKE ALWAYS.

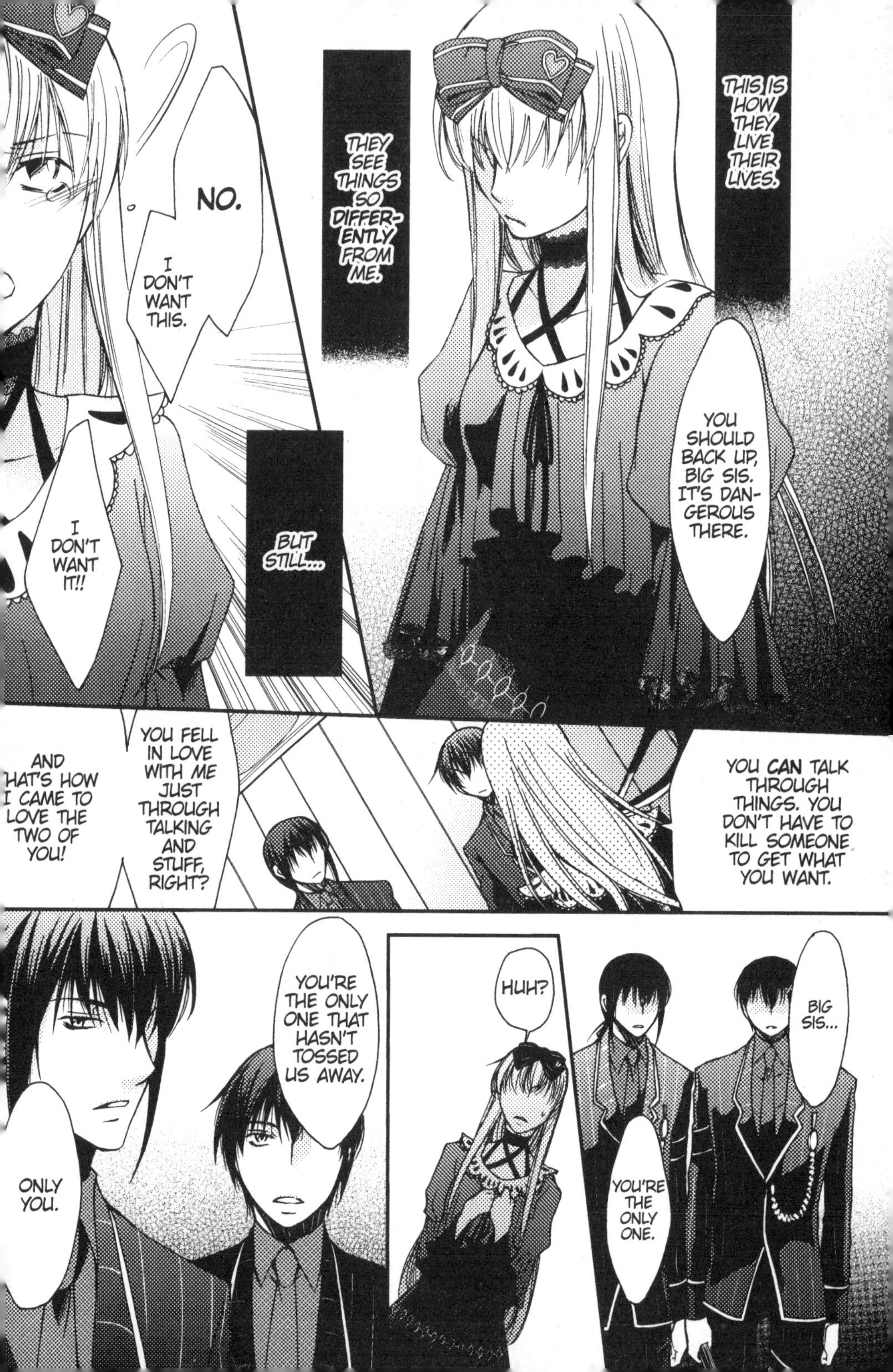
THIS IS HOW THEY LIVE THEIR LIVES.
THEY SEE THINGS SO DIFFERENTLY FROM ME.
YOU SHOULD BACK UP, BIG SIS. IT'S DANGEROUS THERE.
BUT STILL...
NO.
I DON'T WANT THIS.
I DON'T WANT IT!!
YOU CAN TALK THROUGH THINGS. YOU DON'T HAVE TO KILL SOMEONE TO GET WHAT YOU WANT.
YOU FELL IN LOVE WITH ME JUST THROUGH TALKING AND STUFF, RIGHT?
AND HAT'S HOW I CAME TO LOVE THE TWO OF YOU!
BIG SIS...
YOU'RE THE ONLY ONE.
HUH?
YOU'RE THE ONLY ONE THAT HASN'T TOSSED US AWAY.
ONLY YOU.

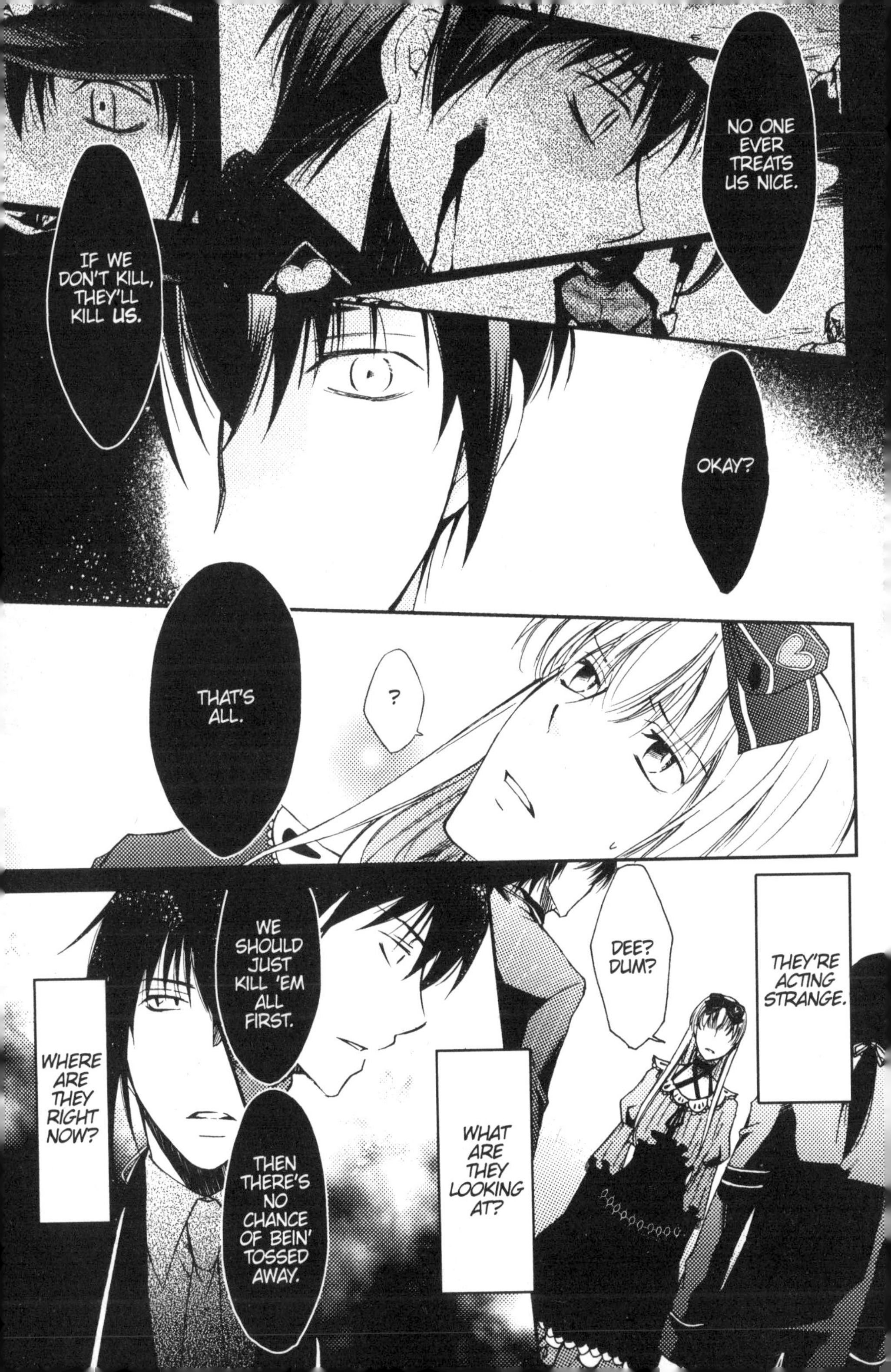
NO ONE EVER TREATS US NICE.
IF WE DON'T KILL, THEY'LL KILL US.
OKAY?
THAT'S ALL.
?
THEY'RE ACTING STRANGE.
DEE? DUM?
WHAT ARE THEY LOOKING AT?
WE SHOULD JUST KILL 'EM ALL FIRST.
THEN THERE'S NO CHANCE OF BEIN' TOSSED AWAY.
WHERE ARE THEY RIGHT NOW?

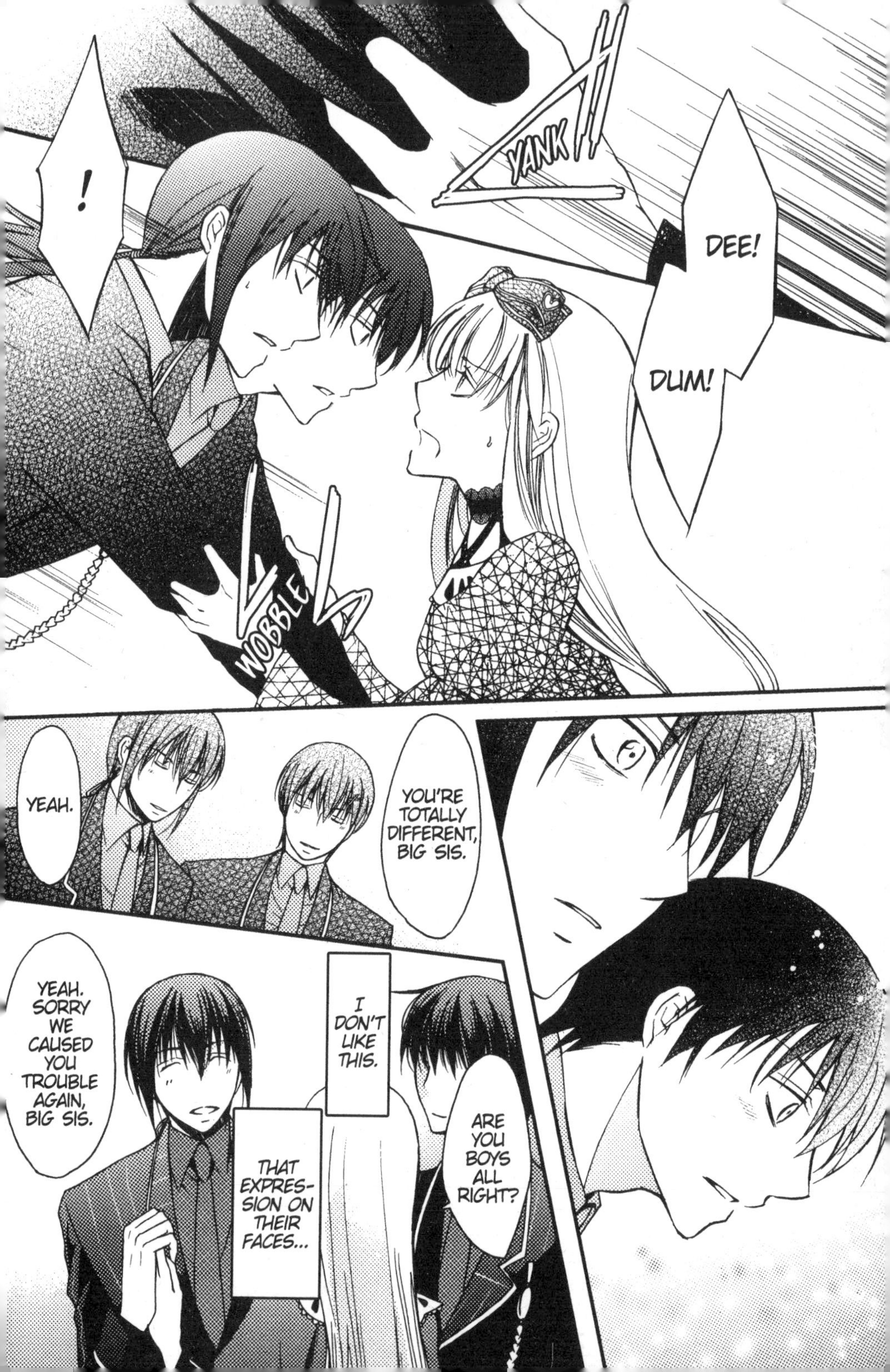
YANK
DEE!
DUM!
!
WOBBLE
ARE YOU BOYS ALL RIGHT?
YOU'RE TOTALLY DIFFERENT, BIG SIS.
YEAH.
I DON'T LIKE THIS.
THAT EXPRESSION ON THEIR FACES...
YEAH. SORRY WE CAUSED YOU TROUBLE AGAIN, BIG SIS.

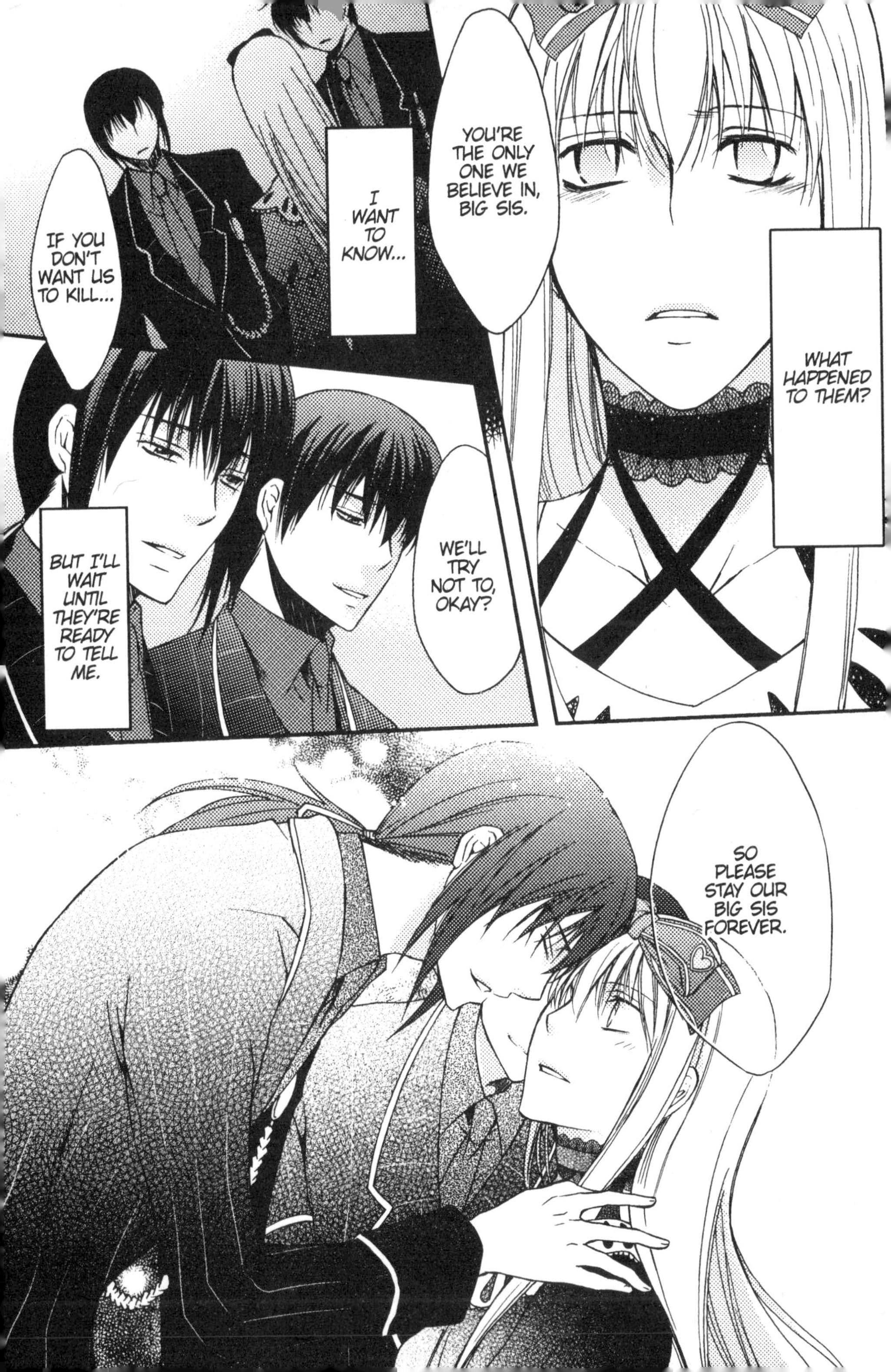
YOU'RE THE ONLY ONE WE BELIEVE IN, BIG SIS.
I WANT TO KNOW...
IF YOU DON'T WANT US TO KILL...
WHAT HAPPENED TO THEM?
WE'LL TRY NOT TO, OKAY?
BUT I'LL WAIT UNTIL THEY'RE READY TO TELL ME.
SO PLEASE STAY OUR BIG SIS FOREVER.

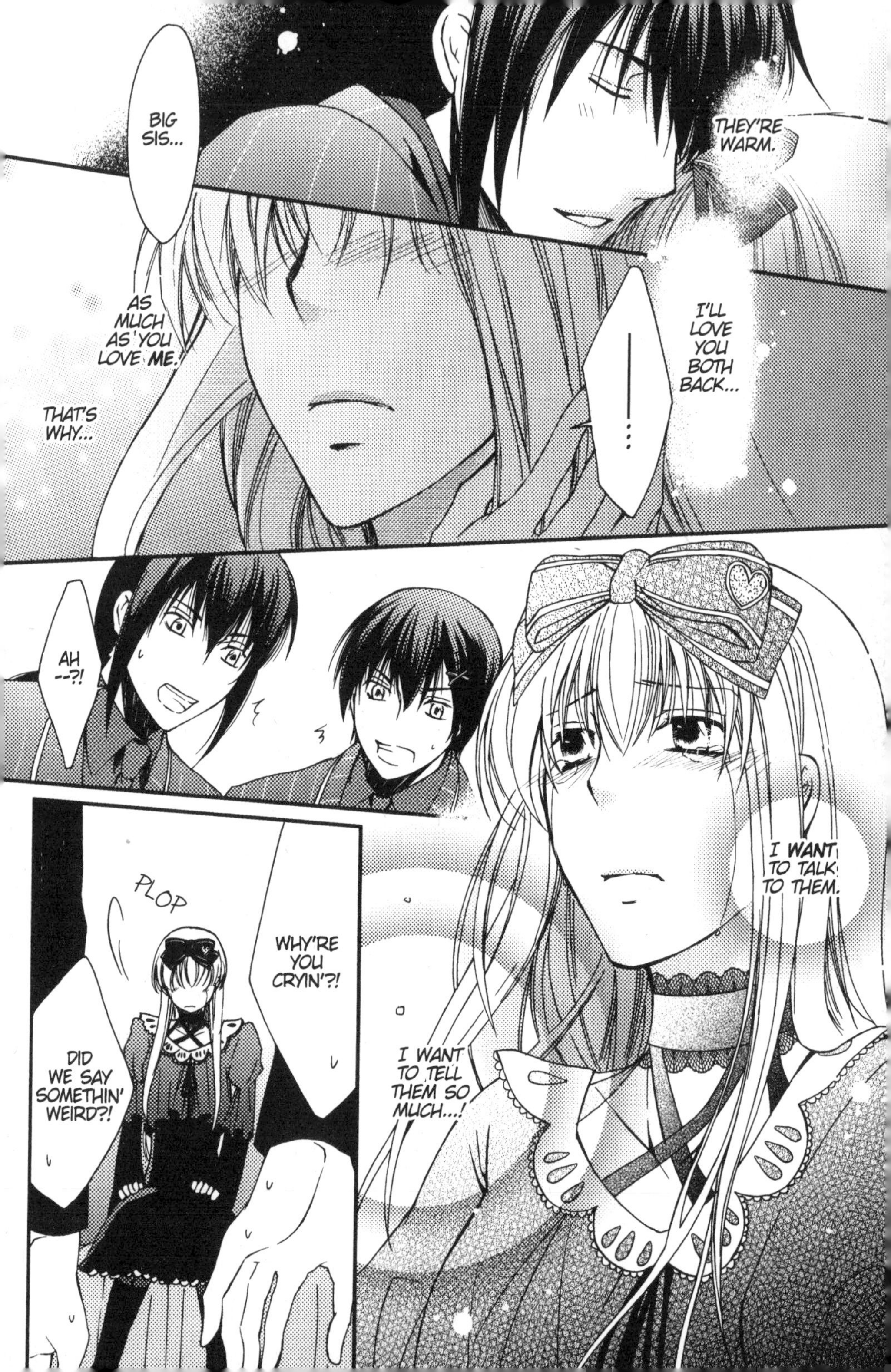
THEY'RE WARM.
BIG SIS...
I'LL LOVE YOU BOTH BACK...
—…
AS MUCH AS YOU LOVE ME.
THAT'S WHY...
I WANT TO TALK TO THEM.
I WANT TO TELL THEM SO MUCH...!
AH --?!
WHY'RE YOU CRYIN'?!
PLOP
DID WE SAY SOMETHIN' WEIRD?!

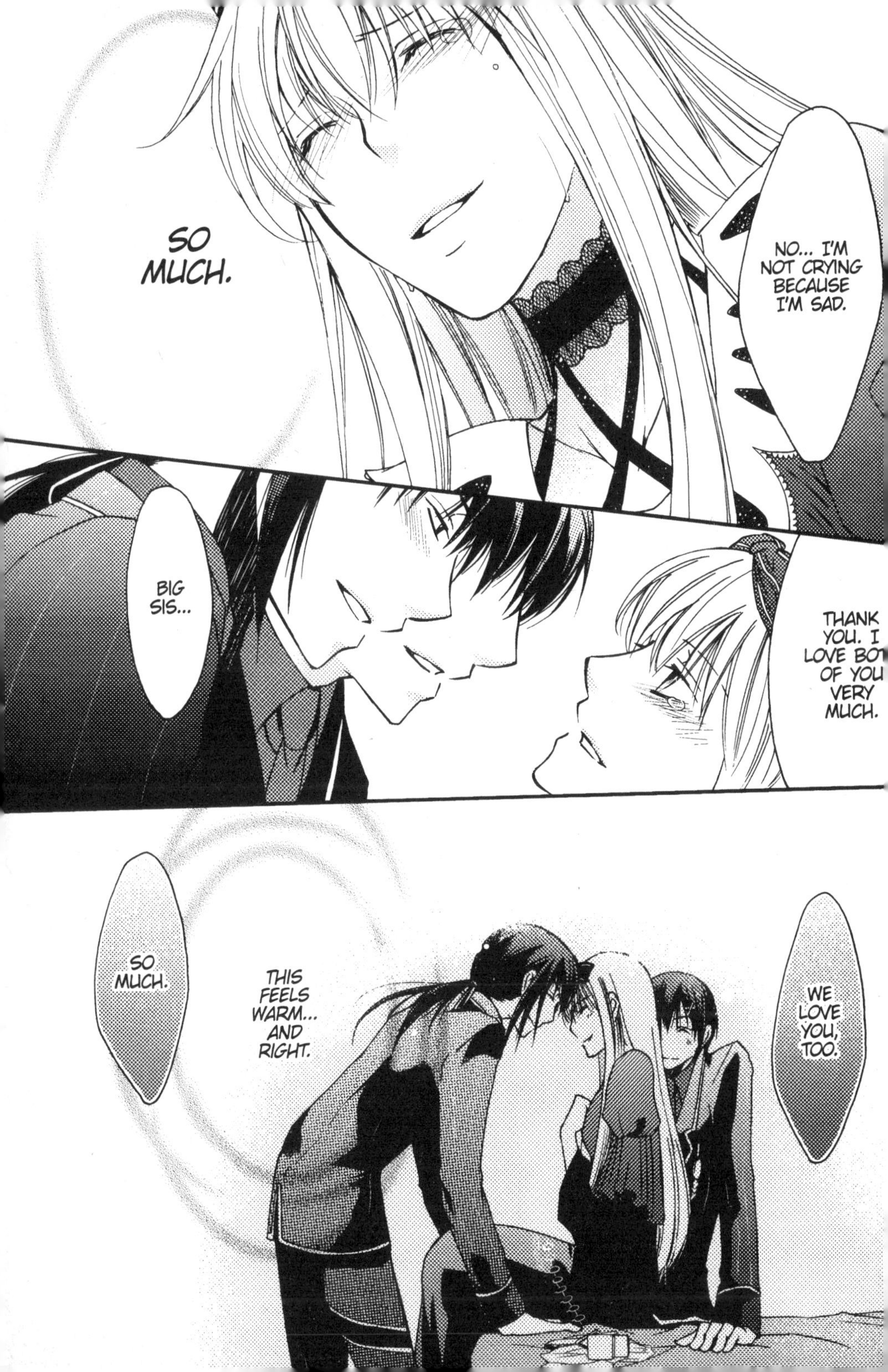
NO... I'M NOT CRYING BECAUSE I'M SAD.
SO MUCH.
THANK YOU. I LOVE BOT OF YOU VERY MUCH.
BIG SIS...
WE LOVE YOU, TOO.
THIS FEELS WARM... AND RIGHT.
SO MUCH.

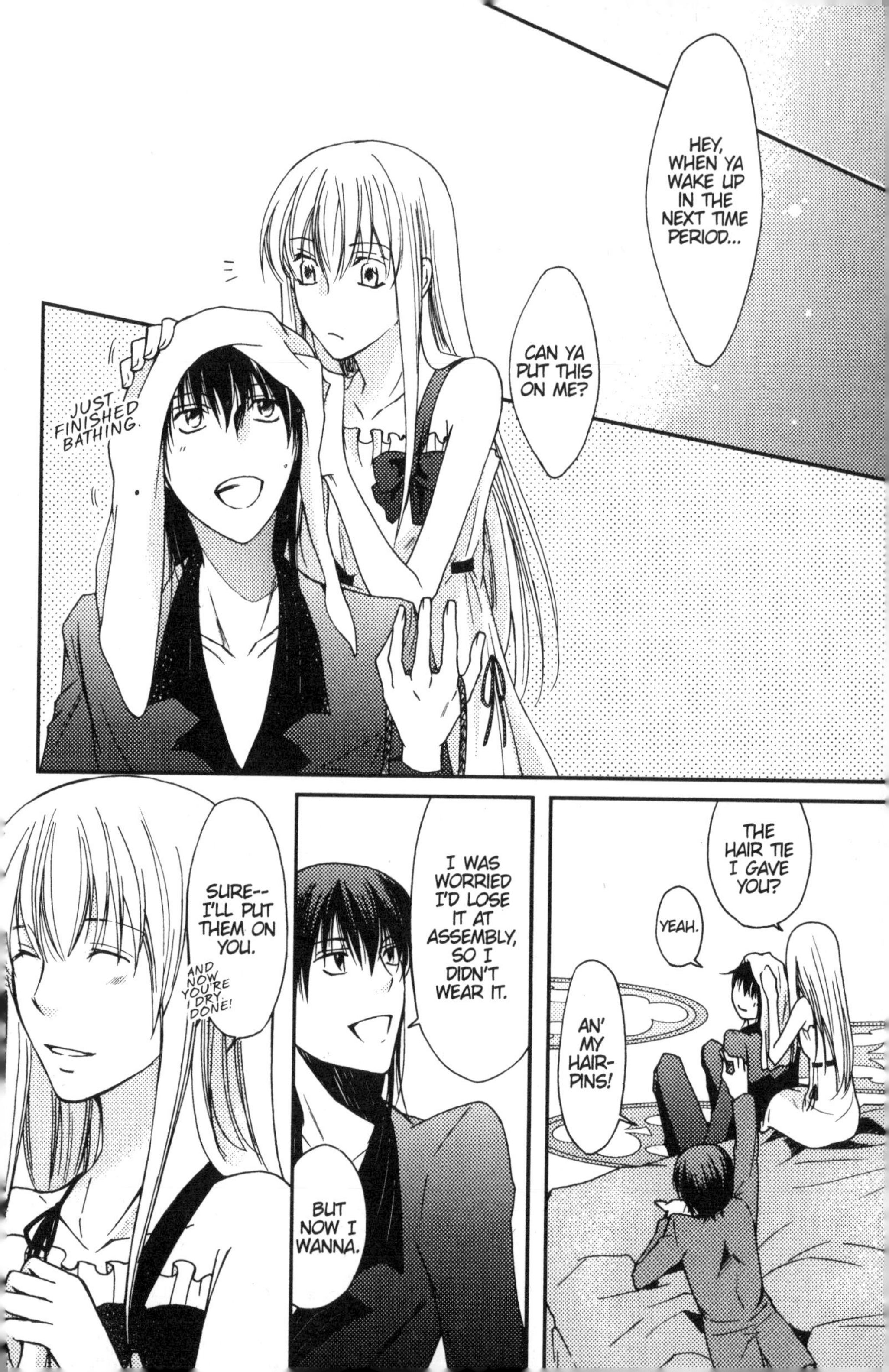
HEY, WHEN YA WAKE UP IN THE NEXT TIME PERIOD...
CAN YA PUT THIS ON ME?
JUST FINISHED BATHING.
THE HAIR TIE I GAVE YOU?
YEAH.
AN' MY HAIR-PINS!
I WAS WORRIED I'D LOSE IT AT ASSEMBLY, SO I DIDN'T WEAR IT.
BUT NOW I WANNA.
SURE-- I'LL PUT THEM ON YOU.
AND NOW YOU'RE DRY. DONE!

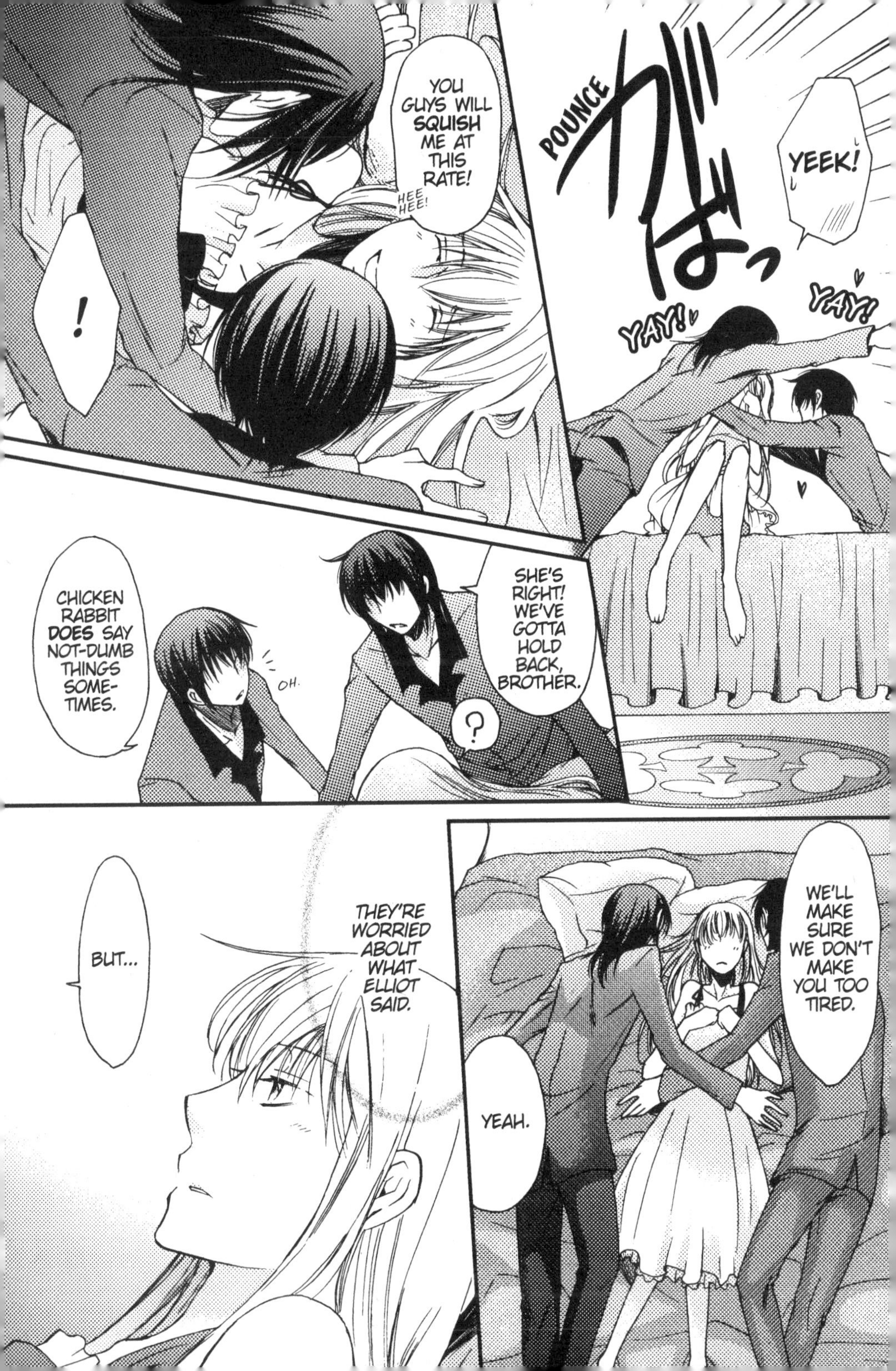
POUNCE
がばっ
YEEK!
YAY!
YAY!
YOU GUYS WILL SQUISH ME AT THIS RATE!
HEE HEE!
!
SHE'S RIGHT! WE'VE GOTTA HOLD BACK, BROTHER.
?
OH.
CHICKEN RABBIT DOES SAY NOT-DUMB THINGS SOME-TIMES.
WE'LL MAKE SURE WE DON'T MAKE YOU TOO TIRED.
YEAH.
THEY'RE WORRIED ABOUT WHAT ELLIOT SAID.
BUT...

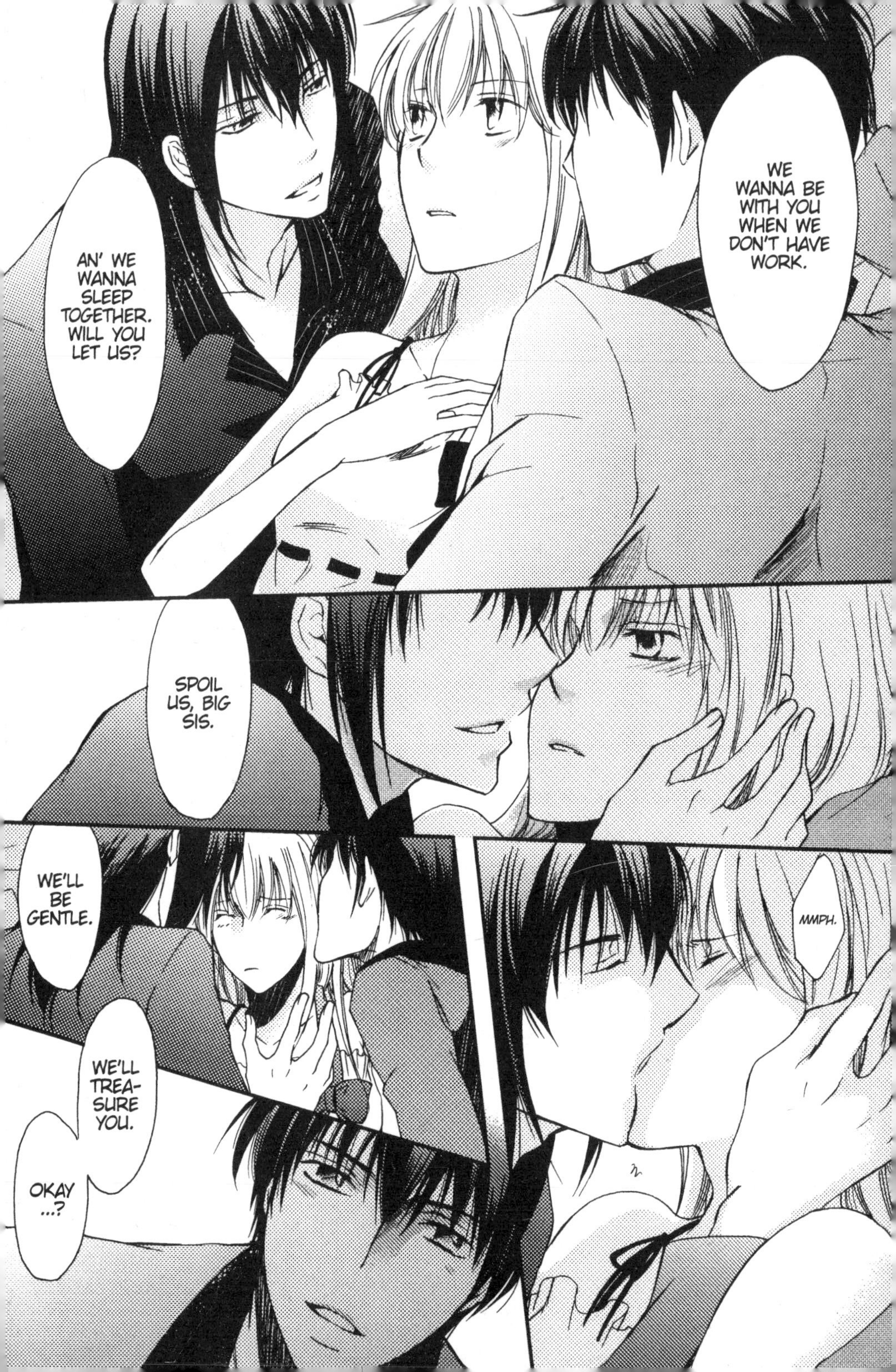
WE WANNA BE WITH YOU WHEN WE DON'T HAVE WORK.
AN' WE WANNA SLEEP TOGETHER. WILL YOU LET US?
SPOIL US, BIG SIS.
MMPH.
WE'LL BE GENTLE.
WE'LL TREA-SURE YOU.
OKAY ...?

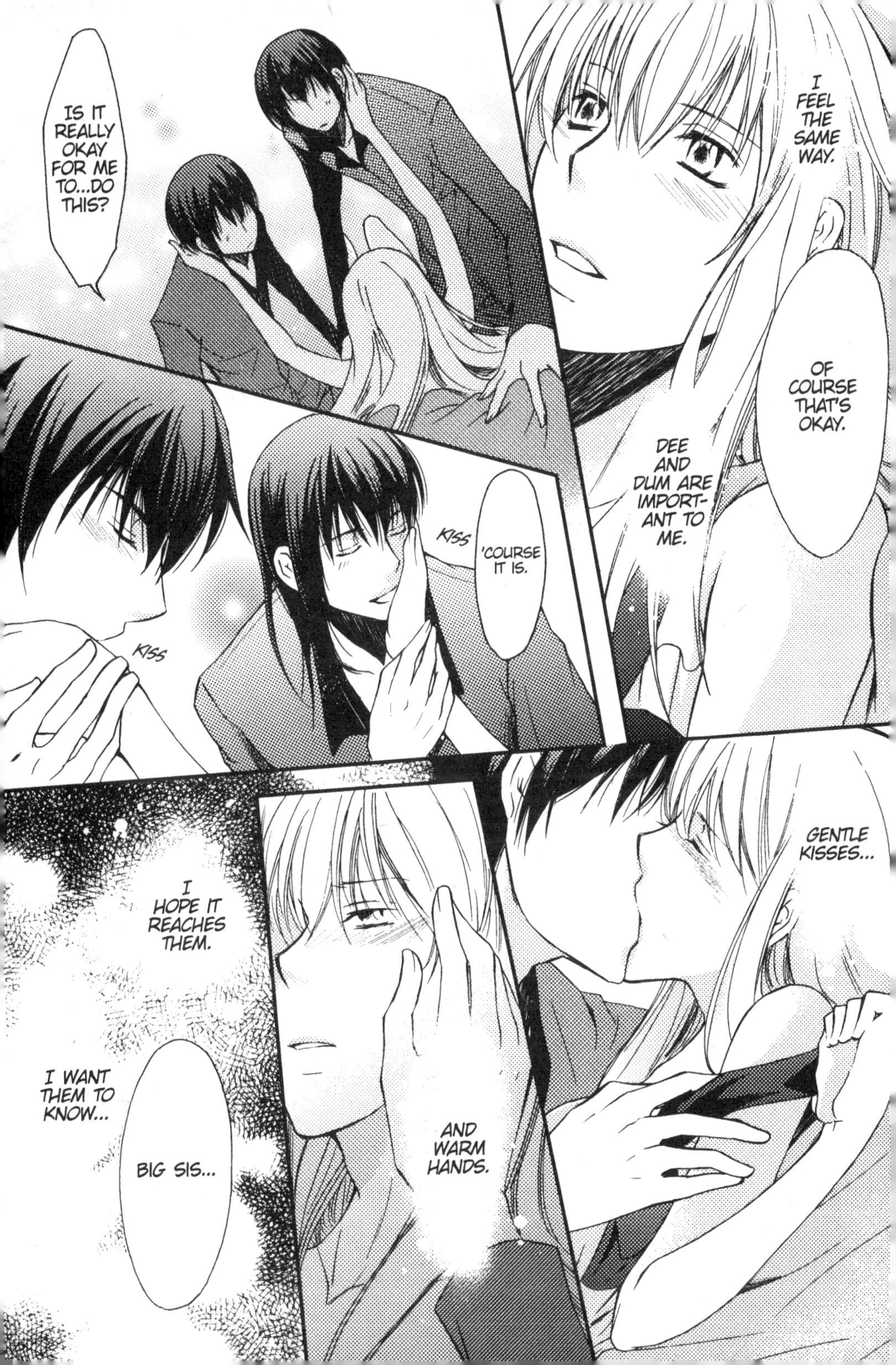
I FEEL THE SAME WAY.
OF COURSE THAT'S OKAY.
DEE AND DUM ARE IMPORT-ANT TO ME.
IS IT REALLY OKAY FOR ME TO...DO THIS?
KISS
'COURSE IT IS.
KISS
GENTLE KISSES...
AND WARM HANDS.
I HOPE IT REACHES THEM.
BIG SIS...
I WANT THEM TO KNOW...

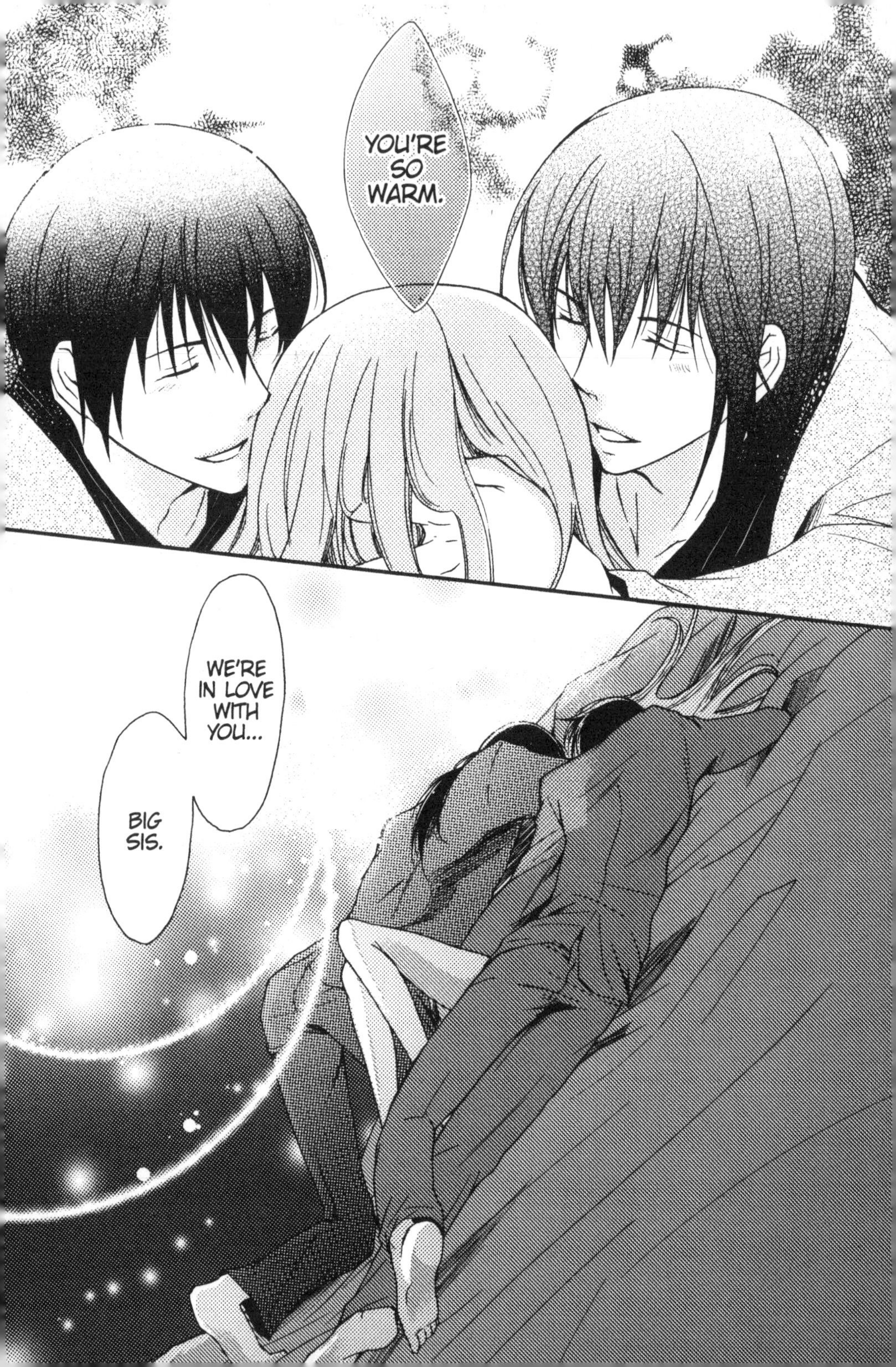
YOU'RE SO WARM.
WE'RE IN LOVE WITH YOU...
BIG SIS.

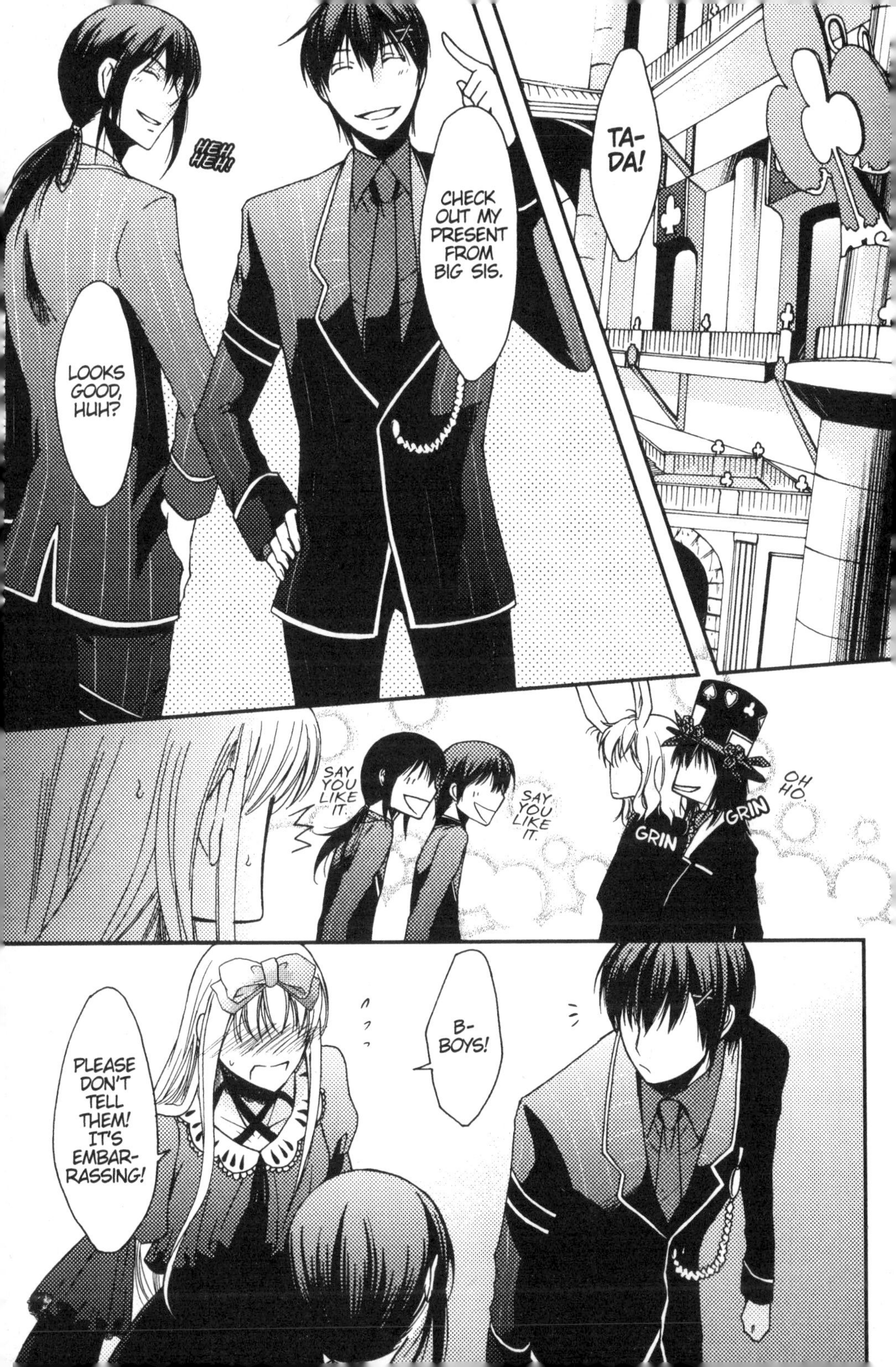
TA-DA!
CHECK OUT MY PRESENT FROM BIG SIS.
HEH HEH!
LOOKS GOOD, HUH?
OH HO.
GRIN
GRIN
SAY YOU LIKE IT.
SAY YOU LIKE IT.
B-BOYS!
PLEASE DON'T TELL THEM! IT'S EMBARRASSING!

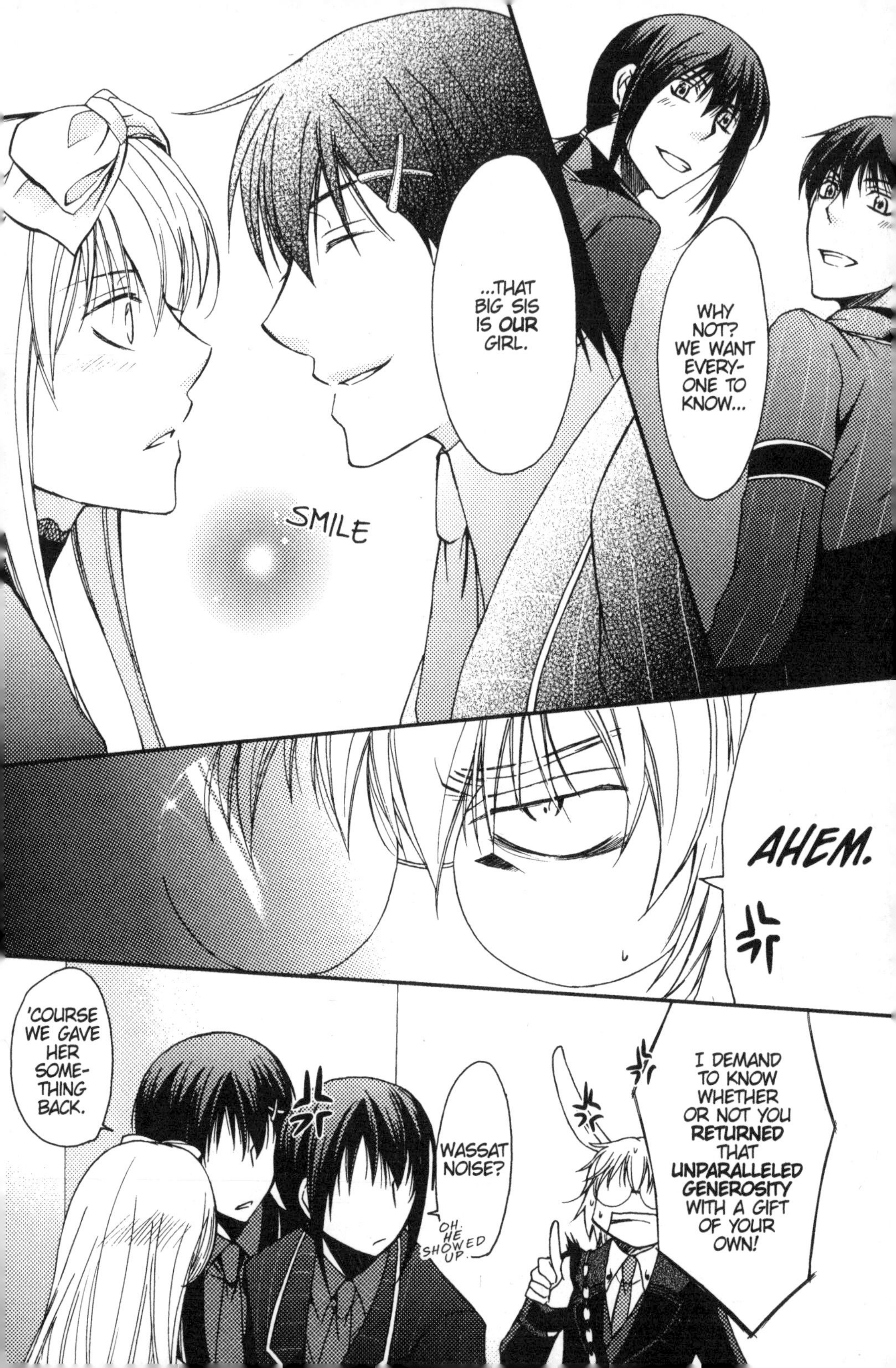
WHY NOT? WE WANT EVERY-ONE TO KNOW...
...THAT BIG SIS IS OUR GIRL.
SMILE
AHEM.
I DEMAND TO KNOW WHETHER OR NOT YOU RETURNED THAT UNPARALLELED GENEROSITY WITH A GIFT OF YOUR OWN!
WASSAT NOISE?
OH. HE SHOWED UP.
'COURSE WE GAVE HER SOMETHING BACK.

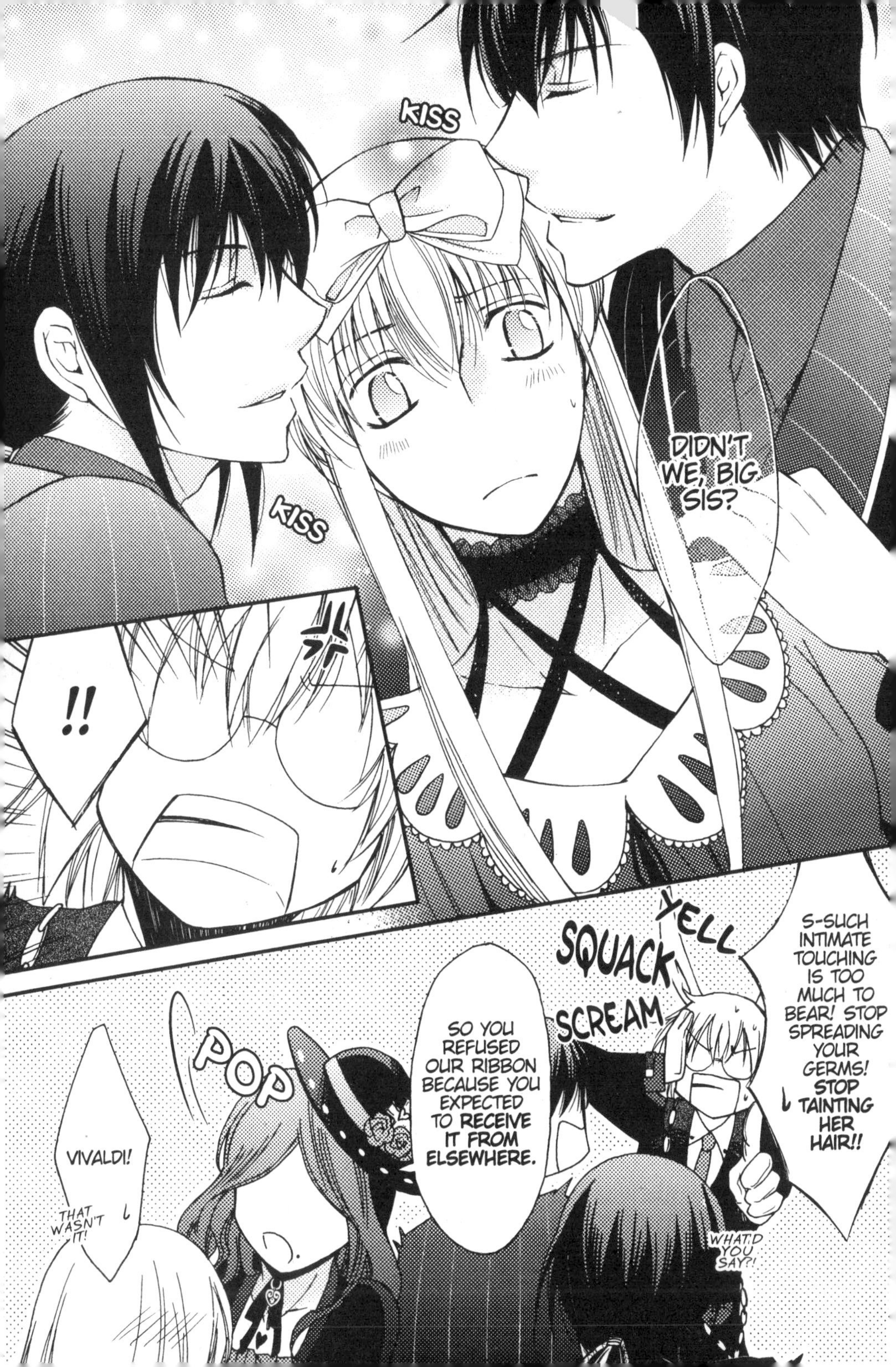
KISS
DIDN'T WE, BIG SIS?
KISS
!!
S-SUCH INTIMATE TOUCHING IS TOO MUCH TO BEAR! STOP SPREADING YOUR GERMS! STOP TAINTING HER HAIR!!
YELL
SQUACK
SCREAM
SO YOU REFUSED OUR RIBBON BECAUSE YOU EXPECTED TO RECEIVE IT FROM ELSEWHERE.
WHAT'D YOU SAY?!
POP
VIVALDI!
THAT WASN'T IT!

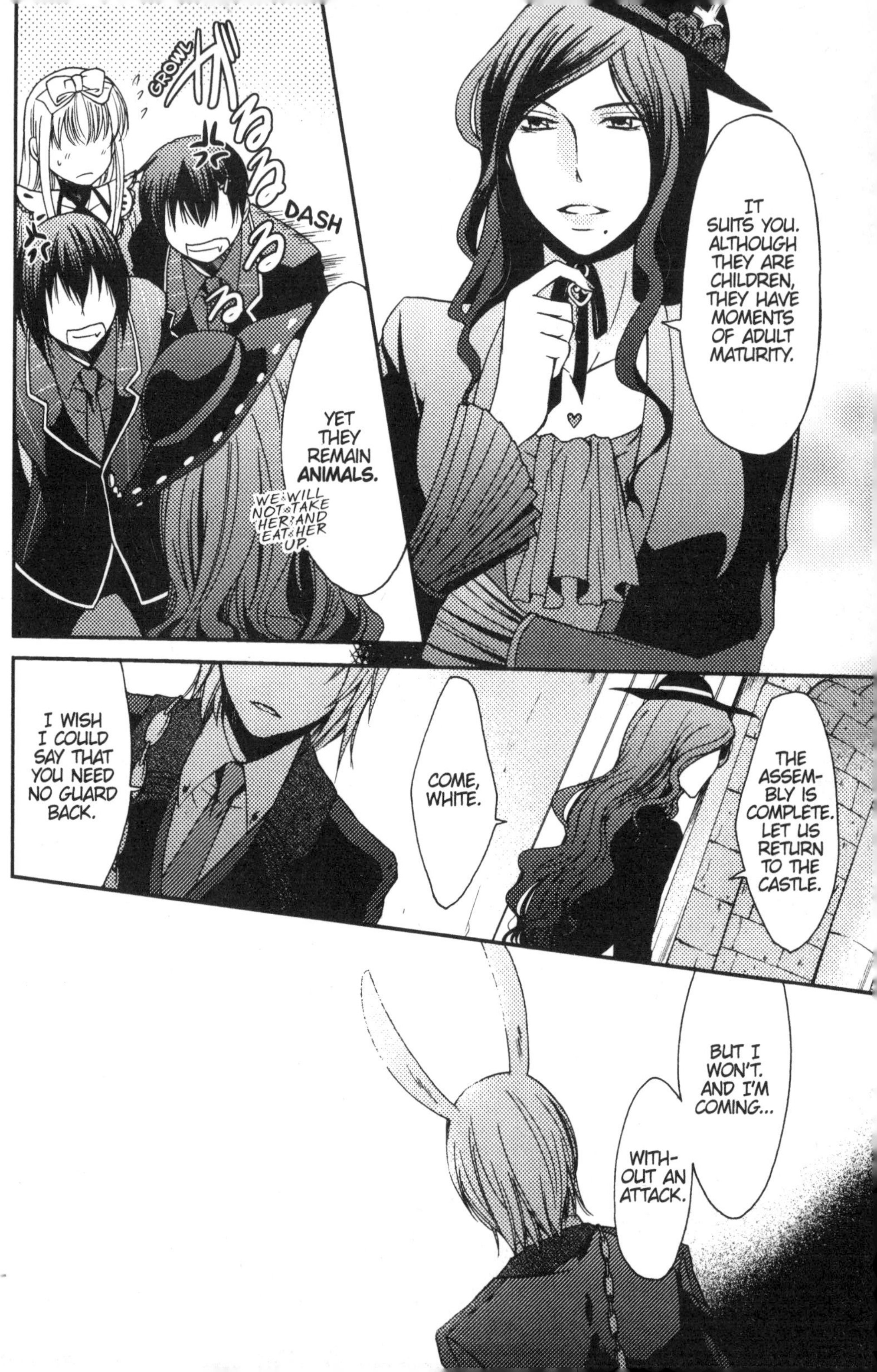
IT SUITS YOU. ALTHOUGH THEY ARE CHILDREN, THEY HAVE MOMENTS OF ADULT MATURITY.
YET THEY REMAIN ANIMALS.
GROWL
DASH
WE WILL NOT TAKE HER AND EAT HER UP.
THE ASSEM-BLY IS COMPLETE. LET US RETURN TO THE CASTLE.
COME, WHITE.
I WISH I COULD SAY THAT YOU NEED NO GUARD BACK.
BUT I WON'T. AND I'M COMING...
WITH-OUT AN ATTACK.

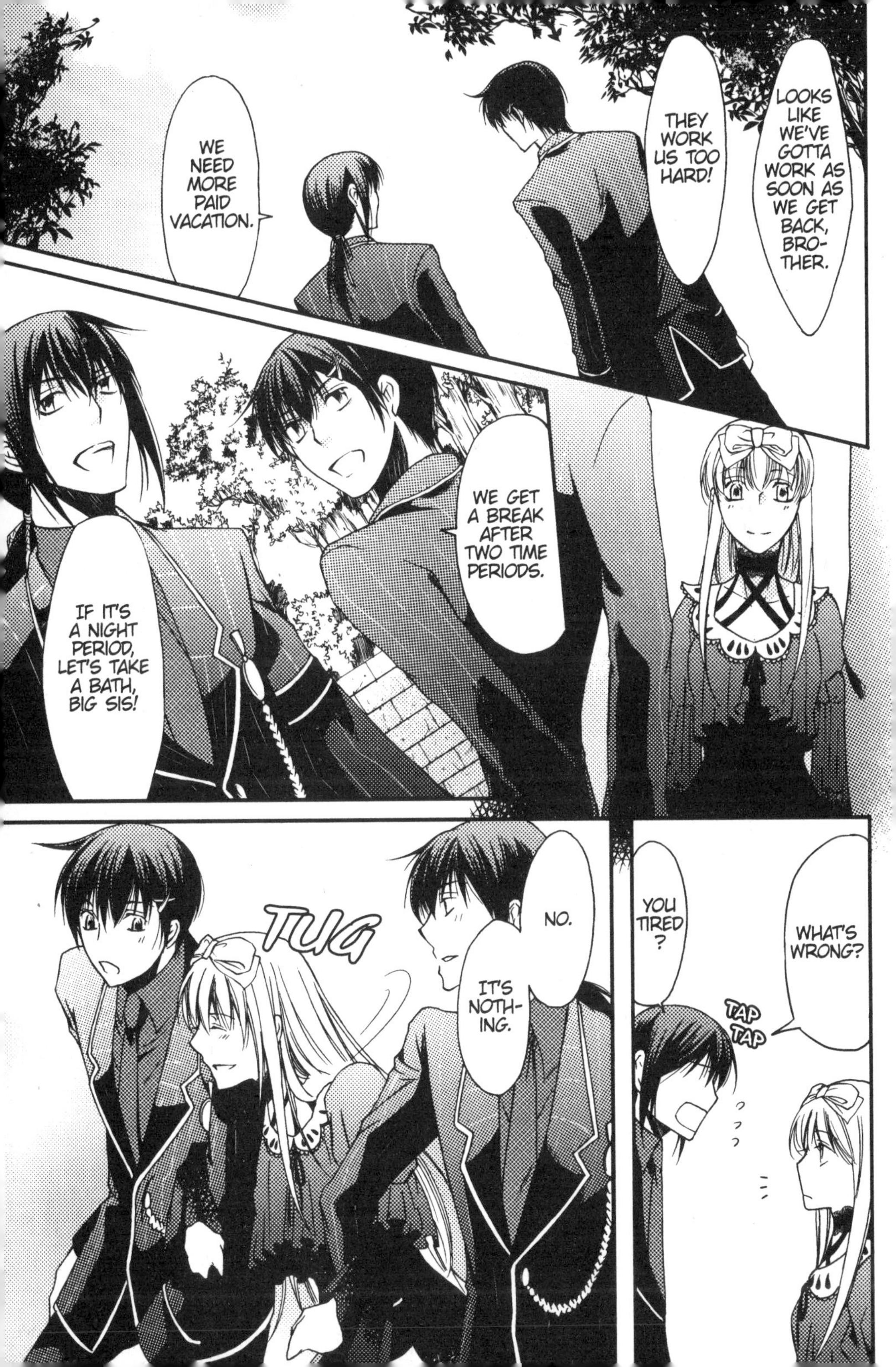
LOOKS LIKE WE'VE GOTTA WORK AS SOON AS WE GET BACK, BRO-THER.
THEY WORK US TOO HARD!
WE NEED MORE PAID VACATION.
WE GET A BREAK AFTER TWO TIME PERIODS.
IF IT'S A NIGHT PERIOD, LET'S TAKE A BATH, BIG SIS!
WHAT'S WRONG?
TAP TAP
YOU TIRED?
NO.
IT'S NOTH-ING.
TUG

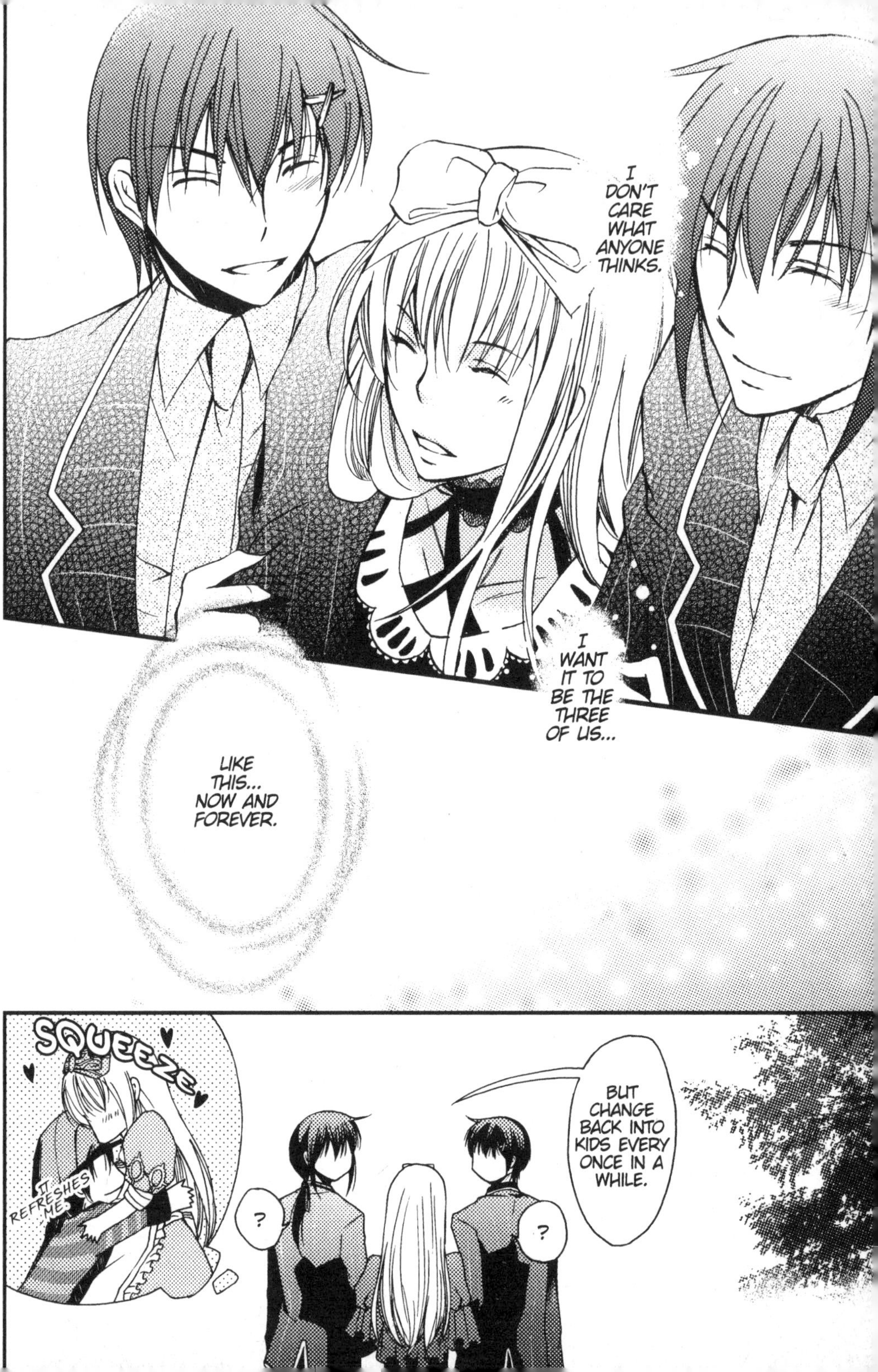
I DON'T CARE WHAT ANYONE THINKS.
I WANT IT TO BE THE THREE OF US...
LIKE THIS... NOW AND FOREVER.
BUT CHANGE BACK INTO KIDS EVERY ONCE IN A WHILE.
?
?
SQUEEZE
IT REFRESHES ME.

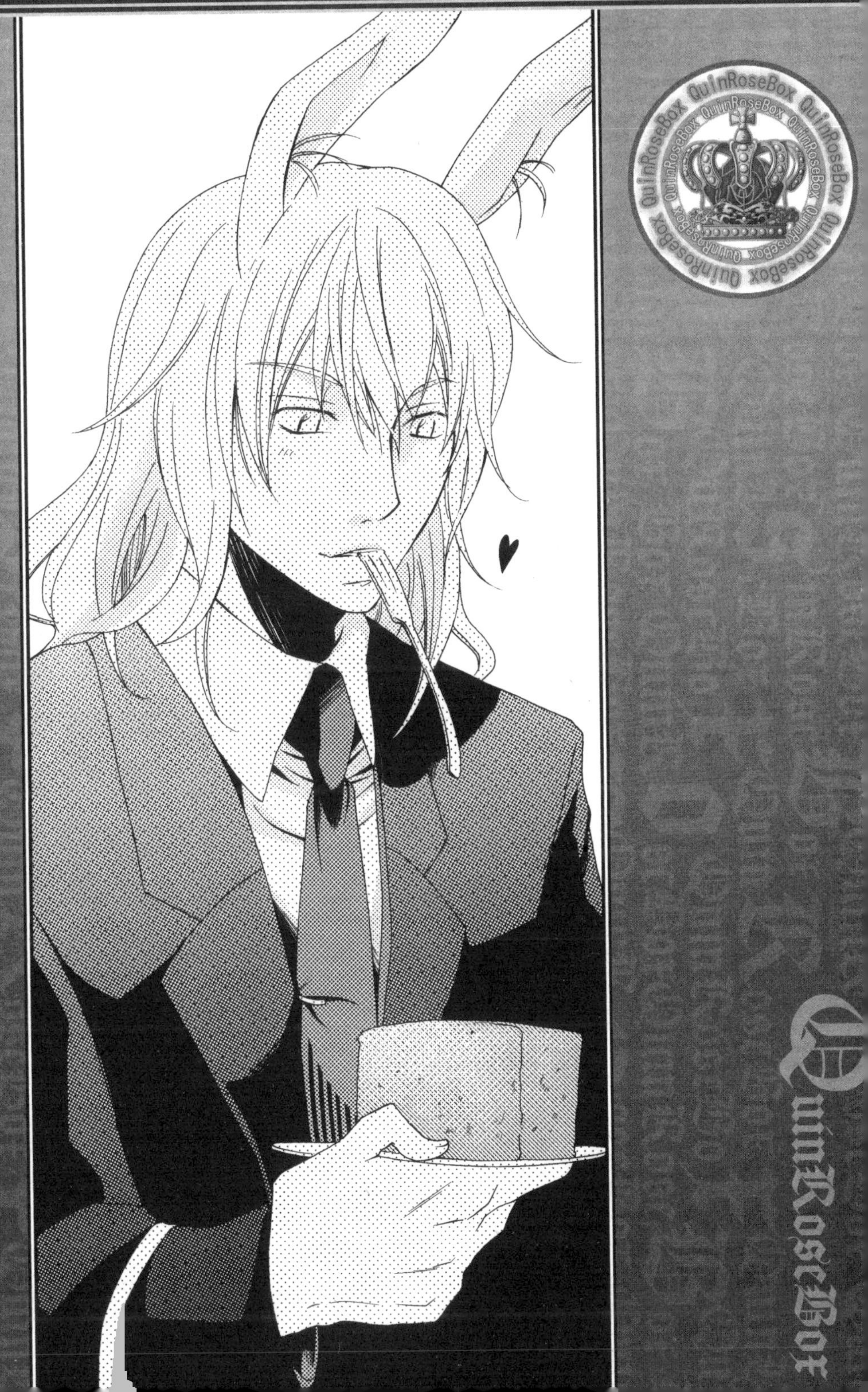
QuinRoseBox

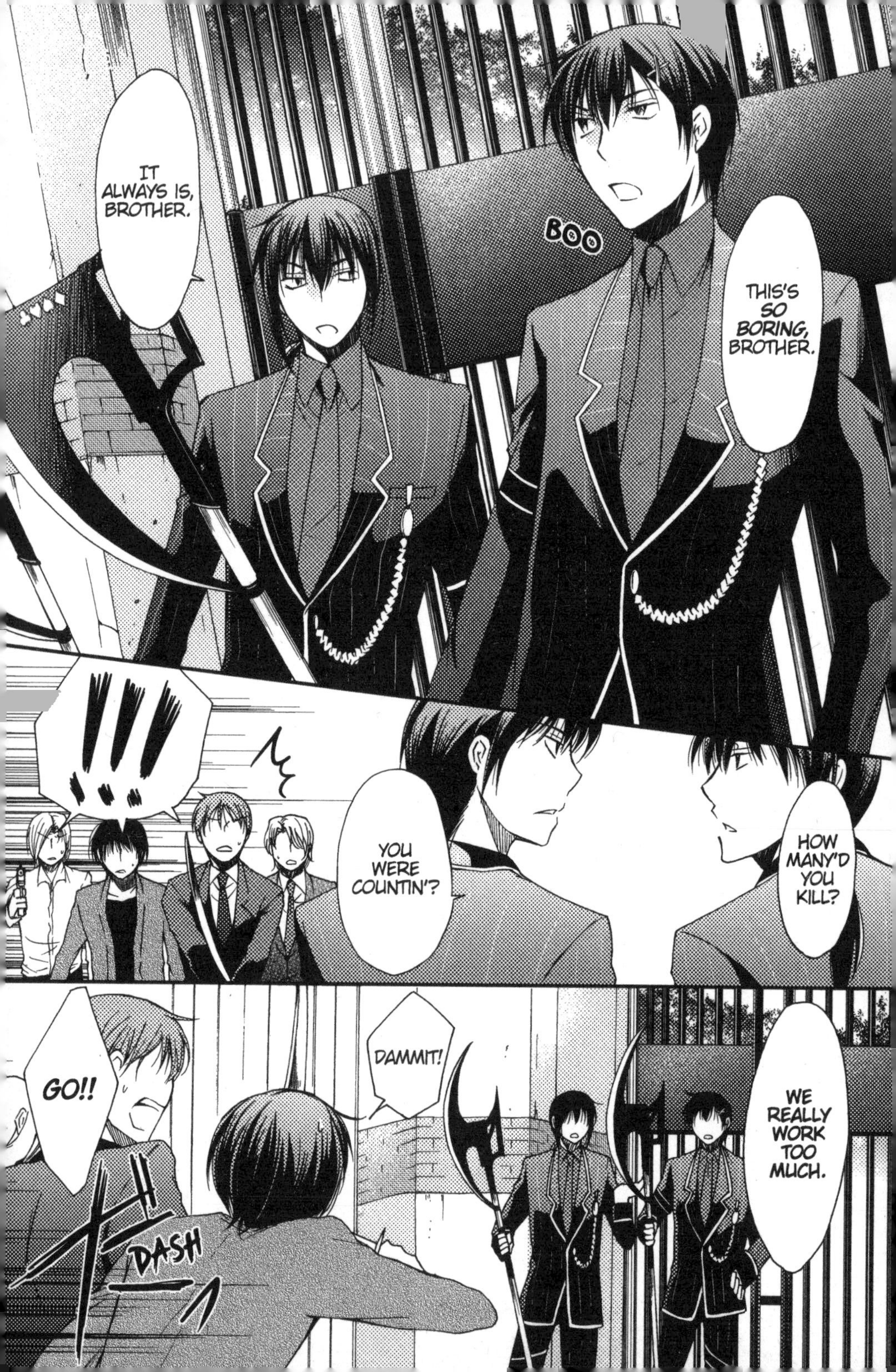
THIS'S SO BORING, BROTHER.
BOO
IT ALWAYS IS, BROTHER.
HOW MANY'D YOU KILL?
YOU WERE COUNTIN'?
!!!
WE REALLY WORK TOO MUCH.
DAMMIT!
GO!!
DASH

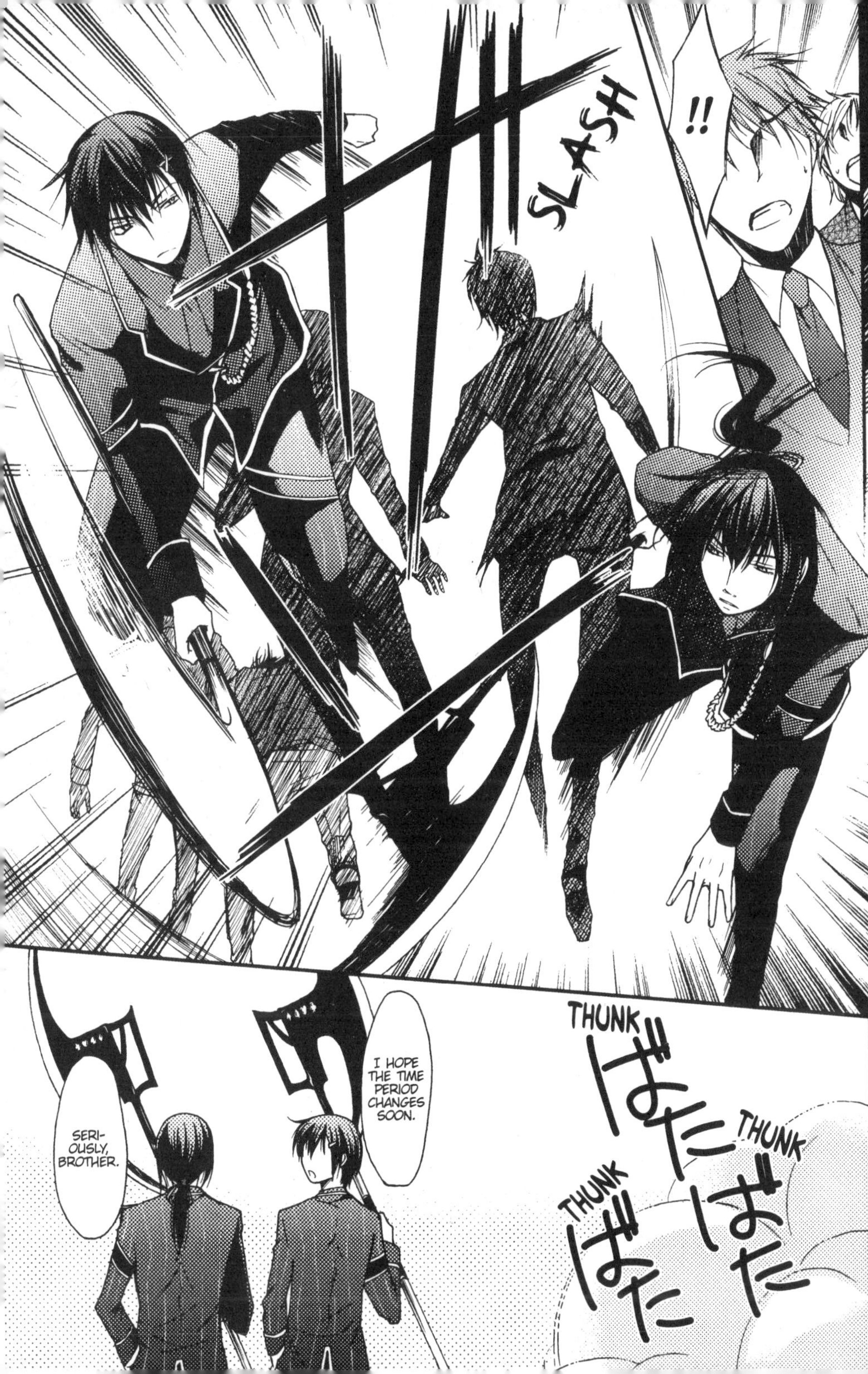
SLASH
!!
THUNK
ばた
THUNK
ばた
THUNK
ばた
I HOPE THE TIME PERIOD CHANGES SOON.
SERI-OUSLY, BROTHER.

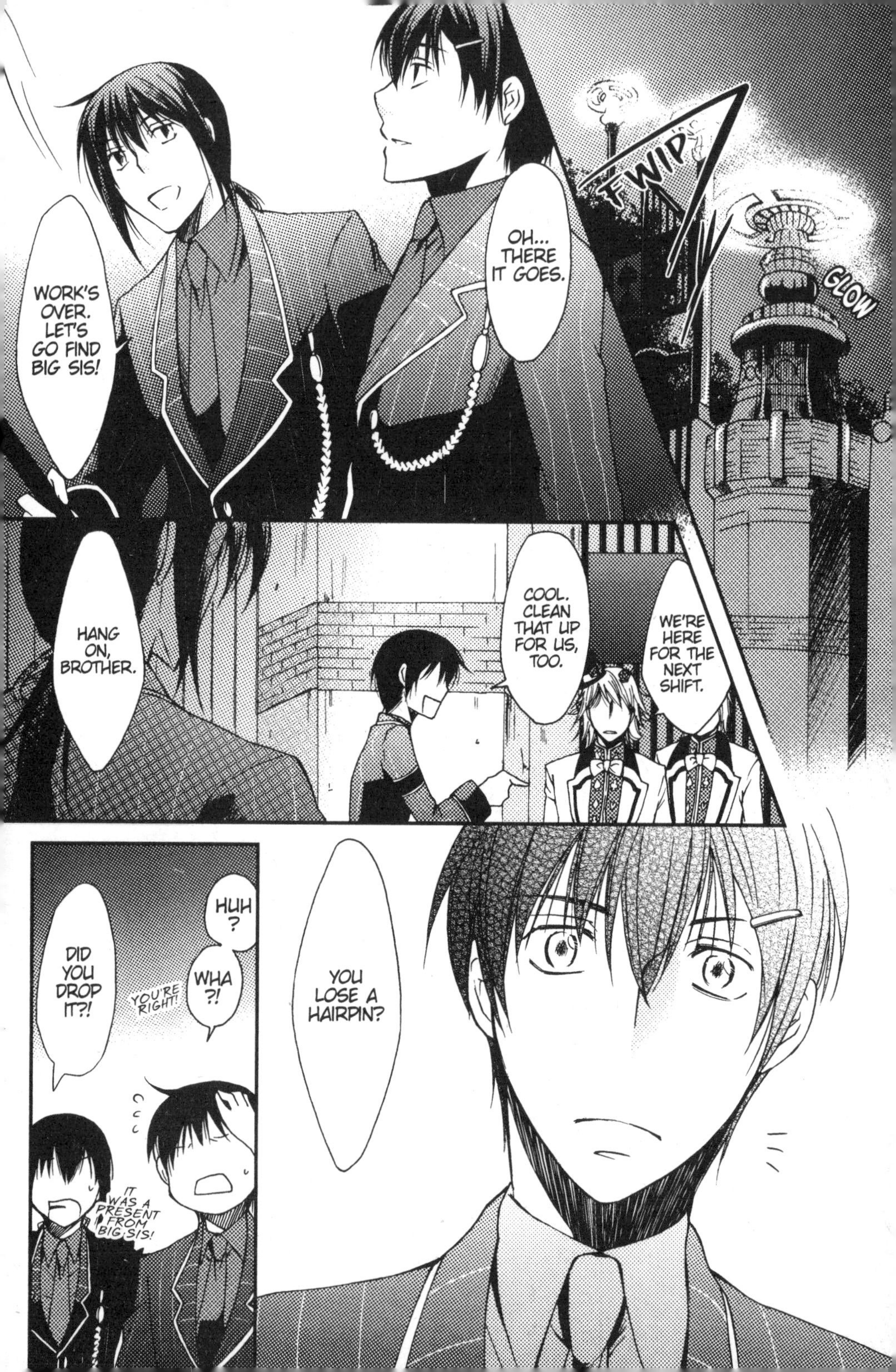

FWIP
GLOW
OH... THERE IT GOES.
WORK'S OVER. LET'S GO FIND BIG SIS!
WE'RE HERE FOR THE NEXT SHIFT.
COOL. CLEAN THAT UP FOR US, TOO.
HANG ON, BROTHER.
YOU LOSE A HAIRPIN?
HUH?
WHA?!
YOU'RE RIGHT!
DID YOU DROP IT?!
IT WAS A PRESENT FROM BIG SIS!

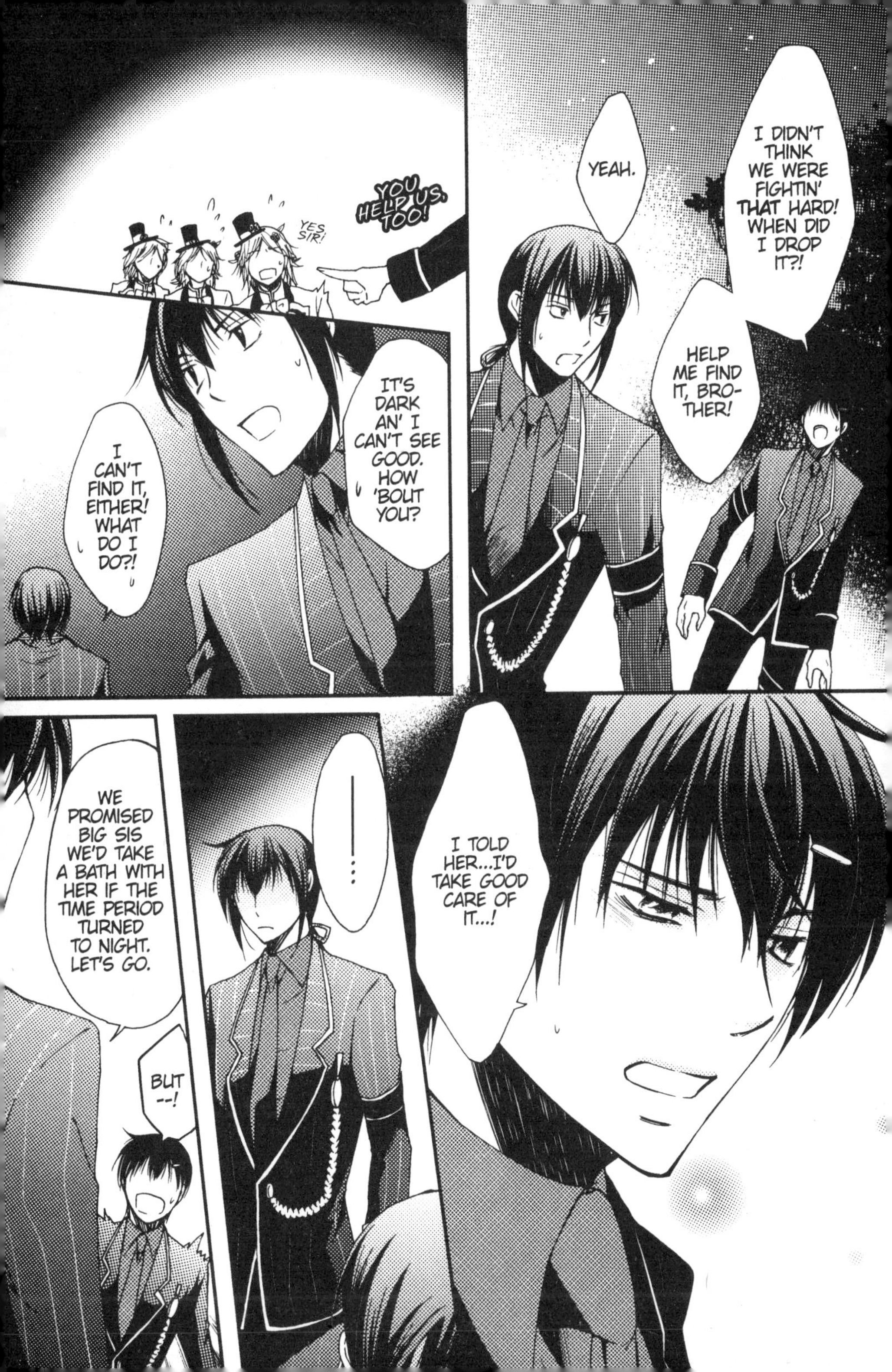
I DIDN'T THINK WE WERE FIGHTIN' THAT HARD! WHEN DID I DROP IT?!
YEAH.
HELP ME FIND IT, BROTHER!
YOU HELP US, TOO!
YES, SIR!
IT'S DARK AN' I CAN'T SEE GOOD. HOW 'BOUT YOU?
I CAN'T FIND IT, EITHER! WHAT DO I DO?!
I TOLD HER...I'D TAKE GOOD CARE OF IT...!
—...
WE PROMISED BIG SIS WE'D TAKE A BATH WITH HER IF THE TIME PERIOD TURNED TO NIGHT. LET'S GO.
BUT --!

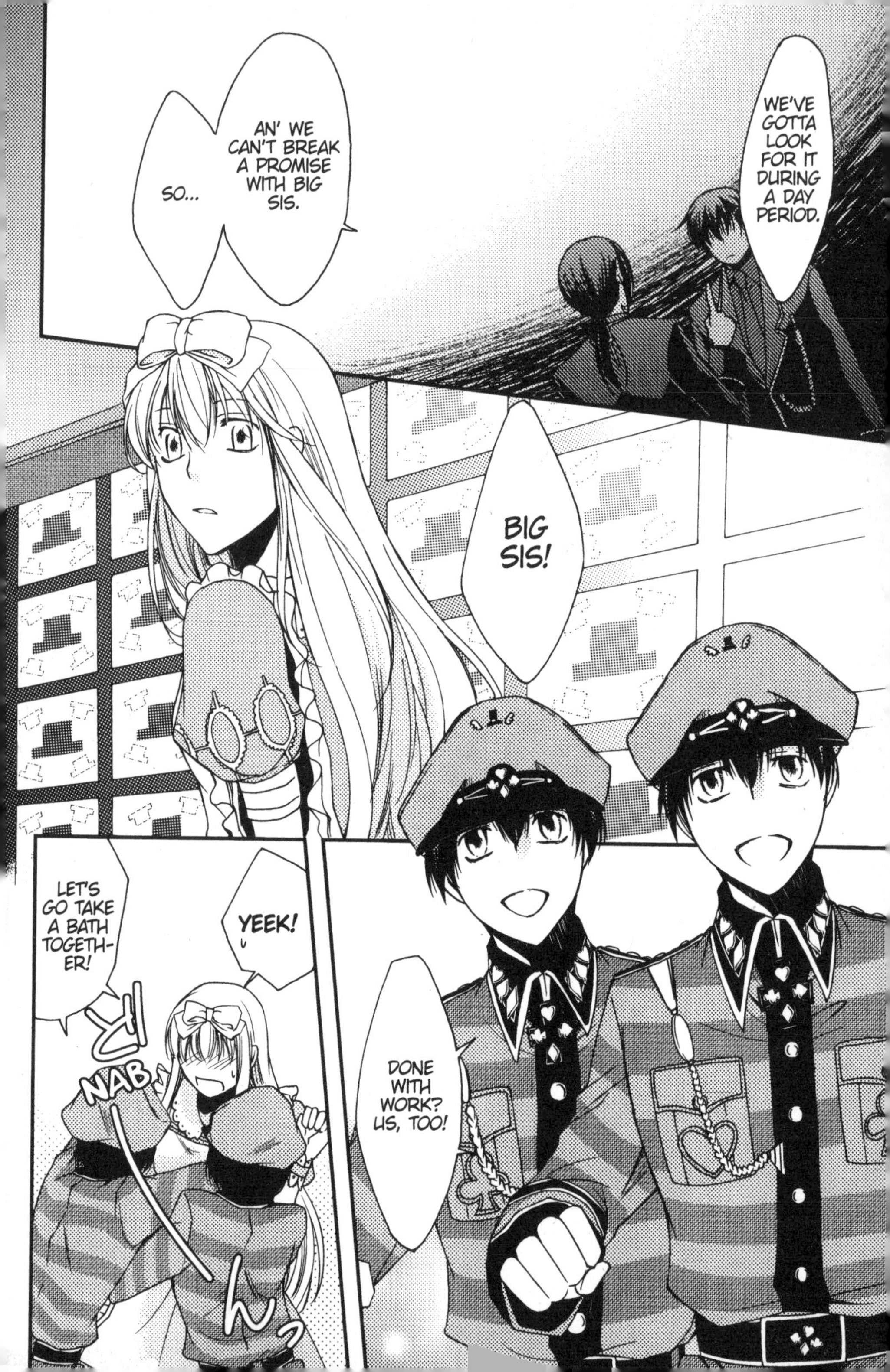

WE'VE GOTTA LOOK FOR IT DURING A DAY PERIOD.
AN' WE CAN'T BREAK A PROMISE WITH BIG SIS. SO...
BIG SIS!
DONE WITH WORK? US, TOO!
YEEK!
LET'S GO TAKE A BATH TOGETHER!
NAB

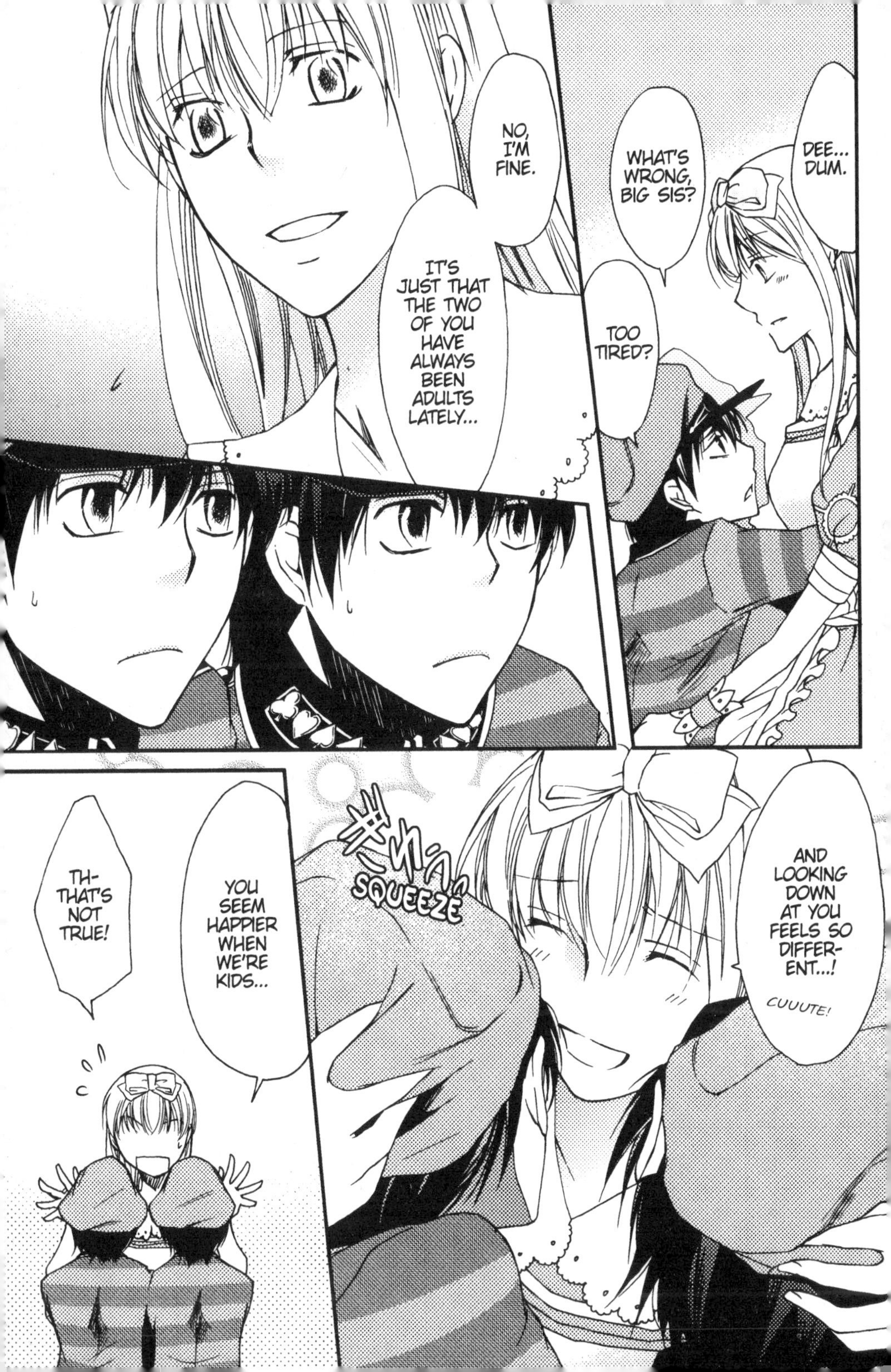
DEE... DUM.
WHAT'S WRONG, BIG SIS?
TOO TIRED?
NO, I'M FINE.
IT'S JUST THAT THE TWO OF YOU HAVE ALWAYS BEEN ADULTS LATELY...
AND LOOKING DOWN AT YOU FEELS SO DIFFER-ENT...!
CUUUTE!
SQUEEZE
YOU SEEM HAPPIER WHEN WE'RE KIDS...
TH-THAT'S NOT TRUE!

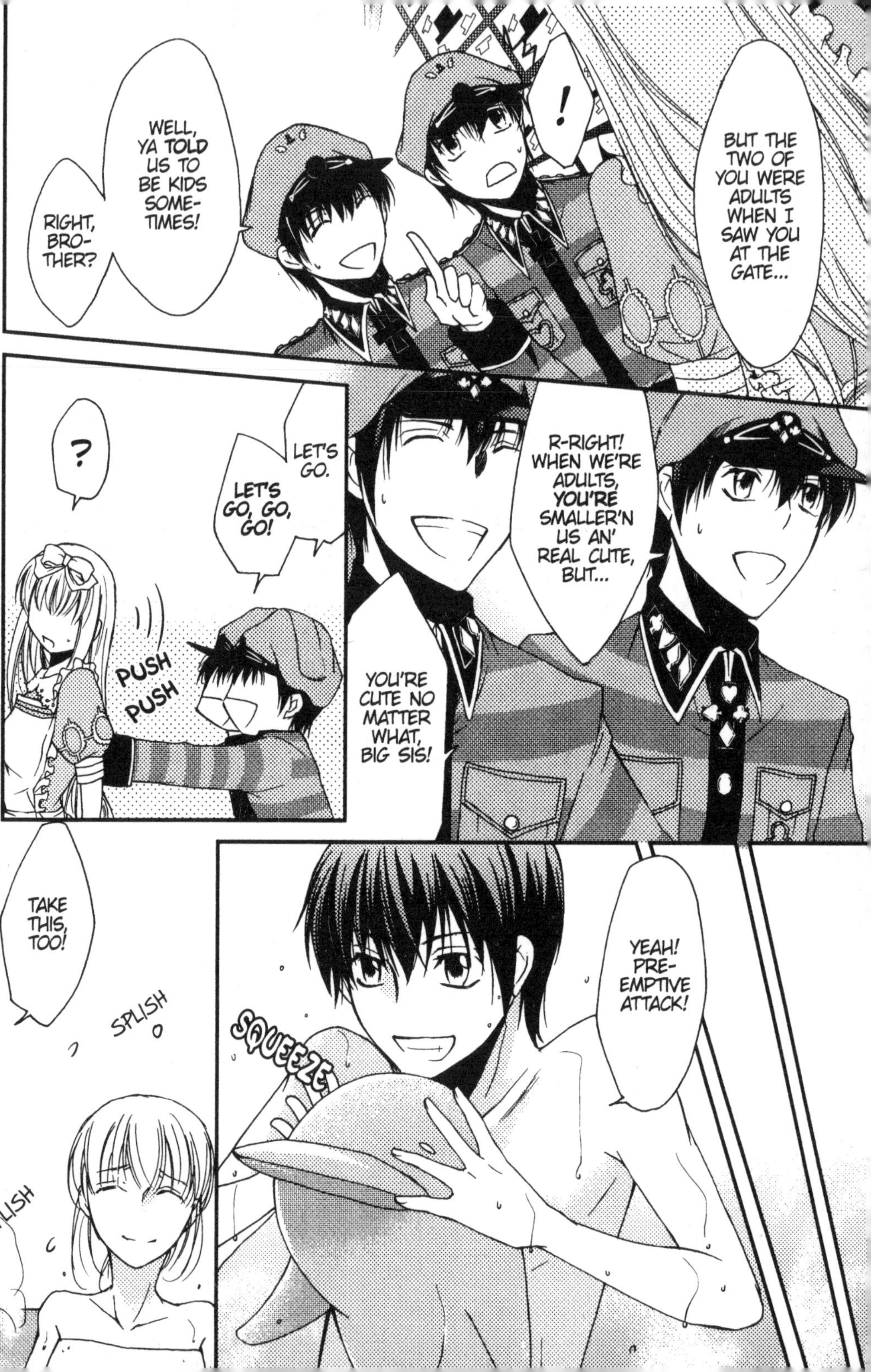
BUT THE TWO OF YOU WERE ADULTS WHEN I SAW YOU AT THE GATE...
!
WELL, YA TOLD US TO BE KIDS SOME-TIMES!
RIGHT, BRO-THER?
R-RIGHT! WHEN WE'RE ADULTS, **YOU'RE** SMALLER'N US AN' REAL CUTE, BUT...
YOU'RE CUTE NO MATTER WHAT, BIG SIS!
LET'S GO.
LET'S GO, GO, GO!
?
PUSH PUSH
YEAH! PRE-EMPTIVE ATTACK!
SQUEEZE
TAKE THIS, TOO!
SPLISH
SPLISH

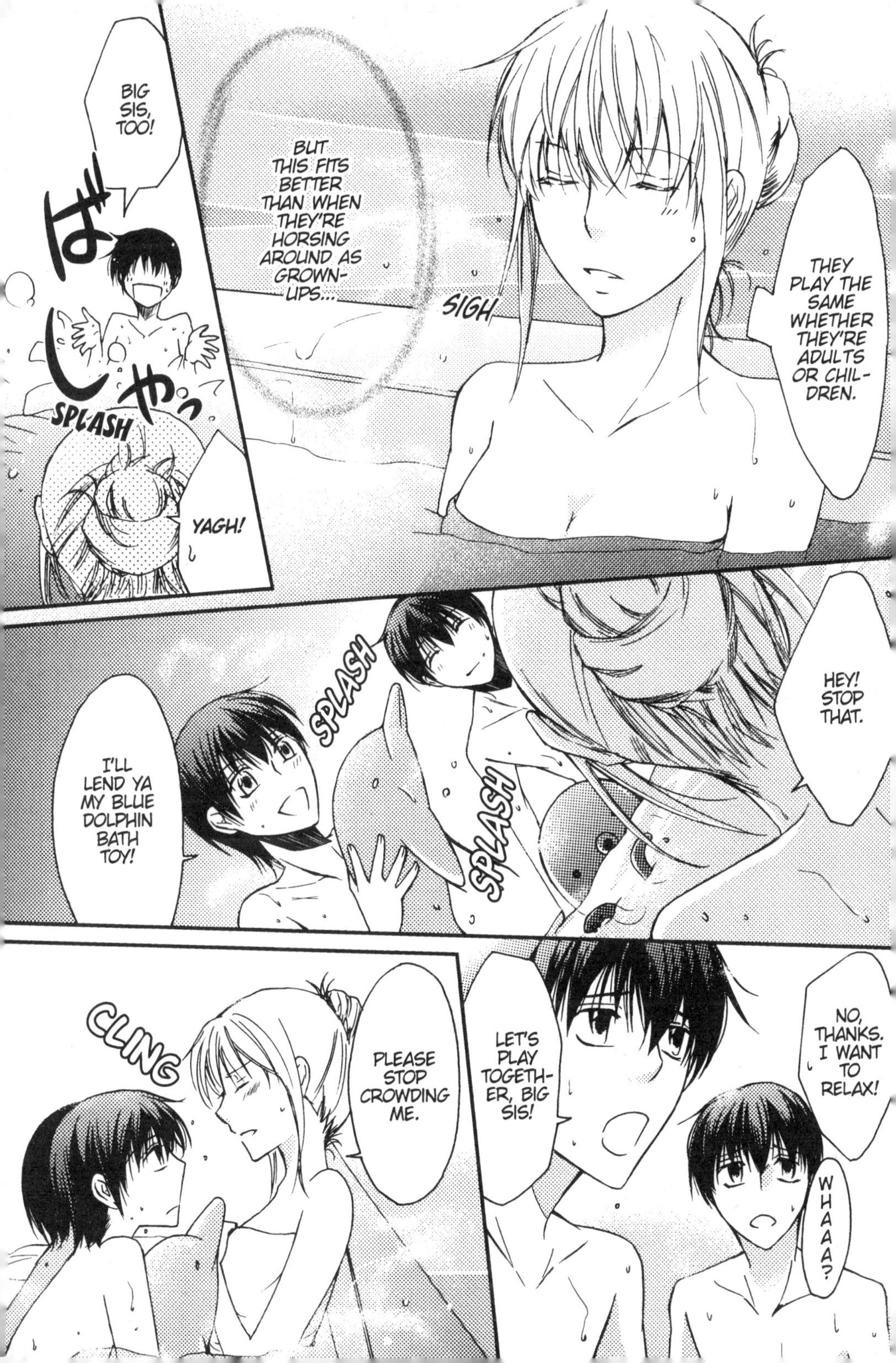
THEY PLAY THE SAME WHETHER THEY'RE ADULTS OR CHIL-DREN.
SIGH
BUT THIS FITS BETTER THAN WHEN THEY'RE HORSING AROUND AS GROWN-UPS...
BIG SIS, TOO!
ばしゃっ
SPLASH
YAGH!
HEY! STOP THAT.
SPLASH
SPLASH
I'LL LEND YA MY BLUE DOLPHIN BATH TOY!
NO, THANKS. I WANT TO RELAX!
LET'S PLAY TOGETH-ER, BIG SIS!
WHAAAA?
PLEASE STOP CROWDING ME.
CLING

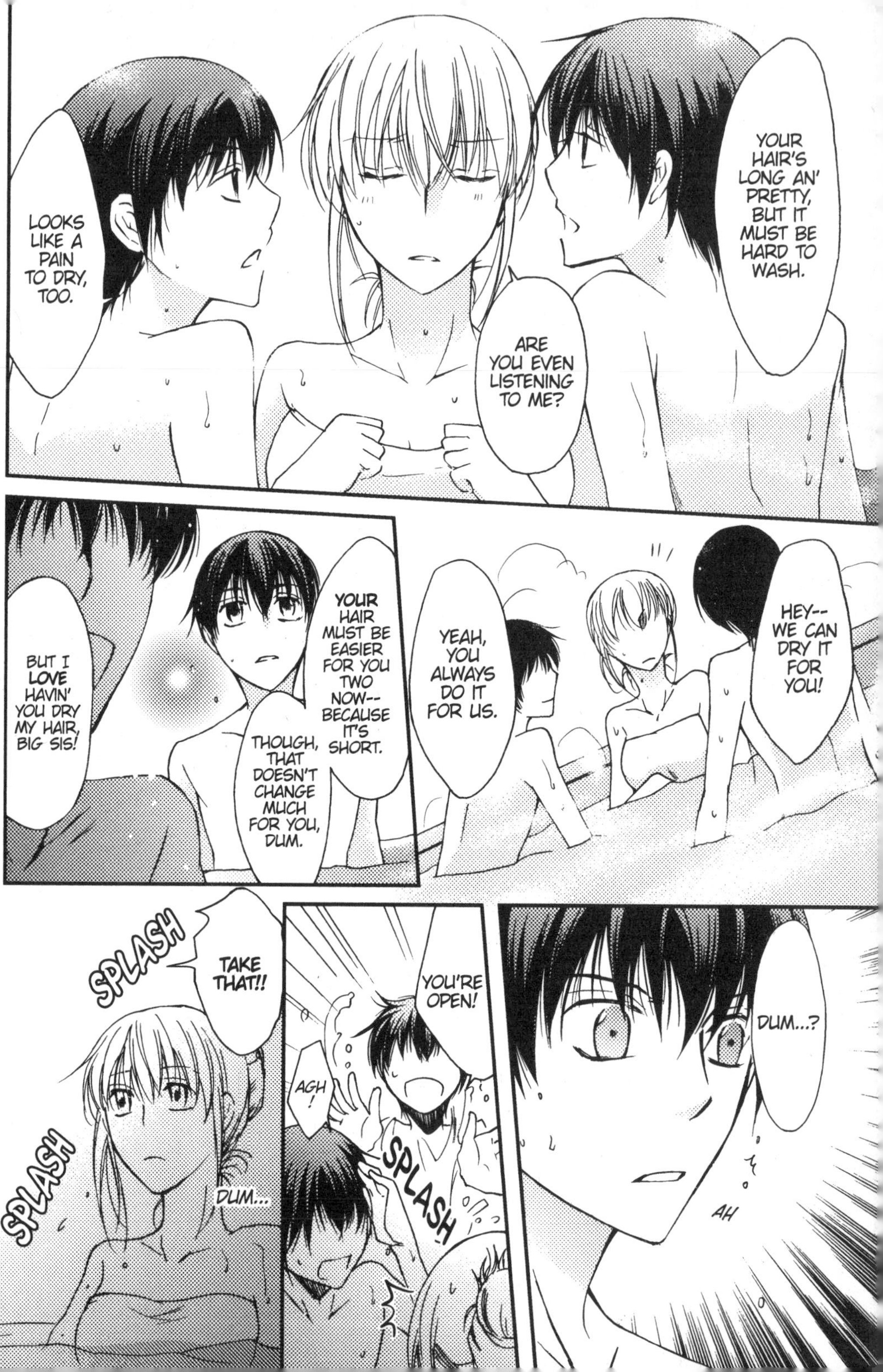
YOUR HAIR'S LONG AN' PRETTY, BUT IT MUST BE HARD TO WASH.
ARE YOU EVEN LISTENING TO ME?
LOOKS LIKE A PAIN TO DRY, TOO.
HEY-- WE CAN DRY IT FOR YOU!
YEAH, YOU ALWAYS DO IT FOR US.
YOUR HAIR MUST BE EASIER FOR YOU TWO NOW-- BECAUSE IT'S SHORT.
THOUGH, THAT DOESN'T CHANGE MUCH FOR YOU, DUM.
BUT I LOVE HAVIN' YOU DRY MY HAIR, BIG SIS!
DUM...?
AH
YOU'RE OPEN!
AGH!
SPLASH
TAKE THAT!!
SPLASH
SPLASH
DUM...

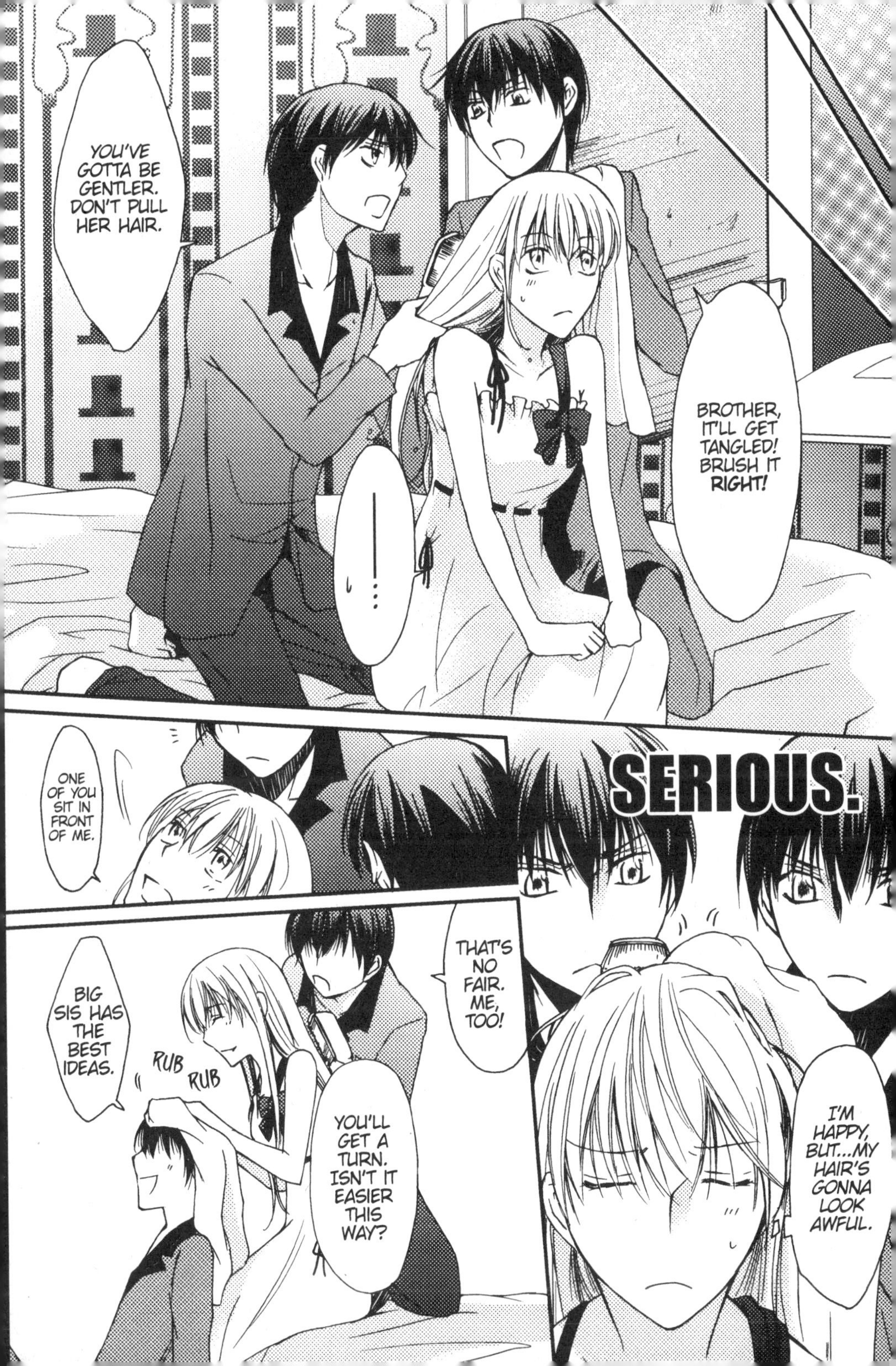
BROTHER, IT'LL GET TANGLED! BRUSH IT RIGHT!
—!...
YOU'VE GOTTA BE GENTLER. DON'T PULL HER HAIR.
SERIOUS.
I'M HAPPY, BUT...MY HAIR'S GONNA LOOK AWFUL.
ONE OF YOU SIT IN FRONT OF ME.
THAT'S NO FAIR. ME, TOO!
YOU'LL GET A TURN. ISN'T IT EASIER THIS WAY?
BIG SIS HAS THE BEST IDEAS.
RUB RUB

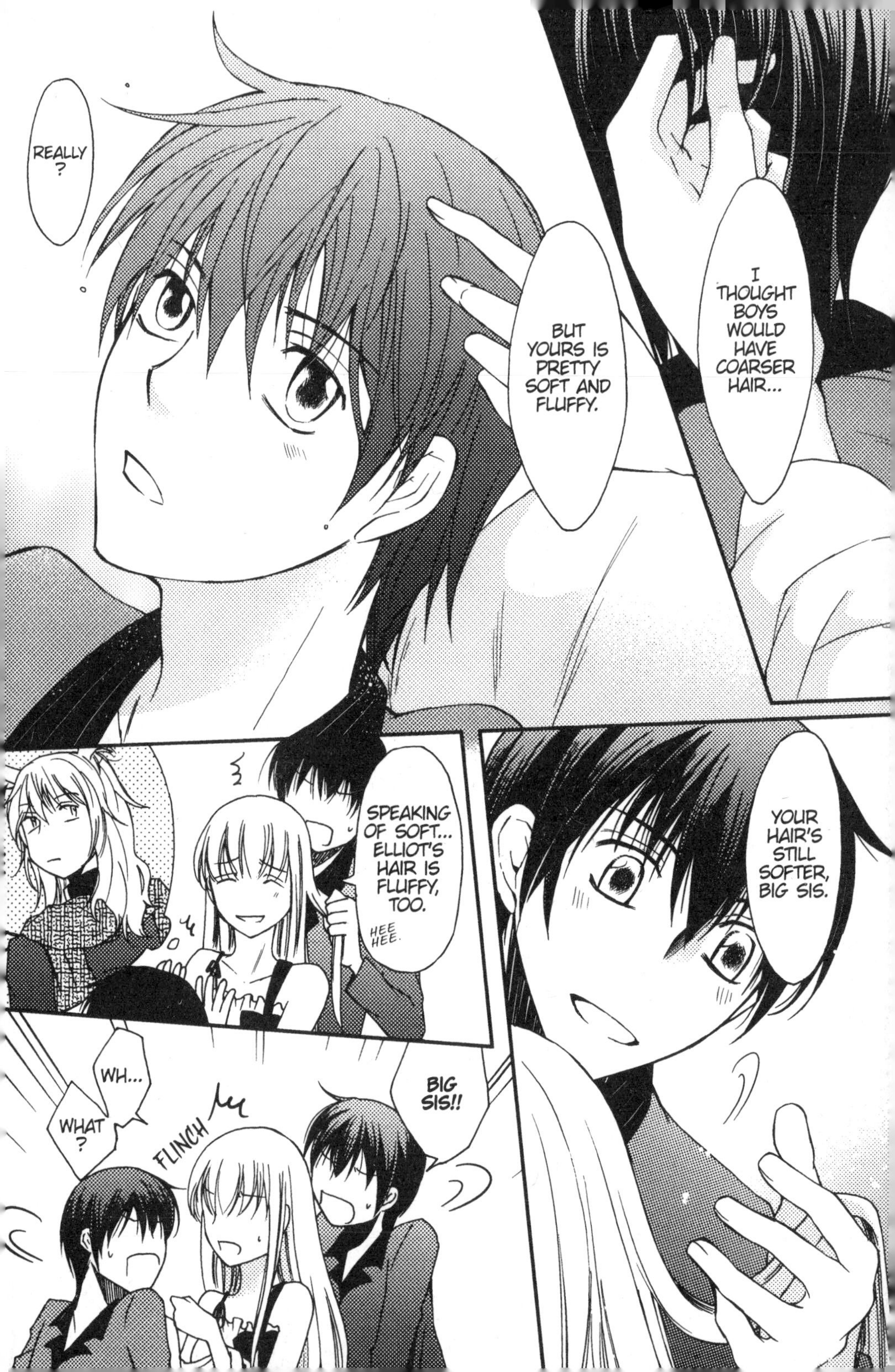
I THOUGHT BOYS WOULD HAVE COARSER HAIR...
BUT YOURS IS PRETTY SOFT AND FLUFFY.
REALLY?
YOUR HAIR'S STILL SOFTER, BIG SIS.
SPEAKING OF SOFT... ELLIOT'S HAIR IS FLUFFY, TOO.
HEE HEE.
BIG SIS!!
FLINCH
WH... WHAT?

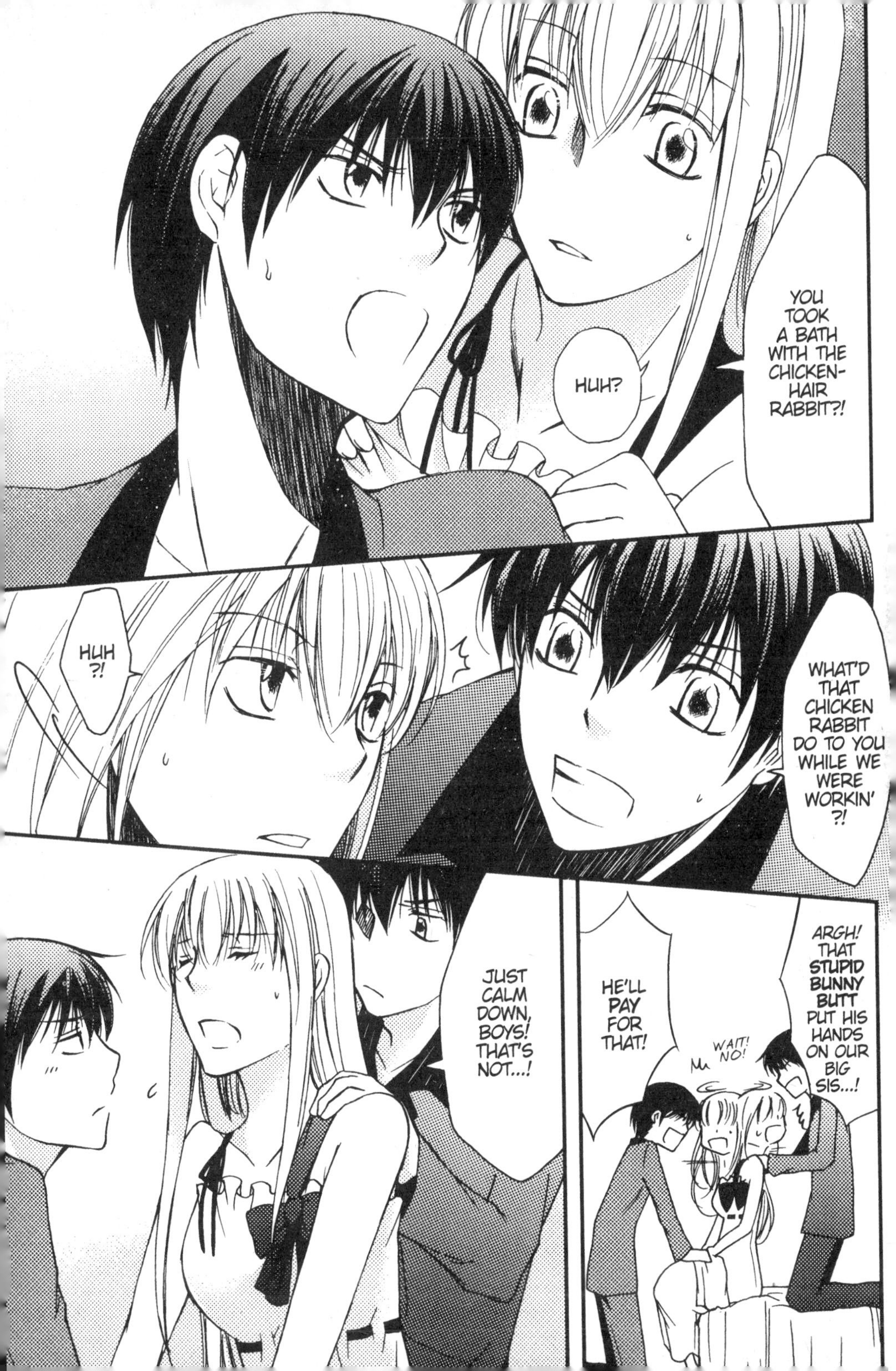
YOU TOOK A BATH WITH THE CHICKEN-HAIR RABBIT?!
HUH?
WHAT'D THAT CHICKEN RABBIT DO TO YOU WHILE WE WERE WORKIN'?!
HUH?!
ARGH! THAT **STUPID BUNNY BUTT** PUT HIS HANDS ON OUR BIG SIS...!
HE'LL **PAY** FOR THAT!
WAIT! NO!
JUST CALM DOWN, BOYS! THAT'S NOT...!

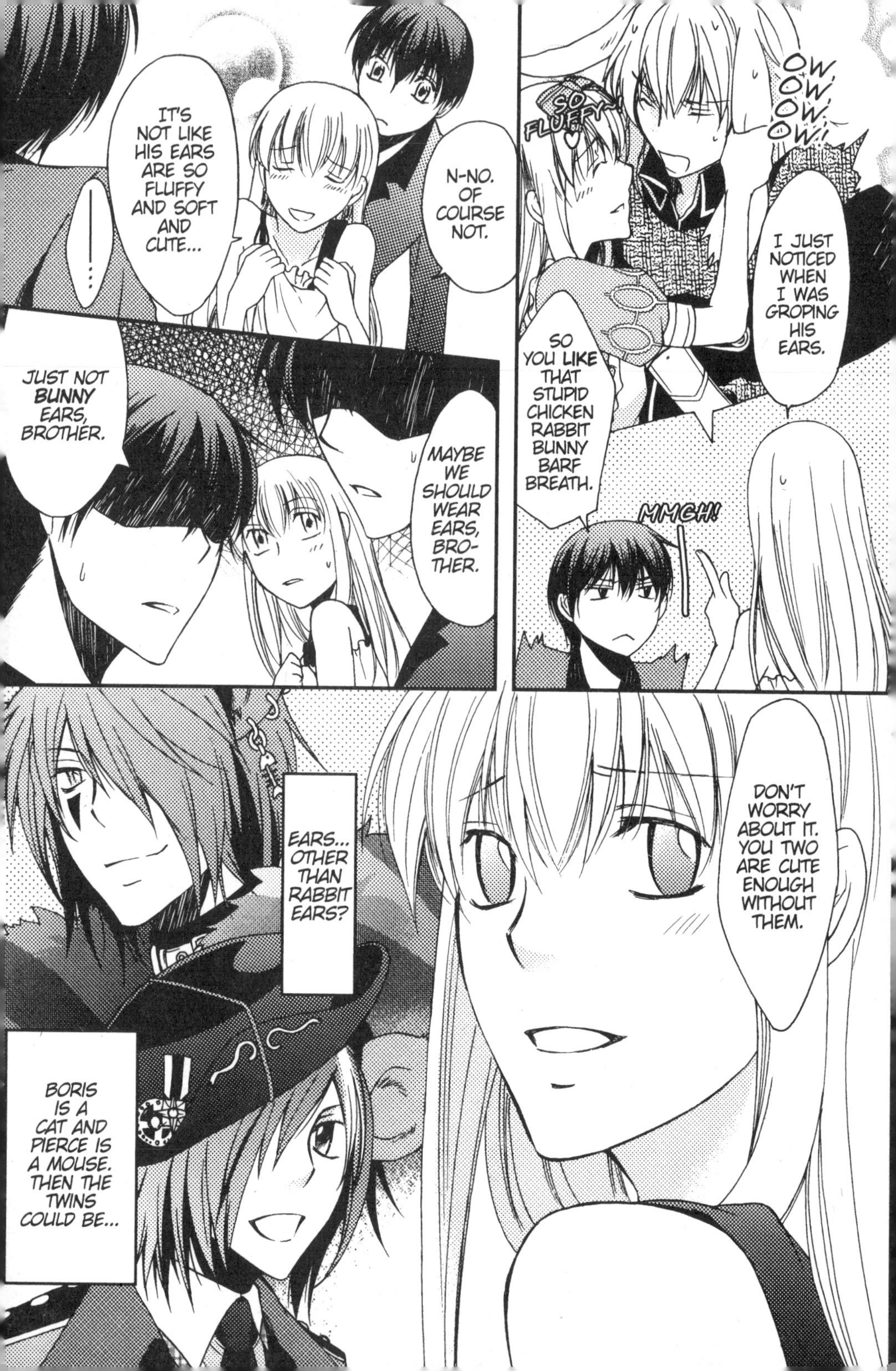
OW, OW, OW, OW!
SO FLUFFY~ ♥
I JUST NOTICED WHEN I WAS GROPING HIS EARS.
SO YOU LIKE THAT STUPID CHICKEN RABBIT BUNNY BARF BREATH.
MMGH!
IT'S NOT LIKE HIS EARS ARE SO FLUFFY AND SOFT AND CUTE...
N-NO. OF COURSE NOT.
...!...
MAYBE WE SHOULD WEAR EARS, BROTHER.
JUST NOT BUNNY EARS, BROTHER.
DON'T WORRY ABOUT IT. YOU TWO ARE CUTE ENOUGH WITHOUT THEM.
EARS... OTHER THAN RABBIT EARS?
BORIS IS A CAT AND PIERCE IS A MOUSE. THEN THE TWINS COULD BE...

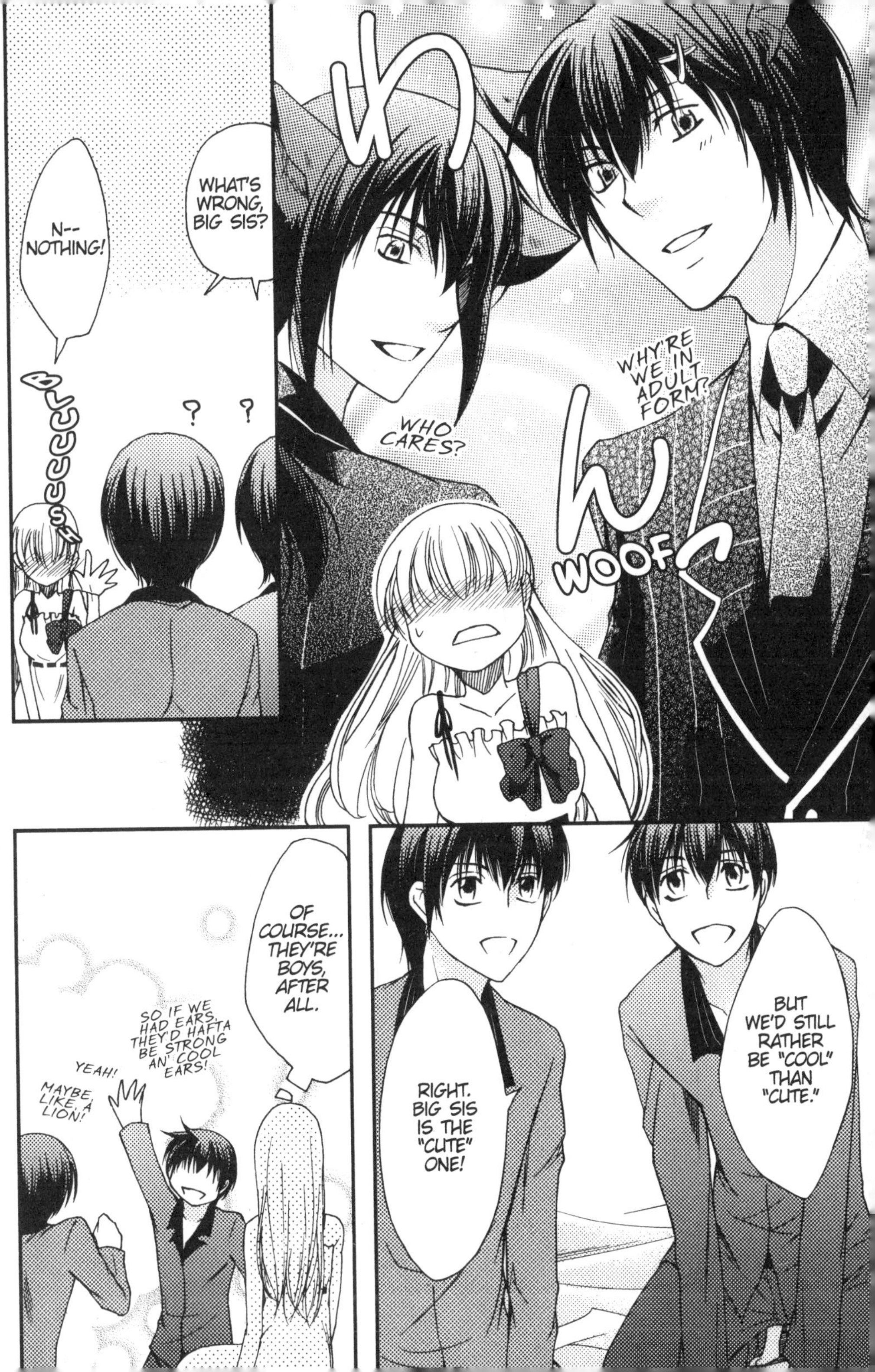
わん
WHY'RE WE IN ADULT FORM?
WHO CARES?
WOOF
WHAT'S WRONG, BIG SIS?
N-- NOTHING!
BLUUUUSH
RIGHT. BIG SIS IS THE "CUTE" ONE!
BUT WE'D STILL RATHER BE "COOL" THAN "CUTE."
OF COURSE... THEY'RE BOYS, AFTER ALL.
SO IF WE HAD EARS, THEY'D HAFTA BE STRONG AN' COOL EARS!
YEAH!
MAYBE, LIKE A LION!

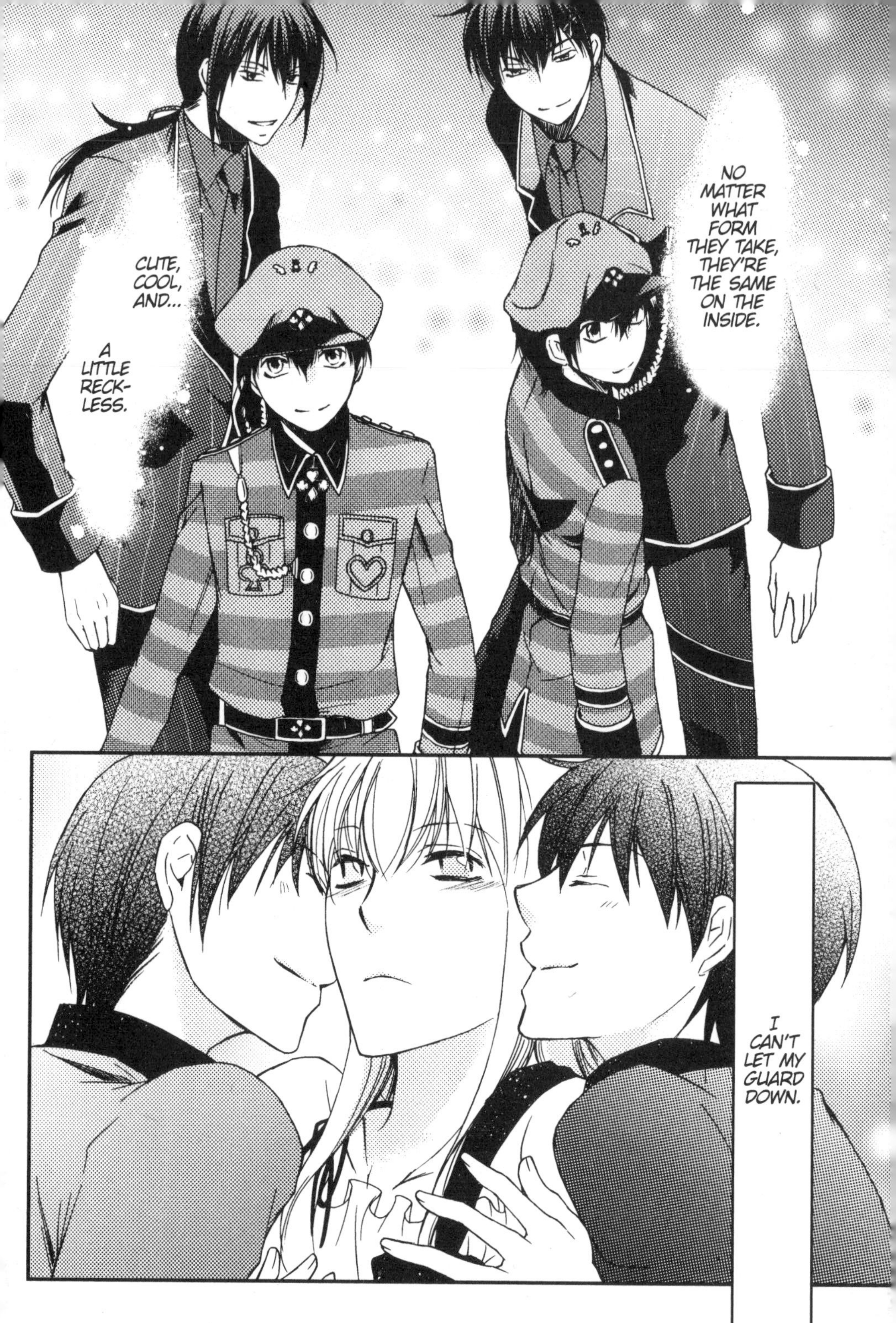
NO MATTER WHAT FORM THEY TAKE, THEY'RE THE SAME ON THE INSIDE.
CUTE, COOL, AND...
A LITTLE RECK-LESS.
I CAN'T LET MY GUARD DOWN.

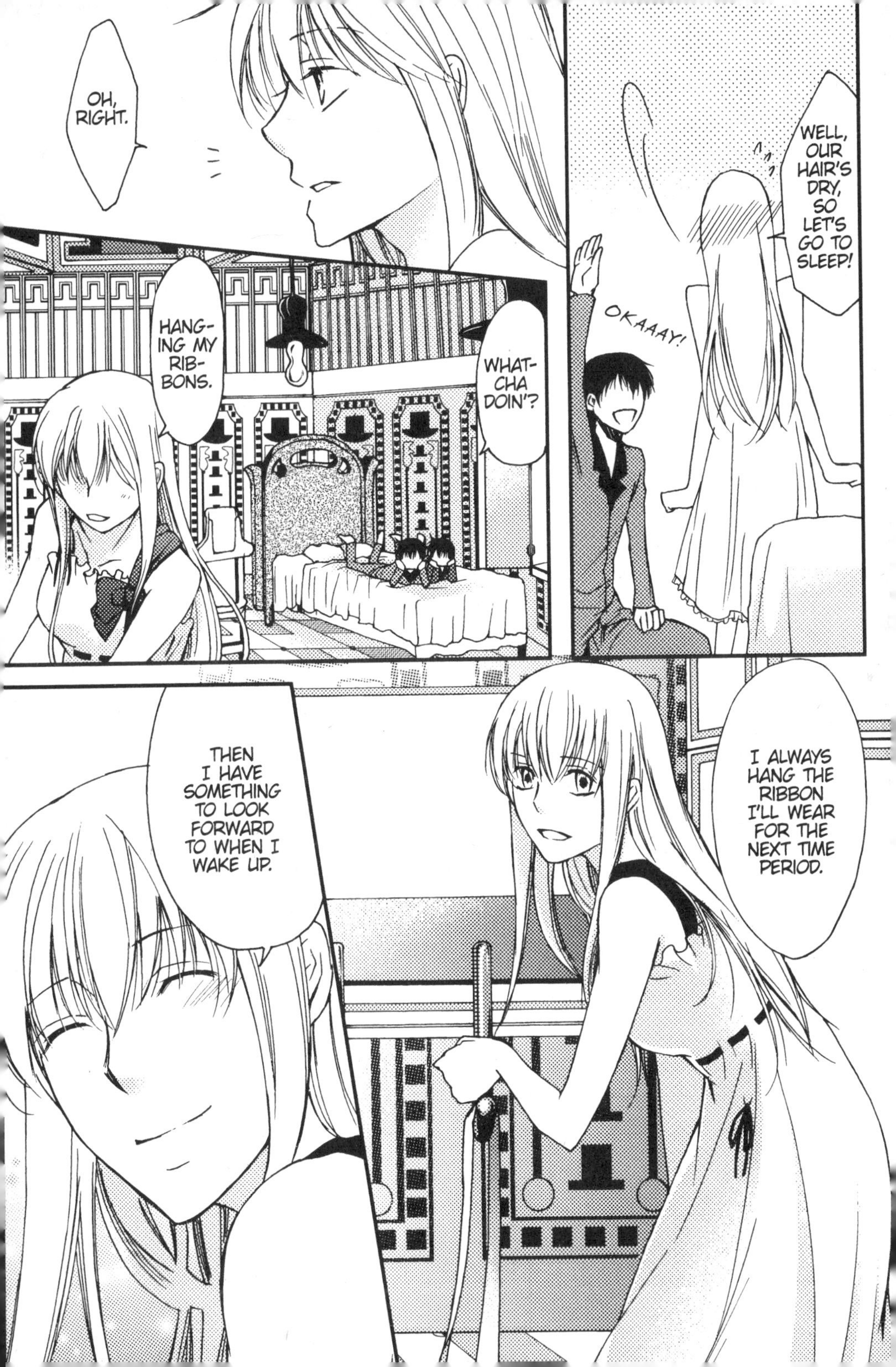

WELL, OUR HAIR'S DRY, SO LET'S GO TO SLEEP!
OKAAAY!
OH, RIGHT.
WHATCHA DOIN'?
HANGING MY RIBBONS.
I ALWAYS HANG THE RIBBON I'LL WEAR FOR THE NEXT TIME PERIOD.
THEN I HAVE SOMETHING TO LOOK FORWARD TO WHEN I WAKE UP.

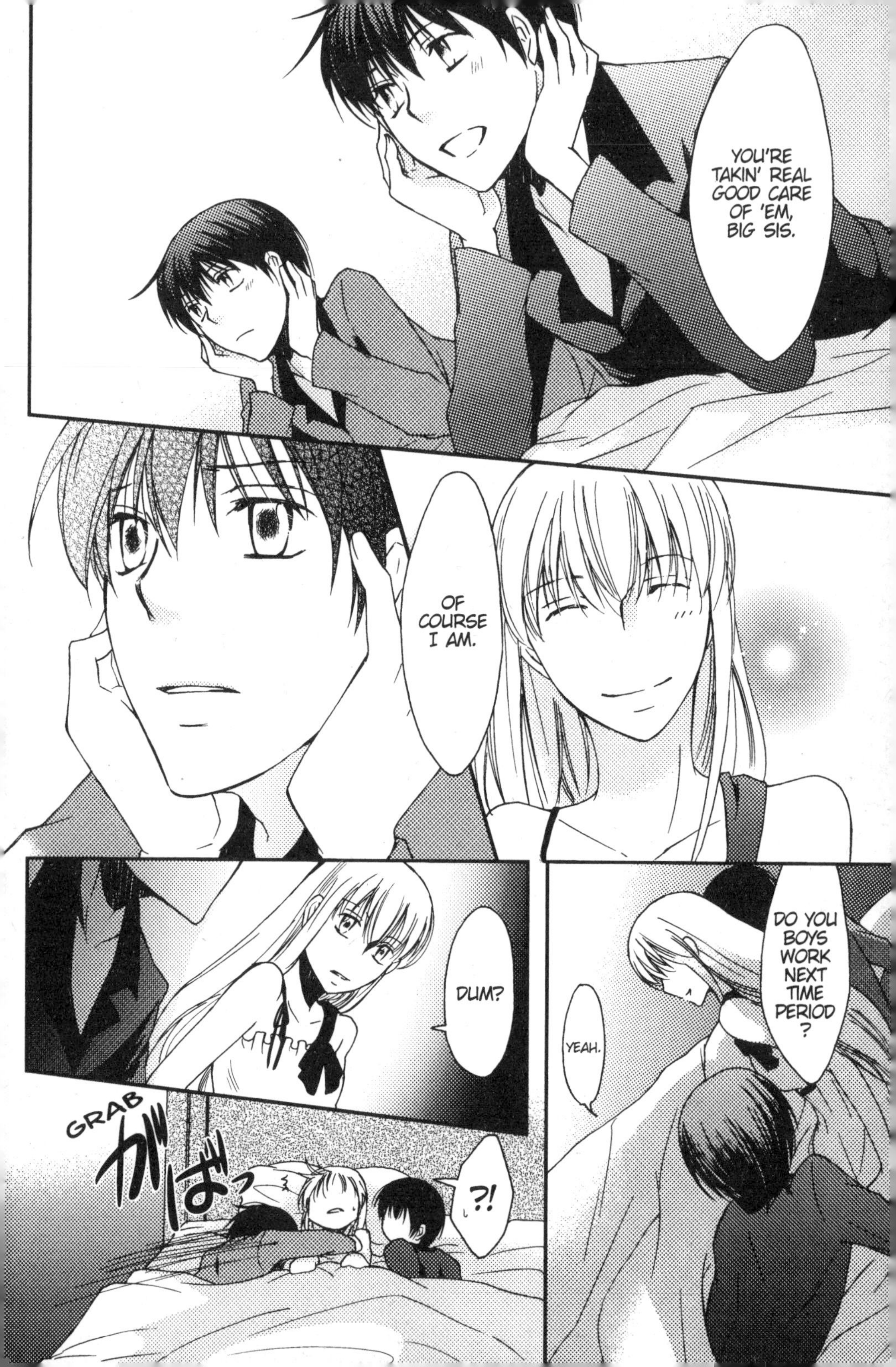
YOU'RE TAKIN' REAL GOOD CARE OF 'EM, BIG SIS.
OF COURSE I AM.
DO YOU BOYS WORK NEXT TIME PERIOD?
YEAH.
DUM?
GRAB
がばっ
?!

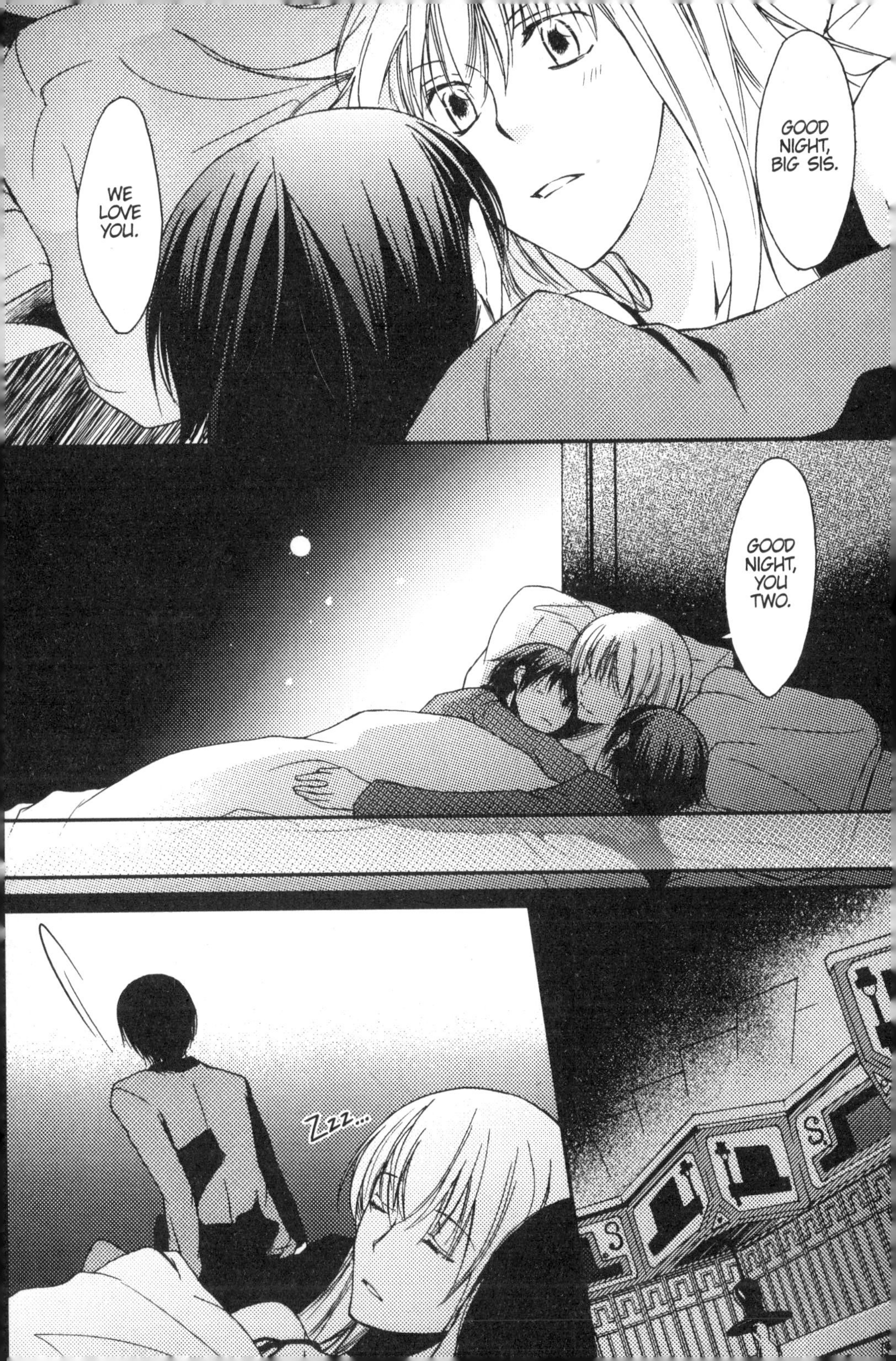
GOOD NIGHT, BIG SIS.
WE LOVE YOU.
GOOD NIGHT, YOU TWO.
Zzz...

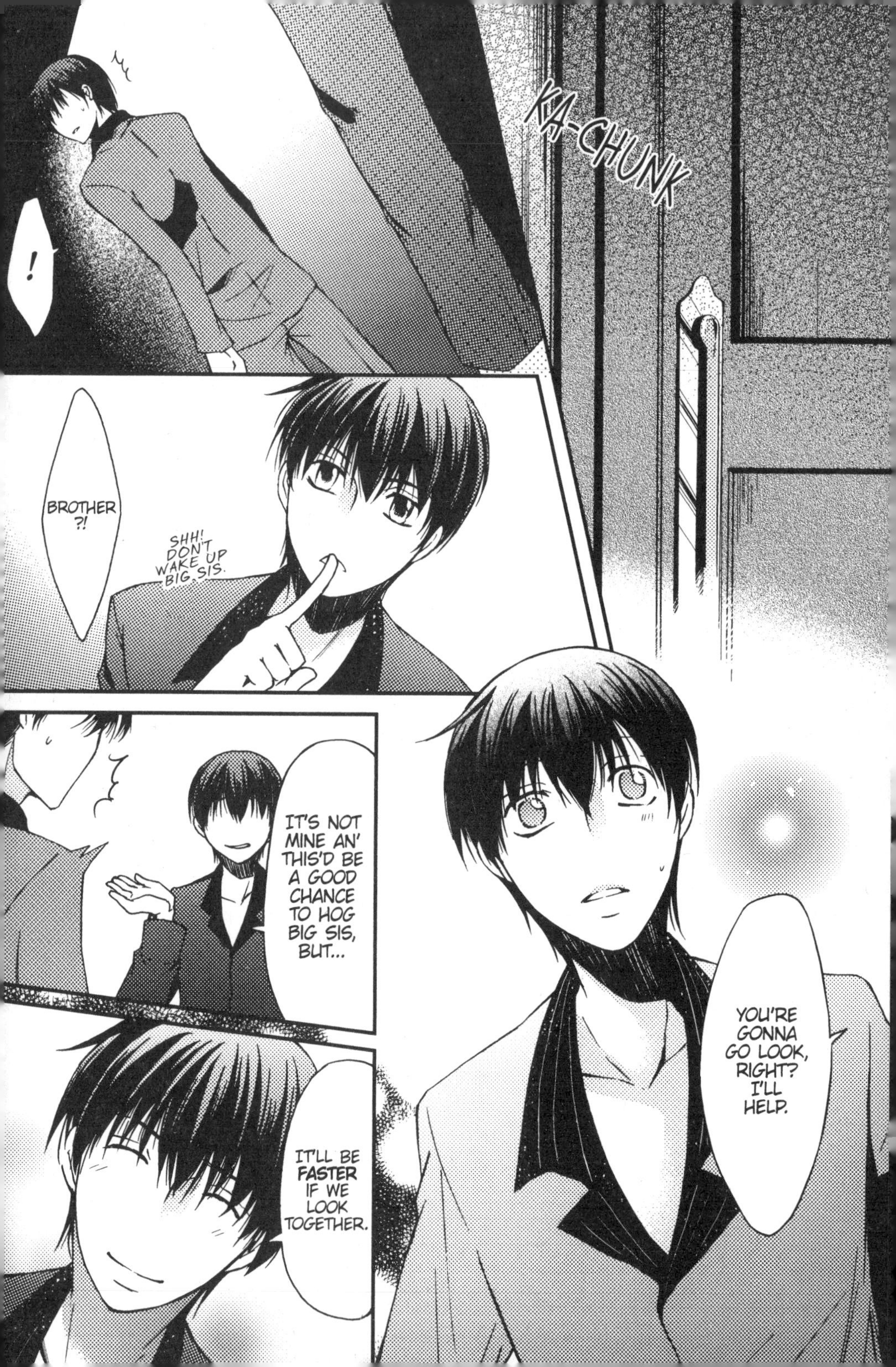
KA-CHUNK
!
BROTHER ?!
SHH! DON'T WAKE UP BIG SIS.
YOU'RE GONNA GO LOOK, RIGHT? I'LL HELP.
IT'S NOT MINE AN' THIS'D BE A GOOD CHANCE TO HOG BIG SIS, BUT...
IT'LL BE **FASTER** IF WE LOOK TOGETHER.

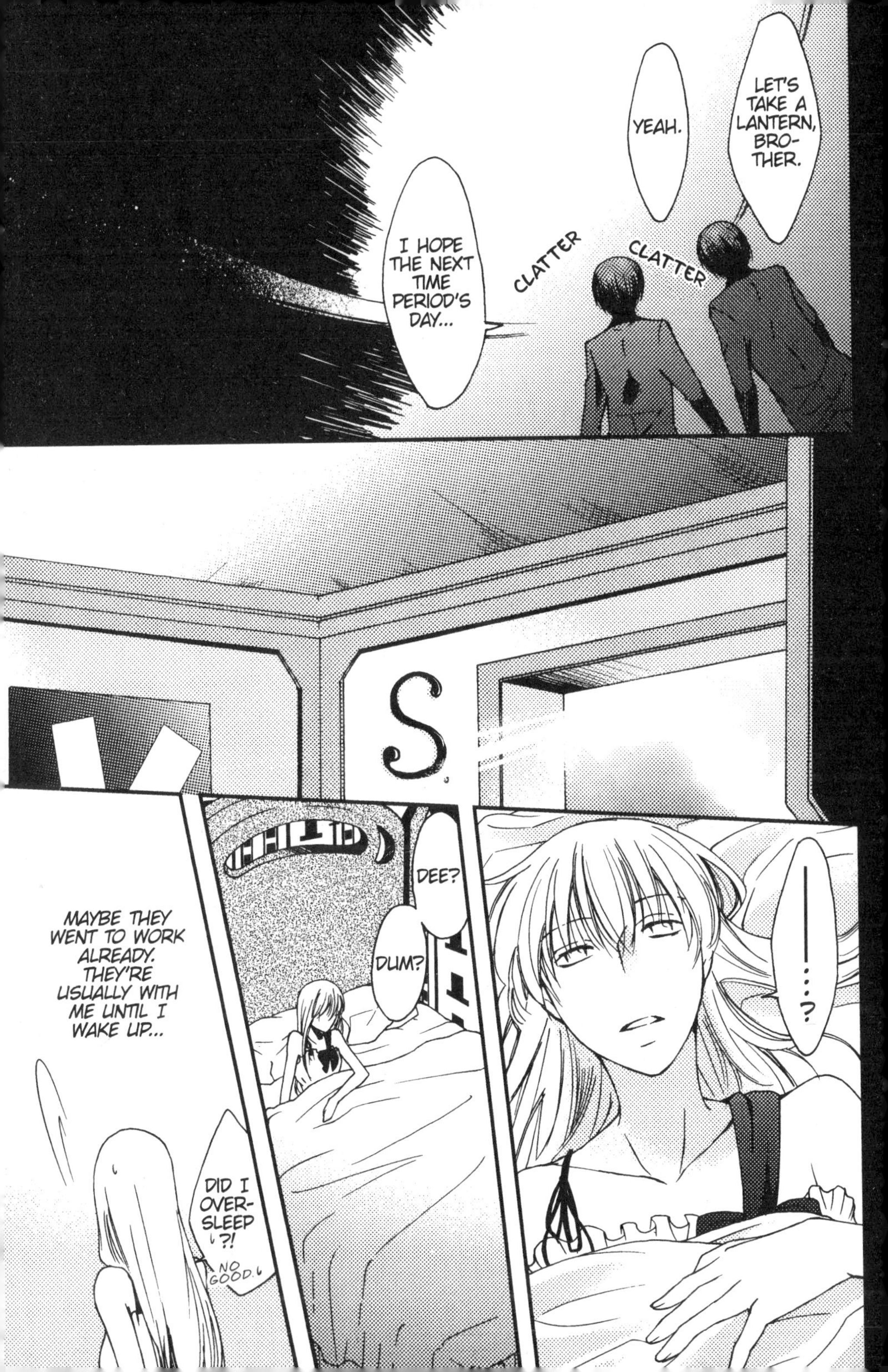

LET'S TAKE A LANTERN, BRO- THER.
YEAH.
CLATTER
CLATTER
I HOPE THE NEXT TIME PERIOD'S DAY...
——...?
DEE?
DUM?
MAYBE THEY WENT TO WORK ALREADY. THEY'RE USUALLY WITH ME UNTIL I WAKE UP...
DID I OVER- SLEEP ?!
NO GOOD.

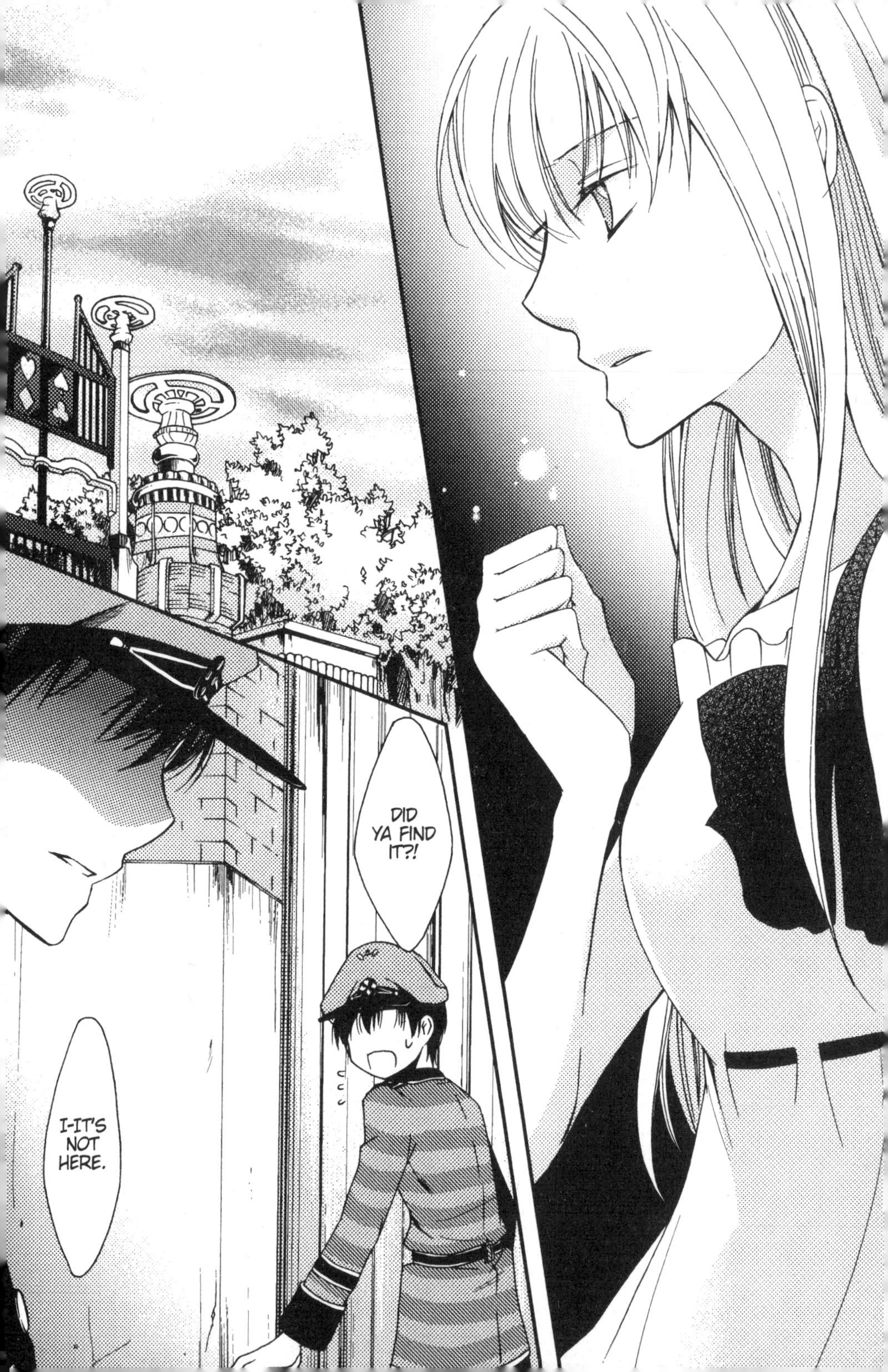
DID YA FIND IT?!
I-IT'S NOT HERE.

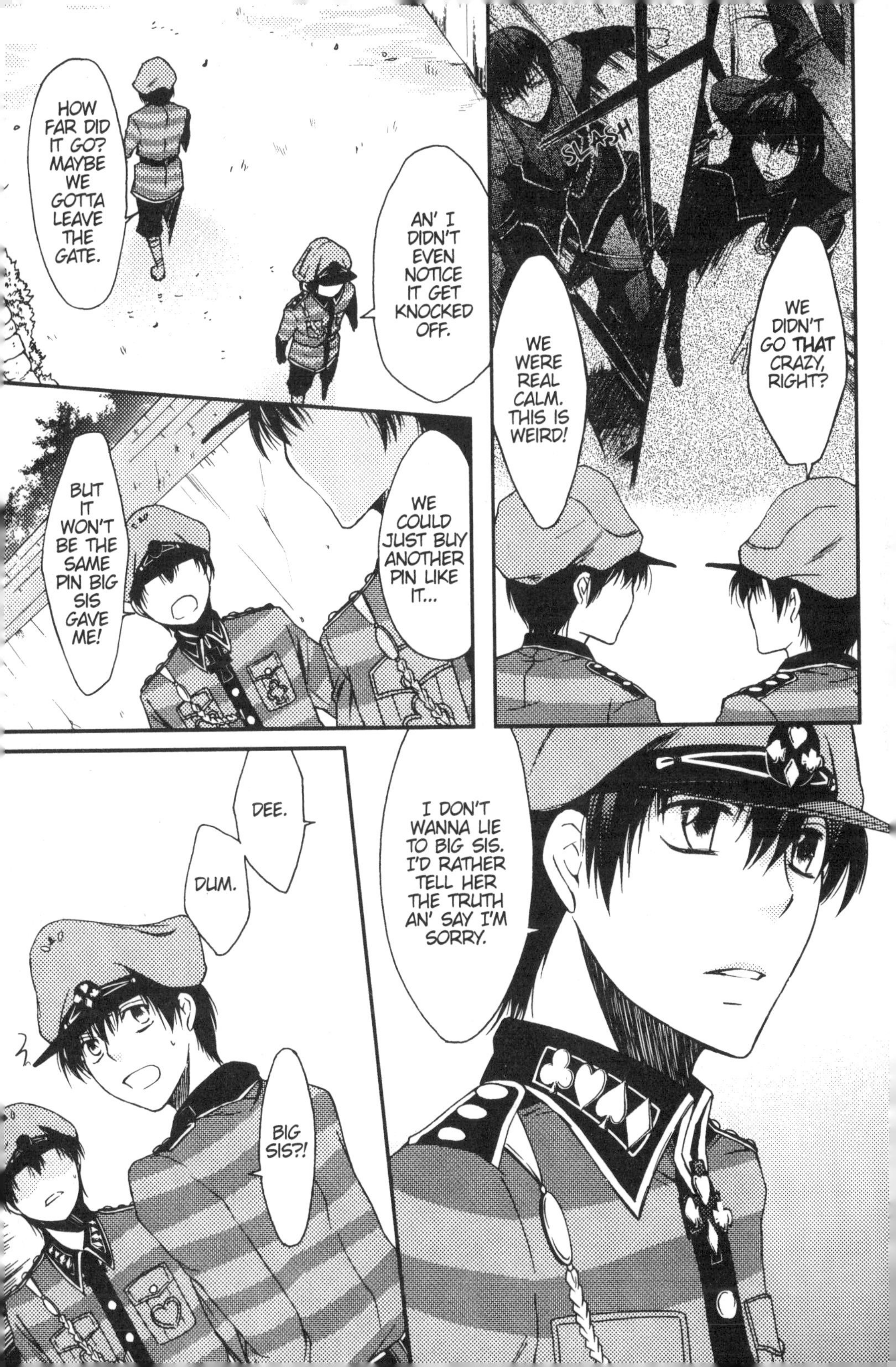
SLASH
WE DIDN'T GO THAT CRAZY, RIGHT?
WE WERE REAL CALM. THIS IS WEIRD!
AN' I DIDN'T EVEN NOTICE IT GET KNOCKED OFF.
HOW FAR DID IT GO? MAYBE WE GOTTA LEAVE THE GATE.
WE COULD JUST BUY ANOTHER PIN LIKE IT...
BUT IT WON'T BE THE SAME PIN BIG SIS GAVE ME!
I DON'T WANNA LIE TO BIG SIS. I'D RATHER TELL HER THE TRUTH AN' SAY I'M SORRY.
DEE.
DUM.
BIG SIS?!

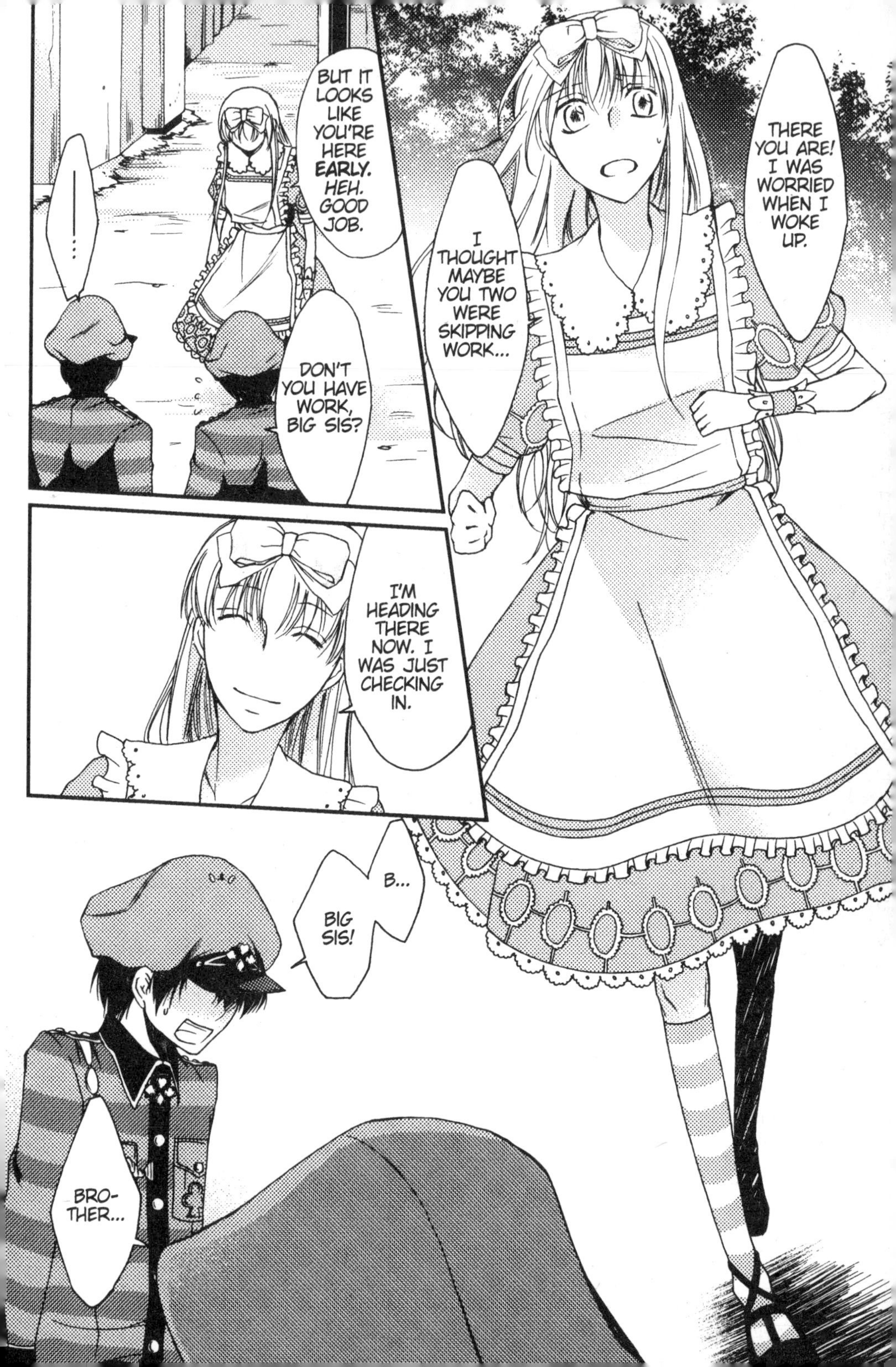
THERE YOU ARE! I WAS WORRIED WHEN I WOKE UP.
I THOUGHT MAYBE YOU TWO WERE SKIPPING WORK...
BUT IT LOOKS LIKE YOU'RE HERE **EARLY.** HEH. GOOD JOB.
—...
DON'T YOU HAVE WORK, BIG SIS?
I'M HEADING THERE NOW. I WAS JUST CHECKING IN.
B...
BIG SIS!
BRO-THER...

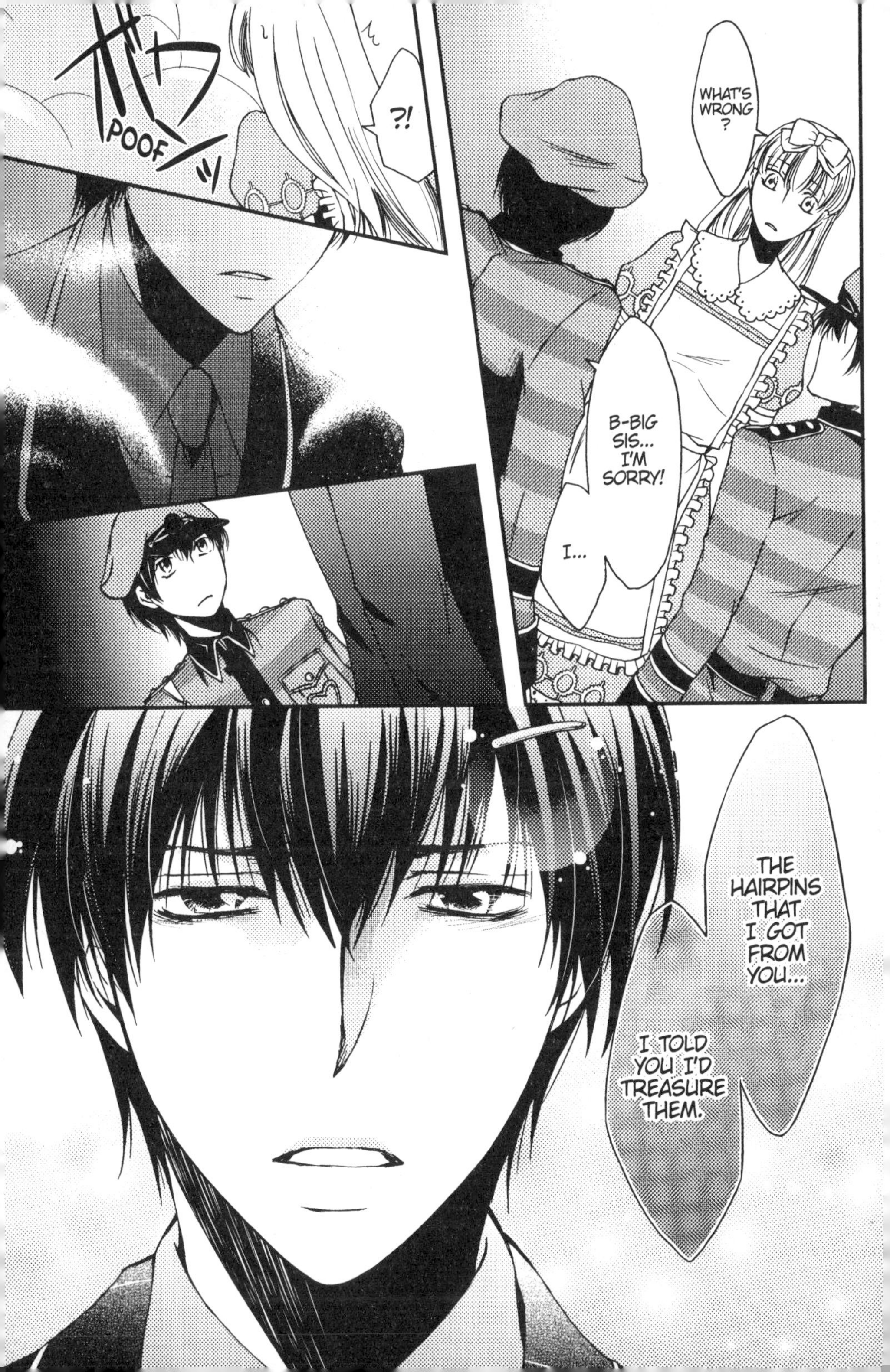

WHAT'S WRONG?
B-BIG SIS... I'M SORRY!
I...
POOF
?!
THE HAIRPINS THAT I GOT FROM YOU...
I TOLD YOU I'D TREASURE THEM.

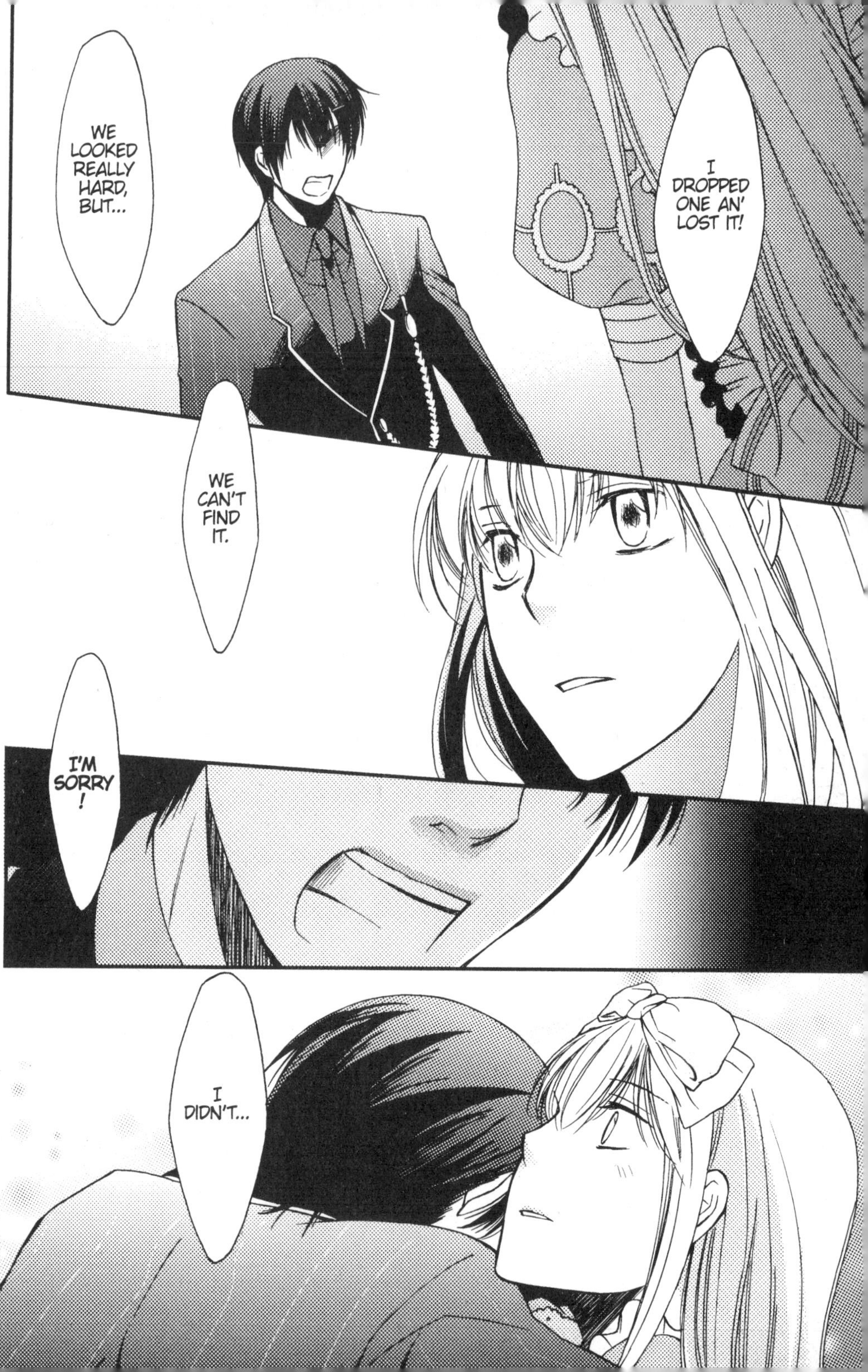
I DROPPED ONE AN' LOST IT!
WE LOOKED REALLY HARD, BUT...
WE CAN'T FIND IT.
I'M SORRY!
I DIDN'T...

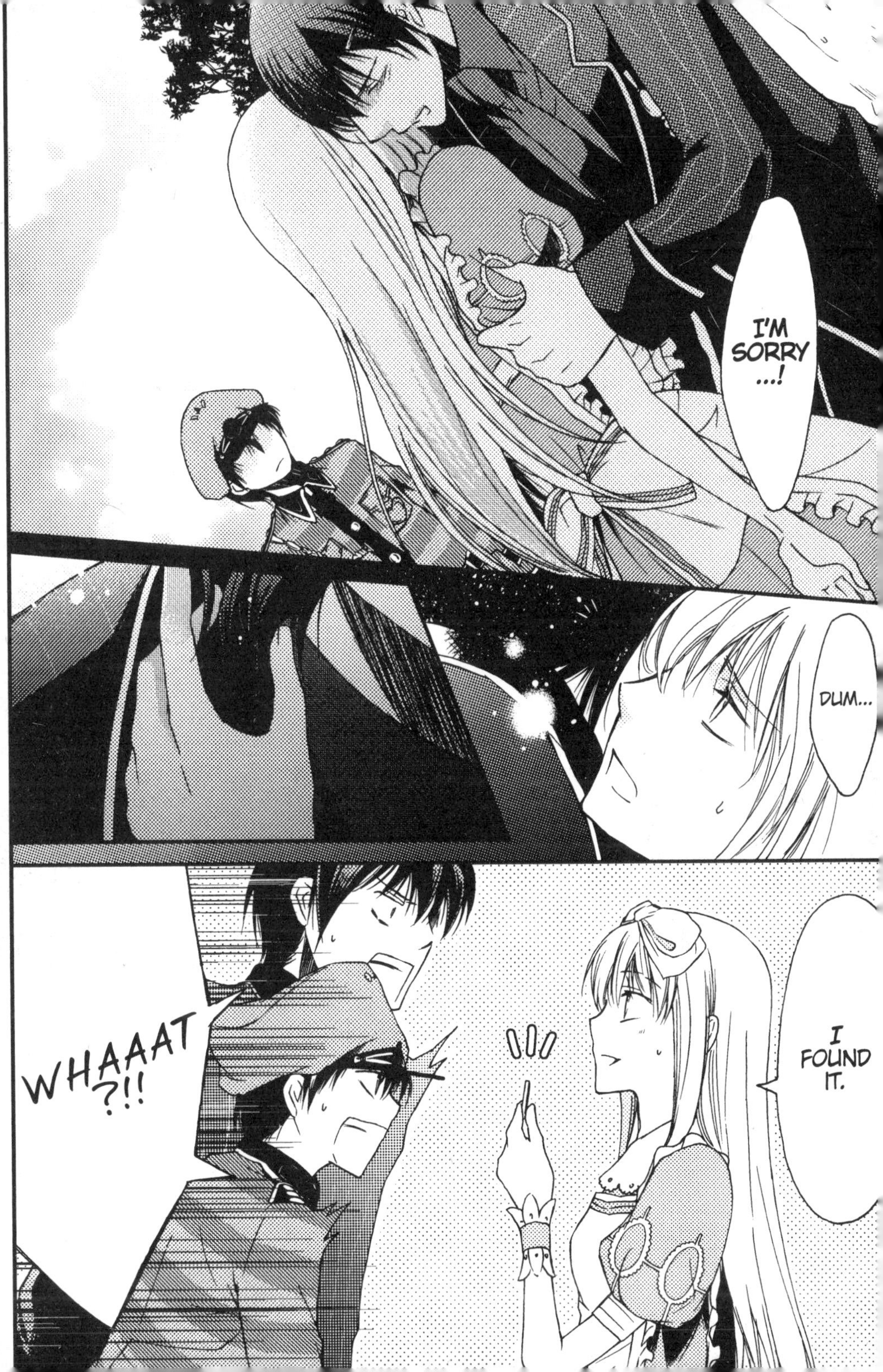
I'M SORRY ...!
UM...
I FOUND IT.
!!!
WHAAAT ?!!

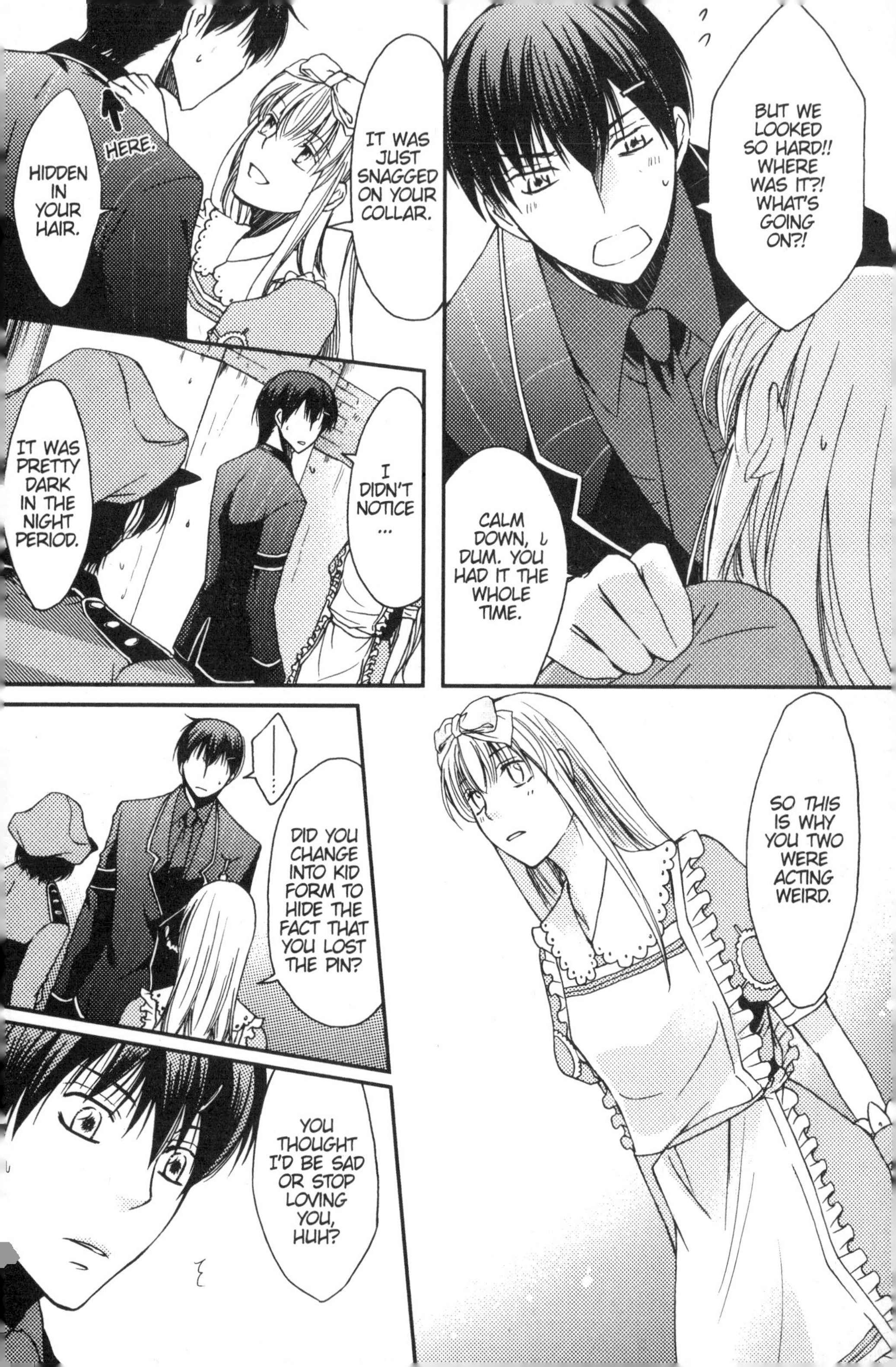
BUT WE LOOKED SO HARD!! WHERE WAS IT?! WHAT'S GOING ON?!
CALM DOWN, DUM. YOU HAD IT THE WHOLE TIME.
IT WAS JUST SNAGGED ON YOUR COLLAR.
HIDDEN IN YOUR HAIR.
HERE.
I DIDN'T NOTICE ...
IT WAS PRETTY DARK IN THE NIGHT PERIOD.
SO THIS IS WHY YOU TWO WERE ACTING WEIRD.
...!
DID YOU CHANGE INTO KID FORM TO HIDE THE FACT THAT YOU LOST THE PIN?
YOU THOUGHT I'D BE SAD OR STOP LOVING YOU, HUH?

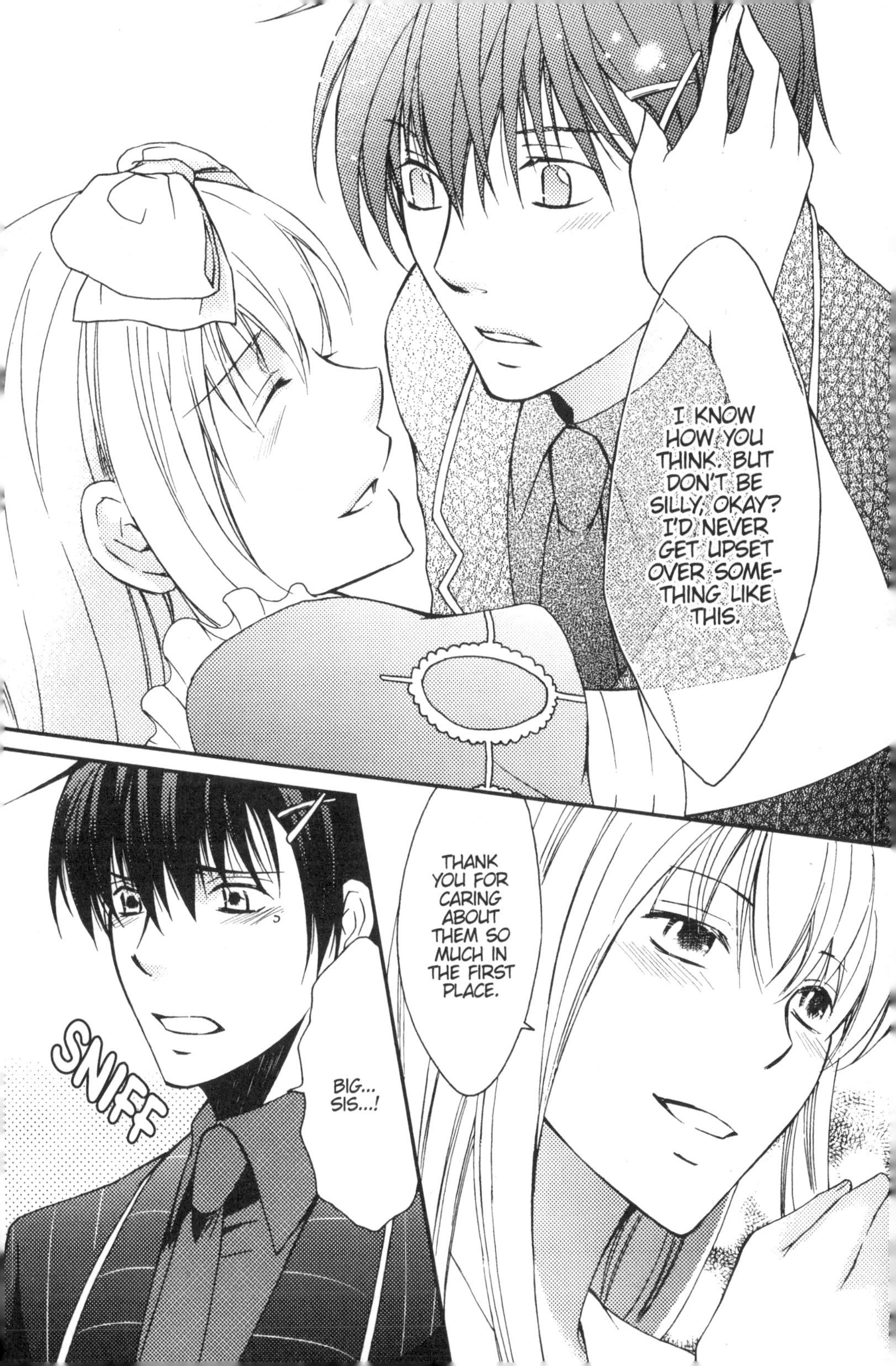
I KNOW HOW YOU THINK. BUT DON'T BE SILLY, OKAY? I'D NEVER GET UPSET OVER SOME-THING LIKE THIS.
THANK YOU FOR CARING ABOUT THEM SO MUCH IN THE FIRST PLACE.
BIG... SIS...!
SNIFF

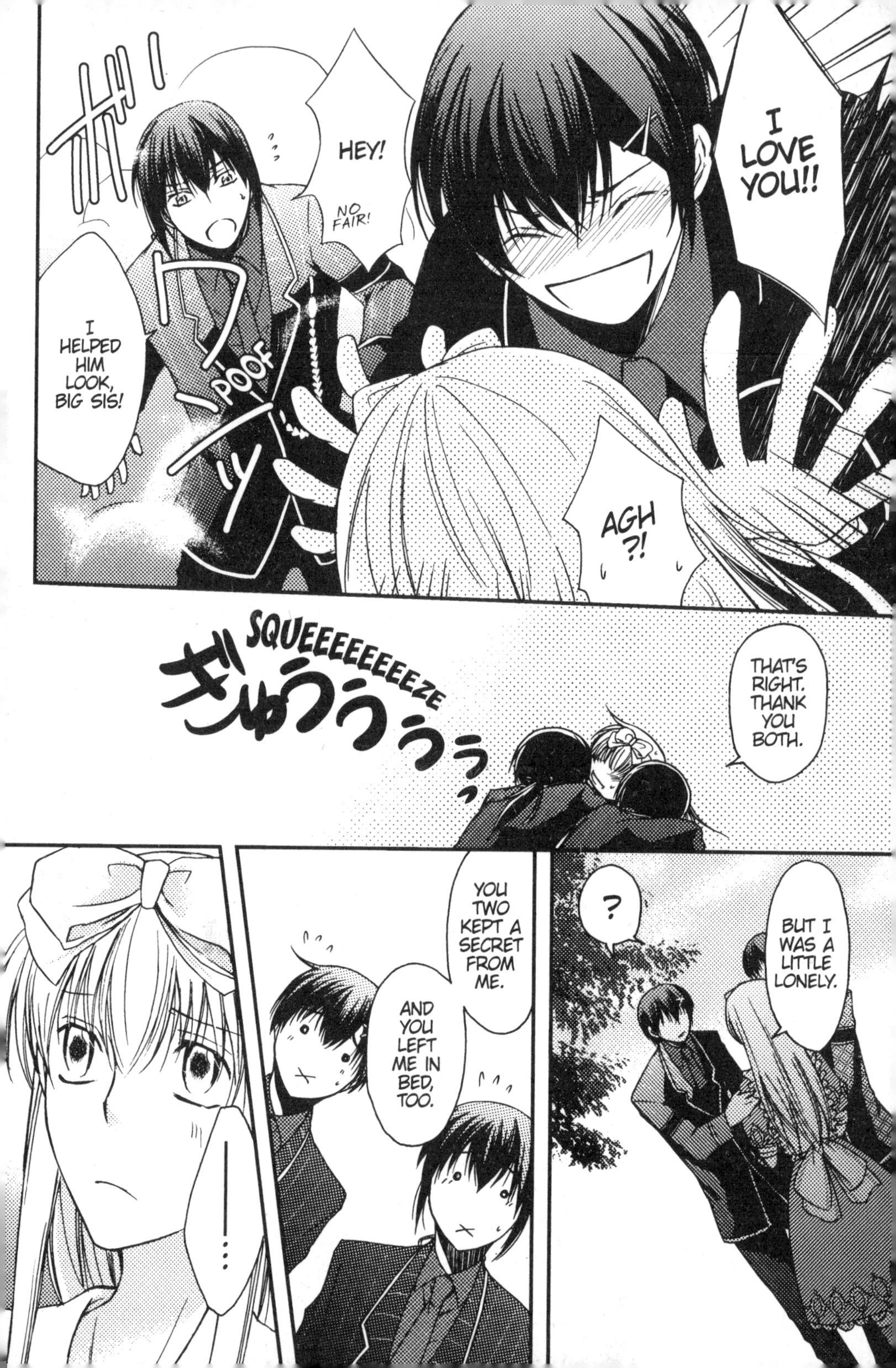
I LOVE YOU!!
AGH ?!
HEY!
NO FAIR!
POOF
I HELPED HIM LOOK, BIG SIS!
THAT'S RIGHT. THANK YOU BOTH.
SQUEEEEEEEEEZE
BUT I WAS A LITTLE LONELY.
?
YOU TWO KEPT A SECRET FROM ME.
AND YOU LEFT ME IN BED, TOO.
......

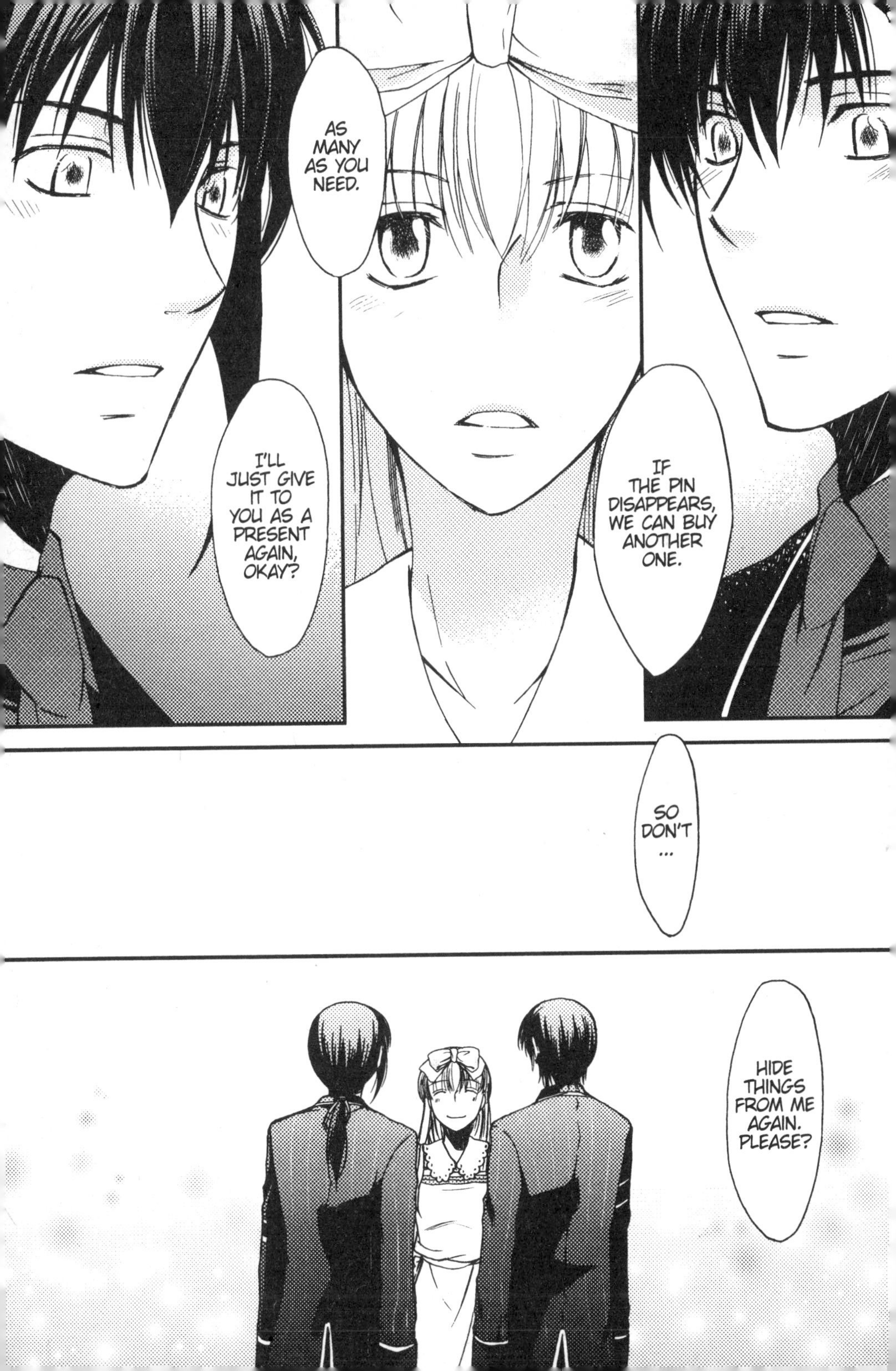
IF THE PIN DISAPPEARS, WE CAN BUY ANOTHER ONE.
AS MANY AS YOU NEED.
I'LL JUST GIVE IT TO YOU AS A PRESENT AGAIN, OKAY?
SO DON'T ...
HIDE THINGS FROM ME AGAIN. PLEASE?

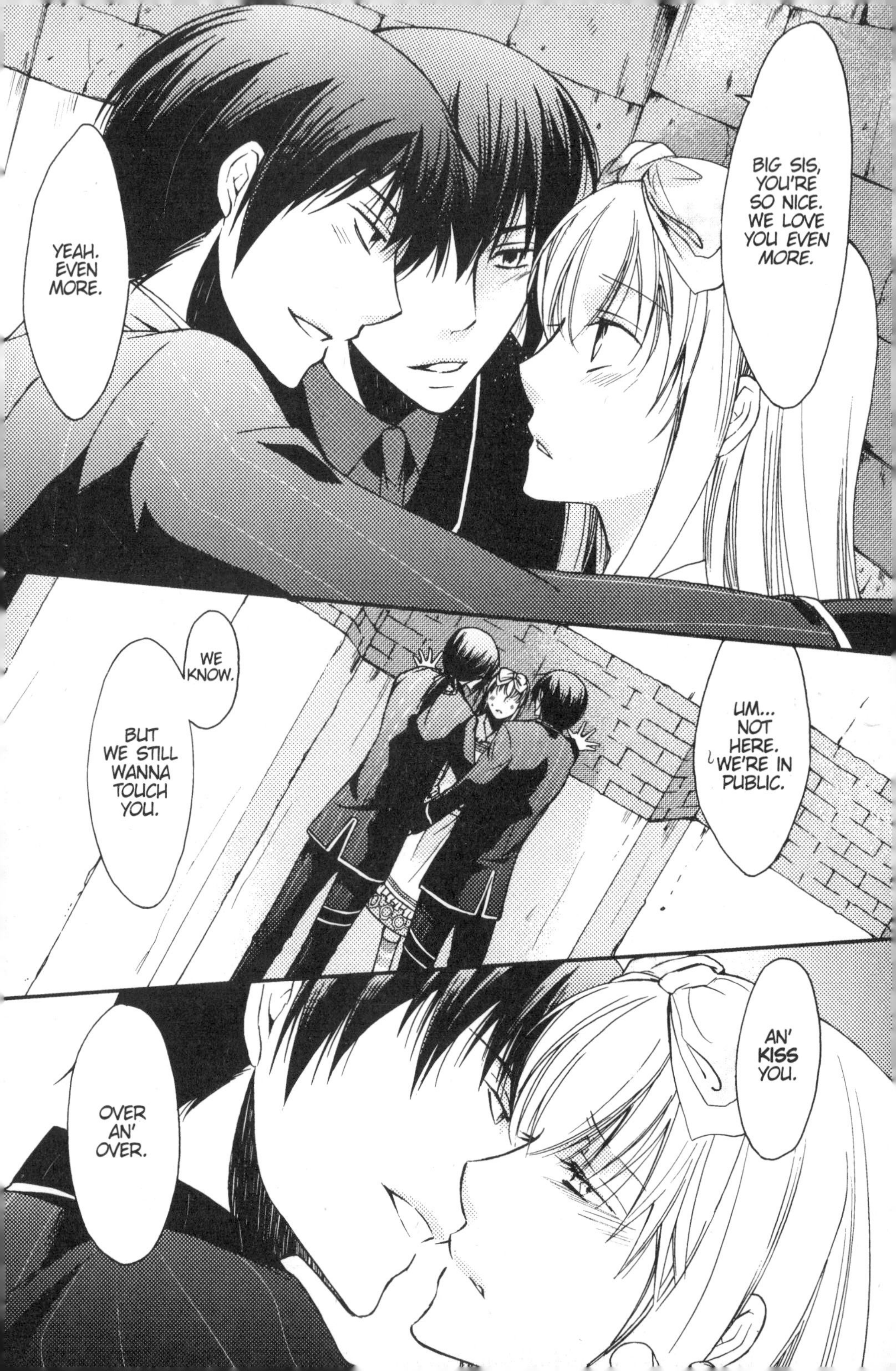
BIG SIS, YOU'RE SO NICE. WE LOVE YOU EVEN MORE.
YEAH. EVEN MORE.
UM... NOT HERE. WE'RE IN PUBLIC.
WE KNOW.
BUT WE STILL WANNA TOUCH YOU.
AN' KISS YOU.
OVER AN' OVER.

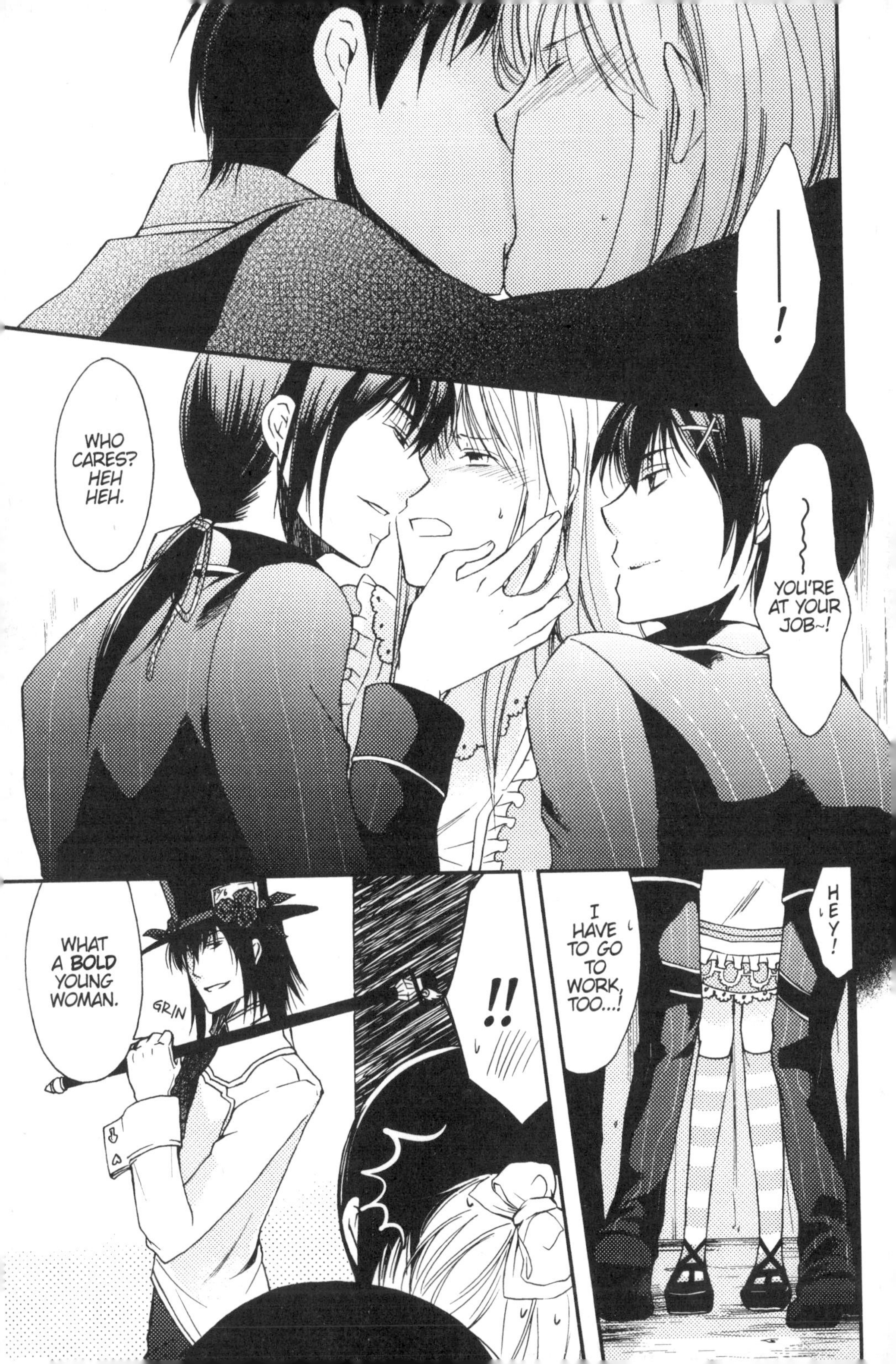
—!
YOU'RE AT YOUR JOB~!
WHO CARES? HEH HEH.
HEY!
I HAVE TO GO TO WORK, TOO...!
!!
WHAT A BOLD YOUNG WOMAN.
GRIN

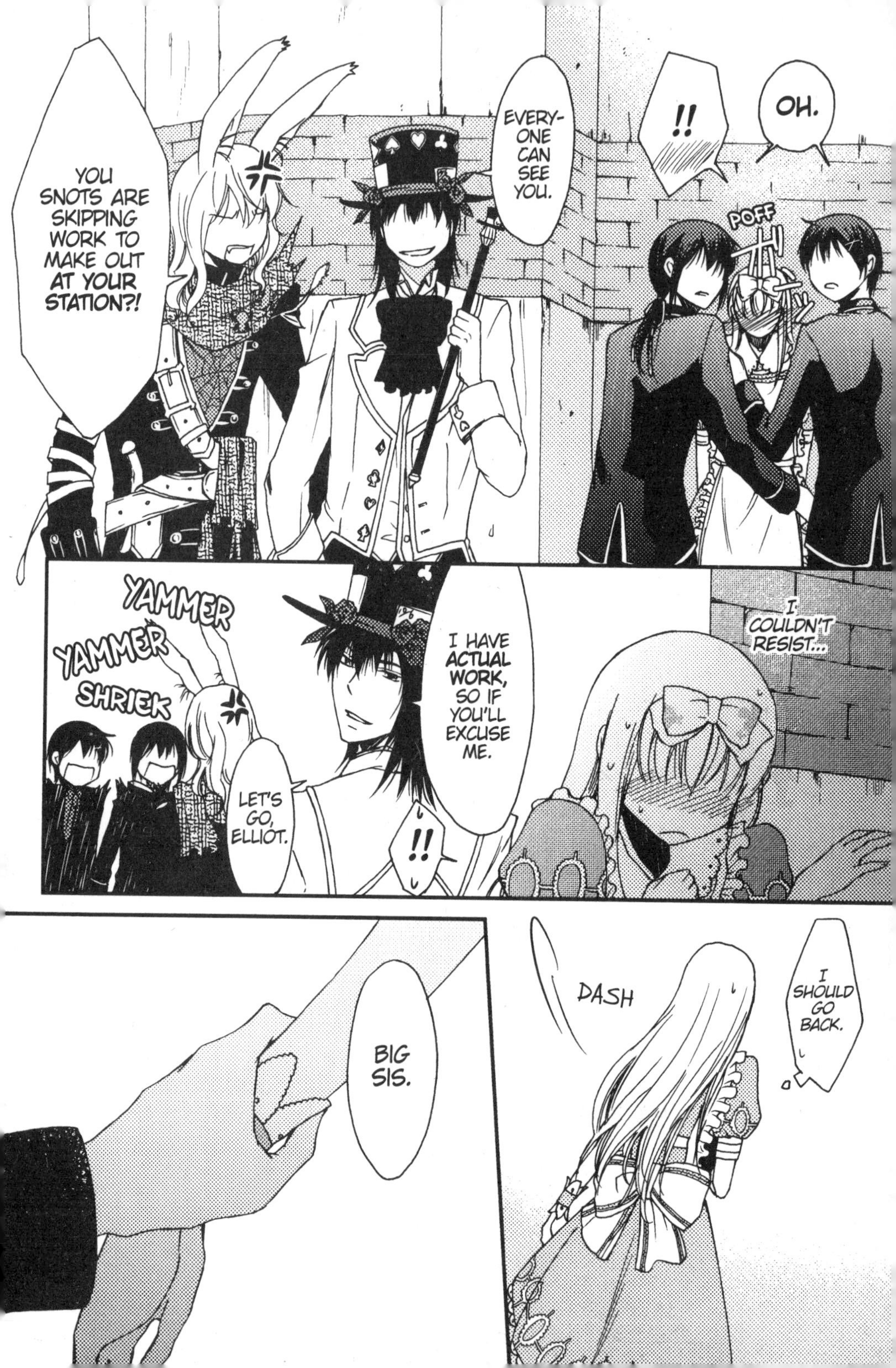

OH.
!!
POFF
EVERY-ONE CAN SEE YOU.
YOU SNOTS ARE SKIPPING WORK TO MAKE OUT AT YOUR STATION?!
I COULDN'T RESIST...
I HAVE ACTUAL WORK, SO IF YOU'LL EXCUSE ME.
LET'S GO, ELLIOT.
!!
YAMMER
YAMMER
SHRIEK
I SHOULD GO BACK.
DASH
BIG SIS.

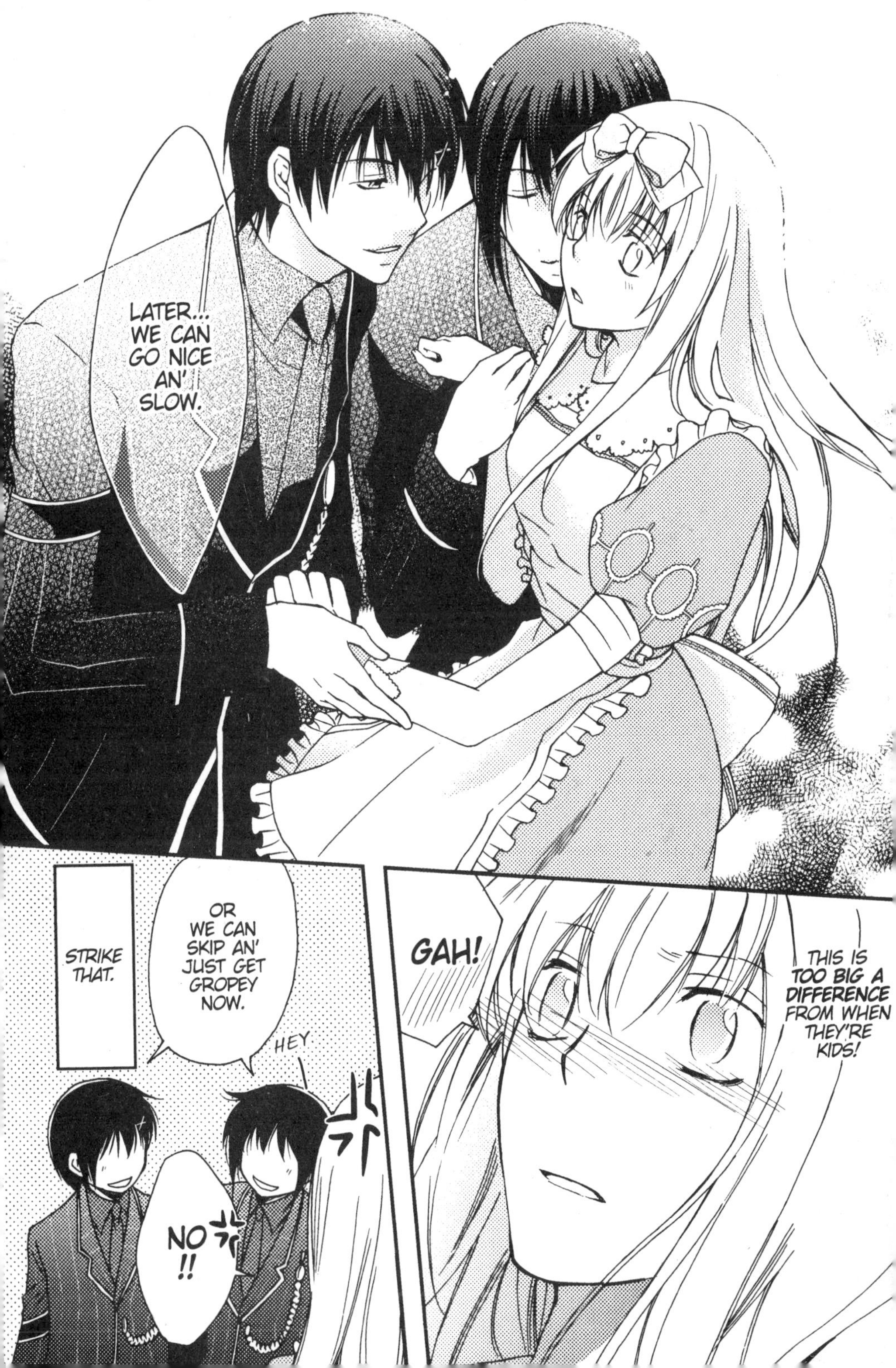
LATER... WE CAN GO NICE AN' SLOW.
THIS IS TOO BIG A DIFFERENCE FROM WHEN THEY'RE KIDS!
GAH!
OR WE CAN SKIP AN' JUST GET GROPEY NOW.
STRIKE THAT.
HEY
NO!!

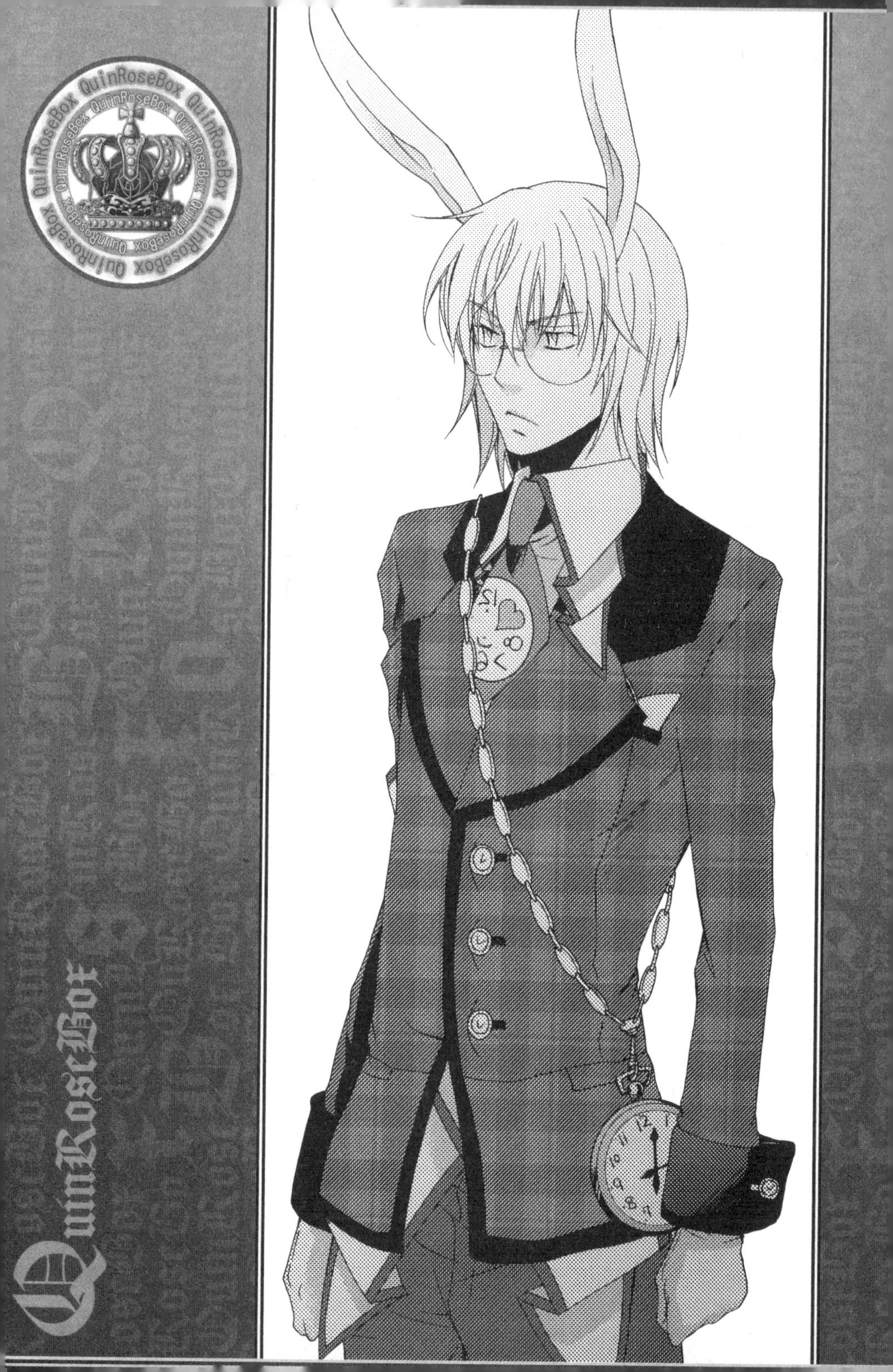
QuinRoseBox

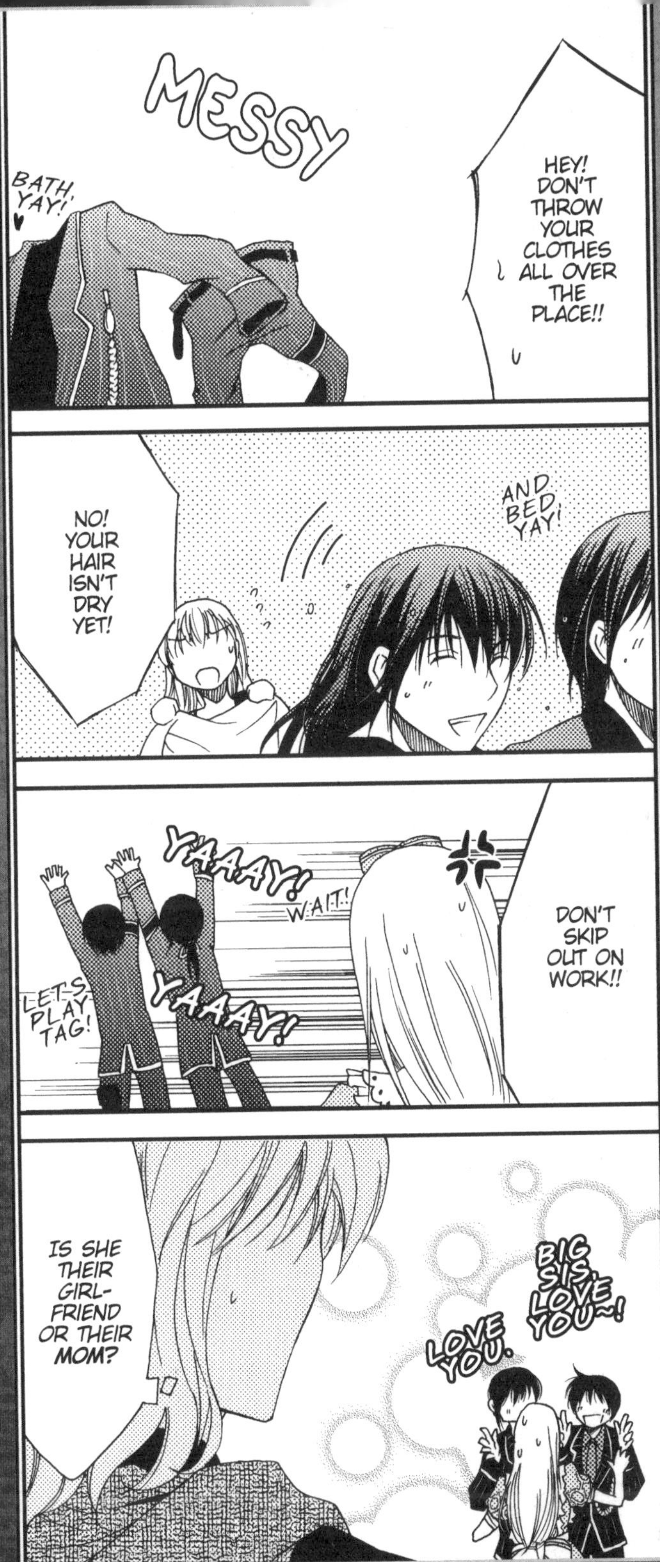
HEY! DON'T THROW YOUR CLOTHES ALL OVER THE PLACE!!
MESSY
BATH, YAY! ♥
AND BED, YAY!
NO! YOUR HAIR ISN'T DRY YET!
DON'T SKIP OUT ON WORK!!
YAAAY!
WAIT!
YAAAY!
LET'S PLAY TAG!
BIG SIS, LOVE YOU~!
LOVE YOU.
IS SHE THEIR GIRL-FRIEND OR THEIR MOM?

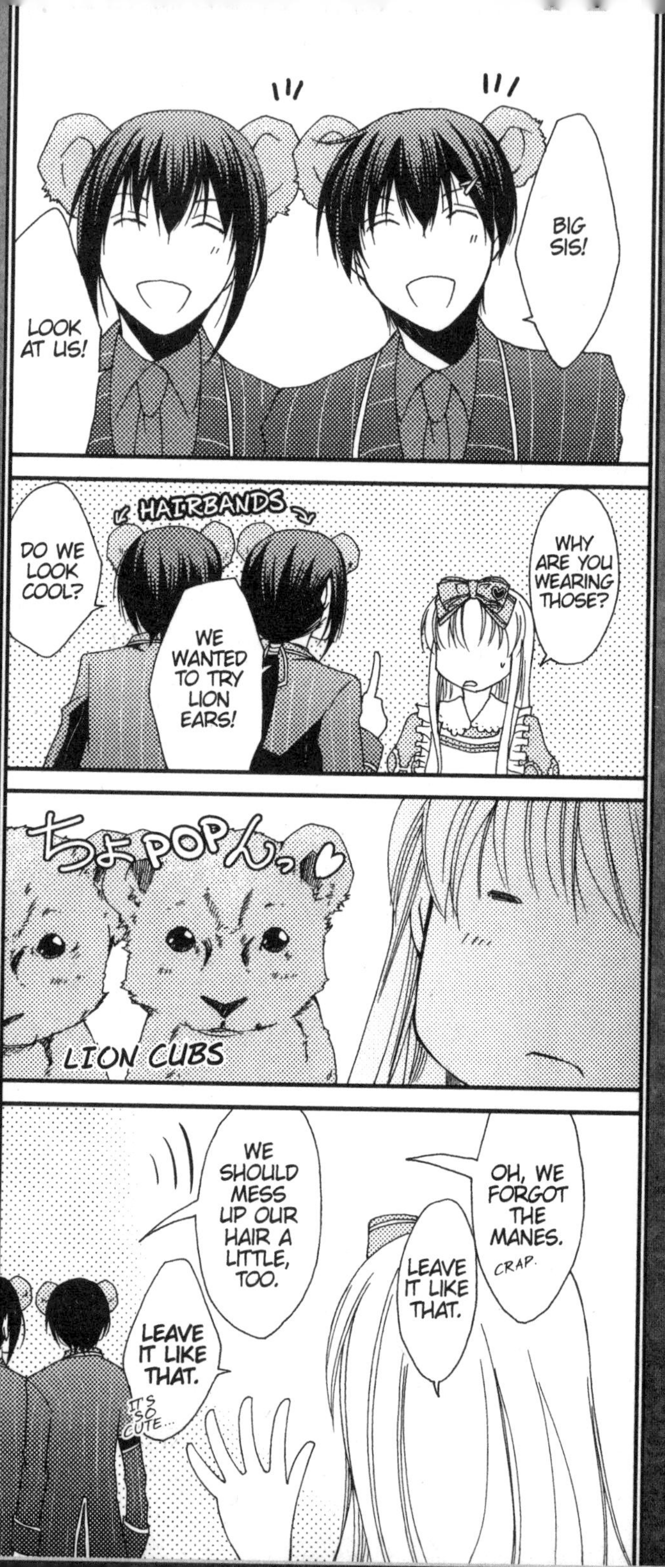
BIG SIS!
LOOK AT US!
WHY ARE YOU WEARING THOSE?
HAIRBANDS
DO WE LOOK COOL?
WE WANTED TO TRY LION EARS!
ちょPOPん
LION CUBS
OH, WE FORGOT THE MANES.
CRAP.
LEAVE IT LIKE THAT.
WE SHOULD MESS UP OUR HAIR A LITTLE, TOO.
LEAVE IT LIKE THAT.
IT'S SO CUTE...

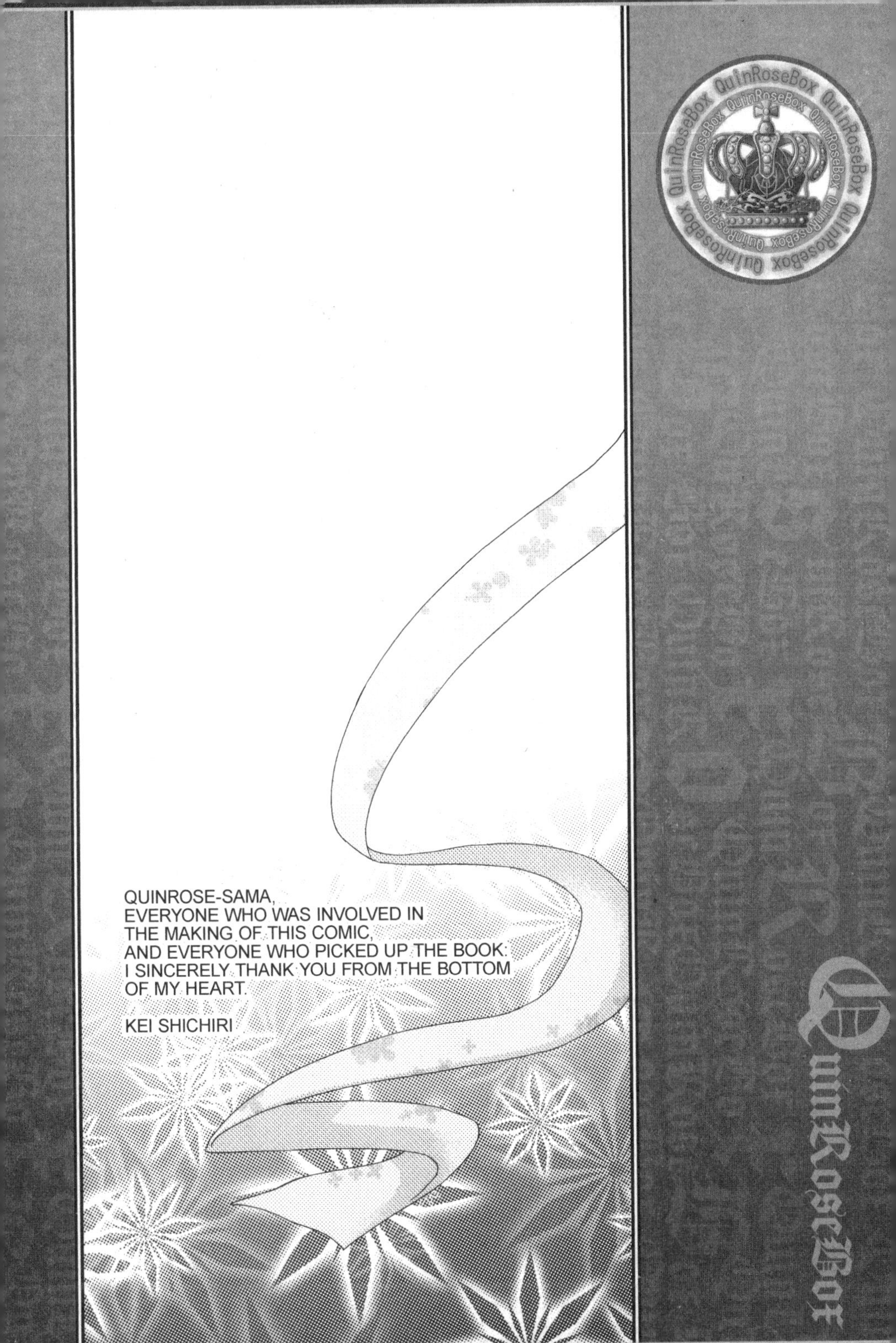
QUINROSE-SAMA,
EVERYONE WHO WAS INVOLVED IN
THE MAKING OF THIS COMIC,
AND EVERYONE WHO PICKED UP THE BOOK:
I SINCERELY THANK YOU FROM THE BOTTOM
OF MY HEART.
KEI SHICHIRI
QuinRoseBox

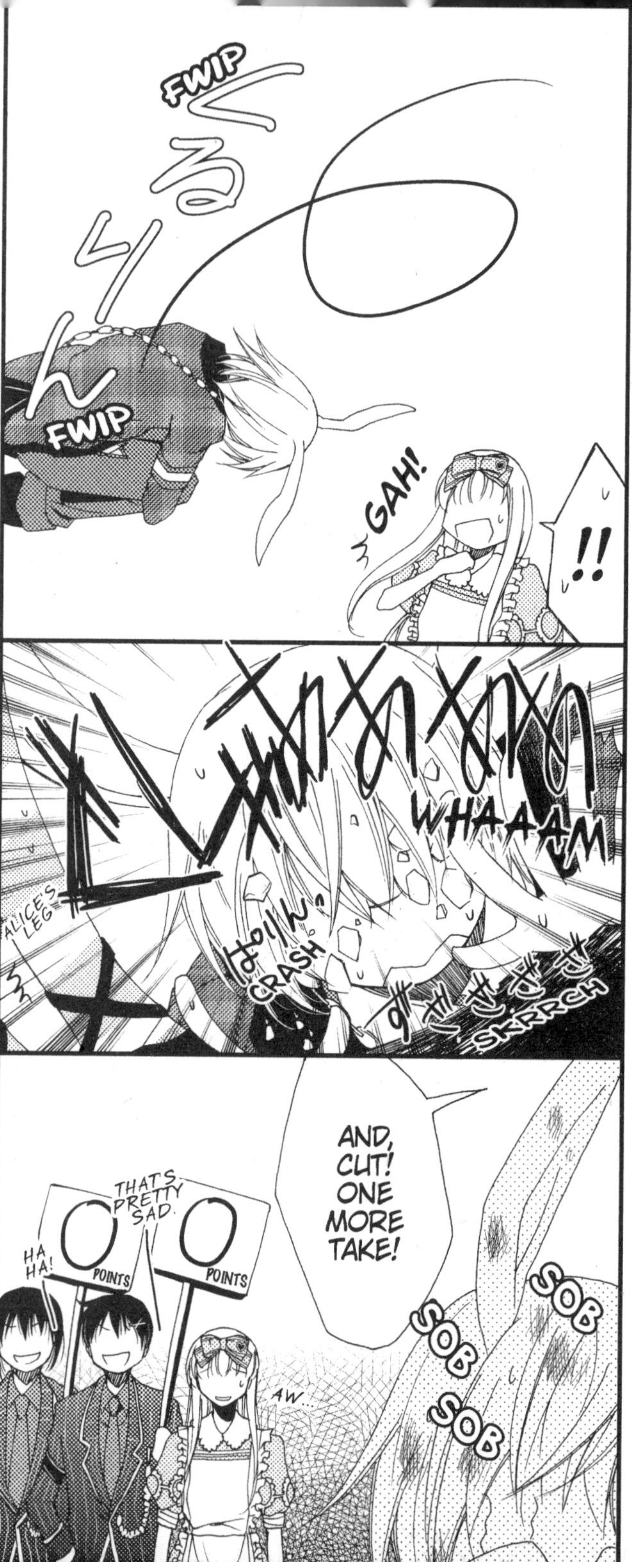
FWIP
くるりん
FWIP
GAH!
!!
WHAAAM
ALICE'S LEG
CRASH
SKRRCH
AND, CUT! ONE MORE TAKE!
SOB
SOB
SOB
SOB
0 POINTS
THAT'S PRETTY SAD.
0 POINTS
HA HA!
AW...

BEHIND THE SCENES OF PAGE 36.

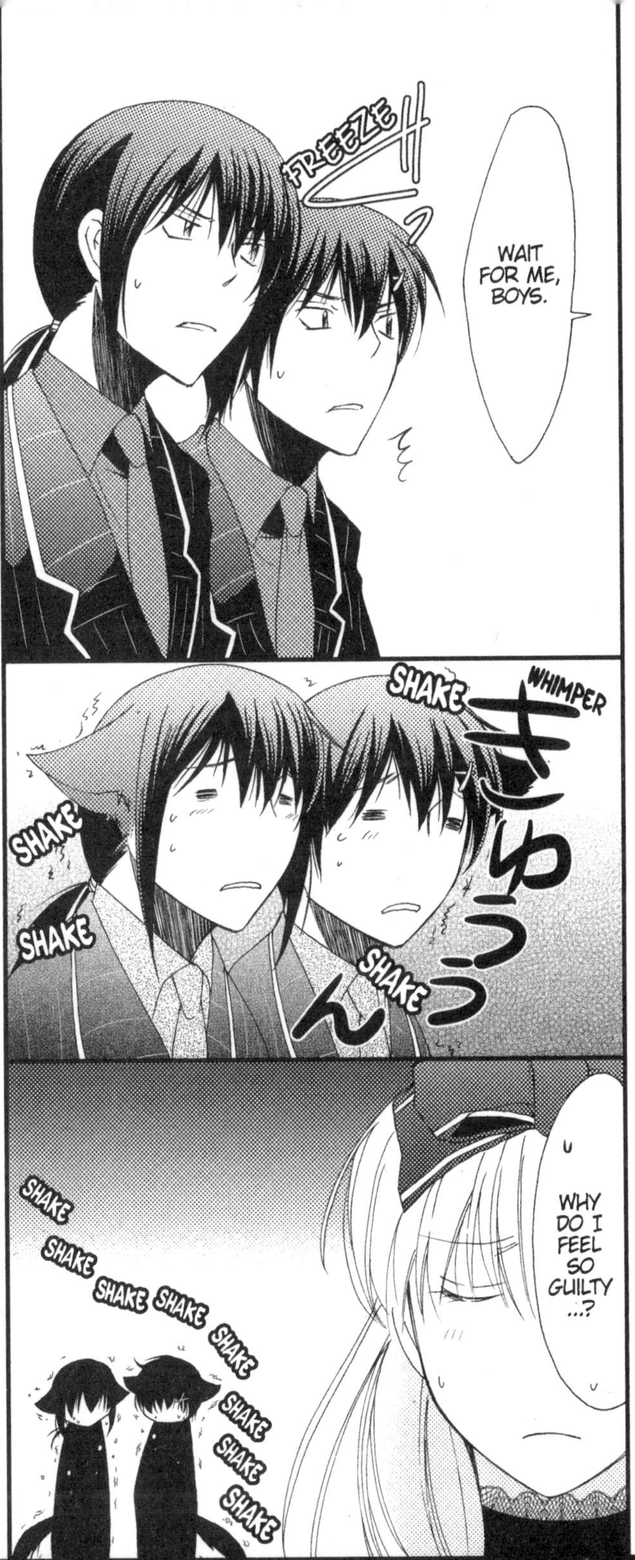
FREEZE
WAIT FOR ME, BOYS.
WHIMPER
きゅううん
SHAKE
SHAKE
SHAKE
SHAKE
SHAKE SHAKE SHAKE SHAKE SHAKE SHAKE SHAKE SHAKE
WHY DO I FEEL SO GUILTY ...?

BEHIND THE SCENES OF PAGE 77.

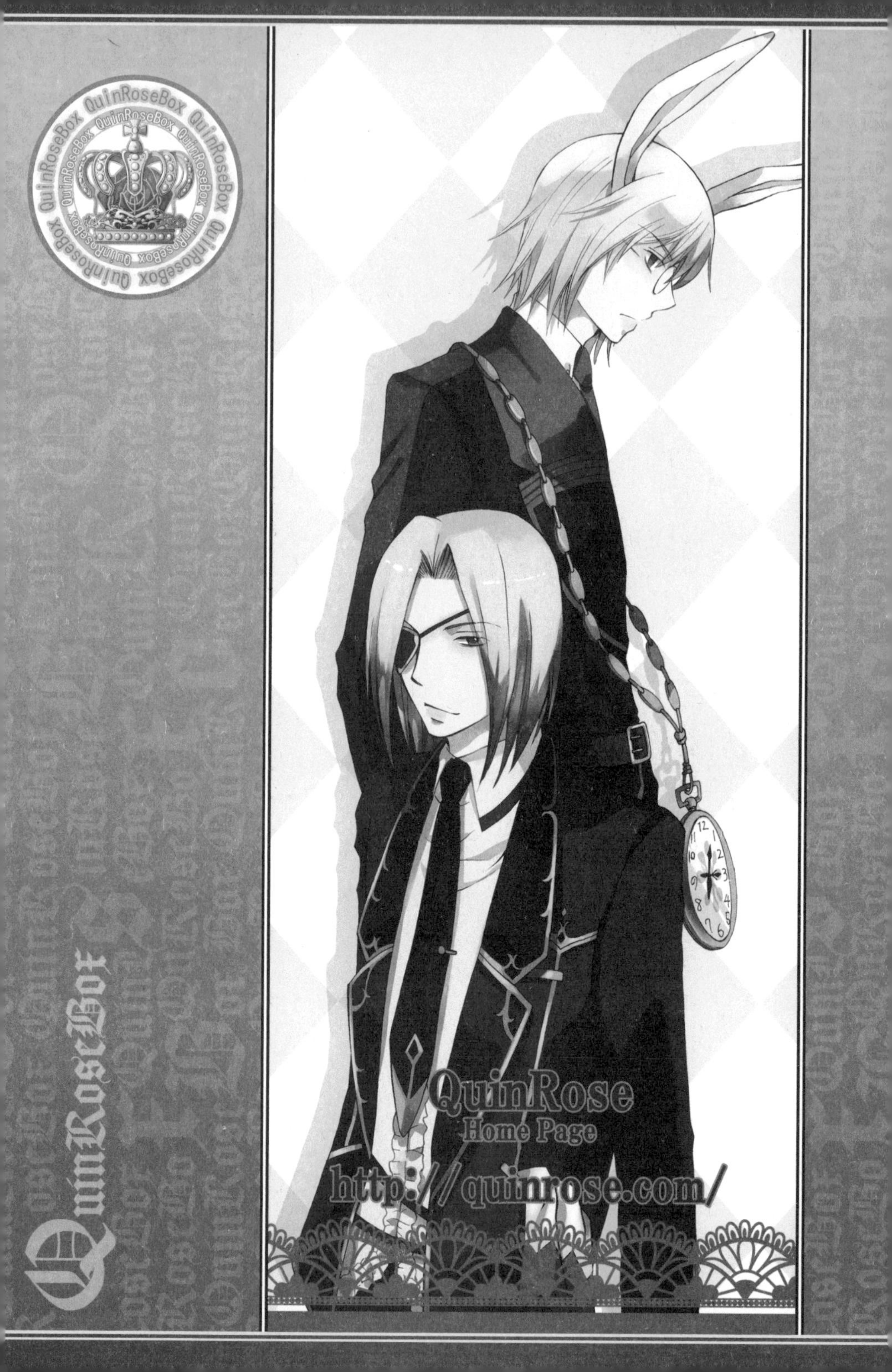
QuinRoseBox
QuinRose
Home Page
http://quinrose.com/
QuinRoseBox

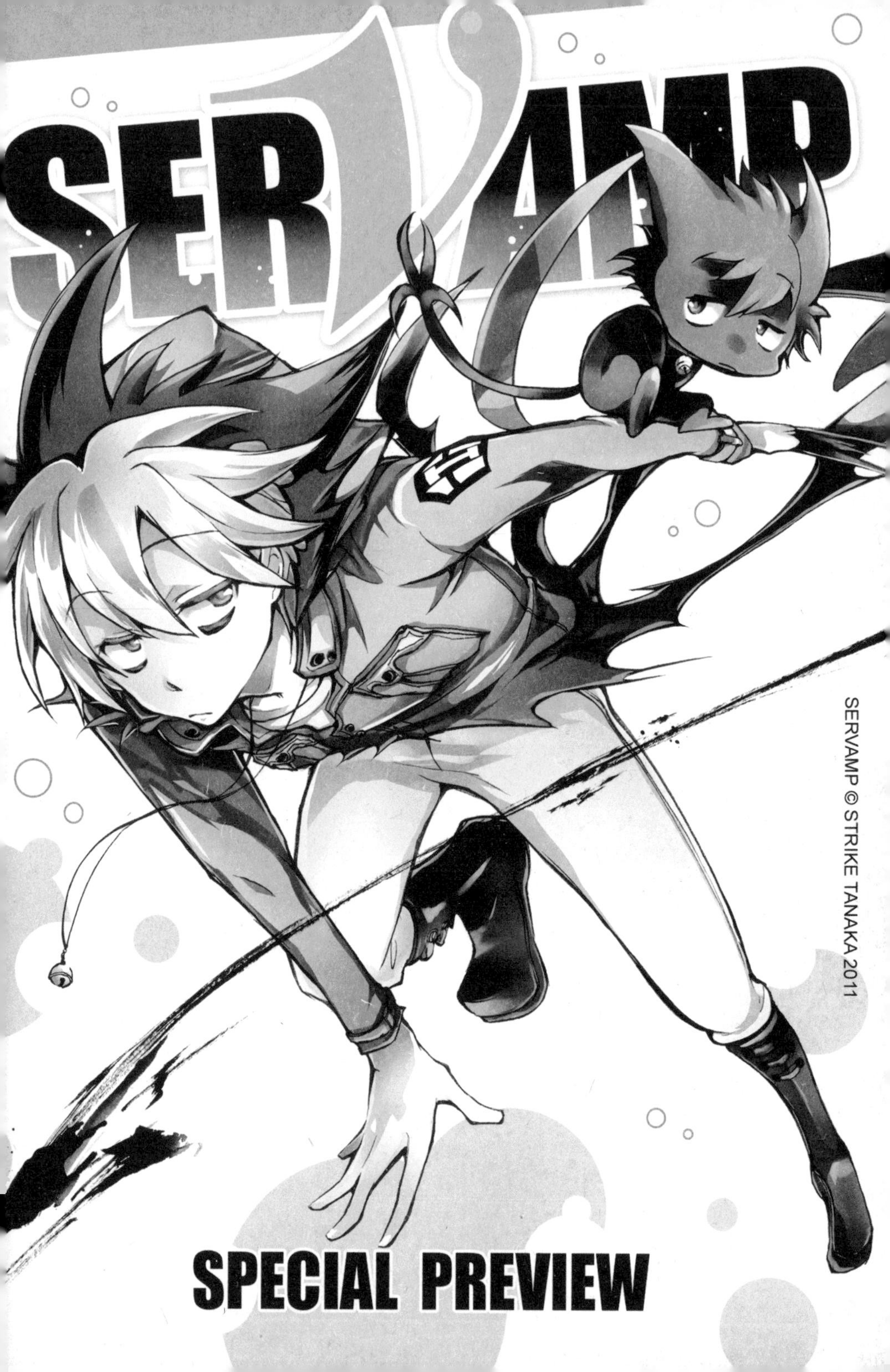
SERVAMP

SPECIAL PREVIEW

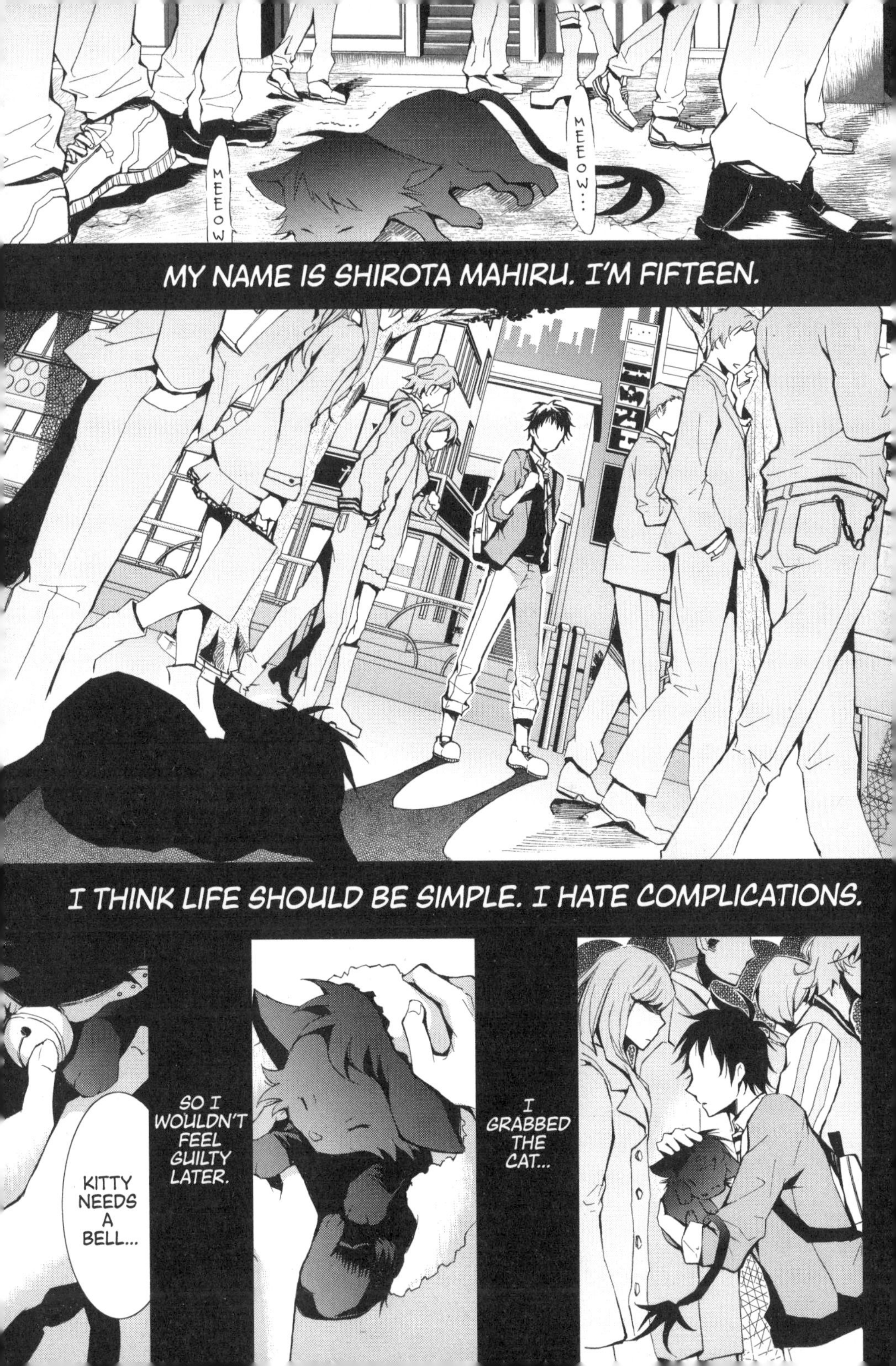
MEEOW...
MEEOW
MY NAME IS SHIROTA MAHIRU. I'M FIFTEEN.
I THINK LIFE SHOULD BE SIMPLE. I HATE COMPLICATIONS.
I GRABBED THE CAT...
SO I WOULDN'T FEEL GUILTY LATER.
KITTY NEEDS A BELL...

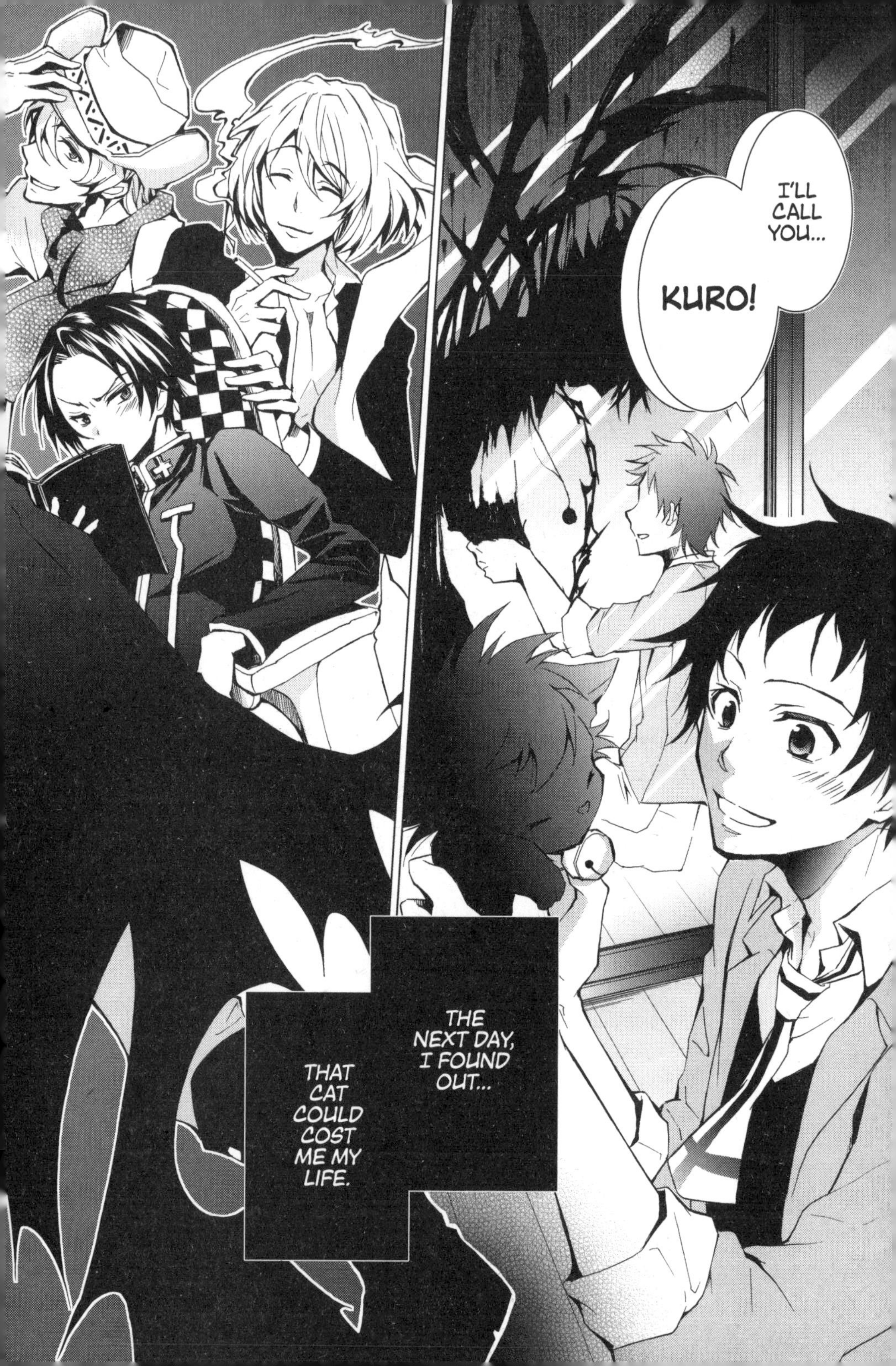
I'LL CALL YOU...
KURO!
THE NEXT DAY, I FOUND OUT...
THAT CAT COULD COST ME MY LIFE.

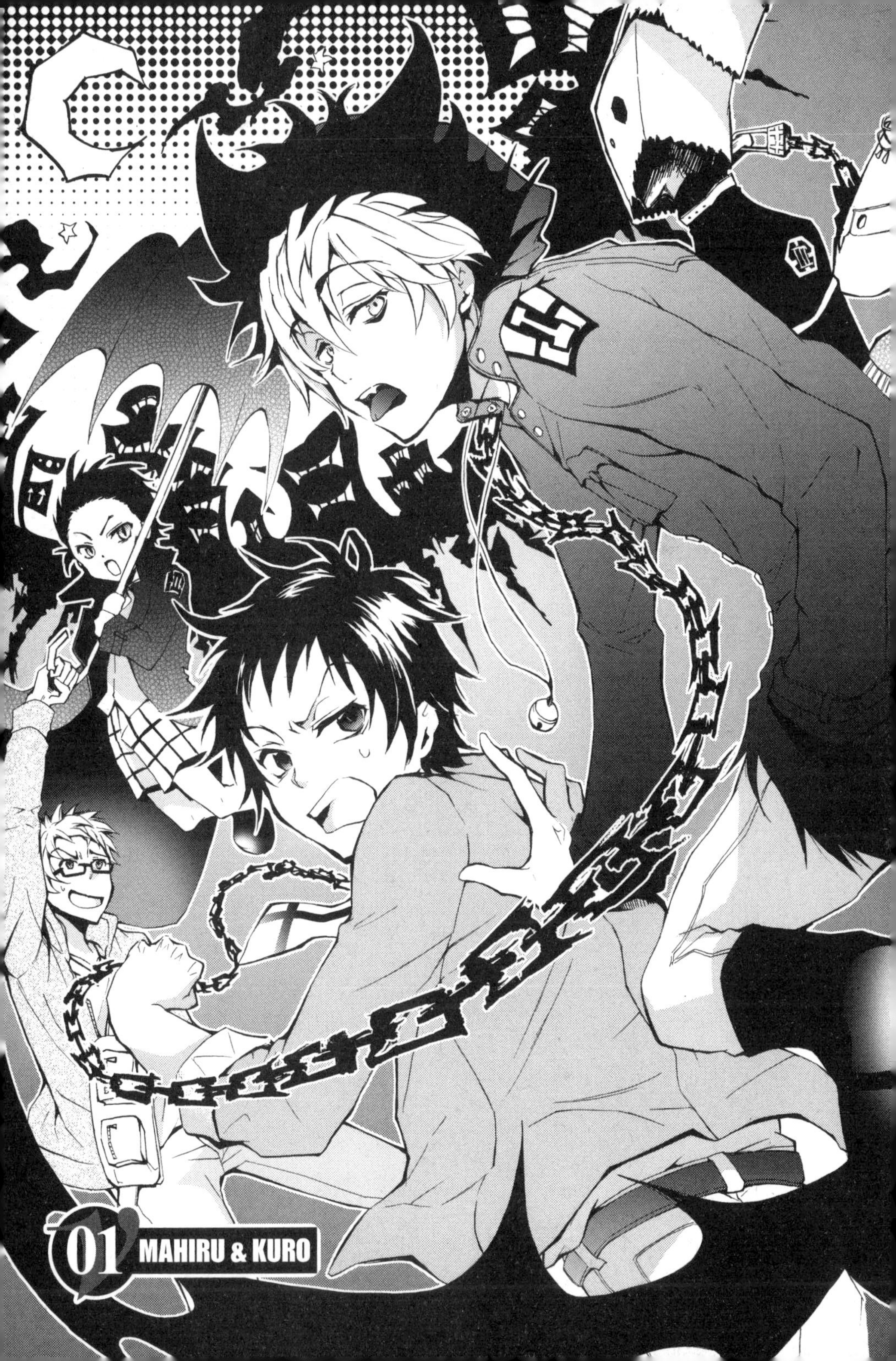
01
MAHIRU & KURO

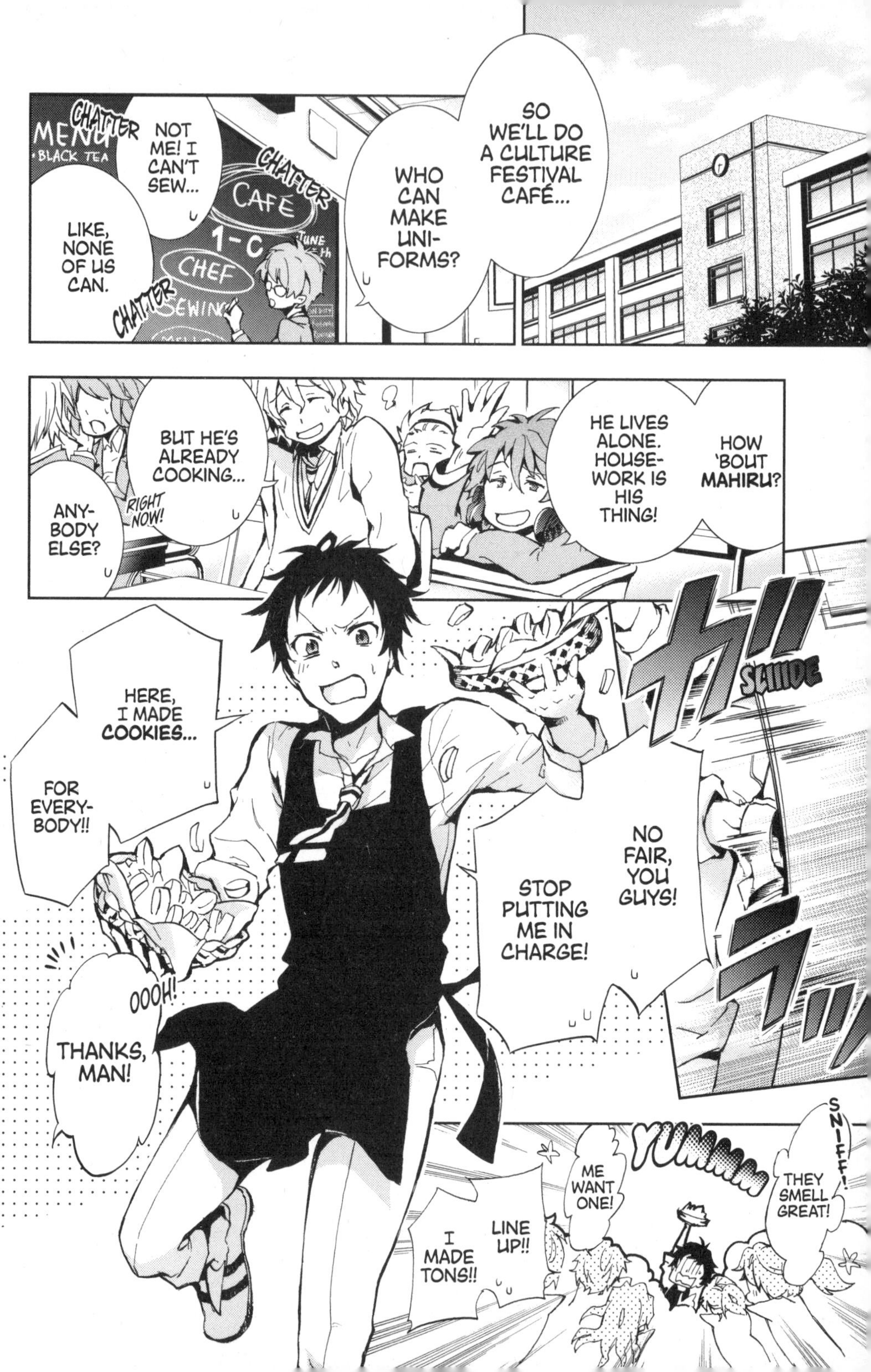
SO WE'LL DO A CULTURE FESTIVAL CAFÉ...
WHO CAN MAKE UNIFORMS?
CHATTER
CHATTER
NOT ME! I CAN'T SEW...
LIKE, NONE OF US CAN.
CHATTER
MENU
BLACK TEA
CAFÉ
1-C
CHEF
HOW 'BOUT MAHIRU?
HE LIVES ALONE. HOUSEWORK IS HIS THING!
BUT HE'S ALREADY COOKING...
RIGHT NOW!
ANYBODY ELSE?
SLIIIDE
NO FAIR, YOU GUYS!
STOP PUTTING ME IN CHARGE!
HERE, I MADE COOKIES...
FOR EVERYBODY!!
OOOH!
THANKS, MAN!
SNIFF!
THEY SMELL GREAT!
YUMMM
ME WANT ONE!
LINE UP!!
I MADE TONS!!

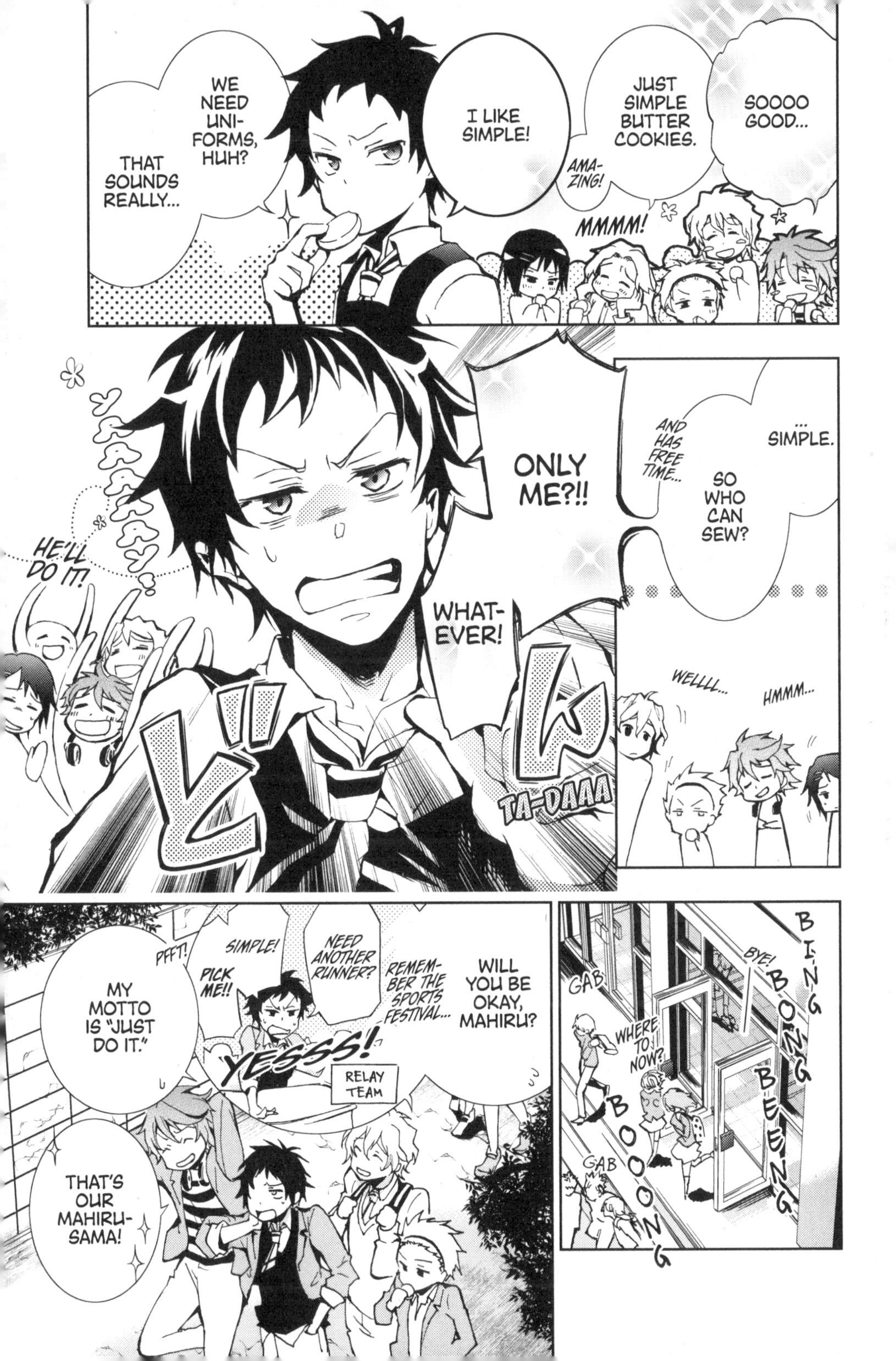
SOOOO GOOD...
JUST SIMPLE BUTTER COOKIES.
AMA-ZING!
MMMM!
I LIKE SIMPLE!
WE NEED UNI-FORMS, HUH?
THAT SOUNDS REALLY...
... SIMPLE.
AND HAS FREE TIME...
SO WHO CAN SEW?
HMMM...
WELLLL...
ONLY ME?!!
WHAT-EVER!
TA-DAAA
HE'LL DO IT!
BING BONG BEENG BOOOONG
BYE!
WHERE TO NOW?
GAB
GAB
WILL YOU BE OKAY, MAHIRU?
REMEM-BER THE SPORTS FESTIVAL...
NEED ANOTHER RUNNER?
SIMPLE!
PICK ME!!
PFFT!
MY MOTTO IS "JUST DO IT."
YESSS!
RELAY TEAM
THAT'S OUR MAHIRU-SAMA!

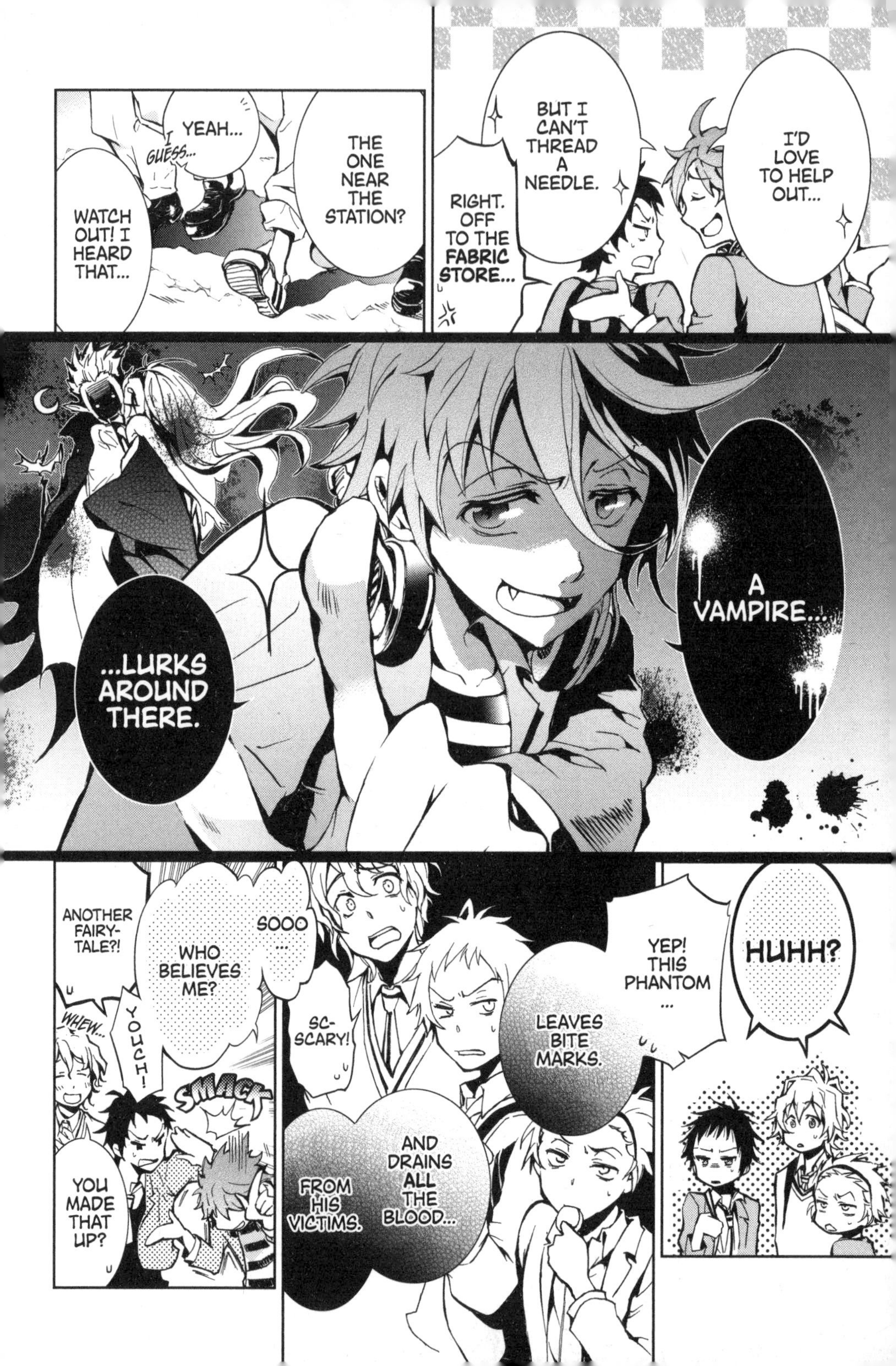

I'D LOVE TO HELP OUT...
BUT I CAN'T THREAD A NEEDLE.
RIGHT. OFF TO THE FABRIC STORE...
THE ONE NEAR THE STATION?
YEAH...
I GUESS...
WATCH OUT! I HEARD THAT...
A VAMPIRE...
...LURKS AROUND THERE.
HUHH?
YEP! THIS PHANTOM ...
LEAVES BITE MARKS.
SC-SCARY!
AND DRAINS ALL THE BLOOD...
FROM HIS VICTIMS.
SOOO ...
WHO BELIEVES ME?
ANOTHER FAIRY-TALE?!
WHEW...
YOUCH!
SMACK
YOU MADE THAT UP?

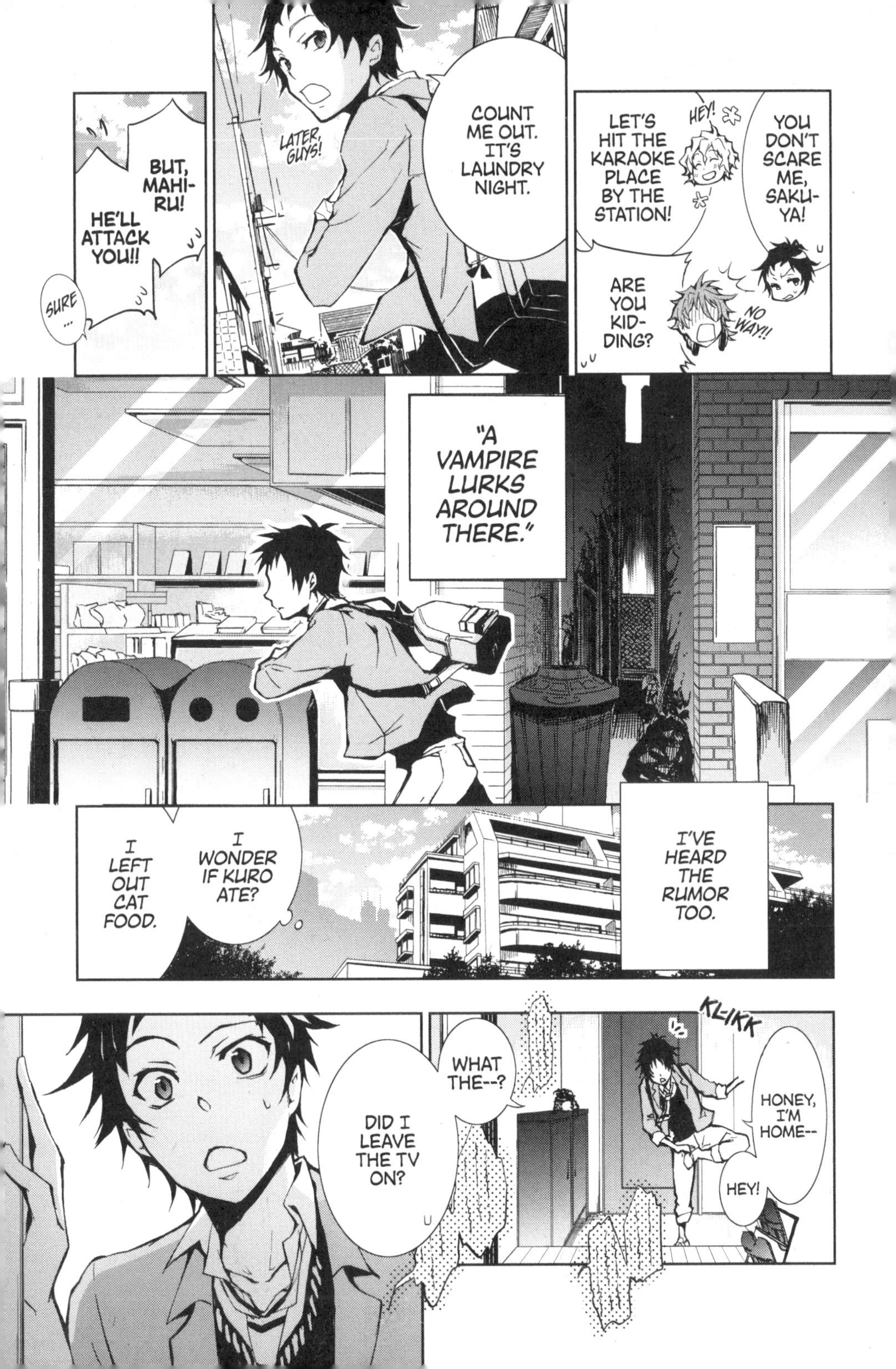
YOU DON'T SCARE ME, SAKUYA!
HEY!
LET'S HIT THE KARAOKE PLACE BY THE STATION!
NO WAY!!
ARE YOU KIDDING?
COUNT ME OUT. IT'S LAUNDRY NIGHT.
LATER, GUYS!
BUT, MAHIRU!
HE'LL ATTACK YOU!!
SURE ...
"A VAMPIRE LURKS AROUND THERE."
I'VE HEARD THE RUMOR TOO.
I WONDER IF KURO ATE?
I LEFT OUT CAT FOOD.
KL-IKK
HONEY, I'M HOME--
HEY!
WHAT THE--?
DID I LEAVE THE TV ON?

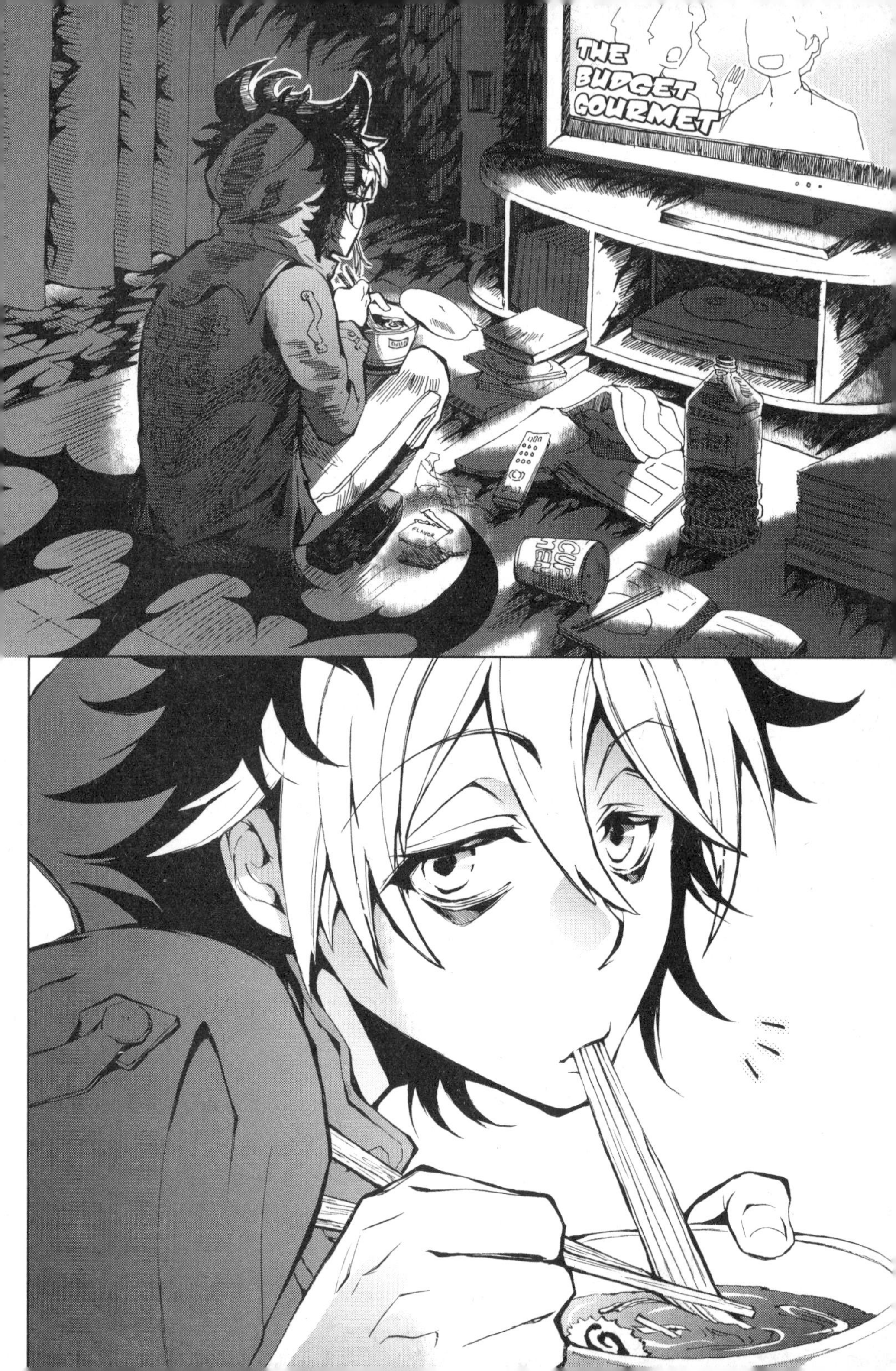
THE BUDGET GOURMET
FLAVOR
CUP

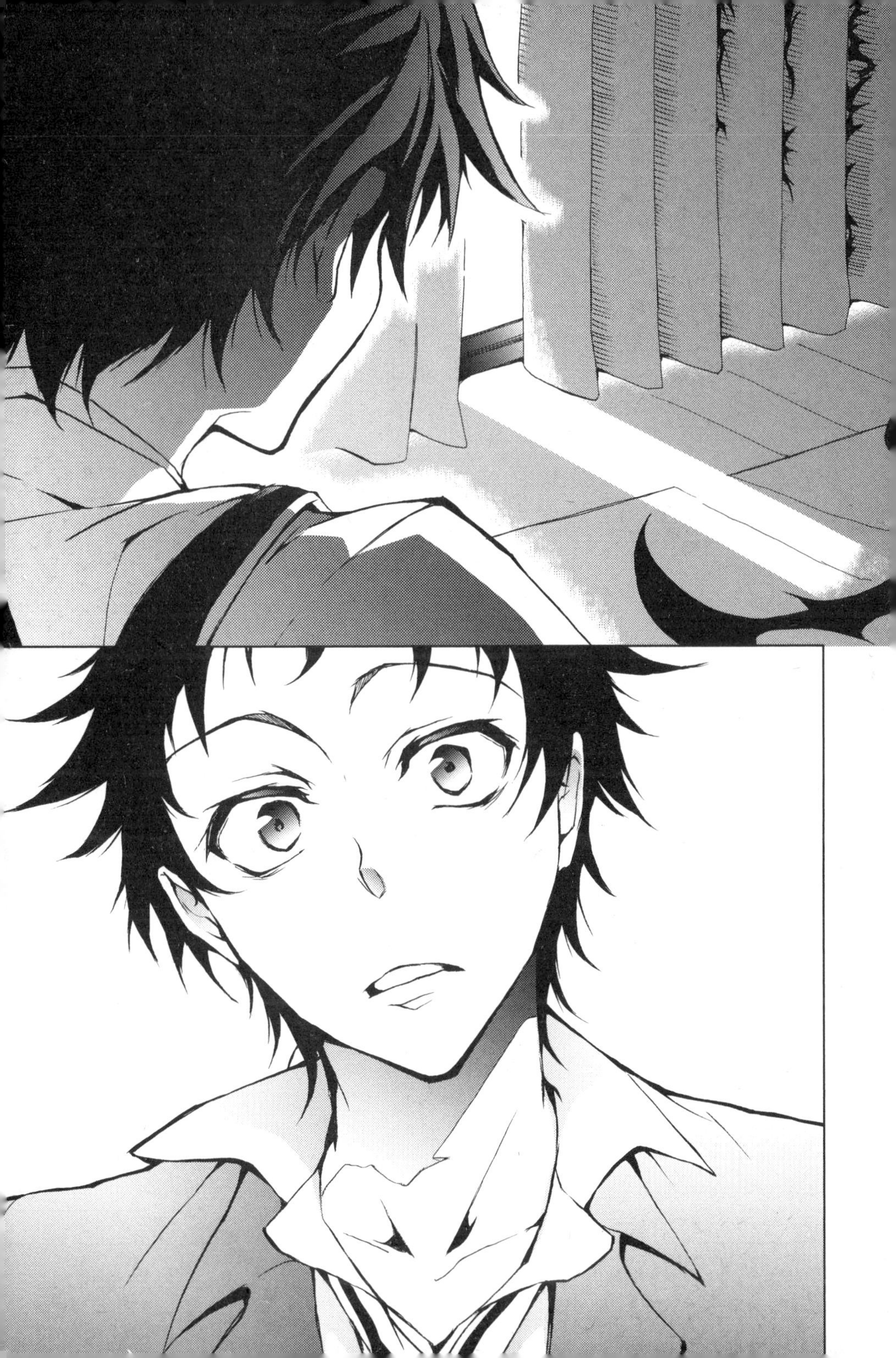

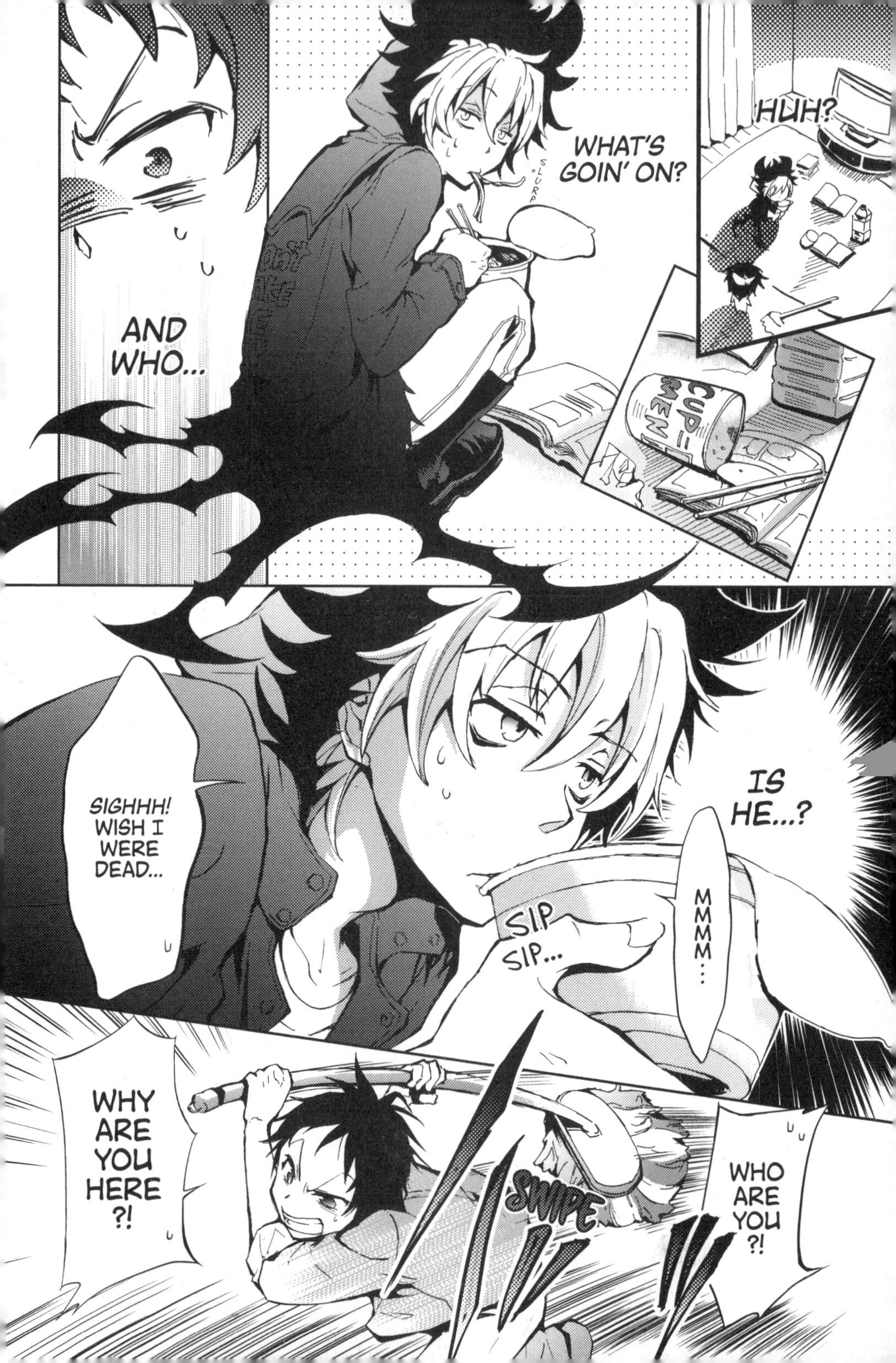

HUH?
CUP MEN
WHAT'S GOIN' ON?
SLURP
AND WHO...
IS HE...?
MMMM...
SIP SIP...
SIGHHH! WISH I WERE DEAD...
WHO ARE YOU ?!
SWIPE
WHY ARE YOU HERE ?!

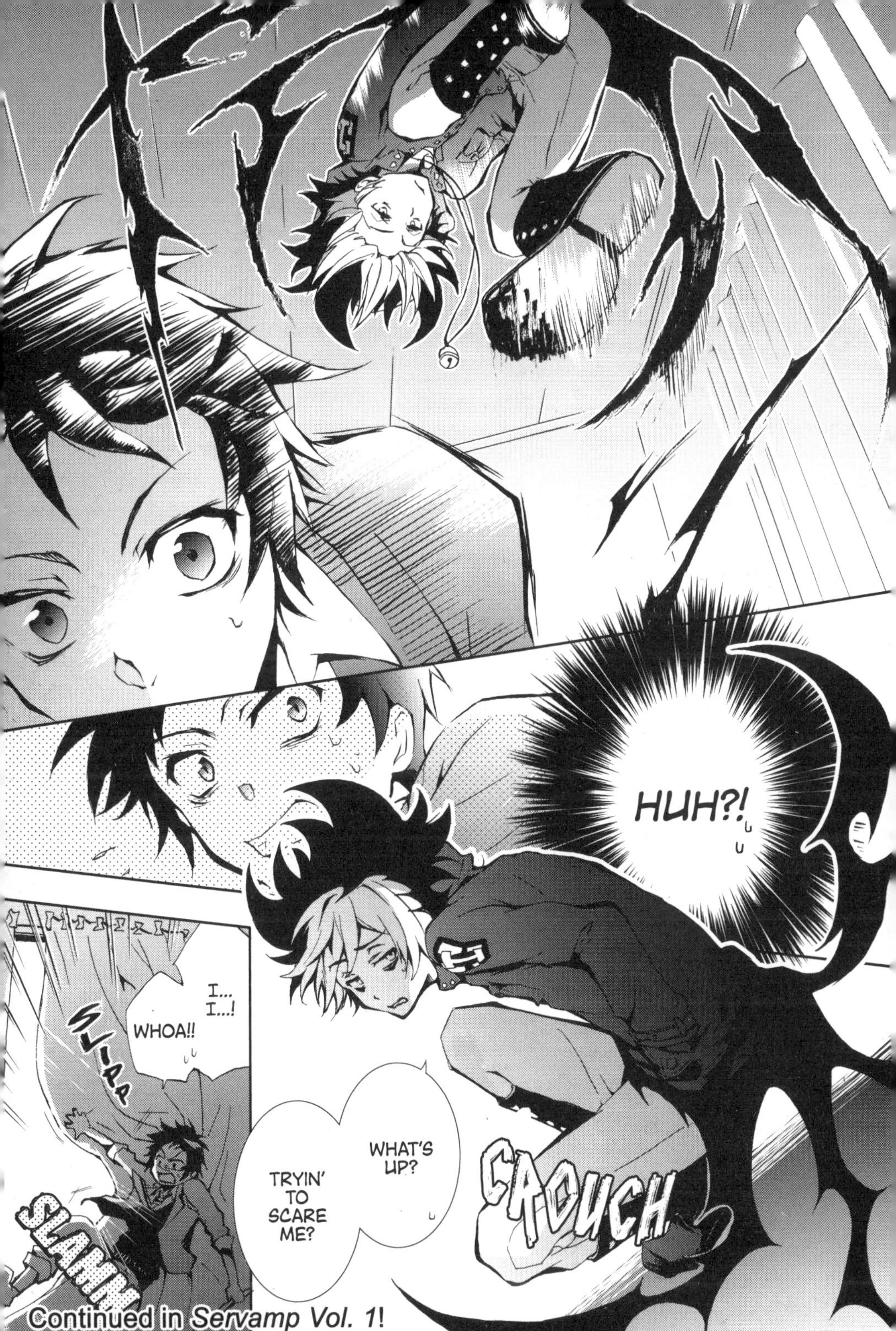
HUH?!
CROUCH
WHAT'S UP?
TRYIN' TO SCARE ME?
I... I...!
WHOA!!
SLIPP
SLAMM

Continued in *Servamp Vol. 1*!

COMING SOON

JUNE 2015
Alice in the Country of Hearts:
Junk Box

JULY 2015
Alice in the Country of Clover:
Black Lizard and
Bitter Taste Vol. 1

AUGUST 2015
Alice in the Country of Hearts:
White Rabbit and
Some Afternoon Tea Part 1

SEPTEMBER 2015
Alice in the Country of Clover:
Black Lizard and
Bitter Taste Vol. 2